A Resource Guide to Themes in Contemporary American Song Lyrics, 1950–1985

B. LEE COOPER

Foreword by Wayne A. Wiegand

GREENWOOD PRESS
New York · Westport, Connecticut · London

Library of Congress Cataloging-in-Publication Data

Cooper, B. Lee
   A resource guide to themes in contemporary American
song lyrics, 1950–1985.

   Discography: p.
   Bibliography: p.
   Includes indexes.
   1.   Music, Popular (Songs, etc.)—United States—
Discography.   2.   Music, Popular (Songs, etc.)—United
States—History and criticism.   3.   Music and society.
I.   Title.
ML156.4.P6C66   1986   016.7899'1245'00973   85–21933
ISBN 0–313–24516–9 (lib. bdg. : alk. paper)

Library of Congress Catalog Card Number: 85–21933
ISBN: 0–313–24516–9

First published in 1986

Greenwood Press, Inc.
88 Post Road West
Westport, Connecticut 06881

Printed in the United States of America

The paper used in this book complies with the
Permanent Paper Standard issued by the National
Information Standards Organization (Z39.48–1984).

10   9   8   7   6   5   4   3   2   1

To
Charles A. Cooper
and
Kathleen M. Cooper

Contents

Tables

Foreword

by Wayne A. Wiegand

Finally scholars are beginning serious analysis of a vast field of study rich in potential—popular culture. Heretofore they largely accepted literary canon and social science paradigms defined by a high-culture elite as standards against which to evaluate popular culture materials. Invariably their efforts neglected a crucial interaction between the popular culture medium and its audience—the act of selection. Why do people choose one form of popular culture over another? As Janice Radway so well argues in her recently published book, *Reading the Romance: Women, Patriarchy and Popular Culture* (Chapel Hill, N.C.: University of North Carolina Press, 1984), one cannot address this question by holding static high-culture standards against the dynamic process that occurs when people select a popular culture product.

Looking at popular culture through the eyes of its patrons offers exciting challenges for scholars. But some preliminary work has to be done, for the ground is still hard from neglect. Popular music is a case in point. We know so little about it, despite the fact that it preoccupies the attention of millions of Americans, especially adolescents and young adults. What permits popular music to command such devotion and loyalty? We cannot begin to answer until we acknowledge the complexity of the system that supports it, a major part of which is represented in the hundreds of themes that weave their way into and out of popular music lyrics. The academic world needs essential tools to identify common threads in popular music lyrics, to facilitate investigations, and to push those investigations in directions that promise immediate results.

"Knowledge is of two kinds," Samuel Johnson once said. "We know a subject ourselves, or we know where we can find information upon it." B. Lee Cooper here provides students and scholars of popular music with an invaluable new source of information. Few scholars have spent as much productive time studying popular music lyrics. Cooper's thematic approach is vital; it allows researchers to identify relevant primary source materials for the examination of scores of subjects by a variety of methods. Scholars and students owe Professor Cooper a debt of gratitude for this highly useful work. It will guide them through the labyrinth of themes in popular music lyrics and at the same time add significantly to the body of knowledge growing up around the study of popular culture.

Acknowledgments

The motivation for creating this resource guide came from Wayne A. Wiegand and Mary R. Sive. Dr. Wiegand, a prize-winning historical researcher and associate professor of library science at the University of Kentucky, has been urging me to create a "song encyclopedia" for more than a decade. He has also been a close personal advisor, a crafty literary critic, and a constant source of insight into the relationships of popular culture and information services. His specific suggestion was that I should compile a theme-directed package of contemporary songs that would enable teachers, librarians, and scholars to examine the social, political, and personal commentaries contained in contemporary music. Beyond recognition here, Dr. Wiegand genuinely longs for future psychological research on the influence of lyrical content on the personal perceptions and the social conceptions of America's listening public. If recordings are really examples of oral history (as several scholars claim), the task of historians, sociologists, psychologists, and literary analysts during the remainder of this century is to determine the public's responses, reactions, and contributions to ideas contained in popular songs. This compilation is a necessary, if very modest, initial step in this complex communication process.

The other person who prompted me to develop this book is Mary R. Sive, acquisitions editor for Greenwood Press. From her initial inquiry letter until the formal contract was issued for this text, Ms. Sive was cordial, constructive, critical, and thoroughly professional. She had a definite idea about the type of reference work she wanted; she was firm in emphasizing the style, structure, and relevance of the resource guide she sought. Such diligence and intelligence among acquisitions personnel is as welcome as it is rare.

Writers benefit from loving, uncritical support of wives, children, parents, and other relatives. This kind of sustenance is indispensable during lengthy research and writing projects, when brief periods of creativity are followed by lengthy times of boring compilation drudgery. My team of familial supporters includes Jill Cooper, Michael Cooper, Laura Cooper, Julie Cooper, Kathleen Cooper, Charles A. Cooper, Patty Douglas, Robert Douglas, Larry Cooper, Elizabeth Cunningham, Judy Jones, and Herb Jones.

Beyond this family circle is another band of support. Writers count on professional colleagues and friends for encouragement, ideas, criticism, examples, reactions, and goodwill. I have benefitted from the thoughtful assistance of a vast network of kind, helpful folks including: Pat Browne, Ray B. Browne, Donna J. Brummett, Gary Burns, Ronald Butchart, George O. Carney, Jim Creeth, Jack Dennis, Howard A. DeWitt, Charles Gritzner, Gordon Henry, Peter Hesbacher, Frank W. Hoffmann, Hugo Keesing, Stephen Kneeshaw, Dennis Loren, Russel B. Nye, Linda Painter, David Pichaske, Charles P. Pruitt, Lawrence Redd, Roger B. Rollin, Fred E. H. Schroeder, Tom Schultheiss, Frank Scott, Virginia Senn, Gordon Stevenson, John E. Sukovich, Stewart Tubbs, Clara Wertz, Chas "Dr. Rock" White, and Brett Williams.

The final type of support that made this study possible was financial. I wish to thank the Division of Fellowships and Seminars of the National Endowment for the Humanities (NEH) for awarding me a Travel to Collections Grant during 1985. This special funding permitted me to gain research access to the literary and audio materials at the Sound Recordings Archive in the Jerome Library at Bowling Green State University. I was also able to consult directly with long-time friend and discographic expert William L. Schurk as a result of the NEH funding.

In conclusion, I wish to echo the disclaimer first stated by music bibliographer Vincent Duckles more than two decades ago. He correctly identified two sources of frustration felt by all reference book compilers. The first is achieving literary closure—submitting a manuscript. The second is acknowledging the inevitability of incompleteness and error. Professor Duckles' own words warrant reiteration:

A bibliographer's work is never done. Even as this edition goes to press, I am troubled by the submerged voices of would be entries which may have been overlooked, and entries which may have been misplaced or misrepresented. . . . But if one were too attentive to such considerations a work of this kind would never reach the point of publication. Now that it has made its appearance, I hope that it will attract collaboration in the form of corrections, additions, or suggestions for improvement, from all who have occasion to use it.*

I support these same sentiments, particularly the invitation for constructive criticism and resource assistance.

*Vincent Duckles, "Introduction to the First Edition," in *Music Reference and Research Materials: An Annotated Bibliography*, 2d ed. (New York: Free Press, 1967), p. x.

Introduction

Popular songs are pieces of oral history. They depict contemporary American culture in the form of an audio collage. The historical perspective they offer resembles that knowledge found in remnants available in an Indian burial mound. An archaeologist must reconstruct ancient cultural reality from fragments of a former civilization—pieces of pottery, projectile points, tools for building, stone drawings, children's toys and games, eating utensils, religious tokens, and death masks; similarly, the contemporary soundscape researcher must examine many, many recordings produced within a defined time span in order to identify persistent lyrical trends.

Some subjects of popular song lyrics are universally available for scrutiny. For example, the standard courtship theme—boy meets girl, boy dates girl, love blooms, marriage beckons, and a wedding occurs—remains a predominate topic in modern music.[1] However, there are also numerous variations to this typical love-and-marriage scenario. Women's liberation, birth control, social mobility, economic independence, the sexual revolution, and dozens of other ideas, trends, and situations in post-1950 American culture have dramatically altered and complicated the previously simple courtship theme in popular song. These social, political, and personal trends have generated an enlarged spectrum of commentary within the lyrics of many hit tunes. This observation is not meant to imply that songs haven't functioned as outlets for personal opinion or as socialization devices throughout human history.[2] But the nature of traditional folk songs, of gospel and spiritual tunes, and even of patriotic hymns differs in quality and quantity from the ubiquitous contemporary popular song. From 1950 to 1985, American society has been verbally photographed by innumeral tunesmiths and displayed in audio galleries across this continent and throughout the world.

Radios, jukeboxes, cable television (MTV), cassette recordings, motion picture soundtracks, compact discs, and millions and millions of records sound a clarion call to prospective oral historians. It is regrettable that so few scholars have tapped these valuable recorded resources.[3]

This resource guide offers a lyrical picture of American society during the late twentieth century. The thirty-five years of sound recordings presented here represent material from the period when popular music was transformed from The Big Band/Swing Era into The Age of Rock. The 1950–1959 decade was provocative, revolutionary, and fun for most pop musicians and their youthful listeners alike. The next ten years, 1960–1969, featured more innovations in song styling, increased levels of performer prestige, and dramatically intensified social commentary in song lyrics.[4] From 1970 to the present, the recording industry has continued to expand on the dynamism of rock's initial two decades. A heroic (if sometimes manipulated) recording star system has emerged, complete with discographic documentation and biographical treatise.[5] Yet it is the songs—those individual popular culture building blocks performed by Elvis Presley, The Beatles, Aretha Franklin, Bob Dylan, Michael Jackson, and Elvis Costello— that still await careful historical analysis. Granted, the task is gigantic. But just as armies of archaeologists have successfully reconstructed the fabric of ancient Indian cultures by carefully examining buried relics, it is vital that modern scholars apply their logical analyses and reasoned perspectives to the vinyl remnants of the American music industry. This task begins here.

This guide presents a limited portion of American popular music. It provides a thematically structured analysis of the lyrics from 3,000 songs performed over the past thirty-five years. Traditional scholars have been consistently hostile toward popular music pundits who ignore the statistical rigors of content analysis and avoid controlled group research while ascribing philosophical or historical meanings to tunes performed by Bob Dylan, Curtis Mayfield, John Lennon, and Joni Mitchell.[6] The central function of this text is not to resolve the dilemma of exactly how popular music affects the American public's perception of itself and contemporary society; instead, this study hinges on a single, unspectacular assumption. American music is a logical product of a pluralistic culture; as such, its lyrics accurately reflect the conflicting social, political, and personal concerns of individuals and groups within that society. The media revolution of the post–World War II era has increased both the quality and the availability of sound recordings. The rise of middle-class financial power, coupled with the growing economic influence of teenagers, has also dramatically expanded the scope of popular music as a social indicator. This milieu of contemporary American life enhances the meaning and value of lyric-based investigation.

This resource guide focuses on the lyrics of commercial recordings released between January 1, 1950 and January 1, 1985. Neither date is historically relevant; both were selected arbitrarily. The 1950–1985 period in the United States was one of accelerating social, political, and personal change.[7] Just as a 1954 Supreme Court decision launched the civil rights movement, the Korean War signalled the beginning of American military involvement in Southeast Asia throughout the next three decades, and the burgeoning youth culture of the fifties became a source of rebellion, financial strength, and leisure time industries over the next three decades—all of American society lurched forward toward new structures, new tempos, and new heroes. The kaleidoscopic nature of this thirty-five–year period is captured and transmitted in the lyrics of popular music. But like the minute glass chips that form the changing face of a kaleidoscope, individual popular recordings rarely give more than a hint of their capacity to depict larger social conditions. Only when these separate black vinyl units of latent oral history are reflectively assembled into thematic patterns and then exposed to the light of critical review do unified forms begin to emerge. This is the method of oral history. It is also the best way of hearing the voice of America's popular culture.

This resource guide contains more than 3,000 popular recordings organized to support fifteen predetermined social, political, and personal themes. Each of these major themes, which form the chapters in this reference work, is subdivided into a number of related sub-themes. A discographic section listing individual songs, performers, record company names and disc numbers, and years of release accompanies each major theme. Preceding these song lists is a brief essay describing each theme. This section examines a variety of songs in the same concise fashion that a bibliographic essay investigates books and articles dealing with a designated topic. That is, specified lyrical ideas and observations are highlighted in the introductory essay in order to define and to clarify the scope of each major theme and the related sub-themes. The function of this resource guide is not to create a totally comprehensive 1950–1985 song compilation. This work is essentially interpretive. It is designed to stimulate further thought and to provide factual material for future examination of lyrics as pieces of oral history.

The quality and frequency of popular music investigations will increase dramatically during the next decade. This prediction is based upon several factors. First, recording industry activities during the past decade have garnered the attention of more and more academic researchers and popular writers.[8] Second, the number of scholars who have established their academic reputations in popular culture and media-related fields since 1970 has increased dramatically. As they train new teachers and researchers in their areas of expertise, the dimensions of popular music study will expand exponentially.[9] Third, the publishing industry will continue to integrate all forms of communication media—electronic, print, video, computer, audio—into marketable systems. Song lyrics—occasionally poetry but more often simply strings of commonly understood phrases, short stories, and idioms—will remain key elements in modern American life. Individual experiences with song, searches for suitable metaphors to interpret identity and meaning, will expand. It was this growing hunger for media knowledge that prompted the initial explosion of literary products related to popular music.[10] Finally, an ever-increasing number of information service specialists believe that more reliable information is needed on the influence of mass communications on public opinion. This area will become a more central research focus, with special attention devoted to the interaction of lyrics, video images (MTV), and human behavior and beliefs.[11] All of these elements will fuel the study of American popular music into the 1990s.

This resource compilation of contemporary recordings presents prearranged groupings of popular songs for the examination of teachers, students, and scholars. As noted previously, recordings cited here are intended to be illustrative rather than definitive, and are selective rather than comprehensive. Sources utilized to identify specific popular recordings for this guide included several of the Record Research, Inc. texts compiled by Joel Whitburn of Menomonee Falls, Wisconsin. These books are:

1. *Bubbling Under the Hot 100, 1969–1981*

2. *Top Country and Western Records, 1949–1971* (Supplements available for 1972–1973, 1974, 1975 to the present)

3. *Top Easy Listening Records, 1961–1974* (Supplements available for 1975, 1976, 1977 to the present)

4. *Top Pop, 1955–1982*

5. *Top Pop Records, 1940–1955*

6. *Top Rhythm and Blues Records, 1949–1971* (Supplements available for 1972–1973, 1974, 1975 to the present)

Other record listing resources consulted were:

1. George Albert and Frank Hoffmann, comps. *The Cash Box Country Singles Charts, 1958–1982*. Metuchen, N.J.: Scarecrow Press, 1984.

2. Peter E. Berry, comp. *". . . And the Hits Just Keep on Comin.' "* Syracuse, N. Y.: Syracuse University Press, 1977.

3. Joe Edwards, comp. *Top Tens and Trivia of Rock and Roll and Rhythm and Blues*. St. Louis: Blueberry Hill, 1981 (supplements available for 1981, 1982, 1983 to the present).

4. Stewart Goldstein and Alan Jacobson, comps. *Oldies but Goodies: The Rock 'N' Roll Years*. New York: Mason/Charter, 1977.

5. Frank Hoffmann, comp. *The Cash Box Singles Charts, 1950–1981*. Metuchen, N. J.: Scarecrow Press, 1983.

6. Bob Macken, Peter Fornatale, and Bill Ayres, comps. *The Rock Music Source Book*. Garden City, N.Y.: Anchor Press/Doubleday, 1980.

7. Jim Quirin and Barry Cohen, comps. *The Chartmasters' Rock 100: An Authoritative Ranking of the 100 Most Popular Songs for Each Year, 1956 through 1981.* Covington, La.: Chartmasters, 1982 (supplements available for 1982, 1983, 1984 to the present).

The selection of particular songs for inclusion in this text was highly subjective. Although the author frequently benefitted from suggestions by friends and fellow rock afficionados, there were also several song compilation books that proved invaluable for gaining a broad perspective on popular music lyrics. These lyric anthologies appear in the bibliography at the end of this text.

Notes

1. James T. Carey, "Changing Courtship Patterns in the Popular Song," *American Journal of Sociology* 74 (May 1969); 720–731; Patricia Freudiger, "Love Lauded and Love Lamented: Men and Women in Popular Music," *Popular Music and Society* 6 (1978): 1–10; and Melvin Wilkinson, "Romantic Love: The Great Equalizer? Sexism in Popular Music," *The Family Coordinator* 25 (April 1976): 161–166.

2. Mark W. Booth, *The Experience of Songs* (New Haven: Yale University Press, 1981), pp. 1–28; R. Serge Denisoff and Richard A. Peterson, "Theories of Culture, Music, and Society," in *The Sounds of Social Change: Studies in Popular Culture* (Chicago: Rand McNally, 1972), pp. 1–12; George O. Carney, ed., *The Sounds of People and Places: Readings in the Geography of Music* (Washington, D.C.: University Press of America, 1979); James H. Cone, *The Spirituals and the Blues: An Interpretation* (New York: Seabury Press, 1972); David Ewen, *All the Years of American Popular Music: A Comprehensive History* (Englewood Cliffs, N.J.: Prentice-Hall, 1977); Charles Hamm, Bruno Nettl, and Ronald Byrnside, *Contemporary Music and Music Cultures* (Englewood Cliffs, N.J.: Prentice-Hall, 1975); Charles Hamm, *Yesterdays: Popular Song in America* (New York: W. W. Norton, 1979); Daniel Kingman, *American Music: A Panorama* (New York: Schirmer Books, 1979); Lawrence W. Levine, *Black Culture and Black Consciousness: Afro-American Folk Thought from Slavery to Freedom* (New York: Oxford University Press, 1977); George McCue, ed., *Music in American Society, 1776–1976: From Puritan Hymn to Synthesizer* (New Brunswick, N.J.: Transaction Books, 1977); John Anthony Scott, *The Ballad of America: The History of the United States in Song and Story* (New York: Bantam Books, 1966); and Eileen Southern, *The Music of Black Americans: A History* (New York: W. W. Norton, 1971).

3. Advocates for sound recordings as historical resources include: Tim Brooks, "ARSC: Association for Recorded Sound Collections—An Unusual Organization," *Goldmine*, no. 81 (February 1983): 22–23; Frank W. Hoffmann, "Documentation of Sound Recordings (Discography)," in *Encyclopedia of Library and Information Science*, ed. Allen Kent, Harold Lancour, and Jay E. Daily (New York: Marcel Dekker, 1980), pp. 117–129; Frank Hoffmann, "Popular Music Collections and Public Libraries," *Southeastern Librarian* 23 (Winter 1974): 26–31; John P. Morgan and Thomas C. Tulloss, "The Jake Walk Blues: A Toxicologic Tragedy Mirrored in American Popular Music," *Annals of Internal Medicine* 85 (December 1976): 804–808; David Pichaske, *A Generation in Motion: Popular Music and Culture in the Sixties* (New York: Schirmer Books, 1979); Carl Ryant, "Oral History as Popular Culture," *Journal of*

Popular Culture 15 (Spring 1982): 60–66; Fred E. H. Schroeder, ed., *Twentieth Century Popular Culture in Museums and Libraries* (Bowling Green, Ohio: Bowling Green University Press, 1981); William L. Schurk, "A Description of the Sound Recordings Archive at Bowling Green State University," *ARSC Journal* 14 (1982): 5–8; Gordon Stevenson, "Race Records: Victims of Benign Neglect in Libraries," *Wilson Library Bulletin* 50 (November 1975): 224–232; Gordon Stevenson, "The Wayward Scholar: Resources and Research in Popular Culture," *Library Trends* 25 (April 1977): 779–818; Susan S. Tamke, "Oral History and Popular Culture: A Method for the Study of the Experience of Culture," *Journal of Popular Culture* 11 (Summer 1977): 267–279; Larry Van Dyne, "Oral History: Sharecroppers and Presidents, Jazz and Texas Oil," *The Chronicle of Higher Education* 8 (December 24, 1973): 9–10; Wayne A. Wiegand, "Popular Culture: A New Frontier for Academic Libraries," *Journal of Academic Librarianship* 5 (September 1979): 200–204; and Wayne A. Wiegand, "Taste Cultures and Librarians: A Position Paper," *Drexel Library Quarterly* 16 (July 1980): 1–11.

4. It is impossible, of course, to apply decade descriptors with any authenticity. For overviews of popular music activities from 1950 to 1970 see: Carl Belz, *The Story of Rock*, 2d ed. (New York: Harper and Row, 1972); Gene Busnar, *It's Rock 'n' Roll: A Musical History of the Fabulous Fifties* (New York: Wanderer Books, 1979); Phyl Garland, *The Sound of Soul: The History of Black Music* (Chicago: Henry Regnery, 1969); Charlie Gillett, *The Sound of the City: The Rise of Rock and Roll* (New York: Outerbridge and Dienstfrey, 1970); Herb Hendler, *Year by Year in the Rock Era: Events and Conditions Shaping the Rock Generations That Reshaped America* (Westport, Conn.: Greenwood Press, 1983); Don J. Hibbard and Carol Kaleialoha, *The Role of Rock* (Englewood Cliffs, N.J.: Prentice-Hall, 1983); Ian Hoare, Tony Cummings, Clive Anderson, and Simon Frith, *The Soul Book* (New York: Dell Publishing Company, 1976); Jerry Hopkins, *The Rock Story* (New York: New American Library, 1970); Greil Marcus, *Mystery Train: Images of America in Rock 'n' Roll Music*, rev. ed. (New York: E. P. Dutton, 1982); Richard Middleton, *Pop Music and the Blues: A Study of the Relationship and Its Significance* (London: Victor Gollancz, 1972); Jim Miller, ed., *The Rolling Stone Illustrated History of Rock and Roll*, rev. ed. (New York: Random House/Rolling Stone Press Book, 1980); Lynda R. Obst, ed., *The Sixties: The Decade Remembered Now, by the People Who Lived It Then* (New York: Random House/Rolling Stone Press, 1977); David Pichaske, *A Generation in Motion: Popular Music and Culture in the Sixties* (New York: Schirmer Books, 1979); David Pichaske, *The Poetry of Rock: The Golden Years* (Peoria, Ill.: Ellis Press, 1981); Bruce Pollock, *When Rock Was Young: A Nostalgic Review of the Top 40 Era* (New York: Holt, Rinehart, and Winston, 1981); Jerome L. Rodnitzky, *Minstrels of the Dawn: The Folk-Protest Singer as a Cultural Hero* (Chicago: Nelson-Hall, 1976); Jacques Vassal, *Electric Children: Roots and Branches of Modern Folkrock* (New York: Taplinger, 1976); Arnold Shaw, *Honkers and Shouters: The Golden Years of Rhythm and Blues* (New York: Collier Books, 1978); Arnold Shaw, *The Rockin' 50s: The Decade That Transformed the Pop Music Scene* (New York: Hawthorn Books, 1974); Arnold Shaw, *The World of Soul* (New York: Paperback Library, 1971); and Ritchie Yorke, *The History of Rock 'n' Roll* (New York: Methuen Press, 1976).

5. Some of the best discographic and biographical studies include: Harry Castleman and Walter J. Podrazik, comps., *All Together Now: The First Complete Beatles Discography, 1961–1975* (New York: Ballantine Books, 1975); Harry Castleman and

Walter J. Podrazik, comps., *The Beatles Again* (Ann Arbor, Mich.: Pierian Press, 1977); Lee Cotten and Howard A. DeWitt, comps., *Jailhouse Rock: The Bootleg Records of Elvis Presley, 1970–1983* (Ann Arbor, Mich.: Pierian Press, 1983); R. Serge Denisoff, *Waylon: A Biography* (Knoxville: University of Tennessee Press, 1983); David Jeffrey Fletcher, comp., *David Robert Jones Bowie: The Discography of a Generalist, 1962–1979*, 3d ed. (Chicago: F. Fergeson Productions, 1979); John Goldrosen, *The Buddy Holly Story* (New York: Quick Fox, 1979); Michael H. Gray, comp., *Bibliography of Discographies—Volume 3: Popular Music* (New York: R. R. Bowker, 1983); Michael Gray, *Song and Dance Man: The Art of Bob Dylan*, rev. ed. (New York: St. Martin's Press, 1981); Jerry Hopkins, *Elvis: A Biography* (New York: Warner Paperback Library, 1971); Jerry Hopkins, *Elvis: The Final Years* (New York: St. Martin's Press, 1980); Terry Hounsome and Tim Chambre, comps., *Rock Record* (New York: Facts on Files, 1981); Myra Lewis, with Murray Silver, *Great Balls of Fire: The Uncensored Story of Jerry Lee Lewis* (New York: Quill Books, 1982); Dave Marsh and John Swenson, eds., *The New Rolling Stone Record Guide*, rev. ed. (New York: Random House/Rolling Stone Press Book, 1983); Jim Miller, ed., *The Rolling Stone Illustrated History of Rock and Roll*, rev. ed. (New York: Random House/Rolling Stone Press Book, 1980); Philip Norman, *Shout! The Beatles in Their Generation* (New York: Simon and Schuster, 1981); Charles Reinhart, comp., *You Can't Do That! Beatles' Bootlegs and Novelty Records, 1963–1980* (Ann Arbor, Mich.: Pierian Press, 1981); Charles Sawyer, *The Arrival of B. B. King: The Authorized Biography* (Garden City, N.Y.: Doubleday, 1980); John Swenson, *Bill Haley: The Daddy of Rock and Roll* (New York: Stein and Day, 1983); and Nick Tosches, *Hellfire: The Jerry Lee Lewis Story* (New York: Dell Publishing Company, 1982). For a critical commentary on star system biographies see: Simon Frith, "Rock Biography: Essay Review," in *Popular Music 3: Producers and Markets*, ed. Richard Middleton and David Horn (Cambridge: Cambridge University Press, 1983), pp. 271–277.

6. R. Serge Denisoff, "Content Analysis: The Achilles Heel of Popular Culture?" *Journal of Sociology* 75 (May 1970): 1035–1038; S. I. Hayakawa, "Popular Songs vs. the Facts of Life," *ETC: A Review of General Semantics* 12 (Winter 1955): 83–95; Leonard B. Meyer, "Meaning in Music and Information Theory," *Aesthetics and Art Criticism* 15 (June 1957): 412–424; and John Robinson and Paul Hirsch, "It's the Sound That Does It," in *Mass Media Issues*, ed. Leonard L. Sellers and William L. Rivers (Englewood Cliffs, N.J.: Prentice-Hall, 1977), pp. 153–158. For more balanced commentaries on the role of popular media on public opinion see: Ronald E. Rice, "The Content of Popular Recordings," *Popular Music and Society* 7 (1980): 140–158; Roger B. Rollin, "Against Evaluation: The Role of the Critic of Popular Culture," *Journal of Popular Culture* 9 (Fall 1975): 355–365; Roger B. Rollin, "Son of 'Against Evaluation': Reply to John Shelton Lawrence," *Journal of Popular Culture* 12 (Summer 1978): 113–117; and Wayne A. Wiegand, "Taste Cultures and Librarians," *Drexel Library Quarterly* 16 (July 1980): 1–11.

7. Glenn A. Baker, "Rock's Angry Voice," *Goldmine* no. 74 (July 1982): 10–11; R. Serge Denisoff, *Sing a Song of Social Significance* (Bowling Green, Ohio: Bowling Green University Popular Press, 1972); John Naisbitt, *Megatrends: Ten New Directions Transforming Our Lives* (New York: Warner Books, 1982); David Pichaske, *A Generation in Motion: Popular Music and Culture in the Sixties* (New York: Schirmer Books, 1979); and Richard A. Rosenstone, " 'The Times They Are a-Changin' ': The Music of Protest," *The Annuals* 381 (March 1969): 131–144.

8. Bruce Anderson, Peter Hesbacher, K. Peter Etzkorn, and R. Serge Denisoff, "Hit Record Trends, 1940–1977," *Journal of Communication* 30 (Spring 1980): 31–43; Gordon C. Bruner II, "The Association between Record Purchase Volume and Other Music-Related Characteristics," *Popular Music and Society* 6 (1979): 234–240; Steve Chapple and Reebee Garfalo, *Rock 'n' Roll Is Here to Pay: The History and Politics of the Music Industry* (Chicago: Nelson-Hall, 1977); R. Serge Denisoff, "Popular Music: Who Are the Recording Artists?" *Journal of Communication* (Winter 1982): 132–142; R. Serge Denisoff, *Solid Gold: The Popular Record Industry* (New Brunswick, N.J.: Transaction Books, 1975); Dave Harker, *One for the Money: Politics and the Popular Song* (London: Hutchinson and Company, 1980): Peter Hesbacher, K. Peter Etzkorn, Bruce Anderson, and David G. Berger, "A Major Manufacturer's Recordings: Shifts by CBS in Artistry and Song," *International Journal of Communication Research* 4 (1978): 375–392; Richard A. Peterson and David G. Berger, "Cycles in Symbol Production: The Case of Popular Music," *American Sociological Review* 40 (April 1975): 158–173; and Stephen S. Treichel, Peter Hesbacher, Paul Snyderman, and Bruce Anderson, "Anthology Albums: Do They Promote or Replace Regular Product?" *Popular Music and Society* 7 (1980): 245–252.

9. B. Lee Cooper, *Images of American Society in Popular Music: A Guide to Reflective Teaching* (Chicago: Nelson-Hall, 1982); Mark Gordon and Jack Nachbar, comps., *Currents of Warm Life: Popular Culture in American Higher Education* (Bowling Green, Ohio: Bowling Green University Popular Press, 1980); Fred E. H. Schroeder, ed., *Twentieth-Century Popular Culture in Museums and Libraries* (Bowling Green, Ohio: Bowling Green University Popular Press, 1981); Gordon Stevenson, "Popular Culture and the Public Library," in *Advances of Librarianship—Volume 7*, ed. Melvin J. Voight and Michael H. Harris (New York: Academic Press, 1977), pp. 177–229; Gordon Stevenson, "The Wayward Scholar: Resources and Research in Popular Culture," *Library Trends* 25 (April 1977): 779–818; Wayne A. Wiegand, ed., *Popular Culture and the Library: Proceedings of Symposium 2* (Lexington: College of Library Science at the University of Kentucky, 1978); and Wayne A. Wiegand, "Popular Culture: A New Frontier for Academic Libraries," *Journal of Academic Librarianship* 5 (September 1979): 200–204.

10. The spectrum of music-related books and articles is depicted in: Mark W. Booth, "Popular Music," in *Handbook of American Popular Culture—Volume One*, ed. M. Thomas Inge (Westport, Conn.: Greenwood Press, 1978), pp. 171–193; Mark W. Booth, comp., *American Popular Music: A Reference Guide* (Westport, Conn.: Greenwood Press, 1983); B. Lee Cooper, comp., *The Popular Music Handbook: A Resource Guide for Teachers, Librarians, and Media Specialists* (Littleton, Colo.: Libraries Unlimited, 1984); R. Serge Denisoff and John Bridges, "The Battered and Neglected Orphan: Popular Music Research and Books," *Popular Music and Society* 8 (1981): 43–59; Simon Frith, Stephen Fry, and David Horn, comps., "Booklist," in *Popular Music 2: Theory and Method*, ed. Richard Middleton and David Horn (Cambridge: Cambridge University Press, 1982), pp. 324–341; Simon Frith, David Horn, et al., comps., "Booklist," in *Popular Music 3: Producers and Markets*, ed. Richard Middleton and David Horn (Cambridge: Cambridge University Press, 1983), pp. 337–363; Frank W. Hoffmann, comp., *The Literature of Rock, 1954–1978* (Metuchen, N.J.: Scarecrow Press, 1981); Frank W. Hoffmann and B. Lee Cooper, comps., *The Literature of Rock II—A Supplement, 1954–1983* (Metuchen, N.J.: Scarecrow Press, 1986); David Horn, comp., *The Literature of American Music in Books*

and Folk Music Collections: A Fully Annotated Bibliography (Metuchen, N.J.: Scarecrow Press, 1977); Hugo A. Keesing, comp., "Annotated Bibliography of Pop/Rock Music," *Popular Culture Methods* 3 (Spring 1976): 4–22; George H. Lewis, "The Sociology of Popular Music," *Popular Music and Society* 7 (1979): 57–68; and Graham Vulliamy and Ed Lee, comps., "Bibliography," in *Pop Music in School* (London: Cambridge University Press, 1976), pp. 181–194. The publishing perspective on this music book avalanche is presented in: Madeleine Morel, "The Phenomenon of Rock Book Publishing," *Publishers Weekly*, 222 (December 17, 1982): 56–59 and Parke Puterbaugh, "Rock of Pages: Book Biz Thriving," *Rolling Stone* (April 14, 1983): 55, 58–59.

11. Madeleine Morel, "Books: Rock's New Partner," *Billboard* (July 31, 1982): 12; Edward Jay Whetmore, *Mediamerica: Form, Content, and Consequence of Mass Communication*, 2d ed. (Belmont, Calif.: Wadsworth Publishing Company, 1982); and Arnold S. Wolfe, "Rock on Cable—On MTV: Music Television, the First Video Music Channel," *Popular Music and Society* 9 (1983): 41–50.

A Resource Guide
to Themes
in Contemporary
American Song Lyrics,
1950–1985

Characters and Personalities

Creating a personal identity is an unending human endeavor. This activity is particularly pressing during adolescent years when there is an urgent need to forge a distinctive personality after years of contacts with family groups, socializing agencies, and childhood peers. Rock 'n' roll music exploded during the 1950s and created a legacy of sound that swept forward through the next three decades. The fact that rock performers such as Chuck Berry, The Who, Paul Simon, Cyndi Lauper, The Beatles, and Stevie Wonder suggest lyrically that individual identity is a significant concern is not co-incidental to their popularity and recording success. Many youth-directed anthems—"My Generation" (1966), "Won't Get Fooled Again" (1971), and "Who Are You" (1978)—examine universal issues of nonconformity, anti-authoritarianism, and personal identification.

Characters and personalities portrayed in popular songs are not always righteous; nor are they always rewarded for principled stands. They are not, as several fundamentalist preachers and feminist extremists believe, strictly satanic or blatantly sexist in their orientations toward life, love, and material possessions, either. The complexity of contemporary social beings is revealed in recorded characterizations. There are winners and losers; hipsters, tricksters, and con men along with squares, dupes, and marks; happy men and joyous women side by side with defeated souls and depressed hearts. The entire spectrum of human emotion is depicted in contemporary songs.

Pleasing others to secure their approval, to establish new friendships, to retain current jobs, or to avoid conflict, pressure, and strain in personal relationships is a common practice. During the 1950s and early 1960s, conformity in personality development was defined by many sociologists as "other-directedness." Although individual assertiveness seemed to rise dramatically during the post-1965 period, there is little evidence in contemporary lyrics that submissive characters disappeared. On the contrary, for every domineering male or powerful female there is a woman or male who opts for a subservient role. It would be unfair to define all submissive personalities as weak, though. The decision not to be assertive, not to make waves, can be a fulfilling, logical sign of inner strength. However, the stereotyping of submissive characters is common in popular songs. Ernie K-Doe's painful suffering at the hands (or actually at the tongue) of his malevolent "Mother-In-Law" (1961) is true to the universal joke pattern. Other songs go beyond this type of humorous statement, though, in depicting submissive characters.

Ironically, the sneering, posturing, swaggering King of Rock 'n' Roll contributed numerous illustrations to the I'll-do-anything-you-say-darling brand of lyrics. Elvis Presley praised flexibility in "Anyway You Want Me (That's How I Will Be)" (1956); he lauded docility in "(Let Me Be Your) Teddy Bear" (1957); and he urged the object of his affection to treat him like a fool—or mean and cruel—in "Love Me" (1956). This sentiment of total personal sacrifice for a loved one pervades popular lyrics. Other songs illustrating this fact are "Baby What You Want Me To Do" (1960), "Bend Me, Shape Me" (1967), "Carpet Man" (1968), "Chain Of Fools" (1967), "I'm Your Puppet" (1966), "Oh Me Oh My (I'm A Fool For You Baby)" (1969), "Piece Of My Heart" (1968), "Snap Your Fingers" (1962), "Under Your Spell Again" (1965), "When A Man Loves A Woman" (1966), and "Where You Lead" (1971).

Many commentators have mistakenly labelled all popular music as overtly "sexist" because women are allegedly always depicted in submissive roles. Upon examining the varying characters and distinctive characteristics of both men and women in contemporary lyrics, a typical interchange of dominant and submissive roles emerges. Does this imply that women aren't ever described as downtrodden? No. Sandy Posey speaks tragically of the trials of female existence in "Born A Woman" (1966) and "Single Girl" (1966); Glen Campbell observes that something less than total personal fulfillment prompts the "Dreams of The Everyday Housewife" (1968); Willie Nelson and Waylon Jennings laud the "Good-Hearted Woman" (1976) who is victimized by her self-centered, good-timin' man; and Linda Ronstadt describes a less-than-in-full-control situation in "When Will I Be Loved" (1975). The male side of submission is also frequently illustrated. Manipulated, frustrated, comical, and inept men appear as bewildered victims in various incidents. Albert King attributes his constant misfortunes to being "Born Under A Bad Sign" (1967); Junior Parker asks his spouse to define his marital role as a "Man Or Mouse" (1966); Jim Croce portrays a laughable loner in "Hard-Time Losin' Man" (1973); Bob Dylan depicts a male teenager's post–high school conundrum in the humorous "Subterranean Homesick Blues" (1965); and Sue Thompson and Phil McLean speak of less-than-dominant male characters in "Norman" (1962) and "Small Sad Sam" (1961). The image of the disheartened, confused male comes through most clearly in situations of unanticipated female assertion. Tyrone Davis asks "Can I Change My Mind" (1968) when a woman unexpectedly calls his bluff and The Drifters vow self-destruction over the loss of a loved one in "If You Don't Come Back" (1963).

Sometimes submission is designed to ease pain rather than to produce pleasure. This situation is depicted sexually by Merrilee Rush in "Angel Of The Morning" (1968), in Sami Smith's "Help Me Make It Through The Night" (1971), in Margie Rayburn's "I'm Available" (1957), and in Dusty Springfield's "You Don't Have to Say You Love Me" (1966). It is also interesting to note the internal frustrations created by self-willed cooperation with accepted social norms or with stated parental controls. Janis Ian testifies to the pressures of conservative parents and wrong-headed peer judgments in "Society's Child (Baby I've Been Thinking)" (1967) and "At Seventeen" (1975). Janis Joplin describes youthful persecution in "Down On Me" (1968). The act of externally following popular, healthful, trendy behavioral patterns in order to be a part of the in-crowd is yet another form of submission. Larry Groce displays a public life of proper dietary control, while he is secretly munching out on Ho-Hos and Ding Dongs, as the notorious "Junk Food Junkie" (1976).

Controlling the lives of others sounds like an ideal situation. Better yet, being in control of one's own life is surely a legitimate goal. The dominant personality can be a role model, a charismatic leader, or a rational decision maker. The problem with this situation, though, is that domination demands submission. A strong character often wills the behavior of others, rather than logically convincing followers or seeking to develop individual independence. Worse yet, domination can be demeaning, belittling, frustrating, and ultimately unhealthy. If a totally submissive stature is less than desirable, then a domineering personality can be deadly.

There is no gender monopoly on strength of character or decisiveness in contemporary lyrics. Just as Sarah Vaughan noted, "Whatever Lola Wants" (1955) she gets, females over the next three decades have demonstrated considerable power and authority over males. Sometimes it was the endless nagging of a "Mother-In-Law" (1961); other times it was a sassy lady proclaiming "These Boots Are Made For Walkin' " (1966) and "How Does That Grab You, Darlin'?" (1966). Peggy Lee affirmed "I'm A Woman" (1963), while Rod Stewart described the zany antics of the rambunctious "Maggie May" (1971). Other male perspectives on and bewildered fascination with female dominance are demonstrated in "Under Your Spell Again" (1965), "Louisiana Anna" (1983), "Gypsy Woman" (1961), "Mary Lou" (1959), "Mustang Sally" (1966), and "Wild Thing" (1966).

Just as physical attractiveness is often an asset that aids women in asserting control over men, so too males laud their own good looks, their reputations for virility, and their personal assuredness as justifications for dominance. During the fifties the distinctive males were "Daddy-O" (1955), a "Brown-Eyed Handsome Man" (1956), and "Daddy Cool" (1957). In the following decades singers like Wilson Pickett proclaimed "I'm A Midnight Mover" (1969) and "A Man And A Half" (1968); Otis Redding bragged that he was "Hard To Handle" (1968); and James Taylor described himself as a "Handy Man" (1977). Hints of domination or allusions to male prowess are also found in "The Boy From New York City" (1965), "Duke Of Earl" (1962), "Killer Joe" (1963), and "Speedo" (1955). These suggestions are confirmed in such paens to sexual domination as "I'm Ready" (1954), "I'm Your Hootchie Coochie Man" (1954), "Long Tall Shorty" (1964), "Magic Man" (1976), "Medicine Man" (1969), "Sixty Minute Man" (1973), and "Steamroller Blues" (1973).

Sometimes dominance is more readily recognized by outsiders. It may be confronted and challenged directly as in Dolly Parton's reaction to the manipulative "Jolene" (1974). The person being dominated can also react, as in "Nadine (Is It You?)" (1964), "Delilah" (1968), and "Evil Woman, Don't Play Your Games With Me" (1969). Claims of legitimate control or strong declarations against interference in personal relationships are also common in popular lyrics. Elvis Presley is a "U.S. Male" (1968) who won't brook any competition for his girlfriend's attentions; The Cookies warn their friends "Don't Say Nothin' Bad (About My Baby)" (1963); and The Marvellettes hiss at other young ladies, warning them "Don't Mess With Bill" (1966). Acknowledgment of the foolish acceptance of subordinate status is presented by Carly Simon in "You're So Vain" (1972), while the stubborn refusal to be dominated is championed by The Marvellettes in "Playboy" (1962) and by Jeannie Knight in "Mr. Big Stuff" (1971). The Cornelius Brothers and Sister Rose describe a more benign form of getting one's way with the opposite sex in "Treat Her Like A Lady" (1971).

Finally, two other types of personal dominance are unique and somewhat uncontrollable. Employment situations often force otherwise self-directed individuals to abandon their desired independence—Lou Rawls' "A Natural Man" (1971)—and to adopt a pattern of eight-hours-per-day subservience. This type of occupational subordination is also described in Jimmy Reed's "Big Boss Man" (1961), in Roy Orbison's "Workin' For The Man" (1962), in Johnny Paycheck's "Take This Job And Shove It" (1977), and in Jonathan Edwards' "Sunshine" (1971). The control of a celebrity over his or her fans is sometimes awesome—although it may be only in the minds of either the performer or a particular follower. Songs asserting such leadership include "Kansas City Star" (1965), "The Guitar Man" (1972), "Agent Double-O-Soul" (1965), "Star Baby" (1974), and "Clap For The Wolfman" (1974).

Popular music lyrics celebrate independence in many ways. Obviously, there is some relationship between personality dominance and self-directed behavior. Independent characters can be defined as "dominant," with the significant qualification that they tend to value the liberty of others too much to force unthinking acquiescence on their friends and associates. They seek freedom for themselves and others; they defy all authority that is irrational and unwarranted. Although the independent person may be un-recognized—neither a public celebrity nor a conquering hero, neither a wild-eyed radical nor a social deviant—he or she illustrates that true identity means continuous choice. The give and take of dominance and submission is secondary to the idea that change is possible in roles, in relationships, and within groups.

Chronologically, the desire for freedom is particularly prominent among those who are "Eighteen" (1971) and "Almost Grown" (1959). Flexibility in the behavior of youthful males is noted in Sheena Easton's "When He Shines" (1982). The same unpredictability among females is the subject of Foreigner's "Women" (1980). But initial thrusts at freedom are sometimes simply experiments with extremes of behavior, symbolic flights from pa-rental control, from real or imagined sexual domination, or from boring, repetitive organizational situations. Humorous examples of acts of inde-pendence are contained in Billy Joel's "Big Shot" (1979), Roger Miller's "Dang Me" (1964), Nancy Sinatra and Lee Hazlewood's "Jackson" (1967), Otis Redding and Carla Thomas' "Tramp" (1967), and B. B. King's "That Evil Child" (1971). Experimental departures are also featured in Mark Lind-say's "Arizona" (1969), Gallery's "Big City Miss Ruth Ann" (1972), Albert Hammond's "The Free Electric Band" (1973), and Billy Joel's "Movin' Out (Anthony's Song)" (1978).

Certain characters seem to be endowed—either by talent, by personality, or by circumstance—with remarkably high degrees of freedom. Other per-sonalities possess strangely disguised, latent forces of independence. As Bo Diddley correctly warns, "You Can't Judge A Book By The Cover" (1962). A teacher like "Abigail Beecher" (1964) defies schoolmarm stereotypes of dress and behavior; a self-driven lady like "Fancy" (1969) exercises her innate physical talents to secure a high level of wealth and independence; and the "Jazzman" (1974) and "Johnny B. Goode" (1958) utilize their musical skills to escape poverty and to encourage others to gain freedom from personal cares.

Many singers express complex notions of independence through lyrics that address the transience of personal relationships. Unlike traditional till-the-end-of-time romantic themes, these pleas are designed to promote emo-tional distance and personal objectivity. Illustrations include Cher's state-ment that "All I Really Want to Do" (1965) is be friends; Linda Ronstadt's acknowledgment that her boyfriend is hopelessly marching to the beat of a "Different Drum" (1967) if he expects their dating to end in a wedding; The Turtles protest that "It Ain't Me Babe" (1965) if a marital relationship is being sought; Diana Ross cautions that an overly serious relationship may produce an unwanted "Love Child" (1968); and Janis Joplin laments her own failure to recognize that freedom and love are not synonymous in "Me And Bobby McGee" (1971).

The most provocative statements of independence to be found in contemporary lyrics are based upon the themes of love and independence. Attacking both sexism and female stereotyping, Helen Reddy's "I Am Woman" (1972) and Maria Muldaur's "I'm A Woman" (1974) punctuate the demand for gender liberation in American society. Aretha Franklin personalized the theme of mutual responsibility in male–female relationships in "Think" (1968) and "Respect" (1967). This same notion was echoed in Dionne Warwick's "Don't Make Me Over" (1962), Otis Redding's "Respect" (1965), and Billy Joel's "Just The Way You Are" (1977). On a less romantic level, there are several other assertions of independence. These statements range from Billy Joel's "My Life" (1978) and Barbra Streisand's "Don't Rain On My Parade" (n.d.), to Sammy Davis, Jr.'s "I've Gotta Be Me" (1968), Frank Sinatra's "My Way" (1969), Lou Rawls' "A Natural Man" (1971), Jim Croce's "I Got A Name" (1973), and Barbra Streisand's "My Heart Belongs To Me" (1977).

In 1970 Bill Anderson wondered aloud "Where Have All The Heroes Gone." For popular music fans, heroes abound—Elvis Presley, Willie Nelson, Marvin Gaye, Stevie Wonder, Barbra Streisand, Michael Jackson, Dolly Parton, Frank Sinatra, Ray Charles, and many, many others. Beyond performers, though, contemporary lyrics offer ample illustrations of both historical and fictional characters who are bigger than life. In the realm of biographical statements, song heroes include figures from motion pictures, salutes to past political leaders, paens to the valor of soldiers, and tales of mythical cowboys, railroaders, and miners.

The acknowledgment of traditional American heroes includes salutes to Andrew Jackson, Davy Crockett, and even Confederate soldiers. Songs illustrating these themes include Johnny Horton's "The Battle Of New Orleans" (1959), Bill Hayes' "The Ballad Of Davy Crockett" (1955), and Johnny Horton's "Johnny Reb" (1959). The most frequently eulogized contemporary political figure is John Fitzgerald Kennedy. The assassinated president's career in the military, in politics, and as a martyred symbol of youthful leadership and social change is depicted in Jimmy Dean's "P.T. 109" (1962), in Connie Francis' "In The Summer Of His Years" (1963), in Dion's "Abraham, Martin, And John" (1968), and in Tommy Cash's "Six White Horses" (1969). American military men, whether courageous or foolhardy, have been lionized in tunes like Red River Dave's "There's A Star Spangled Banner Waving #2 (The Ballad Of Francis Powers)" (1960), SSgt. Barry Sadler's "The Ballad Of The Green Berets" (1966), and Terry Nelson and C Company's "The Battle Hymn Of Lt. Calley" (1971).

Athletes and musicians are also depicted as heroic characters. Examples of this phenomenon include Teresa Brewer's salute to New York Yankee centerfielder Mickey Mantle—"I Love Mickey" (1956)—and Johnny Wakelin and The Kinshasa Band's praise for Louisville's boxing sensation Cassius Clay—"Black Superman—Muhammad Ali" (1975). Tributes to singers and songwriters are even more numerous. Wilson Pickett praises black artists Nat King Cole, Sam Cooke, and Otis Redding in "Cole, Cooke, And Redding" (1970); The Commodores remember Marvin Gaye and Jackie Wilson in "Night Shift" (1984); The Tom Tom Club praises black stars Bootsy Collins, Smokey Robinson, Bob Marley, Kurtis Blow, Bohannon, and James Brown in "Genius Of Love" (1982); Canned Heat salutes Little Richard in "Rockin' With The King" (1972); Stevie Wonder praises Ella Fitzgerald and Duke Ellington in "Sir Duke" (1977); Spyder Turner imitates the vocal stylings of singers Jackie Wilson, David Ruffin, Billy Stewart, Smokey Robinson, and Chuck Jackson in "Stand By Me" (1966); Liverpools' Fab Four are lauded in The Carefrees' "We Love You Beatles" (1964) and in Bruce Foster's "Platinum Heroes" (1977); and Buddy Holly, the Big Bopper, and Ritchie Valens are eulogized in Tommy Dee's "Three Stars" and Don McLean's "American Pie" (1971).

Fictional heroes have been a staple in American music for many decades. Folk songs praising the feats of Casey Jones and John Henry were common throughout the early twentieth century. Willie Nelson identified a long-time set of folk heroes in "My Heroes Have Always Been Cowboys" (1980). But the heroes of popular tunes tend to be a mixed bag of humorous, dedicated, flighty, driven characters including Ray Stevens' "Along Came Jones" (1969), Jimmy Dean's "Big Bad John" (1961), Kenny Rogers' "Coward Of The County" (1979), Elvis Presley's "Guitar Man" (1981), Black Oak Arkansas' "Jim Dandy" (1973), Foreigner's "Juke Box Hero" (1982), Gene Pitney's "(The Man Who Shot) Liberty Valance" (1962), and Ricky Nelson's "Teen Age Idol" (1962).

Just as popular songs depict ranges of submissive, dominant, and independent personalities, they also illustrate some fantastic extremes of human behavior. Heroes are exemplary characters. At the other end of the behavioral spectrum, though, are extreme examples of anti-social persons who can only be described as rebels, renegades, and outcasts.

These individuals vary dramatically from normal modes of social behavior. They are meaner than snakes, more vicious than sharks, and, according to Steppenwolf, "Born To Be Wild" (1968). Their motto is paraphrased by the Ozark Mountain Daredevils: "If You Wanna Get To Heaven" (1974), you've got to raise a little hell. The Rolling Stones refer to individuals of this riot-prone persuasion by various names, including "Jumpin' Jack Flash" (1968) and "Street Fightin' Man" (1968). If, as Elton John contends, "Saturday Night's Alright For Fighting" (1973), the rest of the week is also punctuated with brawls, battles, and imbroglios.

The chaos associated with some rebels is humorous—as in Johnny Cash's "A Boy Named Sue" (1969) and his barroom fisticuffs with his estranged father. Other outcasts are frightening, psychotic murderers. Carole King's "Smackwater Jack" (1971) shotguns a church congregation simply because he was in the mood for a little confrontation. He is clearly a homicidal maniac. Other desperate, hostile characters are described by Jim Croce in "Bad, Bad Leroy Brown" (1973) and "You Don't Mess Around With Jim" (1972), by The Olympics in "Big Boy Pete" (1960), by Quiet Riot in "Bang Your Head (Mental Health)" (1984), by Tony Joe White in "Polk Salad Annie" (1969), and by The Bob Seger System in "Ramblin' Gamblin' Man" (1968).

The legal system establishes the boundary between those who live within accepted social rules and those who elect to lead lives beyond the law. There is an extensive list of recordings, for instance, that deal with prostitution. Viewpoints on this subject vary from female participants, as in LaBelle's self-confident "Lady Marmalade" (1975), to female commentators, as in Donna Summer's "Bad Girls" (1979), and to male observers of prostitutes, as in The Rolling Stones' "Brown Sugar" (1971) and "Honky Tonk Women" (1969), Queen's "Fat Bottom Girls" (1978), The Animals' "The House Of The Rising Sun" (1964), Daryl Hall and John Oates' "Maneater" (1982), and Mountain's "Mississippi Queen" (1970).

Lawbreakers can be depicted as either funny—Jack Scott's "Leroy" (1958) and Jerry Reed's "When You're Hot, You're Hot" (1971)—or frightful and fearsome. They may be renegade businessmen like Jerry Reed's alligator-hunting "Amos Moses" (1970), Robert Mitchum's rum-running driver in "The Ballad Of Thunder Road" (1958), and Bobby Darin's contract killer "Mack The Knife" (1959). Other examples of outlaw behavior are depicted in Georgie Fame's "The Ballad Of Bonnie and Clyde" (1968), Johnny Cash's "Folsom Prison Blues" (1968), Johnny Rivers' "(I Washed My Hands In) Muddy Water" (1966), Lorne Greene's "Ringo" (1964), and The Steve Miller Band's "Take The Money And Run" (1976).

Occasionally, evil is totally personalized. It may appear as pointless murder, as merciless conquest, or as insatiable lust for power. Shirley Bassey's "Goldfinger" (1965) is heartless, materialistic, and absolutely malicious; Al Wilson's "The Snake" (1968) is deadly, consistently hostile, and unable to comprehend compassion; and Jim Stafford's "Swamp Witch" (1973), after seemingly commiting an act of social benevolence, unexpectedly returns to her old homicidal ways. It is intriguing that many of the most mysterious lyrical embodiments of evil are women. These include Santana's "Black Magic Woman" (1970), Queen's "Killer Queen" (1975), Blood, Sweat and Tears' "Lucretia MacEvil" (1970), Bobby Goldsboro's "Lucy And The Stranger" (1982), and Redbone's "Witch Queen of New Orleans" (1971).

CHARACTERS AND PERSONALITIES

"The Logical Song" (A&M 2128)
  by Supertramp

"My Generation" (Decca 31877)
by The Who (1966)

"Who Are You" (MCA 40948)
by The Who (1978)

"Won't Get Fooled Again" (Decca 32846)
by The Who (1971)

Submissive Personalities

"Angel of the Morning"(Bell 705)
by Merrilee Rush (1968)

"Anyway You Want Me (That's How I Will Be)" (RCA 47-6643)
by Elvis Presley (1956)

"At Seventeen" (Columbia 10154)
by Janis Ian (1975)

"Baby What You Want Me To Do" (Vee-Jay 333)
by Jimmy Reed (1960)

"Bad Boy" (Arista 1030)
by Ray Parker, Jr. (1982)

"Bend Me, Shape Me" (Acta 811)
by The American Breed (1967)

"Born A Woman" (MGM 13501)
by Sandy Posey (1966)

"Born Under A Bad Sign" (Stax 217)
by Albert King (1967)

"Can I Change My Mind" (Dakar 602)
by Tyrone Davis (1968)

"Carpet Man" (Soul City 762)
by The Fifth Dimension (1968)

"Chain of Fools" (Atlantic 2464)
by Aretha Franklin (1967)

"The Clown" (Elektra 47302)
by Conway Twitty (1982)

"Down On Me" (Mainstream 662)
by Big Brother and The Holding Company (1968)

"Dreams Of The Everyday Housewife" (Capitol 2224)
by Glen Campbell (1968)

"Eleanor Rigby" (Capitol 5715)
by The Beatles (1966)

"A Girl's Work Is Never Done" (Cadence 1366)
by The Chordettes (1959)

"Good Hearted Woman" (RCA 10529)
by Waylon and Willie (1976)

"Hard-Time Losin' Man" (ABC 11405)
  by Jim Croce (1973)

"Help Me Make It Through The Night" (Mega 0015)
  by Sammi Smith (1971)

"If You Don't Come Back" (Atlantic 2201)
  by The Drifters (1963)

"I'm A Slave" (RCA 13663)
  by Jerry Reed (1983)

"I'm Available" (Liberty 55102)
  by Margie Rayburn (1957)

"I'm Your Puppet" (Bell 648)
  by James and Bobby Purify (1966)

"An Innocent Man" (Columbia 04259)
  by Billy Joel (1983)

"James (Hold The Ladder Steady)" (Hickory 1183)
  by Sue Thompson (1962)

"Junk Food Junkie" (Warner Brothers 8165)
  by Larry Groce (1976)

"Leave Me Alone (Ruby Red Dress)" (Capitol 3768)
  by Helen Reddy (1973)

"(Let Me Be Your) Teddy Bear" (RCA 47-7000)
  by Elvis Presley (1957)

"Like A Rolling Stone" (Columbia 43346)
  by Bob Dylan (1965)

"Love Me" (RCA EPA 992)
  by Elvis Presley (1956)

"Love Theme From 'Eyes of Laura Mars' (Prisoner)" (Columbia 10777)
  by Barbra Streisand (1978)

"Man Or Mouse" (Duke 413)
  by Junior Parker (1966)

"Marianne" (Columbia 40817)
  by Terry Gilkyson and The Easy Riders (1957)

"Mother's Little Helper" (London 902)
  by The Rolling Stones (1966)

"My Girl Sloopy" (Atlantic 2221)
  by The Vibrations (1964)

"My Guy" (Cotillion 47000)
  by Sister Sledge (1982)

"Norman" (Hickory 1159)
  by Sue Thompson (1962)

"Nowhere Man" (Capitol 5587)
  by The Beatles (1966)

"Oh Me Oh My (I'm A Fool For You Baby)" (Atco 6722)
by Lulu (1969)

"Piece Of My Heart" (Columbia 44626)
by Big Brother and The Holding Company (1968)

"Please Come To Boston" (Epic 11115)
by Dave Loggins (1974)

"Rag Doll" (Philips 40211)
by The Four Seasons (1964)

"Ruby Tuesday" (London 904)
by The Rolling Stones (1967)

"Single Girl" (MGM 13612)
by Sandy Posey (1966)

"Single Women" (RCA 13057)
by Dolly Parton (1982)

"Small Sad Sam" (Versatile 107)
by Phil McLean (1961)

"Snap Your Fingers" (Todd 1072)
by Joe Henderson (1962)

"Society's Child (Baby I've Been Thinking)" (Verve 5027)
by Janis Ian (1967)

"Subterranean Homesick Blues" (Columbia 43242)
by Bob Dylan (1965)

"A Sweet Old Fashioned Girl" (Coral 61636)
by Teresa Brewer (1956)

"Under Your Spell Again" (Imperial 66144)
by Johnny Rivers (1965)

"Wake Up Little Susie" (Warner Brothers 50053)
by Simon and Garfunkel (1982)

"When A Man Loves A Woman" (Atlantic 2326)
by Percy Sledge (1966)

"When A Woman Loves A Man" (Atlantic 2335)
by "Little Esther" Phillips (1966)

"When Will I Be Loved" (Capitol 4050)
by Linda Ronstadt (1975)

"Where You Lead" (Columbia 45414)
by Barbra Streisand (1971)

"Workin' At The Car Wash Blues" (ABC 11447)
by Jim Croce (1974)

"You Don't Have To Say You Love Me" (Philips 40371)
by Dusty Springfield (1966)

Dominant Personalities

"Agent Double-O-Soul" (Ric-Tic 103)
by Edwin Starr (1965)

"Automatic Man" (Warner Brothers 20153)
by Michael Sembello (1983)

"Big Boss Man" (Vee-Jay 380)
by Jimmy Reed (1961)

"The Boy From New York City" (Blue Cat 102)
by Ad Libs (1965)

"Brown-Eyed Handsome Man" (Chess 1635)
by Chuck Berry (1956)

"Clap For The Wolfman" (RCA 0324)
by The Guess Who (1974)

"Daddy Cool" (Cameo 117)
by The Rays (1957)

"Daddy-O" (Dot 15428)
by The Fontane Sisters (1955)

"Delilah" (Parrot 40025)
by Tom Jones (1968)

"Dizzy, Miss Lizzy" (Specialty 626)
by Larry Williams (1958)

"Donna The Prima Donna" (Columbia 42852)
by Dion (1963)

"Don't Mess With Bill" (Tamla 54126)
by The Marvelettes (1966)

"Don't Say Nothin' Bad (About My Baby)" (Dimension 1008)
by The Cookies (1963)

"Duke Of Earl" (Vee-Jay 416)
by Gene Chandler (1962)

"Evil Woman Don't Play Your Games With Me" (Amaret 112)
by Crow (1969)

"Green-Eyed Lady" (Liberty 56183)
by Sugarloaf (1970)

"The Guitar Man" (Elektra 45803)
by Bread (1972)

"Gypsy Woman" (ABC-Paramount 10241)
by The Impressions (1961)

"Handy Man" (Columbia 10557)
by James Taylor (1977)

"Hard To Handle" (Atco 6592)
by Otis Redding (1968)

"Hardhearted Hannah" (ABC–Paramount 10164)
by Ray Charles (1960)

"How Does That Grab You, Darlin'?" (Reprise 0461)
by Nancy Sinatra (1966)

"I Get Around" (Capitol 5174)
by The Beach Boys (1964)

"I'm A Midnight Mover" (Atlantic 2528)
by Wilson Pickett (1969)

"I'm A Woman" (Capitol 4888)
by Peggy Lee (1963)

"I'm Ready" (Chess 1579)
by Muddy Waters (1954)

"I'm Your Hootchie Coochie Man" (Chess 1560)
by Muddy Waters (1954)

"Jolene" (RCA 0145)
by Dolly Parton (1974)

"Josie" (ABC 12404)
by Steely Dan (1978)

"Kansas City Star" (Smash 1998)
by Roger Miller (1965)

"Killer Joe" (Scepter 1246)
by The Rocky Fellers (1963)

"Long Tall Shorty" (Checker 1075)
by Tommy Tucker (1964)

"Louisiana Anna" (Mercury 814561)
by The Maines Brothers Band (1983)

"Maggie May" (Mercury 73224)
by Rod Stewart (1971)

"Magic Man" (Mushroom 7011)
by Heart (1976)

"A Man And A Half" (Atlantic 2575)
by Wilson Pickett (1968)

"Mary Lou" (Roulette 4177)
by Ronnie Hawkins and The Hawks (1959)

"Mean Woman Blues" (Monument 824)
by Roy Orbison (1963)

"Medicine Man" (Event 3302)
by The Buchanan Brothers (1969)

"Moody Woman" (Mercury 72929)
by Jerry Butler (1969)

"Mother-In-Law" (Minit 623)
by Ernie K-Doe (1961)

"Mr. Big Stuff" (Stax 0088)
by Jean Knight (1971)

"Mustang Sally" (Atlantic 2365)
by Wilson Pickett (1966)

"The Pied Piper" (Jamie 1320)
by Crispian St. Peters (1966)

"Playboy" (Tamla 54060)
by The Marvelettes (1962)

"Pretty Little Angel Eyes" (Dunes 2007)
by Curtis Lee (1961)

"Queen Of The House" (Capitol 5402)
by Jody Miller (1965)

"Redneck Girl" (Warner/Curb 29923)
by The Bellamy Brothers (1982)

"Rhumba Girl" (Warner Brothers 8795)
by Nicolette Larson (1979)

"Riding The Tiger" (Arista 9023)
by Phyllis Hyman (1983)

"Ruby" (ABC–Paramount 10164)
by Ray Charles (1960)

"Short Fat Fannie" (Specialty 608)
by Larry Williams (1957)

"Since I Met You Baby" (Atlantic 1111)
by Ivory Joe Hunter (1956)

"Sixty Minute Man" (Fame 250)
by Clarence Carter (1973)

"Speedo" (Josie 785)
by The Cadillacs (1955)

"Star Baby" (RCA 0217)
by The Guess Who (1974)

"Steamroller Blues" (RCA 74-0910)
by Elvis Presley (1973)

"Sunshine" (Capricorn 8021)
by Jonathan Edwards (1971)

"Superwoman (Where Were You When I Needed You)" (Tamla 54216)
by Stevie Wonder (1972)

"Take This Job And Shove It" (Epic 60569)
by Johnny Paycheck (1977)

"These Boots Are Made For Walkin' " (Reprise 0432)
by Nancy Sinatra (1966)

"Treat Her Like A Lady" (United Artists 50721)
by The Cornelius Brothers and Sister Rose (1971)

"Under Your Spell Again" (Imperial 66144)
  by Johnny Rivers (1965)

"U.S. Male" (RCA 47-9465)
  by Elvis Presley (1968)

"Whatever Lola Wants" (Mercury 70595)
  by Sarah Vaughan (1955)

"Wild One" (Cameo 171)
  by Bobby Rydell (1960)

"Wild Thing" (Fontana 1548)
  by The Troggs (1966)

"Workin' For The Man" (Monument 467)
  by Roy Orbison (1962)

"You're So Vain" (Elektra 45824)
  by Carly Simon (1972)

Independent Characters

"Abigail Beecher" (Warner Brothers 5409)
  by Freddy Cannon (1964)

"All I Really Want To Do" (Imperial 66114)
  by Cher (1965)

"All My Rowdy Friends (Have Settled Down)" (Elektra 47191)
  by Hank Williams, Jr. (1981)

"Almost Grown" (Chess 1722)
  by Chuck Berry (1959)

"Arizona" (Columbia 45037)
  by Mark Lindsay (1969)

"Big City Miss Ruth Ann" (Sussex 248)
  by Gallery (1972)

"Big Shot" (Columbia 10913)
  by Billy Joel (1979)

"Bold Soul Sister" (Blue Thumb 104)
  by Ike and Tina Turner (1969)

"The Cheater" (Musicland 20001)
  by Bob Kuban and The In-Men (1966)

"Clean Up Woman" (Alston 4601)
  by Betty Wright (1971)

"Come Together" (Apple 2654)
  by The Beatles (1969)

"Country Girl–City Man" (Atlantic 2480)
  by Billy Vera and Judy Clay (1968)

"Crazy Mama" (Shelter 7314)
  by J. J. Cale (1972)

"Daddy Cool" (Cameo 117)
   by The Rays (1957)

"Dang Me" (Smash 1881)
   by Roger Miller (1964)

"Devil Or Angel" (Liberty 55270)
   by Bobby Vee (1960)

"Different Drum" (Capitol 2004)
   by Linda Ronstadt and The Stone Poneys (1967)

"Disco Lady" (Columbia 10281)
   by Johnnie Taylor (1976)

"Don't Make Me Over" (Scepter 1239)
   by Dionne Warwick (1962)

"Don't Rain On My Parade" (Columbia 33161)
   by Barbra Streisand (n.d.)

"Don't Touch Me" (Capitol 2382)
   by Bettye Swann (1969)

"Eighteen" (Warner Brothers 7449)
   by Alice Cooper (1971)

"Elected" (Warner Brothers 7631)
   by Alice Cooper (1972)

"Evil Ways" (Columbia 45069)
   by Santana (1970)

"Fancy" (Capitol 2675)
   by Bobbie Gentry (1969)

"Fancy Dancer" (Motown 1408)
   by The Commodores (1977)

"Fever" (Capitol 3998)
   by Peggy Lee (1958)

"The Fightin' Side Of Me" (Capitol 2719)
   by Merle Haggard (1970)

"Foxey Lady" (Reprise 0641)
   by Jimi Hendrix (1967)

"The Free Electric Band" (Mums 6018)
   by Albert Hammond (1973)

"The Girl Can't Help It" (Specialty 591)
   by Little Richard (1957)

"Gloria" (Atlantic 4048)
   by Laura Branigan (1982)

"Gloria" (Dunwich 116)
   by Shadows of Knight (1966)

"Gypsy Woman" (Uni 55240)
   by Brian Hyland (1970)

"Half-Breed" (MGM 12803)
  by Marvin Rainwater (1959)

"Handy Man" (Amy 905)
  by Del Shannon (1964)

"The Happiest Girl In The Whole U.S.A." (Dot 17409)
  by Donna Fargo (1972)

"Harper Valley P.T.A." (Plantation 3)
  by Jeannie C. Riley (1968)

"Heartbreaker" (Arista 1015)
  by Dionne Warwick (1982)

"Henrietta" (Dot 15664)
  by Jimmy Dee (1958)

"I Am Woman" (Capitol 3350)
  by Helen Reddy (1972)

"I Got A Name" (ABC 11389)
  by Jim Croce (1973)

"I Heard It Through The Grapevine" (Soul 35039)
  by Gladys Knight and The Pips (1967)

"I'm A Happy Man" (United Artists 853)
  by The Jive Five (1965)

"I'm A Man" (United Artists 50149)
  by The Spencer Davis Group (1967)

"I'm A Woman" (Reprise 1319)
  by Maria Muldaur (1974)

"I'm Every Woman" (Warner Brothers 8683)
  by Chaka Khan (1978)

"It Ain't Me Babe" (White Whale 222)
  by The Turtles (1965)

"It's A Man's Man's Man's World" (King 6035)
  by James Brown (1966)

"It's Hard To Be Humble" (Casablanca 2244)
  by Mac Davis (1980)

"I've Gotta Be Me" (Reprise 0779)
  by Sammy Davis, Jr. (1968)

"Jackson" (Reprise 0595)
  by Nancy Sinatra and Lee Hazlewood (1967)

"Jazzman" (Ode 66101)
  by Carole King (1974)

"Johnny B. Goode" (Chess 1691)
  by Chuck Berry (1958)

"The Joker" (Capitol 3732)
  by The Steve Miller Band (1973)

"Just The Way You Are" (Columbia 10646)
  by Billy Joel (1977)

"Justine" (Moonglow 242)
  by The Righteous Brothers (1965)

"Kentucky Woman" (Bang 551)
  by Neil Diamond (1967)

"Lady" (Liberty 1380)
  by Kenny Rogers (1980)

"Lady Godiva" (Capitol 5740)
  by Peter and Gordon (1966)

"Let A Woman Be A Woman—Let A Man Be A Man" (Original Sound 89)
  by Dyke and The Blazers (1969)

"Light My Fire" (RCA 9950)
  by Jose Feliciano (1968)

"Little Diane" (Laurie 3134)
  by Dion (1962)

"Little Egypt (Ying-Yang)" (Atco 6192)
  by The Coasters (1961)

"Little Latin Lupe Lu" (Wand 157)
  by The Kingsmen (1964)

"Little Queenie" (Chess 1722)
  by Chuck Berry (1959)

"Long Cool Woman (In A Black Dress)" (Epic 10871)
  by The Hollies (1972)

"Love Child" (Motown 1135)
  by Diana Ross and The Supremes (1968)

"Lucille" (Specialty 598)
  by Little Richard (1957)

"Macho Man" (Casablanca 922)
  by The Village People (1978)

"Maniac" (Casablanca 812516)
  by Michael Sembello (1983)

"Manish Boy" (Chess 1602)
  by Muddy Waters (1955)

"Me And Bobby McGee" (Columbia 45314)
  by Janis Joplin (1971)

"Mercy, Mercy, Mercy" (Columbia 44182)
  by The Buckinghams (1967)

"Michael" (United Artists 258)
  by The Highwaymen (1961)

"Movin' Out (Anthony's Song)" (Columbia 10708)
  by Billy Joel (1978)

"Mr. Big Stuff" (Stax 0088)
by Jean Knight (1971)

"Mr. Bojangles" (Liberty 56197)
by The Nitty Gritty Dirt Band (1970)

"Mr. Businessman" (Monument 1083)
by Ray Stevens (1968)

"My Heart Belongs To Me" (Columbia 10555)
by Barbra Streisand (1977)

"My Life" (Columbia 10853)
by Billy Joel (1978)

"My Way" (Reprise 0817)
by Frank Sinatra (1969)

"Nadine (Is It You?)" (Chess 1883)
by Chuck Berry (1964)

"A Natural Man" (MGM 14262)
by Lou Rawls (1971)

"A Natural Woman (You Make Me Feel Like)" (Atlantic 2441)
by Aretha Franklin (1967)

"Nature Boy" (Atco 6196)
by Bobby Darin (1961)

"Ninety-Nine And A Half (Won't Do)" (Atlantic 2334)
by Wilson Pickett (1966)

"Nobody But Me" (Capitol 5990)
by The Human Beinz (1967)

"Oh, Pretty Woman" (Monument 851)
by Roy Orbison (1964)

"Okie From Muskogee" (Capitol 2626)
by Merle Haggard (1969)

"One Hell Of A Woman" (Columbia 46004)
by Mac Davis (1974)

"One Man Woman/One Woman Man" (United Artists 569)
by Paul Anka and Odia Coates (1974)

"Patty Baby" (Swan 4139)
by Freddy Cannon (1963)

"Priscilla" (Royal Roost 621)
by Eddie Cooley (1956)

"Queen Of The Roller Derby" (Shelter 7337)
by Leon Russell (1973)

"The Rapper" (Kama Sutra 502)
by The Jaggerz (1970)

"Respect" (Atlantic 2403)
by Aretha Franklin (1967)

"Respect" (Volt 128)
by Otis Redding (1965)

"Rio" (Capitol 5215)
by Duran Duran (1983)

"Road Runner" (Checker 942)
by Bo Diddley (1960)

"Rocket Man" (Uni 55328)
by Elton John (1972)

"A Satisfied Mind" (Philips 40400)
by Bobby Hebb (1966)

"Secret Agent Man" (Imperial 66159)
by Johnny Rivers (1966)

"Seventh Son" (Imperial 6612)
by Johnny Rivers (1965)

"Shakin' " (Columbia 03252)
by Eddie Money (1982)

"She Belongs to Me" (Decca 32550)
by Rick Nelson (1969)

"She's A Heartbreaker" (Musicor 1306)
by Gene Pitney (1968)

"She's About A Mover" (Trite 8308)
by The Sir Douglas Quintet (1965)

"She's A Lady" (Parrot 40058)
by Tom Jones (1971)

"She's Always A Woman" (Columbia 10788)
by Billy Joel (1978)

"Signs" (Lionel 3213)
by The Five Man Electrical Band (1971)

"Sixteen Tons" (Atlantic 3323)
by The Don Harrison Band (1976)

"Soul Man" (Stax 231)
by Sam and Dave (1967)

"Steel Men" (Columbia 42483)
by Jimmy Dean (1962)

"Stray Cat Strut" (EMI America 8122)
by The Stray Cats (1982)

"Strut" (EMI America 8227)
by Sheena Easton (1984)

"Super Bad" (King 6329)
by James Brown (1970)

"Superman" (Warner Brothers 7403)
by The Ides of March (1970)

"Susie-Q" (Checker 863)
  by Dale Hawkins (1957)

"Sweet Hitch-Hiker" (Fantasy 665)
  by Creedence Clearwater Revival (1971)

"Sweet Little Sixteen" (Sun 379)
  by Jerry Lee Lewis (1962)

"That Evil Child" (Kent 4542)
  by B. B. King (1971)

"Theme From Shaft" (Enterprise 9083)
  by Isaac Hayes (1971)

"Think" (Atlantic 2518)
  by Aretha Franklin (1968)

"Tony Rome" (Reprise 0636)
  by Nancy Sinatra (1967)

"Tramp" (Stax 216)
  by Otis and Carla (1967)

"Transistor Sister" (Swan 4078)
  by Freddy Cannon (1961)

"Travelin' Man" (Imperial 5741)
  by Ricky Nelson (1961)

"When He Shines" (EMI America 8113)
  by Sheena Easton (1982)

"Woman Is A Man's Best Friend" (Swan 4102)
  by Teddy and The Twilights (1962)

"Women" (Atlantic 3651)
  by Foreigner (1980)

"Women In Love" (Liberty 1469)
  by Kin Vassy (1982)

"You Can't Judge A Book By The Cover" (Checker 1019)
  by Bo Diddley (1962)

"You Don't Own Me" (Mercury 72206)
  by Lesley Gore (1963)

"(You're So Square) Baby, I Don't Care" (Geffen 29849)
  by Joni Mitchell (1982)

"(You're The) Devil In Disguise" (RCA 47-8188)
  by Elvis Presley (1963)

Heroes

"Abraham, Martin And John" (Laurie 3464)
  by Dion (1968)

"All My Rowdy Friends (Have Settled Down)" (Elektra 47191)
  by Hank Williams, Jr. (1981)

"Along Came Jones" (Monument 1150)
by Ray Stevens (1969)

"American Pie" (United Artists 50856)
by Don McLean (1971)

"The Ballad Of Davy Crockett" (Cadence 1256)
by Bill Hayes (1955)

"Ballad Of John Dillinger" (Mercury 72836)
by Billy Grammer (1968)

"The Ballad Of The Green Berets" (RCA 8739)
by SSgt. Barry Saddler (1966)

"The Battle Hymn Of Lt. Calley" (Plantation 73)
by Terry Nelson and C Company (1971)

"The Battle Of New Orleans" (Columbia 41339)
by Johnny Horton (1959)

"Big Bad John" (Columbia 42175)
by Jimmy Dean (1961)

"Black Superman—Muhammad Ali" (Pye 71012)
by Johnny Wakelin and The Kinshasa Band (1975)

"Cole, Cooke, And Redding" (Atlantic 2722)
by Wilson Pickett (1970)

"Coward Of The County" (United Artists 1327)
by Kenny Rogers (1979)

"Elvis Presley Blvd." (Columbia 03413)
by Billy Joel (1982)

"Genius of Love" (Sire 49882)
by The Tom Tom Club (1982)

"George Jackson" (Columbia 45516)
by Bob Dylan (1971)

"Guitar Man" (RCA PB 12158)
by Elvis Presley (1981)

"Heroes" (Motown 1495)
by The Commodores (1980)

"Heroes And Villains" (Brother 1001)
by The Beach Boys (1967)

"Honky Tonk Man" (Warner/Viva 29847)
by Marty Robbins (1982)

"I Hear You Knocking" (MAM 3601)
by Dave Edmunds (1970)

"I Love Mickey" (Coral 61700)
by Teresa Brewer (1956)

"In The Summer Of His Years" (MGM 13203)
by Connie Francis (1963)

"Jim Dandy" (Atco 6948)
  by Black Oak Arkansas (1973)

"Johnny Reb" (Columbia 41437)
  by Johnny Horton (1959)

"Juke Box Hero" (Atlantic 4017)
  by Foreigner (1982)

"Leave Them Boys Alone" (Warner Brothers 29633)
  by Hank Williams, Jr. (1983)

"Lefty" (Warner/Viva 49778)
  by David Frizzell (1981)

"(The Man Who Shot) Liberty Valance" (Musicor 1020)
  by Gene Pitney (1962)

"The Man With The Golden Thumb" (RCA 13081)
  by Jerry Reed (1982)

"My Heroes Have Always Been Cowboys" (Columbia 11186)
  by Willie Nelson (1980)

"Night Shift" (Motown 1773)
  by The Commodores (1984)

"Platinum Heroes" (Millennium 602)
  by Bruce Foster (1977)

"P.T. 109" (Columbia 42338)
  by Jimmy Dean (1962)

"The Ride" (Columbia 03778)
  by David Allen Coe (1983)

"Rockin' With The King" (United Artists 50892)
  by Canned Heat (1972)

"Sir Duke" (Tamla 54281)
  by Stevie Wonder (1977)

"Six White Horses" (Epic 10540)
  by Tommy Cash (1969)

"Stand By Me" (MGM 13617)
  by Spyder Turner (1966)

"Stars On 45 II" (Radio 3830)
  by Stars on 45 (1981)

"Stars On 45 III" (Radio 4019)
  by Stars on 45 (1982)

"Teen Age Idol" (Imperial 5864)
  by Ricky Nelson (1962)

"There's A Star Spangled Banner Waving #2 (The Ballad of Francis Powers)"
  (Savoy 3020)
  by Red River Dave (1960)

"This Cowboy's Hat" (Warner Brothers 29772)
  by Porter Wagoner (1983)

"Three Stars" (Crest 1057)
  by Tommy Dee, with Carol Kay and The Teen-Aires (1959)

"Tribute To A King" (Stax 248)
  by William Bell (1968)

"Vincent" (United Artists 50887)
  by Don McLean (1972)

"We Love You Beatles" (London International 10614)
  by The Carefrees (1964)

"Where Have All The Heroes Gone" (Decca 32744)
  by Bill Anderson (1970)

Rebels and Outcasts

"Alabama Wild Man" (RCA 0738)
  by Jerry Reed (1972)

"Amos Moses" (RCA 9904)
  by Jerry Reed (1970)

"Authority Song" (Riva 216)
  by John Cougar Mellencamp (1983)

"Bad, Bad Leroy Brown" (ABC 11359)
  by Jim Croce (1973)

"Bad Boy" (Savoy 1508)
  by The Jive Bombers (1957)

"Bad Boys" (Columbia 03932)
  by Wham! U.K. (1983)

"Bad Girls" (Casablanca 988)
  by Donna Summer (1979)

"Bad Girls" (Geffen 29627)
  by Junior Tucker (1983)

"Bad Motorcycle" (Cameo 126)
  by The Storey Sisters (1958)

"The Ballad Of Bonnie And Clyde" (Epic 10283)
  by Georgie Fame (1968)

"The Ballad of Thunder Road" (Capitol 3986)
  by Robert Mitchum (1958)

"Bang Your Head (Mental Health)" (Pasha 04267)
  by Quiet Riot (1984)

"Barracuda" (Portrait 70004)
  by Heart (1977)

"Big Boy Pete" (Arvee 595)
  by The Olympics (1960)

"Big Iron" (Columbia 41589)
by Marty Robbins (1960)

"Black Magic Woman" (Columbia 45270)
by Santana (1970)

"Blue Money" (Warner Brothers 7462)
by Van Morrison (1971)

"Bohemian Rhapsody" (Elektra 45297)
by Queen (1976)

"Born To Be Wild" (Dunhill 4138)
by Steppenwolf (1968)

"Born To Run" (Columbia 10209)
by Bruce Springsteen (1975)

"A Boy Named Sue" (Columbia 44944)
by Johnny Cash (1969)

"Break It To Them Gently" (Portrait 70016)
by Burton Cummings (1978)

"Brown Sugar" (Rolling Stone 19100)
by The Rolling Stones (1971)

"Caribbean Queen" (Jive 9199)
by Billy Ocean (1984)

"Chain Gang" (RCA 7783)
by Sam Cooke (1960)

"Dark Lady" (MCA 40161)
by Cher (1974)

"Daughter Of Darkness" (Parrot 40048)
by Tom Jones (1970)

"Desperado" (Warner Brothers 7529)
by Alice Cooper (1971)

"Devil Woman" (Columbia 42486)
by Marty Robbins (1962)

"Dirty White Boy" (Atlantic 3618)
by Foreigner (1979)

"Don't Take Your Guns To Town" (Columbia 41313)
by Johnny Cash (1959)

"(Don't Worry) If There's A Hell Below We're All Going To Go"
(Curtom 1955)
by Curtis Mayfield (1970)

"Fantasy" (Portrait 02799)
by Aldo Nova (1982)

"Fat Bottomed Girls" (Elektra 45541)
by Queen (1978)

"Folsom Prison Blues" (Columbia 44513)
by Johnny Cash (1968)

"For The Love Of Money" (Philadelphia International 3544)
   by The O'Jays (1974)

"Gloria" (Elektra 69770)
   by The Doors (1983)

"Goldfinger" (United Artists 790)
   by Shirley Bassey (1965)

"Good Ole Boys" (RCA 13527)
   by Jerry Reed (1983)

"Guns For Hire" (Atlantic 89664)
   by AC/DC (1983)

"Gypsys, Tramps, And Thieves" (Kapp 2146)
   by Cher (1971)

"Half-Breed" (MCA 40102)
   by Cher (1973)

"Hell Cat" (Warner Brothers 8220)
   by The Bellamy Brothers (1976)

"He's A Rebel" (Philles 106)
   by The Crystals (1962)

"Hi-Heel Sneakers" (Checker 1067)
   by Tommy Tucker (1964)

"Highway To Hell" (Atlantic 3617)
   by AC/DC (1979)

"Honky Tonk Queen" (Columbia 02198)
   by Moe Bandy and Joe Stampley (1981)

"Honky Tonk Women" (London 910)
   by The Rolling Stones (1969)

"House Of Blue Lights" (Mercury 70627)
   by Chuck Miller (1955)

"House Of The Rising Sun" (MGM 13264)
   by The Animals (1964)

"I Got Stripes" (Columbia 41427)
   by Johnny Cash (1959)

"If You Wanna Get To Heaven" (A & M 1515)
   by The Ozark Mountain Daredevils (1974)

"I'm A Man" (Checker 814)
   by Bo Diddley (1955)

"I'm A Ramblin' Man" (RCA 10020)
   by Waylon Jennings (1974)

"In The Jailhouse Now" (Columbia 03231)
   by Willie Nelson and Webb Pierce (1982)

"Iron Man" (Warner Brothers 7530)
  by Black Sabbath (1972)

"(I Washed My Hands In) Muddy Water" (Imperial 66175)
  by Johnny Rivers (1966)

"Jumpin' Jack Flash" (London 908)
  by The Rolling Stones (1968)

"Just Dropped In (To See What Condition My Condition Was In)"
  (Reprise 0655)
  by Kenny Rogers and The First Edition (1968)

"Killer Queen" (Elektra 45226)
  by Queen (1975)

"The Lady Came From Baltimore" (Atlantic 2395)
  by Bobby Darin (1967)

"Lady Marmalade" (Epic 50048)
  by LaBelle (1975)

"Leader Of The Pack" (Red Bird 014)
  by The Shangri-Las (1964)

"Leroy" (Carlton 462)
  by Jack Scott (1958)

"Lizzie Borden" (Kapp 439)
  by The Chad Mitchell Trio (1962)

"Lucretia MacEvil" (Columbia 45235)
  by Blood, Sweat and Tears (1970)

"Lucy And The Stranger" (Curb 02726)
  by Bobby Goldsboro (1982)

"Lyin', Cheatin', Woman Chasin', Honky Tonkin', Whiskey Drinkin' You"
  (MCA 52219)
  by Loretta Lynn (1983)

"Mack The Knife" (ATCO 6147)
  by Bobby Darin (1959)

"Maneater" (RCA 13354)
  by Daryl Hall and John Oates (1982)

"Midnight Rider" (Capricorn 0035)
  by Gregg Allman (1973)

"Midnight Rider" (A&M 1370)
  by Joe Cocker (1972)

"Midnight Special" (Guaranteed 205)
  by Paul Evans (1960)

"Mississippi Queen" (Windfall 532)
  by Mountain (1970)

"Motorcycle Mama" (Elektra 45782)
  by Sailcat (1972)

"Never On Sunday" (Cadence 1402)
by The Chordettes (1961)

"No More Mr. Nice Guy" (Warner Brothers 7691)
by Alice Cooper (1973)

"Outlaw Man" (Asylum 11025)
by The Eagles (1973)

"Papa Was A Rollin' Stone" (Gordy 7121)
by The Temptations (1972)

"Polk Salad Annie" (Monument 1104)
by Tony Joe White (1969)

"Psycho Killer" (Sire 1013)
by Talking Heads (1978)

"The Rambler" (Epic 50965)
by Molly Hatchet (1981)

"Ramblin' Gamblin' Man" (Capitol 2297)
by The Bob Seger System (1968)

"Ramblin' Man" (Capricorn 0027)
by The Allman Brothers (1973)

"Rebel" (Dot 15586)
by Carol Jarvis (1957)

"Renegade" (Epic 50184)
by Michael Murphy (1976)

"Renegade" (A&M 2110)
by Styx (1979)

"Ringo" (RCA 8444)
by Lorne Greene (1964)

"Rolene" (Capitol 4765)
by Moon Martin (1979)

"Rough Boys" (ATCO 7318)
by Pete Townshend (1980)

"Ruby, Don't Take Your Love To Town" (Reprise 0829)
by Kenny Rogers and The First Edition (1969)

"Runnin' From The Law" (Warner Brothers 49165)
by Stargard (1980)

"Running On Empty" (Asylum 45460)
by Jackson Browne (1978)

"Saturday Night's Alright For Fighting" (MCA 40105)
by Elton John (1973)

"Say, Has Anybody Seen My Sweet Gypsy Rose" (Bell 45374)
by Tony Orlando and Dawn (1973)

"She Came In Through The Bathroom Window" (A&M 1147)
by Joe Cocker (1969)

"Sixteen Tons" (Capitol 3262)
by Tennessee Ernie Ford (1955)

"Smackwater Jack" (Ode 66019)
by Carole King (1971)

"Smokey Joe's Cafe" (ATCO 6059)
by The Robins (1955)

"The Snake" (Soul City 767)
by Al Wilson (1968)

"The Son Of Hickory Holler's Tramp" (Columbia 44425)
by O. C. Smith (1968)

"Stagger Lee" (ABC 9972)
by Lloyd Price (1958)

"Stag-O-Lee" (Atlantic 2448)
by Wilson Pickett (1967)

"Street Fightin' Man" (London 909)
by The Rolling Stones (1968)

"Superfly" (Curtom 1978)
by Curtis Mayfield (1972)

"Super Freak" (Gordy 7205)
by Rick James (1981)

"Suzanne" (Reprise 0615)
by Noel Harrison (1967)

"Swamp Witch" (MGM 14496)
by Jim Stafford (1973)

"Sweet Cream Ladies, Forward March" (Mala 12035)
by The Box Tops (1968)

"Take The Money And Run" (Capitol 4260)
by The Steve Miller Band (1976)

"Trouble Man" (Tamla 54218)
by Marvin Gaye (1972)

"20th Century Fox" (Southern Tracks 1021)
by Bill Anderson (1983)

"Voodoo Woman" (Elektra 45670)
by Simon Stokes and The Nighthawks (1969)

"Walk On The Wild Side" (Mercury 71925)
by Brook Benton (1962)

"Wang Dang Doodle" (Checker 1135)
by Ko Ko Taylor (1966)

"Werewolf" (Polydor 14221)
by The Five Man Electrical Band (1974)

"Werewolf" (Dolton 16)
by The Frantics (1960)

"Werewolves Of London" (Asylum 45472)
by Warren Zevon (1978)

"When You're Hot, You're Hot" (RCA 9976)
by Jerry Reed (1971)

"Witch Queen Of New Orleans" (Epic 10749)
by Redbone (1971)

"Witchy Woman" (Asylum 11008)
by The Eagles (1972)

"You Don't Mess Around With Jim" (ABC 11328)
by Jim Croce (1972)

"Young Turks" (Warner Brothers 49843)
by Rod Stewart (1981)

2

Communications Media

Throughout history mankind has utilized oral and written communications to transmit feelings of love and hate, to preserve documents of public significance and ideas of personal value, and to provide individuals and groups with resources for examining themselves and their predecessors. Both songs and books should be central to historical investigation. Contemporary man lives at a time when different mediums of communication (radio, telephone, television, and motion pictures) dramatically affect, and in some cases even become, intellectual messages. Writers like Marshall McLuhan have speculated that human senses (of which all media are merely extensions) function to configure the awareness and the experiences of each of us. Thus, the products of modern electronic technology frequently become the content of learning and understanding in late twentieth-century America. When one medium of communication—the popular song/hit recording—either comments on or draws its imagery from yet another media, the perception of individuals is broadened by both the technology and the mediated thought. The ability of human beings to conceive and interpret ideas, issues, and problems through films, newspapers, magazines, radio programs, telephones, and television shows is often illustrated in popular lyrics.

In 1919 Billy Murray urged frustrated suitors to "Take Your Girlie To The Movies" if she can't be induced to cooperate at home. A decade later a more amorous Belle Baker crooned "If I Had A Talking Picture Of You" (1929). By 1934 the Ziegfeld Follies introduced the universal idea "You Oughta Be In Pictures." Tony Alamo and Judy Johnson, singing with the Sammy Kay Orchestra in 1950, repeated the same sentiments. But it was Johnny "Scat" Davis, backed by Benny Goodman and his band in 1937,

who had trumpeted the most famous paen to the motion picture capital—
"Hooray For Hollywood." The silver screen was so deeply ingrained in
American popular culture by the mid-twentieth century that many film
celebrities' names were more readily recognized by the general public than
those of wealthy businessmen or successful politicians.

Between 1950 and 1985 motion pictures have assumed a dominant position in American thought and life. Attendance at films is chronicled in a
variety of recordings. Eddie Cochran urged his girl to join him at a "Drive
In Show" (1957); he also suggested that they could enjoy undescribed adolescent delights while "Sittin' In The Balcony" (1957) on the very last
row. Carl Perkins attempted to hide from the overly watchful eyes of a
suspicious, gun-toting father by taking his girlfriend to a show in "Movie
Magg" (1955). The Drifters echoed Cochran's suggestive sentiments in
"Saturday Night At The Movies" (1964), while The Steve Miller Band
reminisced about a first romance that began in the back seat of a car at the
drive-in movie show in "Circle Of Love" (1982). The most humorous tale
of movie-related teenage problems is related in "Wake Up Little Susie"
(1957, 1982), where a couple falls asleep during a film and finally awakes
to discover the movie's over, it's four o'clock and they're in deep trouble.

Motion pictures, aside from providing excuses for meeting friends and
loved ones or for escaping from suspicious parents, offer a world of personal
fantasy to each viewer. Individual satisfaction with film images varies greatly.
In "Sad Movies (Make Me Cry)" (1961), Sue Thompson reflects on personal
affairs that have failed, while in "Are You Getting Enough Happiness"
(1982), Hot Chocolate notes that every time they go to the movies all they
see is happy love on the silver screen. Obviously, fantasy expectations often
dictate interest in particular films. The most traditional hero–wins–out–over–
villain scenes are laughingly recalled by The Coasters (1959) and again by
Ray Stevens (1969) in the novelty tune "Along Came Jones." Bertie Higgins
depicts his own love life in "Key Largo" (1981) when he contends that he
and his girl had it all, just like Bogey and Bacall, starring in their own late,
late show. Humphrey Bogart and Lauren Bacall are only two of an innumerable list of movie stars who are mentioned in popular recordings. Marilyn Monroe was idealized by Teddy and the Twilights in "Woman Is A
Man's Best Friend" (1962), while Kim Carnes used a distinctive facial feature
to conjure up a mysterious female persona in "Bette Davis Eyes" (1981).
And if Michael Jackson viewed "Billie Jean" (1983) as a beauty queen from
the movie screen, he only echoed the thoughts of The Bellamy Brothers
who, after admitting that they go to the movies to see Sophia Loren and
Brigitte Bardot, still assert loyalty to their hometown girl in "You're My
Favorite Star" (1981).

Hollywood offers a get-rich-quick, become-a-celebrity-overnight myth
to many Americans. This idea is reinforced in films, through media hype
on radio and television, and by authentic (although statistically rare) in-

stances of a pretty girl or handsome boy from Peoria achieving fame and fortune in Los Angeles. Chuck Berry (1965) and Elvis Presley (1974) both described Southern California's movie sets as "The Promised Land" for aspiring performers. The Beatles noted that all you've got to do to be successful in films is just "Act Naturally" (1965). The exciting West Coast lifestyle is lauded by Carl Perkins in "Hollywood City" (1961) and by Kool and The Gang in "Hollywood Swinging" (1974). But in the pursuit of John Stewart's "Gold" (1979) and in the excitement of chasing "Star Baby" (1974) with The Guess Who, the movie capital of America also harbors rejection, failure, and lost hope. These sentiments are contained in Gladys Knight and The Pips' "Midnight Train To Georgia" (1973), Eric Clapton's "Tulsa Time" (1980), and Don Williams' "If Hollywood Don't Need You (Honey, I Still Do)" (1982).

In terms of hourly contact, Americans view television to a far greater extent than they attend motion picture theaters. However, with the advent of cable movie networks, there has been considerable blurring of the notions of feature films versus TV programs as distinct media sources. Clearly, the ideas, images, personalities, and techniques of communication between motion pictures and television dramatically overlap during the 1980s. The Statler Brothers, in "A Child Of The Fifties" (1982), nostalgically recall the early days of black-and-white broadcasting when television was their friend—particularly "I Love Lucy" and "Rin Tin Tin." It is interesting to note that Lucille Ball reruns were united with a late 1970s dance fad to enable The Wilton Place Street Band to produce the hit recording "Disco Lucy (I Love Lucy Theme)" (1977).

However, the lyrical depiction of television as a social force varies significantly from 1950 to the present. The humor of The Coasters employing all of the tricks of TV detectives while "Searchin' " (1957) for their missing sweetheart was echoed by The Olympics who were frustrated by girls who prefer sitting at home watching lawmen and desperadoes in "Western Movies" (1958) to dating, dancing, and romancing. With considerable remorse Mac Davis declared that you can't even look at television these days without getting scared to death. Regrettably, the image presented in his "The Beer Drinkin' Song" (1982) is the product of contemporary visual horror ranging from napalm atrocities in Vietnam to kidnapping and mass hysteria in Iran to saturation bombing in Lebanon to any number of domestic war zones within American cities. Mac Davis concludes this early 1980s analysis by admitting that the eyewitness news leaves him abused and gasping for breath.

Only Don Henley's "Dirty Laundry" (1982) presents a more caustic indictment of broadcast journalism run amuck. Henley notes that television news is presented by an attractive female reporter who can describe a grisly plane crash with a gleam in her eye. He notes that morbidity, scandal, sensationalism, death, and other sub-human values seem to motivate the ratings chase within the television news industry. Other recent recordings offer only two solutions to the constant flow of bad news. Junior rejoices that the television's out of order so he won't see the news at ten in "Communication Breakdown" (1983) and Joe Jackson pleads with his girlfriend to leave the television and radio behind and go "Steppin' Out" (1982) for an evening unencumbered by reports of international warfare or domestic tragedy. The rock group Styx carries George Orwell's vision of television as a mind control device into 1984. In "High Times" (1983), they note with sinister fear that the mind police are coming.

In terms of public communication, both motion pictures and television programs are overshadowed by ubiquitous radio broadcasts. From the morning bedside chatter of a wake-up disc jockey, through a day-long experience of transistorized portable tunes, news, and weather reports, toward home in a car humming with AM-FM stereo, unwinding in the early evening with AOR/Country Rock/MOR/Rock Sounds, and finally retiring to quiet sounds by The Beatles, Bread, Three Dog Night—radio is omnipresent. It is undeniable, though, that there is an element of public unrest about the dirty laundry being pushed by the radio as well as by the video media. Songs such as "Silent Night/Seven O'Clock News" (n.d.) by Simon and Garfunkel and "In Times Like These" (1983) by Barbara Mandrell convey this feeling.

Somehow there is a more controllable sense and a more personalized connection between listeners and broadcast celebrities in lyrics that assess radio as a communication medium. Mark Dinning notes that the essentials of pop radio programming are "Top Forty, News, Weather, And Sports" (1961). Throughout the 1950–1985 period, various personalities have ruled the airwaves. From Alan Freed and Wolfman Jack to Norm Nite and Casey Kasem, the identifiable platter chatter of a friendly disc jockey has set the tempo for modern musical messages. Rene and Angela comment fondly about the comforting voice on the radio—your favorite D.J., just going with the flow in "Banging The Boogie" (1983). Other salutes to disc jockeys include "Kansas City Star" (1965) by Roger Miller, "Clap For The Wolfman" (1974) by The Guess Who, and "#1 Dee Jay" (1978) by Goody Goody. The 1959–1960 scandal involving bribes paid to radio station managers and disc jockeys to promote specific records is humorously chronicled by Stan Freberg in "The Old Payola Roll Blues" (1960). But for the most part, radio personalities—even the zany fictional jocks at "WKRP In Cincinnati" (1981)—deliver satisfying musical interludes to individuals who are "Wired For Sound" (1981) and persons listening to "FM (No Static At All)" (1978). There is an overtly sexist—or at least somewhat sexy—tone to other images of broadcast music. Freddy Cannon describes a radio-listening fanatic as "Transistor Sister" (1961). And Dexy's Midnight Runners remind their date that Johnny Ray sounded sad upon the radio as he moved a million hearts in "Come On Eileen" (1983). This kind of airplay foreplay is extended by Don Williams in "Listen To The Radio" (1982) and by The Younger Brothers, who reminisce about how good their date looked with "Nothing But The Radio On" (1982).

Movies and television programs present visual imagery; the radio offers audio perspectives and oral persuasion; but it is the telephone that transmits private, personal feelings. Communication by telephone is immediate, intimate, and by choice; it is also oral and conducted at some distance. The telephone, even after the breakup of AT&T's monopoly during the early 1980s, it a timeless symbol of personal interaction. Since 1950, song lyrics have contained innumerable references to telephone conversations (real or imagined), and it is perhaps fitting that Ma Bell selected a popular song title—"Reach Out And Touch (Somebody's Hand)" (1980) by Diana Ross—for one of their advertising campaigns.

The spectrum of messages delivered by phone is fascinating. Although Karla Bonoff claims that she's got someting for her love that must be delivered "Personally" (1982), most lyrics remain telephone intimate and sensitive. Jim Reeves pleads by telephone "He'll Have To Go" (1959). Stevie Wonder, in "Do I Do" (1982), declares when he talks to his girl on the phone that her sweet sexy voice turns him on. For Cymarron, telephone "Rings" (1971) mean invitations to romantic relationships. However, for Webb Pierce in "I Ain't Never" (1959), his calls lead only to increased frustration caused by a fickle female. The Four Tops are unable to muster the nerve to telephone a loved one in "Just Seven Numbers (Can Straighten Out My Life)" (1971), while The Orlons plead with an angry friend "Don't Hang Up" (1962). Steely Dan urges "Rikki Don't Lose That Number" (1974) and other singers simply make their phone numbers available—The Marvelettes' "Beachwood 4–5789" (1962), Wilson Pickett's "634–5789 (Soulsville, U.S.A.)" (1966), The Carpenters' "Beechwood 4–5789" (1982), and Tommy Tutone's "867–5309/Jenny" (1982).

Love, expectation, exhilaration, and the mending of damaged relationships are not the only topics of lyrical telephone conversations. Sugarloaf gains sweet, ironic revenge on a haughty talent agent that mocked them with a "Don't Call Us, We'll Call You" (1974) putdown. Telephone operators function as marriage counselors for Chuck Berry, Johnny Rivers, and Fred Knoblock in "Memphis, Tennessee" (1959, 1964, 1981); as amateur psychologists for Jim Croce in "Operator (That's Not The Way It Feels)" (1972), and as religious go-betweens in Manhattan Transfer's metaphorical "Operator" (1975). Jealousy also exists via long distance lines. Freddy Cannon is vexed when he encounters a continuing busy signal from his girlfriend's phone in "Buzz Buzz A-Diddle-It" (1961). He concludes that some hound dog is sweet talking his sweet angel. Bobby Darin is more direct in warning his girl that "If A Man Answers" (1962) her phone when he calls, then their romance is through. Finally, Dr. Hook faces the most frustrating dilemma of all. When his girlfriend's phone rings and he answers it, there is only silence on the caller's part. Dr. Hook's conclusion is that, "When You're In Love With A Beautiful Woman" (1979), you can't trust any of your male companions.

Beyond the realm of the "hot" electronic media, lyrical attention has also been focused on newspapers, books, and magazines. Recordings illustrating print media activities are far less numerous than those examining or alluding to motion pictures, television shows, or radio programs. This is perhaps indicative of the nonprint style of the post–1960 period, particularly in regard to the more youthful generation. Neil Diamond observes that heartbreak isn't a "Front Page Story" (1983) and probably won't even make the papers, while Christopher Cross says just the opposite in "No Time For Talk" (1983). Although The Silhouettes seemed content to search the want ads just to "Get A Job" (1958), Rupert Holmes felt compelled to seek a new relationship via print advertisement in "Escape (The Pina Colada Song)" (1979). Beauty is assessed by The J. Geils Band in terms of making a magazine "Centerfold" (1981). For George Jones in "Shine On (Shine All Your Sweet Love On Me)" (1983), the judgment that his girl will never grace the centerfold of *Playboy* magazine is followed by his criterion for physical excellence—in her jeans she's as sexy as a dream. The ultimate print market achievement for a rock band is not just to be lauded in *Playboy*, *Variety*, *Billboard*, *Cash Box*, or *The New Musical Express*. Dr. Hook emphasizes that the goal of his band is to have their picture on "The Cover Of 'Rolling Stone' " (1972).

COMMUNICATIONS MEDIA

Motion Pictures

"Act Naturally" (Capitol 5498)
   by The Beatles (1965)

"Along Came Jones" (Atco 6141)
   by The Coasters (1959)

"Along Came Jones" (Monument 1150)
   by Ray Stevens (1969)

"Are You Getting Enough Happiness" (EMI America 8143)
   by Hot Chocolate (1982)

" 'B' Movie" (Arista 0647)
   by Gil Scott-Heron (1981)

"Bette Davis Eyes" (EMI America 8077)
   by Kim Carnes (1981)

"Billie Jean" (Epic 03509)
   by Michael Jackson (1983)

"Circle of Love" (Capitol 5086)
by The Steve Miller Band (1982)

"Drive In Show" (Liberty 55087)
by Eddie Cochran (1957)

"Gold" (RSO 931)
by John Stewart (1979)

"Good Guys Only Win In The Movies" (Bamboo 109)
by Mel and Tim (1970)

"Hollywood" (MGM 13039)
by Connie Francis (1961)

"Hollywood" (ABC 12269)
by Rufus, featuring Chaka Khan (1977)

"Hollywood" (Columbia 10679)
by Boz Scaggs (1978)

"Hollywood" (Epic 02755)
by Shooting Star (1982)

"Hollywood City" (Columbia 42045)
by Carl Perkins (1961)

"Hollywood Hot" (20th Century 2215)
by Eleventh Hour (1975)

"Hollywood Nights" (Capitol 4618)
by Bob Seger and The Silver Bullet Band (1978)

"Hollywood Swinging" (DeLite 561)
by Kool and The Gang (1974)

"If Hollywood Don't Need You (Honey, I Still Do)" (MCA 52152)
by Don Williams (1982)

"If You Could Read My Mind" (Reprise 0974)
by Gordon Lightfoot (1970)

"Just Like In The Movies (Swan 4010)
by The Upbeats (1958)

"Key Largo" (Kat Family 02524)
by Bertie Higgins (1981)

"Last Of The Silver Screen Cowboys" (Warner Brothers 50035)
by Rex Allen, Jr. (1982)

"Like An Old Time Movie" (Ode 105)
by Scott McKenzie (1967)

"Midnight Train to Georgia" (Buddah 383)
by Gladys Knight and The Pips (1973)

"Movie Day" (Kapp 936)
by Don Scardino (1968)

"Movie Magg" (Flip 501)
by Carl Perkins (1955)

"Movie Star Song" (Epic 10640)
  by Georgie Fame (1970)

"The Movies" (Mercury 73877)
  by The Statler Brothers (1977)

"Norma Jean Wants To Be A Movie Star" (Polydor 14312)
  by Sundown Company (1976)

"Pop Goes The Movies" (Arista 0660)
  by Meco (1982)

"Promised Land" (Chess 1916)
  by Chuck Berry (1965)

"Promised Land" (RCA PB–10074)
  by Elvis Presley (1974)

"Sad Movies (Make Me Cry)" (Hickory 1153)
  by Sue Thompson (1961)

"Saturday Night At The Movies" (Atlantic 2260)
  by the Drifters (1964)

"Say Goodbye To Hollywood" (Columbia 02518)
  by Billy Joel (1981)

"Sittin' In The Balcony" (Liberty 55056)
  by Eddie Cochran (1957)

"Star Baby" (RCA 0217)
  by The Guess Who (1974)

"Tulsa Time" (RSO 1039)
  by Eric Clapton (1980)

"Wake Up Little Susie" (Cadence 1337)
  by The Everly Brothers (1957)

"Wake Up Little Susie" (Warner Brothers 50053)
  by Simon and Garfunkel (1982)

"Woman Is A Man's Best Friend" (Swan 4102)
  by Teddy and The Twilights (1962)

"You're My Favorite Star" (Warner/Curb 49815)
  by The Bellamy Brothers (1981)

Newspapers, Books, and Magazines

"Centerfold" (EMI America 8102)
  by The J. Geils Band (1981)

"The Cover Of 'Rolling Stone' " (Columbia 45732)
  by Dr. Hook (1972)

"Escape (The Pina Colada Song)" (Infinity 50035)
  by Rupert Holmes (1979)

"Front Page Story" (Columbia 03801)
  by Neil Diamond (1983)

"Get A Job" (Ember 1029)
  by The Silhouettes (1958)

"The Girl On Page 44" (Columbia 41310)
  by The Four Lads (1959)

"Headline News" (Ric-Tic 114)
  by Edwin Starr (1966)

"A Little Good News" (Capitol 5264)
  by Ann Murray (1983)

"Movie Magazine, Stars In Her Eyes" (Playboy 6043)
  by Barbi Benton (1975)

"No Time For Talk" (Warner Brothers 29662)
  by Christopher Cross (1983)

"Put It In A Magazine" (Highrise 2001)
  by Sonny Charles (1982)

"Shine On (Shine All Your Sweet Love On Me)" (Epic 03489)
  by George Jones (1983)

"Want Ads" (Hot Wax 7011)
  by Honey Cone (1971)

Phonographs

"Hit Record" (Mercury 71962)
  by Brook Benton (1962)

"If I Didn't Have A Dime (To Play The Jukebox)" (Musicor 1022)
  by Gene Pitney (1962)

"The Jukebox Never Plays Home Sweet Home" (EMH 0016)
  by Jack Greene (1983)

"Juke Box Saturday Night" (Madison 166)
  by Nino and the Ebb Tides (1961)

"The Old Songs" (Arista 0633)
  by Barry Manilow (1981)

Photographs

"8 × 10" (Decca 31521)
  by Bill Anderson (1963)

"Photograph" (Mercury 811215)
  by Def Leppard (1983)

"Snap Shot" (Cotillion 46022)
  by Slave (1981)

"Snapshot" (RCA 13501)
  by Sylvia (1983)

"Take Another Picture" (Geffen 29523)
   by Quarterflash (1983)
"Wishing (If I Had A Photograph Of You)" (Jive 2006)
   by Flock of Seagulls (1983)

Radio

"Banging The Boogie" (Capitol 5220)
   by Rene and Angela (1983)
"Clap For The Wolfman" (RCA 0324)
   by The Guess Who (1974)
"Come On Eileen" (Mercury 76189)
   by Dexy's Midnight Runners (1983)
"Dear Mr. D.J. Play It Again" (Mercury 71852)
   by Tina Robin (1961)
" 'DJ' Man" (Prelude 8066)
   by Secret Weapon (1983)
"FM (No Static At All)" (MCA 40894)
   by Steely Dan (1978)
"H.A.P.P.Y. Radio" (20th Century 2408)
   by Edwin Starr (1979)
"In Times Like These" (MCA 52206)
   by Barbara Mandrell (1983)
"Juke Box Baby" (RCA 6427)
   by Perry Como (1956)
"Juke Box Hero" (Atlantic 4017)
   by Foreigner (1982)
"Kansas City Star" (Smash 1998)
   by Roger Miller (1965)
"Last Night A D.J. Saved My Life" (Sound New York 602)
   by Indeep (1983)
"Listen To The Radio" (MCA 52037)
   by Don Williams (1982)
"Love On The Airwaves" (Planet 47921)
   by Night (1981)
"Mexican Radio" (I.R.S. 9912)
   by Wall of Voodoo (1983)
"Mr. D.J. (5 For The D.J.)" (Atlantic 3289)
   by Aretha Franklin (1975)
"Nothing But The Radio On" (MCA 52076)
   by The Younger Brothers (1982)
"#1 Dee Jay" (Atlantic 3504)
   by Goody Goody (1978)

"The Old Payola Roll Blues" (Capitol 4329)
by Stan Freberg (1960)

"Old Songs" (Juana 3700)
by Frederick Knight (1981)

"Old Time Rock And Roll" (Capitol 5276)
by Bob Seger and The Silver Bullet Band (1983)

"On The Radio" (Casablanca 2236)
by Donna Summer (1980)

"Play That Beat Mr. D.J." (Tommy Boy 836)
by G.L.O.B.E. and Whiz Kid (1983)

"A Prayer And A Juke Box" (End 1047)
by Little Anthony and The Imperials (1959)

"Radio Activity (Part 1)" (Sutra 126)
by Royalcash (1983)

"Radio Free Europe" (I.R.S. 9916)
by R.E.M. (1983)

"Radio Ga Ga" (Capitol 5317)
by Queen (1984)

"Radio Man" (Island 791)
by World's Famous Supreme Team (1984)

"Rock Radio" (Capitol 4996)
by Gene Dunlap (1981)

"Rockin' Radio" (Arista 9088)
by Tom Browne (1983)

"Silent Night/Seven O'Clock News" (Columbia album)
by Simon and Garfunkel (n.d.)

"Sleepin' With The Radio On" (Epic 02421)
by Charly McClain (1981)

"Song On The Radio" (Arista 0389)
by Al Stewart (1979)

"The Spirit Of Radio" (Mercury 76044)
by Rush (1981)

"That Old Song (Arista 0616)
by Ray Parker, Jr. and Raydio (1981)

"Top Forty, News, Weather And Sports" (MGM 12980)
by Mark Dinning (1961)

"Transistor Sister" (Swan 4078)
by Freddy Cannon (1961)

"Union Of The Snake" (Capitol 5290)
by Duran Duran (1983)

"Video Killed The Radio Star" (Island 49114)
by The Buggles (1979)

"Voice On The Radio" (Montage 1210)
  by Conductor (1982)

"Who Listens To The Radio" (Arista 0468)
  by The Sports (1979)

"Wired For Sound" (EMI America 8095)
  by Cliff Richard (1981)

"WKRP In Cincinnati" (MCA 51205)
  by Steve Carlisle (1981)

"You Can't Judge A Book By The Cover" (Checker 1019)
  by Bo Diddley (1962)

"You Turn Me On, I'm A Radio" (Asylum 11010)
  by Joni Mitchell (1972)

Telephones

"Answering Machine" (MCA 41235)
  by Rupert Holmes (1980)

"Baby, Hang Up The Phone" (A & M 1620)
  by Carl Graves (1974)

"Beechwood 4–5789" (Tamla 54065)
  by The Marvelettes (1962)

"Beechwood 4–5789" (A & M 2405)
  by The Carpenters (1982)

"Beep A Freak" (Total Experience 2405)
  by The Gap Band (1984)

"Buzz Buzz A-Diddle-It" (Swan 4071)
  by Freddy Cannon (1961)

"Call Me" (Chrysalis 2414)
  by Blondie (1980)

"Call Me" (Atlantic 2706)
  by Aretha Franklin (1970)

"Call Me" (Columbia 41253)
  by Johnny Mathis (1958)

"Call Me" (A&M 780)
  by Chris Montez (1966)

"Call Me" (Salsoul 2152)
  by Skyy (1982)

"Call Me (Come Back Home)" (Hi 2235)
  by Al Green (1973)

"(Call Me) When The Spirit Moves You" (Atco 7222)
  by Touch (1980)

"Can't Hang Up The Phone" (Columbia 42628)
  by Stonewall Jackson (1963)

"Chantilly Lace" (Mercury 71343)
  by The Big Bopper (1958)

"Chantilly Lace" (Mercury 73273)
  by Jerry Lee Lewis (1972)

"Death By Phone" (Yoyo 12249)
  by Scott Puffer (1979)

"Do I Do" (Tamla 1612)
  by Stevie Wonder (1982)

"Don't Call Us, We'll Call You" (Claridge 402)
  by Sugarloaf (1974)

"Don't Hang Up" (Cameo 231)
  by The Orlons (1962)

"867–5309/Jenny" (Columbia 02646)
  by Tommy Tutone (1982)

"Ghostbusters" (Arista 9212)
  by Ray Parker, Jr. (1984)

"Heart On The Line (Operator, Operator)" (Atlantic Arts 99826)
  by Larry Willoughby (1983)

"He'll Have To Go" (RCA 7643)
  by Jim Reeves (1959)

"Hot Line" (Capitol 4336)
  by The Sylvers (1976)

"I Ain't Never" (Decca 30923)
  by Webb Pierce (1959)

"I Just Called To Say I Love You" (Motown 1745)
  by Steve Wonder (1984)

"If A Man Answers" (Capitol 4837)
  by Bobby Darin (1962)

"If A Woman Answers (Hang Up The Phone)" (Mercury 71926)
  by Leroy Van Dyke (1962)

"Just Seven Numbers (Can Straighten Out My Life)" (Motown 1175)
  by The Four Tops (1971)

"Kissin' On The Phone" (ABC-Paramount 10239)
  by Paul Anka (1961)

"Lonesome 7–7203" (Audiograph 474)
  by Darrell Clanton (1983)

"Love On The Phone" (Casablanca 2242)
  by Suzanne Fellini (1980)

"Memorize Your Number" (Scotti Brothers 510)
  by Leif Garrett (1980)

"Memphis" (Imperial 66032)
  by Johnny Rivers (1964)

"Memphis, Tennessee" (Chess 1729)
by Chuck Berry (1959)

"Memphis, Tennessee" (Scotti Brothers 02434)
by Fred Knoblock (1981)

"Mr. Telephone Man" (MCA 52484)
by The New Edition (1984)

"Obscene Phone Caller" (Motown 1731)
by Rockwell (1984)

"Operator" (Tamla 54115)
by Brenda Holloway (1965)

"Operator" (Furry 1064)
by Gladys Knight and The Pips (1962)

"Operator" (Atlantic 3292)
by Manhattan Transfer (1975)

"Operator" (Solar 69684)
by Midnight Star (1984)

"Operator" (RCA 13265)
by The Tennessee Express (1982)

"Operator, Long Distance Please" (MCA 52111)
by Barbara Mandrell (1982)

"Operator (That's Not The Way It Feels)" (ABC 11335)
by Jim Croce (1972)

"Personally" (Columbia 02805)
by Karla Bonoff (1982)

"Please Come To Boston" (Epic 11115)
by Dave Loggins (1974)

"Rikki Don't Lose That Number" (ABC 11439)
by Steely Dan (1974)

"Ring My Phone" (Capitol 3723)
by Tommy Sands (1957)

"Rings" (Entrance 7500)
by Cymarron (1971)

"777–9311" (Warner Brothers 29952)
by Time (1982)

"634–5789" (RCA 13347)
by Marlow Tackett (1982)

"634–5789" (Soulsville, U.S.A.)" (Atlantic 2320)
by Wilson Pickett (1966)

"Telefone (Long Distance Love Affair)" (EMI American 8172)
by Sheena Easton (1983)

"Telephone" (RCA PB 14032)
by Diana Ross (1984)

"The Telephone" (Kapp 198)
　　by Stan Boreson and Doug Setterberg (1957)

"Telephone Baby" (Capitol 4168)
　　by Johnny Otis and Marci Lee (1959)

"Telephone Bill" (DMJ 1305)
　　by Johnny Guitar Watson (1980)

"Telephone Man" (GRT 127)
　　by Meri Wilson (1977)

"Telephone Operator" (Arista 730)
　　by Pete Shelley (1983)

"The Telephone Song" (Decca 27310)
　　by The Andrews Sisters (1951)

"What's Your Name, What's Your Number" (Buddah 582)
　　by The Andrea True Connection (1978)

"When You're In Love With A Beautiful Woman" (Capitol 4705)
　　by Dr. Hook (1979)

"Wichita Lineman" (Capitol 2302)
　　by Glen Campbell (1968)

Television

"The Beer Drinkin' Song" (Mercury 2355)
　　by Mac Davis (1982)

"A Child Of The Fifties" (Mercury 76184)
　　by The Statler Brothers (1982)

"Communication Breakdown" (Mercury 812397)
　　by Junior (1983)

"Dirty Laundry" (Asylum 69894)
　　by Don Henley (1982)

"Disco Lucy (I Love Lucy Theme)" (Island 078)
　　by The Wilton Place Street Band (1977)

"High Time" (A&M 2568)
　　by Styx (1983)

"Love Busted" (Capricorn 5139)
　　by Billy "Crash" Craddock (1982)

"Searchin' " (Atco 6087)
　　by The Coasters (1957)

"Star On A TV Show" (AVCO 4549)
　　by The Stylistics (1975)

"Steppin' Out" (A&M 2428)
　　by Joe Jackson (1982)

"T.V. Mama" (Casablanca 814217)
　　by Leon Haywood (1983)

"TV Mama" (Atlantic 1016)
  by Joe Turner (1953)
"Video Baby" (Boardwalk 179)
  by Earons (1983)
"Western Movies" (Demon 1508)
  by The Olympics (1958)

3

Death

"The Late Great Johnny Ace" is the most thought-provoking song on Paul Simon's 1983 *Hearts and Bones* album (Columbia 23942–1). This tune, reminiscent of the reflective death songs "American Pie" (1971) and "Abraham, Martin, And John" (1968), offers a lament to the brevity and frailty of human existence. More than just eulogies, though, these three songs depict the psychological impact of death on an entire generation's perception of life. This sounds extremely serious—hardly typical of popular music fare. Yet Paul Simon, Don McLean, and Dion DiMucci, along with a variety of other contemporary singers, have succeeded in delivering different visions of mortality in order to preach universal ideas.

The death theme has been omnipresent in popular music since 1950. Several scholars who have investigated this topic focus on the relatively narrow topic of "teenage coffin songs." These studies, which examine narrative ballads that describe youthful experiences with suicide or accidental death, have generally examined recordings such as Mark Dinning's "Teen Angel" (1960), Jody Reynolds' "Endless Sleep" (1958), Ray Peterson's "Tell Laura I Love Her" (1960), The Shangri-Las' "Leader Of The Pack" (1964), and Dickey Lee's "Patches" (1962). R. Serge Denisoff, a perceptive popular music analyst, notes that the popularity of romantic songs of love lost through death fell victim to rapid cultural and political change during the mid-sixties. Specifically, he observed:

Several death songs in the latter half of the 1960s—"Ode to Billy Joe" and "Honey"—sold quite well. Still, the teenage coffin song did not return after 1965. The demise of the coffin song correlates with the introduction of overt statements of social dissent as found in Barry McGuire's "Eve Of Destruction" and Glen Campbell's version of "Universal Soldier." Conversely, the "He's A Rebel," "Tell Laura I Love Her," "Patches" oriented songs were *passe* with the event of the counterculture and its disavowal of the social ethic of the 1950s.[1]

Just as the notion of courtly love diminished during the sixties and was replaced by more direct commentaries about overt physical attraction, spoken sexual desires, and frequent premarital liaisons, the death theme became more visible and more realistically explored in lyrics after 1965. Of course, there were songs of death and dying that were not simply teenage laments that also had been popular in the fifties. These songs examined more than just dejected drownings or accidental car deaths. Premeditated homicides, brutal spur-of-the-moment shootings, and suicides can be found in many songs from 1950 to the present.[2] Even the gentle Beatles produced the delightfully sinister "Maxwell's Silver Hammer" (n.d.), a tune that rivals Alfred Hitchcock for murderous psychotic impact. But what is more interesting is the fact that the death theme appears in such a variety of visages over the past thirty-five years. Among these different perspectives are: (a) aging and dying as natural life-cycle events; (b) tragic, unexpected airline crashes or automobile accidents; (c) death as an accepted religious or existential event; (d) debilitation and demise from drug abuse; (e) the passing of heroes and villains; (f) the act of murder and the pursuit of murderers; (g) deaths of soldiers and other war-time casualties; and (h) suicide. As noted at the beginning of this chapter, there are also a small group of epic hero songs that use the assassinations or accidental deaths of prominent political or musical figures as backdrops for generation-defining commentaries.

There is considerable discussion about aging in contemporary songs. From the tender side of thirty, The Who proclaim that they hope they die before they grow old. But "My Generation" (1966) isn't typical of the more reflective songs about reaching maturity. Frank Sinatra offers two different assessments of fulfilled lives in "It Was A Very Good Year" (1966) and "My Way" (1969). The former tune chronicles the amorous evolution of a highly successful womanizer. The latter song, authored by Paul Anka and today more often associated with Elvis Presley (1977) than Sinatra, is a classic paen to individualism, freedom, and independence. Anticipating old age and hoping to establish a lifelong relationship of caring is the theme of The Beatles' classic "When I'm Sixty-Four" (n.d.). But for those who are

1. R. Serge Denisoff, " 'Teen Angel': Resistance, Rebellion, and Death—Revisited," *Journal of Popular Culture* 16 (Spring 1983): 121. Also see: R. Serge Denisoff, "Death Songs and Teenage Roles," in *Sing a Song of Social Significance* (Bowling Green, Ohio: Bowling Green University Popular Press, 1972), pp. 171–176.

2. This thematic expansion is investigated in John C. Thrush and George S. Paulus, "The Concept of Death in Popular Music: A Social Psychological Perspective," *Popular Music and Society* 6 (1979): 219–228.

close to retirement age already, images of unfulfilled expectations seem more common. Roy Clark longs for "Yesterday, When I Was Young" (1969), while Peggy Lee asks in a somewhat disillusioned fashion "Is That All There Is?" (1969). The most frightening image of the aged—shoddy clothes, greasy hands, and snot running down his nose—is presented in Jethro Tull's "Aqualung" (n.d.).

Death related to spectacular accidents is the backbone of many heroic tales. Train wreck stories of Casey Jones are legion in folk music. Within the popular song realm, automobile accidents and airplane crashes are events that best illustrate the unexpected loss of life. The tragedy of losing a loved one to a flight disaster is reported by The Everly Brothers in "Ebony Eyes" (1961). In addition to the previously mentioned car death songs by Mark Dinning and Ray Peterson, the foremost examples of four-wheel disaster are J. Frank Wilson and The Cavaliers' "Last Kiss" (1964), The Shangri-Las' "Give Us Your Blessing" (1965), and Jan and Dean's "Dead Man's Curve" (1964).

Death interrupts anticipated continuity. It is a complete surprise, a bitter shock. Death fosters grief, reverie, and a reminder of each person's mortality. Individual responses to life's finality vary in popular songs just as they do in poetry, in literature, and in other forms of popular media. David Clayton-Thomas of Blood, Sweat and Tears expressed confidence that there'll be one child born to carry on when he passes away. This peace of mind found in "And When I Die" (1969) is lost in the short-term anguish over a personal loss in Thomas Wayne's "Tragedy" (1965), Bobby Goldsboro's "Honey" (1968), and Kenny Rogers and The First Edition's "Ruben James" (1969).

Some songs present the death theme in an obscure or peculiar fashion. The 1960 Elvis Presley hit "Are You Lonesome Tonight?" was reissued after his untimely passing in 1977 and became more of a deep personal eulogy than a simple hymn of lost love. David Geddes presents a son-performing-in-honor-of-his-deceased-dad tale in "The Last Game Of The Season (A Blind Man In The Bleachers)" (1975). Paul McCartney and Wings salute the murderous inclinations of daring secret agents in "Live And Let Die" (1973), while Kenny Rogers secures wisdom from a dying "Gambler" (1978) as they travel together on a train bound to nowhere. Joe South sardonically observes that it doesn't matter what "Games People Play" (1969) because everyone will eventually wind up riding in the back of a black hearse. Other recordings that focus on impending death include Blue Oyster Cult's "(Don't Fear) The Reaper" (1976), The Beatles' "Eleanor Rigby" (1966), Pacific Gas and Electric's "Are You Ready?" (1970), The Byrds' "Turn! Turn! Turn!" (1965), and Norman Greenbaum's "Spirit In The Sky" (1970).

Beyond traditional images of the natural life cycle, beyond misfortunes of accidental demise, and beyond all other observations about inevitable mortality there are series of unmercifully violent lyrical perceptions. Death is not serene. It sometimes comes in a chemical disguise that is offered by Steppenwolf's dreaded "Pusher" (n.d.) to a "Snow Blind Friend" (1971). But drug abuse is usually a lonely, solitary form of victimization. The passing of figures that are larger than life—whether they are heroes or villains—is always noteworthy. In 1956 Lonnie Donegan and His Skiffle Group resurrected the classic tale of the powerful, independent spike driver "John Henry." Only a year before "The Ballad Of Davy Crockett" (1955) eulogized an American hero of historic and mythic import. Fess Parker's song of heroism was echoed by Marty Robbins' "Ballad Of The Alamo" (1960). Death remained the focus of lyrical historical exploration for the British soldiers in Johnny Horton's "The Battle Of New Orleans" (1959), and for the Cain family in Joan Baez's "The Night They Drove Old Dixie Down" (1971). The police and National Guard are viewed as contemporary death merchants rather than protectors of peace and justice in "Ohio" (1970) by Crosby, Stills, Nash, and Young, in "Mad Dog" (n.d.) by Lee Michaels, and in "The Ballad Of Bonnie and Clyde" (1968) by Georgie Fame. Heroes die, too. The soft-spoken giant of a man who saved his fellow miners from a cold, dark grave by sacrificing his own life is lauded by Jimmy Dean in "Big Bad John" (1961). Gene Pitney praises the killer of an outlaw who needed to be killed in "(The Man Who Shot) Liberty Valance" (1962). And Jim Stafford even offers praise for the cruel, cunning, mysterious, death-dealing "Swamp Witch" (1973) who provided a special potion to save an entire town from plague.

Murder and mayhem seem miles away from sadly serene teenage coffin songs. Yet homicide is a common feature in hit tunes throughout the past three decades. Traditional vengeance songs such as "Frankie And Johnny" (1963) and "Stagger Lee" (1958) were revived by Sam Cooke and Lloyd Price. But even more cold-blooded characters found their way into vinyl immortality after 1950. The wicked, killer-for-hire exploits of Bobby Darin's "Mack The Knife" (1959) were exceeded by the ungrateful, unprovoked, murderous attack of Al Wilson's "The Snake" (1968); and the bloody ?deeds of Marty Robbins' "Big Iron" (1960) and Lorne Greene's "Ringo" (1964) don't begin to match the psychotic bloodlust illustrated by Carole King's shotgun-wielding "Smackwater Jack" (1971) and The Beatles' mallet-carrying Maxwell.

Country music continues to foster lyrical images of two-gun justice, violence, and death in the contemporary song arena. Johnny Cash sings the "Folsom Prison Blues" (1968) because he shot a man in Reno, just to watch him die. Casual homicide doesn't pay. In addition to Johnny Cash's unheeded warning—"Don't Take Your Guns To Town" (1959)—the ancient streets of the Laredo death scene is reenacted in several songs by Marty Robbins, in the Kingston Trio's "Tom Dooley" (1958), in Eric Clapton's

"I Shot The Sheriff" (1974), and in dozens of other country ballads. Of course, there are other reasons for committing murder. Vicki Lawrence seeks personal vengeance in "The Night The Lights Went Out In Georgia" (1973); Steve Miller describes a man killed during a robbery in "Take The Money And Run" (1976); Bobby Marchan depicts a jealous suitor who shoots his lover when he finds her entertaining his friends in "There's Something On Your Mind" (1960); and, in a frightening example of cannibalism, The Buoys speculate on the unspeakable disappearance of "Timothy" (1971).

Death at an elderly age is regrettable; death by an accident is shocking and unexpected; murder is a singular event of individual violence motivated by greed, vengeance, fear, envy, anger, or insanity. But American society has reserved the most deliberate death-dealing activity for young men. War is organized homicide, murder by carefully calculated plans, annihilation orchestrated by politicians, diplomats, generals, black marketeers, and the numerous "Masters Of War" (n.d.) according to Bob Dylan. While Peter, Paul, and Mary chided "The Cruel War" (1966) and sadly asked how many more times cannon balls would fly in "Blowing' In The Wind" (1963), The Kingston Trio stated an even harsher truth. They acknowledged that the best soldiers have all gone to graveyards. The refrain to "Where Have All The Flowers Gone" (1962) indicts the military fighters, the politicians and diplomats, and the entire human race by asking when will mankind learn to halt warfare. The victims of war include not only soldiers as in "Billy, Don't Be A Hero" (1974) by B. Donaldson and the Heywoods, in "Billy And Sue" (1966) by B. J. Thomas, and in "2 + 2 = ?" (n.d.) by The Bob Seger System, but also their friends and loved ones who are left to mourn battlefield deaths. Although Terry Nelson and C Company intended to defend the trauma-motivated soldiers in Vietnam, the "Battle Hymn Of Lt. Calley" (1971) is actually a grisly reminder of the brutality, the arbitrariness, and the universal pain and death inflicted by military madness. As Edwin Starr shouted in 1970, war is good for absolutely nothing! His conclusion in "War" was that only the undertaker benefitted from such organized mass killing.

The ultimate act of cowardice or of bravery, of defiance or of lunacy, is suicide. The individual decision to choose death over life is the ultimate existential act. Songs that recount self-inflicted death are numerous, but generally melancholy and somewhat mysterious. Most often, a suicide is described by a forlorn lover, a remaining relative, or a sad and confused friend. Don McLean eulogizes Van Gogh's misanthropic artistic genius in "Vincent" (1972); unidentified lovers mourn the loss of mates in "Endless Sleep" (1958), "Emma" (1975), and "Moody River" (1961); an Indian couple produce a watery Romeo and Juliet death scene in "Running Bear" (1959); Bobbie Gentry taunted her listeners with the tale of a young man who jumped off the Tallahachie Bridge in "Ode To Billie Joe" (1967); and

The Kinks and Simon and Garfunkel describe some very strange victims of society in "Richard Cory" (n.d.), "A Well Respected Man" (1965), and "A Most Peculiar Man" (n.d.).

A postscript to the death theme in popular music is found in the coda of tributes to political and singing/songwriting heroes who have died since 1950. Although John Lennon and Elvis Presley have been praised in vinyl in every imaginable fashion, no single popular music artist has yet garnered a more well-crafted, skillfully performed, and positively received recorded eulogy than Buddy Holly. The Don McLean tune "American Pie" (1971) was not only a remembrance of the passing of a brilliant 1950s tunesmith, but also a metaphoric exploration of the changes in American music from 1955 until the early 1970s. A song of similar historic scope, though totally political in nature and import, was Dion DiMucci's lament to the assassinated leaders Abraham Lincoln, Martin Luther King, Jr., John F. Kennedy, and Robert F. Kennedy. The folkish song "Abraham, Martin And John" (1968) was also issued by Moms Mabley (1969), Smokey Robinson and The Miracles, and Tom Clay (1971) to cover all record-purchasing publics with versions of this popular sentimental hymn. Of course, the most all-inclusive tributes to contemporary musical artists have been produced by Tex Ritter in "I Dreamed Of A Hill-Billy Heaven" (1971) and by The Righteous Brothers in "Rock And Roll Heaven" (1974).

In "American Pie" Don McLean utilizes the death of an individual popular music figure to symbolize the end of American innocence. Since Buddy Holly was killed in 1959, a year that marked the termination of rock's golden age (1956–1959), McLean's commentary actually focuses on the evolution of popular song during the sixties. As in most epic tales, there are obscure references to a broad spectrum of historical characters. In this case, nearly all of them are musicians. The lyrical chronology includes references to The Monotones ("The Book Of Love"), Marty Robbins ("A White Sport Coat And A Pink Carnation"), Elvis Presley, Bob Dylan, John Lennon, The Byrds, The Beatles, Mick Jagger ("Jumpin' Jack Flash"), The Rolling Stones, and Janis Joplin. For McLean, the passing of Buddy Holly— along with lesser-known artists J. P. "The Big Bopper" Richardson and Ritchie Valens—was an ignition point of youthful consciousness. A decade later the last vestiges of innocence were shredded by the horror of motorcycle gang murders during the Altamount Music Festival in California. The image of Mick Jagger as Satan contrasted with Buddy Holly's more angelic demeanor is obvious. But mortality remains the central haunting spectre to the singer.

Paul Simon, master songsmith, perceptive social analyst, and self-proclaimed child of the rock generation, seized the same historic scope as Don McLean to comment on death as a shaper of social psyche. The song "The Late Great Johnny Ace" (1983) covers the 1954–1980 period. This tune focuses on three deaths. The strange Russian roulette, accidental suicide of rhythm and blues performer Johnny Ace is depicted as an unexplainably significant moment in an adolescent's life. Ten years later the same music enthusiast thinks of 1964 as the year of The Beatles, the year of The Stones. Yet the underlying event in the storyteller's image of the successful British musical invasion occurred in November 1963. Simon also refers to 1964 as a year after JFK. He and his girl, obviously far removed from the scene of the Dallas assassination in London, are staying up all night and partying in mock Left Bank revelry. The concluding element in this brief tune is a stranger's 1980 announcement that John Lennon has died. No details of the New York City murder are mentioned. The singer adjourns to a bar, pumps coins into a jukebox with the stranger, and dedicates each song played to the late great Johnny Ace. The cycle of death is universal. It is complete from Ace to Lennon. This song updates Don McLean's meaning—yet another music legend has passed.

DEATH

Accidental Deaths

"Dead Man's Curve" (Liberty 55672)
  by Jan and Dean (1964)

"Ebony Eyes" (Warner Brothers 5199)
  by The Everly Brothers (1961)

"Fire And Rain" (Warner Brothers 7423)
  by James Taylor (1970)

"Give Us Your Blessing" (Red Bird 030)
  by The Shangri-Las (1965)

"Last Kiss" (Josie 923)
  by J. Frank Wilson and The Cavaliers (1964)

"Leader Of The Pack" (Red Bird 014)
  by The Shangri-Las (1964)

"The Pusher" (Dunhill album)
  by Steppenwolf, (n.d.)

"Snow Blind Friend" (Dunhill 4269)
  by Steppenwolf (1971)

"Teen Angel" (MGM 12845)
  by Mark Dinning (1960)

"Tell Laura I Love Her" (RCA 7745)
  by Ray Peterson (1960)

Dead Soldiers And Other War-Time Casualties

"The Ballad Of The Green Berets" (RCA 8739)
by SSgt. Barry Sadler (1966)

"Battle Hymn Of Lt. Calley" (Plantation 73)
by Terry Nelson and C Company (1971)

"The Battle Of New Orleans" (Columbia 41339)
by Johnny Horton (1959)

"Billy And Sue" (Hickory 1395)
by B. J. Thomas (1966)

"Billy, Don't Be A Hero" (ABC 11435)
by Bo Donaldson and The Heywoods (1974)

"Blowin' In The Wind" (Warner Brothers 5368)
by Peter, Paul, and Mary (1963)

"The Cruel War" (Warner Brothers 5809)
by Peter, Paul, and Mary (1966)

"Eve Of Destruction" (Dunhill 4009)
by Barry McGuire (1965)

"Masters of War" (Columbia album)
by Bob Dylan (n.d.)

"The Night They Drove Old Dixie Down (Vanguard 35138)
by Joan Baez (1971)

"2 + 2 = ?" (Capitol 2143)
by The Bob Seger System (n.d.)

"Undercover Of The Night" (Rolling Stones 99813)
by the Rolling Stones (1983)

"War" (Gordy 71010)
by Edwin Starr (1970)

"Where Have All The Flowers Gone?" (Capitol 4671)
by The Kingston Trio (1962)

Loss Of A Loved One

"Alone Again (Naturally)" (Mam 3619)
by Gilbert O'Sullivan (1972)

"Death Of An Angel" (Wand 164)
by The Kingsmen (1964)

"Don't Cry Daddy" (RCA 47–9768)
by Elvis Presley (1969)

"Eighteen Yellow Roses" (Capitol 4970)
by Bobby Darin (1963)

"Everything I Own" (Elektra 45765)
by Bread (1972)

"He Stopped Loving Her Today" (Epic 50867)
by George Jones (1980)

"Honey" (United Artists 50283)
by Bobby Goldsboro (1968)

"The Last Game Of The Season (A Blind Man In The Bleachers)"
(Big Tree 16052)
by David Geddes (1975)

"Old Rivers" (Liberty 55436)
by Walter Brennan (1962)

"Papa Was A Rollin' Stone" (Gordy 7121)
by The Temptations (1972)

"Patches" (Atlantic 2748)
by Clarence Carter (1962)

"Ruben James" (Reprise 0854)
by Kenny Rogers and The First Edition (1969)

"Seasons In The Sun" (Bell 45432)
by Terry Jacks (1974)

"Tragedy" (Fernwood 109)
by Thomas Wayne (1959)

Maturing, Aging, and Dying

"Age Ain't Nothin' But A Number"(MCA 52184)
by Little Milton (1983)

"Aqualung" (Reprise album)
by Jethro Tull (1971).

"Autumn Of My Life" (United Artists 50318)
by Bobby Goldsboro (1968)

"Daisy A Day" (MGM 14463)
by Jud Strunk (1973)

"Dearie" (Decca 24873)
by Ray Bolger and Ethel Merman (1950)

"Eleanor Rigby" (Capitol 5715)
by The Beatles (1966)

"Forty And Fadin' " (Dimension 1031)
by Ray Price (1982)

"Goin' Down Slow" (Dunhill 4379)
by Bobby Bland (1974)

"Grandma's Song" (Warner Brothers 49790)
by Gail Davies (1981)

"Hey Nineteen" (MCA 51036)
by Steely Dan (1980)

"I Wish I Was Eighteen Again" (Mercury 57011)
by George Burns (1980)

"I'm Livin' In Shame" (Motown 1139)
  by Diana Ross and The Supremes (1969)

"In My Eyes" (MCA 52282)
  by John Conlee (1983)

"Is That All There Is?" (Capitol 2602)
  by Peggy Lee (1969)

"It Was A Very Good Year" (Reprise 0429)
  by Frank Sinatra (1966)

"Live Your Life Before You Die" (Blue Thumb 262)
  by The Pointer Sisters (1975)

"Moments To Remember" (Columbia 40539)
  by The Four Lads (1955)

"My Generation" (Decca 31877)
  by The Who (1966)

"My Way" (RCA PB–11165)
  by Elvis Presley (1977)

"My Way" (Reprise 0817)
  by Frank Sinatra (1969)

"Old And Wise" (Arista 1048)
  by The Alan Parsons Project (1983)

"Over Thirty (Not Over The Hill)" (MCA 52032)
  by Conway Twitty (1982)

"Puff The Magic Dragon" (Warner Brothers 5348)
  by Peter, Paul, and Mary (1963)

"Thirty-Nine And Holding" (Elektra 47095)
  by Jerry Lee Lewis (1981)

"Through The Years" (Liberty 1444)
  by Kenny Rogers (1981)

"The Way We Were/Try To Remember" (Buddah 463)
  by Gladys Knight and The Pips (1975)

"When I Die" (Buddah 131)
  by Motherlode (1969)

"When I'm Dead And Gone" (Capitol 3014)
  by McGuinness Flint (1971)

"When I'm Sixty-Four" (Capitol album)
  by The Beatles (1967)

"When I Was Young" (MGM 13721)
  by the Animals (1967)

"Yes" (Epic 03917)
  by Billy Swan (1983)

"Yesterday Once More/Nothing Remains The Same" (Atlantic 3798)
  by The Spinners (1981)

"Yesterday, When I Was Young" (Dot 17246)
by Roy Clark (1969)

Murder

"Big Iron" (Columbia 41589)
by Marty Robbins (1960)

"Bohemian Rhapsody" (Elektra 45297)
by Queen (1976)

"Copacabana (At The Copa)" (Arista 0339)
by Barry Manilow (1978)

"Delilah" (Parrot 40025)
by Tom Jones (1968)

"Don't Take Your Guns To Town" (Columbia 41313)
by Johnny Cash (1959)

"El Paso" (Columbia 41511)
by Marty Robbins (1959)

"Electricland" (Swan Song 99966)
by Bad Company (1982)

"Folsom Prison Blues" (Columbia 44513)
by Johnny Cash (1968)

"Frankie and Johnny" (RCA 8215)
by Sam Cooke (1963)

"Freddie's Dead" (Curtom 1975)
by Curtis Mayfield (1972)

"Give Up Your Guns" (Scepter 12318)
by The Buoys (1971)

"Green, Green Grass of Home" (Parrot 40009)
by Tom Jones (1966)

"Guns, Guns, Guns" (RCA 0708)
by The Guess Who (1972)

"The Hanging Tree" (Columbia 41325)
by Marty Robbins (1959)

"I Fought The Law" (Mustang 3014)
by The Bobby Fuller Four (1966)

"I Shot The Sheriff" (RSO 409)
by Eric Clapton (1974)

"In The Ghetto" (RCA 47–9741)
by Elvis Presley (1969)

"Indiana Wants Me" (Rare Earth 5013)
by R. Dean Taylor (1970)

"I've Got To Get A Message To You" (Atco 6603)
by The Bee Gees (1968)

"Killing Of Georgie" (Warner Brothers 8386)
  by Rod Stewart (1977)

"Live And Let Die" (Apple 1863)
  by Paul McCartney and Wings (1973)

"Mack The Knife" (Atco 6147)
  by Bobby Darin (1959)

"Maxwell's Silver Hammer" (Apple album)
  by The Beatles (n.d.)

"Midnight Rider" (Capricorn 0035)
  by Gregg Allman (1973)

"The Night Chicago Died" (Mercury 73492)
  by Paper Lace (1974)

"The Night The Lights Went Out In Georgia" (Bell 45303)
  by Vicki Lawrence (1973)

"Outlaw Man" (Asylum 11025)
  by The Eagles (1973)

"Ringo" (RCA 8444)
  by Lorne Greene (1964)

"Ruby, Don't Take Your Love To Town" (Reprise 0829)
  by Kenny Rogers and The First Edition (1969)

"Sixteen Tons" (Atlantic 3323)
  by The Don Harrison Band (1976)

"Sixteen Tons" (Capitol 3252)
  by Tennessee Ernie Ford (1955)

"Smackwater Jack" (Ode 66019)
  by Carole King (1971)

"The Snake" (Soul City 767)
  by Al Wilson (1968)

"Spirit In The Sky" (Reprise 0885)
  by Norman Greenbaum (1970)

"Stagger Lee" (ABC-Paramount 9972)
  by Lloyd Price (1958)

"Swamp Witch" (MGM 14496)
  by Jim Stafford (1973)

"Take The Money And Run" (Capitol 4260)
  by The Steve Miller Band (1976)

"There's Something On Your Mind" (Fire 1022)
  by Bobby Marchan (1960)

"Timothy" (Scepter 12275)
  by The Buoys (1971)

"Tom Dooley" (Capitol 4049)
  by The Kingston Trio (1958)

Speculating On Death As A Natural Event

"And When I Die" (Columbia 45008)
  by Blood, Sweat and Tears (1969)
"Are You Ready?" (Columbia 45158)
  by Pacific Gas and Electric (1970)
"(Don't Fear) The Reaper" (Columbia 10384)
  by Blue Oyster Cult (1976)
"The Gambler" (United Artists 1250)
  by Kenny Rogers (1978)
"Games People Play" (Capitol 2248)
  by Joe South (1969)
"Instant Karma (We All Shine On)" (Apple 1818)
  by John Lennon (1970)
"Let's Live For Today" (Dunhill 4084)
  by The Grass Roots (1967)
"Turn! Turn! Turn!" (Columbia 43424)
  by The Byrds (1965)

Suicide

"Alone Again (Naturally)" (Mam 3619)
  by Gilbert O'Sullivan (1972)
"Emma" (Big Tree 16031)
  by Hot Chocolate (1975)
"Endless Sleep" (Demon 1507)
  by Jody Reynolds (1958)
"I Think I'm Gonna Kill Myself" (Roulette 4140)
  by Buddy Knox (1959)
"Moody River" (Dot 16209)
  by Pat Boone (1961)
"A Most Peculiar Man" (Columbia album)
  by Simon and Garfunkel (n.d.)
"Ode To Billie Joe" (Capitol 5950)
  by Bobbie Gentry (1967)
"Patches" (Smash 1758)
  by Dickey Lee (1962)
"Richard Cory" (Columbia album)
  by Simon and Garfunkel (n.d.)
"Running Bear" (Mercury 71474)
  by Johnny Preston (1959)
"A Well Respected Man" (Reprise 0420)
  by The Kinks (1965)

Tributes to Deceased Heroes and Villains (Historical and Legendary)

"Abraham, Martin And John" (Laurie 3464)
by Dion (1968)

"Abraham, Martin And John" (Mercury 72935)
by Moms Mabley (1969)

"Abraham, Martin And John" (Tamla 54184)
by Smokey Robinson and The Miracles (1969)

"American Pie" (United Artists 50856)
by Don McLean (1971)

"Are You Lonesome Tonight?" (RCA 47–7810)
by Elvis Presley (1960)

"The Ballad Of Bonnie and Clyde" (Epic 10283)
by George Fame (1968)

"The Ballad Of Davy Crockett" (Columbia 40449)
by Fess Parker (1955)

"Ballad Of Easy Rider" (Columbia 44990)
by The Byrds (1969)

"Ballad Of John Dillinger" (Mercury 72836)
by Billy Grammer (1968)

"Ballad Of The Alamo" (Columbia 41809)
by Marty Robbins (1960)

"Big Bad John" (Columbia 42175)
by Jimmy Dean (1961)

"Cole, Cooke, And Redding" (Atlantic 2722)
by Wilson Pickett (1970)

"Conquistador" (A&M 1347)
by Procol Harum (1972)

"The Death Of Hank Williams" (King 1172)
by Jack Cardwell (1953)

"Done Too Soon" (Uni 55278)
by Neil Young (1971)

"From Graceland To The Promised Land" (MCA 40804)
by Merle Haggard and the Strangers (1977)

"George Jackson" (Columbia 45516)
by Bob Dylan (1971)

"High Noon" (Columbia 39770)
by Frankie Lane (1952)

"I Dreamed Of A Hill-Billy Heaven" (Capitol 4567)
by Tex Ritter (1971)

"In The Quiet Morning (For Janis Joplin)" (A&M 1362)
by Joan Baez (1972)

"In The Summer Of His Years" (MGM 13203)
by Connie Francis (1963)

"James Dean" (Asylum 45202)
by The Eagles (1974)

"John Henry" (London 1650)
by Lonnie Donegan and His Skiffle Group (1956)

"The King Is Gone" (Scorpion 135)
by Ronnie McDowell (1977)

"The Late Great Johnny Ace" (Columbia album)
by Paul Simon (1983)

"Lefty" (Viva 49778)
by David Frizzell (1981)

"Mad Dog" (A&M album)
by Lee Michaels (n.d.)

"(The Man Who Shot) Liberty Valance" (Musicor 1020)
by Gene Pitney (1962)

"Night Shift" (Motown 1773)
by The Commodores (1984)

"Ohio" (Atlantic 2740)
by Crosby, Stills, Nash, and Young (1970)

"P.T. 109" (Columbia 42338)
by Jimmy Dean (1962)

"The Ride" (Columbia 03778)
by David Allan Coe (1983)

"Rock And Roll Heaven" (Haven 7002)
by The Righteous Brothers (1974)

"Sir Duke" (Tamla 54281)
by Stevie Wonder (1977)

"Six White Horses" (Epic 10540)
by Tommy Cash (1969)

"Three Stars" (Crest 1057)
by Tommy Dee, with Carol Kay and The Teen-Aires (1959)

"A Tribute To A King" (Stax 248)
by William Bell (1968)

"Trouble Man" (Tamla 54218)
by Marvin Gaye (1972)

"Vincent" (United Artists 50887)
by Don McLean (1972)

"What The World Needs Now Is Love/Abraham, Martin And John"
(Mowest 5002)
by Tom Clay (1971)

4

Education

Music maintains a highly visible role in American public education. Every secondary school has an athletic fight song and an alma mater, a choral director and an instrumental music teacher, a marching band and a glee club, and usually several other organized musical activities. In addition, lunchroom record hops, piped-in cafeteria music, post-game sock hops, disc jockey dances, proms, and spring, formal, big-band extravaganzas are common social elements at most high schools. It is particularly intriguing to note the depiction of American public education in the lyrics of songs released since 1950. Not only are specific attitudes about schools, teaching, and peer relations frequently presented in contemporary tunes, but an array of critical commentary about the means and ends of formal learning activities surfaces regularly in pop lyrics.

Rock era music has enlisted more and more singers and songwriters who articulate the values of youth. The observations, ideals, and images contained in their songs are uncompromisingly youth oriented. This means that public schools, the physical environment of so much teenage involvement, are depicted, scrutinized, and analyzed in numerous songs. The meaning of this lyrical examination of American schooling is staggering. Internal verifications of educational practices are replacing external expectations and ideals concerning the nature of public school learning. Neither truth nor reality is guaranteed by this change in commentators. However, the perspective of current student experience is undeniably sharper in assessing the behavior and functions of principals, teachers, PTOs, student groups, and individual learners than the more philosophical criticisms of Sidney Hook, Paul Goodman, and legions of other public school analysts.

No comprehensive ideology of public school criticism exists in the grooves of popular recordings. Nevertheless, several key ideas do emerge. Lyrical idealism is not totally absent, of course. Admiration for the teacher who is bright, deeply committed to learning, concerned about his or her pupils, and engaged in a constant battle to overcome ignorance is presented in a few tunes like "To Sir With Love" (1967) and "Welcome Back" (1976). But a much more critical tone dominates the majority of lyrical commentary about schooling. Teachers are generally condemned for being ignorant of student feelings ("Bird Dog"—1958), for pursuing irrelevant classroom topics ("(What A) Wonderful World"—1978), for corrupting student idealism ("The Logical Song"—1979), and for intentionally stifling the development of their pupils' social and political perspectives ("Another Brick In The Wall"—1980). It is difficult to imagine a more blatant denunciation of the entire public educational system than Paul Simon's introductory lines in "Kodachrome" (1973).

The lyrical images of American public education are diverse, lively, colorful, direct, and generally critical. "School" is depicted in contemporary lyrics as a state of mind as well as a physical entity. A few songs beckon students to "(Remember The Days Of The) Old School Yard" (1977). Cat Stevens' nostalgic reverie is echoed by the spirited twenty-eight versions of "High School U.S.A." (1959) recorded by Tommy Faceda, by The Beach Boys' loyalty hymn "Be True To Your School" (1963), and by The Arbors' nostalgic "Graduation Day" (1967). But these tunes are atypical of the genre. The majority of lyrics portraying school life posit the buildings and grounds as a sinister series of segregated compartments that unrelentingly dictate student behavior.

The classroom is generally depicted as the domain of a teaching tyrant. The teacher doesn't know how mean she looks, notes Chuck Berry in "School Day" (1957). The activities that occur in classrooms are conducted in lock-step, intimidating, teacher-directed fashion. A student like The Coasters' "Charlie Brown" (1959) may walk into the classroom cool and slow, but then he'd better be quiet, orderly, and without guile. In contrast, the hallways are always alive with noise. Rigidly enforced classroom silence and cerebral irrelevance give way to cacaphonous peer chatter and delirious social interaction. Discussions of cars, sex, smokes, food, movies, and immediate wants and needs occur in the jostling, locker-slamming hallway atmosphere. The school's corridors also lead to freedom: to a discreet cigarette break in the restroom ("Smokin' In The Boy's Room"—1974); to a luncheon record hop "High School Dance"—1977); to more private activities in recreation areas ("Me And Julio Down By The Schoolyard"—1972); and to parking lots filled with cars and vans. The key word to describe lyrical observations about the school building is escape. Even the songs that laud memories of bygone secondary school experiences—such as Adrian Kimberly's "Pomp And Circumstance" (1961)—praise commencement as the relief felt by all alumni. This escapist theme is most clearly delineated in the numerous songs that depict the annual vacation period for June through August: Gary "U.S." Bonds' "School Is Out" (1961), The Jamies' "Summertime, Summertime" (1958), and Alice Cooper's "School's Out" (1972).

Lyrical images of students vary greatly. A clear recognition of both peer pressures and of the dominance of special interest groups in school is illustrated in songs such as The Beach Boys' "I Get Around" (1964), Dobie Gray's "In Crowd" (1965), and Connie Francis' "Where The Boys Are"(1961). The isolation of individuals and out groups is depicted in The Crystals' "He's A Rebel" (1962), The Shangri-Las' "Leader Of The Pack" (1964), Carol Jarvis' "Rebel" (1957), and Janis Ian's "At Seventeen" (1975) and "Society's Child" (1967). Although they comprise the most heterogeneous group within the educational system, students are also characterized as the least franchised ("Summertime Blues"—1968), most harrassed ("Yakety Yak"—1958), most regimented ("Another Brick In The Wall"—1980), least trusted ("Smokin' In The Boy's Room"—1974), most humorous ("Charlie Brown"—1959 and "My Boy–Flat Top"—1955), most victimized ("My Generation"—1966 and "Society's Child"—1967), and least understood ("It Hurts To Be Sixteen"—1963 and "You And Me Against The World"—1974).

The sense of educational futility is a dominant element in popular lyrics. Paul Simon's 1973 song "Kodachrome," which contains a stunning indictment of academic irrelevance, was followed three years later by an even more negative analysis of post–high school life in "Still Crazy After All These Years" (1976). This self-assessment was shared with a former girlfriend. Still other songs capture poignant vignettes of post–high school reflections. Tunes like Bob Seger's "2 + 2 = ?" (n.d.) question the meaning of a school friend's senseless death in Vietnam; Alice Cooper's "Eighteen" (1971) examines the maturity predicament of a recent high school graduate; and Bob Dylan's "Subterranean Homesick Blues" (1965) presents the image of an illogical society that awaits a formally educated but non–street-wise youth.

The adults that control the environment within public schools are neither admired nor respected. Even those few songs that praise teachers—"Mr. Lee" (1957) by The Bobbettes, "To Sir With Love" (1967) by Lulu, and "Abigail Beecher" (1964) by Freddy Cannon—offer sharp, derogatory contrasts between the caring behavior and independent actions of their favored instructors and the general demeanor of the majority of teachers who are portrayed as boobs, bumpkins, and boors. Chuck Berry, Supertramp, The Coasters, The Who, Janis Ian, Paul Simon, and dozens of other singers acknowledge in simple tones the 1980 message chanted by Pink Floyd in "Another Brick In The Wall."

If teachers are fools, antiquarians, babysitters, and persons generally out of touch with reality, principals are outright villains with malevolent motives and totalitarian drives. Although very few lyrical commentaries are assigned solely to the chief administrative officers of the schools, the implications of their rule-making authority and enforcement abound. The jangling bell system of lock-step, class-to-class routine, the de-personalized hall passes, the regimented class changes, the overly brief lunch periods, and dozens of other system-defining annoyances are attributed to the principal, though usually enforced by the teachers.

Most distressing is the fact that teachers are universally defined in negative images by their students. They lack common sense ("Bird Dog"—1958), are cynical ("The Logical Song"—1979), humorless ("School Day"—1957 and "Charlie Brown"—1959), out of touch with personal problems ("Don't Stand So Close To Me"—1980), and represent a system of thought and action that hides from rather than confronts genuine social problems ("Another Brick In The Wall"—1980 and "Allentown"—1983). Even John Sebastian's laudatory "Welcome Back" (1976)—a tribute to teacher responsibility—specifically notes this behavior to be an exception to the norm.

Students tend to regard the public school system as a reflection of the policy-making power and educational goals of parents and other members of the local community. The lyrics of contemporary songs depict the parental/principal/community nexus as the primary source of conformity, authoritarianism, hypocrisy, and frustration. At best, a student dwells in a world where he's "Almost Grown" (1959). But parents and the community seem unwilling to accept the occasional mistakes that are a normal part of personal maturation and social development. Schools do not function as experimental stages for reflective consideration of alternative social, political, economic, and personal ideas and behaviors; instead, they are cloisters, cells, and societal buffers. Deviant behavior is harshly labelled ("I'm Not A Juvenile Deliquent"—n.d., "Rebel"—1957, and "Leader Of The Pack"—1964) by a unified adult population ("Town Without Pity"—1962, "Sticks And Stones"—1960, and "Society's Child"—1967). Insensitivity to growing pains ("At Seventeen"—1975) is compounded by intense social pressure to conform in thought, word, and deed ("Fortunate Son"—1969 and "The Free Electric Band"'"—1973). Despite occasional public lapses between preachment and practice among community members ("Harper Valley P.T.A."—1968) and parents ("That's The Way I Always Heard It Should Be"—1971), schools remain bastions of patriotic ("Okie From Muskogee"—1969), local ("Be True To Your School"—1963), and moral ("Me and Julio Down By The Schoolyard"—1972) direction. Such a strong parental/community stance obviously renders democratic processes, instructional independence, intellectual objectivity, and open communication among students and teachers impossible. The smothering hand of community control is lyrically chided in the Simon and Garfunkel ballad "My Little Town" (1975).

Please tell me who I am? This question paraphrases Socrates' more positively stated dictum, "Know thyself." But the question is part of the lyrical criticism of formal education posed by the British rock group Supertramp in their 1979 hit "The Logical Song." Echoing Rousseau's naturalistic educational premise, the lyric depicts an untutored youngster who views life as wonderful, a miracle, beautiful, and magical. Then he is sent away to school where he learns to be clinical, logical, cynical, sensible, responsible, and practical. Pink Floyd's "Another Brick In The Wall" (1980) also challenges the formal educational system with a stinging, chanting attack against thought control in the classroom.

The Supertramp Pink Floyd challenges seem far more deep rooted and radical than the humourous, exasperated 1950s commentaries of Chuck Berry and The Coasters. Yet they are logical extensions of critiques presented by Janis Ian, Paul Simon, and several others who are understandably appalled by the failure of American education to meet or even approach in practice its oft-repeated ideals. The laudable goals of fostering human dignity, creativity, freedom, individualism, knowledge, diversity, and objectivity are submerged in public schools beneath a miasma of regimentation, indoctrination, illiteracy, cynicism, arbitrariness, authoritarianism, and local morality and cultural bias. The disembodied voice of youth—popular recordings—chant a consistent sad tale.

If public schools are not effective sources of learning, then how do young people gain their knowledge? Although contemporary tunesmiths provide a variety of answers, they concur on one point. Most valuable ideas, information, social contacts, feelings, beliefs, and personal values are secured through individual experience beyond the classroom. Recorded commentaries argue "I've Gotta Be Me" (1968), "My Way" (1969), "Just The Way You Are" (1977) and "You May Be Right" (1980). The individualistic road through life is not necessarily solipsistic or alienating or narcissistic. Once again, the lyrical images of community pressures ("Town Without Pity"—1962), peer criticisms ("Sticks And Stones"—1960), parental restraints "(Yakety Yak"—1958 and "Summertime Blues"—1968), church irrelevance ("Only The Good Die Young"—1978), political skullduggery ("Won't Get Fooled Again"—1971), and wage labor meaninglessness ("Wake Me, Shake Me"—1960, "Get A Job"—1958, "Take This Job And Shove It"—1977 and "Workin' At The Carwash Blues"—1974) tend to hinder personal development through outside-of-school contacts, too.

One should not conclude that contemporary songs are devoid of paens to the joy of intellectual growth and discovery. Abundant examples illustrate constructive personal experiences. Some are humorous, such as "Spiders And Snakes" (1974), "Mr. Businessman" (1968), and "Dead End Street" (1967); some are serious, such as "Taxi" (1972), "Skip A Rope" (1968), and "Cat's In The Cradle" (1974); some are unresolved, such as "Question" (1970), "Who Will Answer?" (1968), and the "Eve Of Destruction" (1965);

and some are poignant, such as "Color Him Father" (1969), "Son Of Hickory Holler's Tramp" (1968), and "Patches" (1970). In each of these instances the learning is directly connected to individual perceptions of random but personally meaningful life events.

EDUCATION

School

"After School" (Decca 29946)
 by Tommy Charles (1956)

"After School" (Dale 100)
 by Randy Starr (1957)

"Back To School" (Checker 1158)
 by Bo Diddley (1967)

"Back To School Again" (Cameo 116)
 by Timmie Rogers (1957)

"Be True To Your School" (Capitol 5069)
 by The Beach Boys (1963)

"Graduation Day" (Date 1561)
 by The Arbors (1967)

"Graduation's Here" (Dolton 3)
 by The Fleetwoods (1959)

"High School Confidential" (Sun 296)
 by Jerry Lee Lewis (1958)

"High School U.S.A." (Atlantic 51–78)
 by Tommy Facenda (1959)

"I'm Going Back To School" (Vee Jay 462)
 by Dee Clark (1962)

"Kodachrome" (Columbia 45859)
 by Paul Simon (1973)

"The Logical Song" (A&M 2128)
 by Supertramp (1979)

"My Old School" (ABC 11396)
 by Steely Dan (1973)

"Pomp And Circumstance (The Graduation Song)" (Calliope 6501)
 by Adrian Kimberly (1961)

"(Remember The Days Of The) Old Schoolyard" (A&M 1948)
 by Cat Stevens (1977)

"School Bell Rock" (King 5247)
 by Roy Brown (1959)

"School Bus" (Leader 808)
  by Kris Jensen (1960)

"School Busin' " (Mallard 8)
  by Guy Drake (1971)

"School Days Are Back Again" (Imperial 5478)
  by Smiley Lewis (1957)

"School Daze" (Magic 93000)
  by Funn (1981)

"School Is In" (LeGrand 1012)
  by Gary "U.S." Bonds (1961)

"School Is Out" (LeGrand 1009)
  by Gary "U.S." Bonds (1961)

"Schoolbells" (Gone 5039)
  by Nicky and The Nobles (1959)

"Schooldays, Oh Schooldays" (Parkway 804)
  by Chubby Checker (n.d.)

"School's All Over" (World 10)
  by The Adorables (1964)

"School's Out" (Warner Brothers 7596)
  by Alice Cooper (1972)

Teachers and Principals

"Abigail Beecher" (Warner Brothers 5409)
  by Freddy Cannon (1964)

"Another Brick In The Wall" (Columbia 11187)
  by Pink Floyd (1980)

"Bird Dog" (Cadence 1350)
  by The Everly Brothers (1958)

"Don't Stand So Close To Me" (A&M 2301)
  by The Police (1980)

"(I Wanna) Dance With the Teacher" (Demon 1512)
  by The Olympics (1959)

"Mr. Lee" (Atlantic 1144)
  by The Bobbettes (1957)

"School Day" (Chess 1653)
  by Chuck Berry (1957)

"School Teacher" (Reprise 1069)
  by Kenny Rogers and The First Edition (1972)

"Teacher" (Reprise 0899)
  by Jethro Tull (1970)

"Teacher, Teacher" (Columbia 41152)
  by Johnny Mathis (1958)

"Teacher's Pet" (Columbia 41123)
  by Doris Day (1958)

"To Sir With Love" (Epic 10187)
  by Lulu (1967)

"Welcome Back" (Reprise 1349)
  by John Sebastian (1976)

Students

"Almost Grown" (Chess 1722)
  by Chuck Berry (1959)

"At Seventeen" (Columbia 10154)
  by Janis Ian (1975)

"Bennie And The Jets" (MCA 40198)
  by Elton John (1974)

"Charlie Brown" (Atco 6132)
  by The Coasters (1959)

"The Class" (Parkway 804)
  by Chubby Checker (1959)

"Class Of '57" (Mercury 73315)
  by The Statler Brothers (1972)

"Class Of '49" (Starday 779)
  by Red Sovine (1966)

"Department Of Youth" (Atlantic 3280)
  by Alice Cooper (1975)

"Dialogue (Part I and II)" (Columbia 45717)
  by Chicago (1972)

"Don't Be A Drop-Out" (King 6056)
  by James Brown (1966)

"Eighteen" (Warner Brothers 7449)
  by Alice Cooper (1971)

"Everybody's Talkin' " (RCA 0161)
  by Harry Nilsson (1969)

"From A School Ring To A Wedding Ring" (ABC-Paramount 9732)
  by The Rover Boys (1956)

"From The Teacher To The Preacher" (Brunswick 55387)
  by Gene Chandler and Barbara Acklin (1968)

"Graduation Day" (Capitol 3410)
  by The Four Freshmen (1956)

"He's A Rebel" (Philles 106)
  by The Crystals (1962)

"Hey Little Girl" (Abner 1029)
  by Dee Clark (1959)

"Hey, Schoolgirl" (Big 613)
by Tom and Jerry (1958)

"High School Dance" (Capitol 4405)
by The Sylvers (1977)

"High School Dance" (Specialty 608)
by Larry Williams (1957)

"High School Days" (Fairlane 21020)
by Bill Erwin and The Four Jacks (1962)

"High School Romance" (ABC-Paramount 9838)
by George Hamilton IV (1957)

"I Get Around" (Capitol 5174)
by The Beach Boys (1964)

"I'm Not A Juvenile Delinquent" (Gee album)
by Frankie Lymon and the Teenagers (n.d.)

"The 'In' Crowd" (Charger 105)
by Dobie Gray (1965)

"It Hurts To Be Sixteen" (Big Top 3156)
by Andrea Carroll (1963)

"Leader Of The Pack" (Red Bird 014)
by The Shangri-Las (1964)

"Little School Girl" (Modern 704)
by Smokey Hogg (1949)

"Lonely School Days" (Chess 1926)
by Chuck Berry (1965)

"Lonely School Year" (Rocket 40464)
by The Hudson Brothers (1965)

"Me And Julio Down By The Schoolyard" (Columbia 45585)
by Paul Simon (1972)

"My Boy–Flat Top" (King 1494)
by Boyd Bennett and His Rockets (1955)

"My Generation" (Decca 31877)
by The Who (1966)

"New Girl In School" (Liberty 55672)
by Jan and Dean (1964)

"New Kid In Town" (Asylum 45373)
by The Eagles (1977)

"Only Sixteen" (Capitol 4171)
by Dr. Hook (1976)

"An Open Letter To My Teenage Son" (Liberty 55996)
by Victor Lundberg (1967)

"Queen Of The Senior Prom" (Decca 30299)
by The Mills Brothers (1957)

"Rebel" (Dot 15586)
  by Carol Jarvis (1957)

"A Rose And A Baby Ruth" (ABC-Paramount 9765)
  by George Hamilton IV (1956)

"Roses Are Red (My Love)" (Epic 9509)
  by Bobby Vinton (1962)

"School Boy Crush" (Atlantic 3304)
  by The Average White Band (1975)

"School Boy Romance" (ABC-Paramount 9888)
  by Danny and The Juniors (1958)

"School Dance" (ABC-Paramount 9908)
  by Dwayne Hickman (1958)

"School Day Crush" (Gone 5039)
  by Nicky and The Nobles (1959)

"School Fool" (Mam 12553)
  by Mark Dinning (1957)

"Seventeen" (King 1470)
  by Boyd Bennett and His Rockets (1955)

"She Was Only Seventeen (He Was One Year More)" (Columbia 41209)
  by Marty Robbins (1958)

"Short Fat Fannie" (Specialty 608)
  by Larry Williams (1957)

"Smokin' In The Boy's Room" (Big Tree 16011)
  by Brownsville Station (1974)

"Society's Child (Baby I've Been Thinking)" (Verve 5027)
  by Janis Ian (1967)

"Stood Up" (Imperial 5483)
  by Ricky Nelson (1958)

"Summertime Blues" (Liberty 55144)
  by Eddie Cochran (1958)

"Summertime, Summertime" (Epic 9281)
  by The Jamies (1958)

"Swingin' On A Star" (Dimension 1010)
  by Big Dee Irwin (1963)

"Swingin' School" (Cameo 175)
  by Bobby Rydell (1960)

"Talk Of The School" (Capitol 4178)
  by Sonny James (1959)

"The Teacher And The Pet" (AGP 110)
  by Johnny Christopher (1969)

"Teenage Lament '74" (Warner Brothers 7762)
  by Alice Cooper (1974)

"To Be Young, Gifted And Black" (RCA 0269)
by Nina Simone (1969)

"Venus In Blue Jeans" (Ace 8001)
by Jimmy Clanton (1962)

"Waitin' In School" (Imperial 5483)
by Ricky Nelson (1958)

"Wake Up Little Susie" (Cadence 1337)
by The Everly Brothers (1957)

"(What A) Wonderful World" (Columbia 10676)
by Art Garfunkel, James Taylor, and Paul Simon (1978)

"What Is A Teenage Boy?" (Coral 61773)
by Tommy Edwards (1957)

"What Is A Teenage Girl?" (Coral 61773)
by Tommy Edwards (1957)

"Whenever A Teenager Cries" (World 1036)
by Reparata and The Delrons (1965)

"Where The Boys Are" (MGM 12971)
by Connie Francis (1961)

"A White Sport Coat (And A Pink Carnation)" (Columbia 40864)
by Marty Robbins (1957)

"Wonderful World" (Kleen 2112)
by Sam Cooke (1960)

"Young Blood" (Swan Song 70108)
by Bad Company (1976)

"Young School Girl" (Imperial 5537)
by Fats Domino (1958)

"Your Teenage Dreams" (Mercury 72184)
by Johnny Mathis (1963)

"You're Sixteen" (Apple 1870)
by Ringo Starr (1974)

Parents and the Community

"Cat's In The Cradle" (Elektra 45203)
by Harry Chapin (1974)

"Color Him Father" (Metromedia 117)
by The Winstons (1969)

"Fortunate Son" (Fantasy 634)
by Creedence Clearwater Revival (1969)

"The Free Electric Band" (Mums 6018)
by Albert Hammond (1973)

"Harper Valley P.T.A." (Plantation 3)
  by Jeannie C. Riley (1968)

"I Think We're Alone Now" (Roulette 4720)
  by Tommy James and The Shondells (1966)

"The Last Game Of The Season (A Blind Man In The Bleachers)"
  (Big Tree 16052)
  by David Geddes (1975)

"Mama Told Me (Not To Come)" (Dunhill 4239)
  by Three Dog Night (1970)

"My Little Town" (Columbia 10230)
  by Simon and Garfunkel (1975)

"Okie From Muskogee" (Capitol 2626)
  by Merle Haggard and The Strangers (1969)

"Skip A Rope" (Monument 1041)
  by Henson Cargill (1968)

"Sticks And Stones" (ABC-Paramount 10118)
  by Ray Charles (1960)

"Summertime Blues" (Philips 40516)
  by Blue Cheer (1968)

"Sylvia's Mother" (Columbia 45562)
  by Dr. Hook (1972)

"Teach Your Children" (Atlantic 2735)
  by Crosby, Stills, Nash, and Young (1970)

"That's The Way I've Always Heard It Should Be" (Elektra 45724)
  by Carly Simon (1971)

"Town Without Pity" (Musicor 1009)
  by Gene Pitney (1962)

"Why Don't They Understand" (ABC-Paramount 9862)
  by George Hamilton IV (1958)

"Yakety Yak" (Atco 6116)
  by The Coasters (1958)

"You And Me Against The World" (Imperial 5537)
  by Helen Reddy (1974)

"You Never Can Tell" (Chess 1906)
  by Chuck Berry (1964)

"Your Mama Don't Dance" (Columbia 45719)
  by Loggins and Messina (1973)

Noninstitutionalized Learning

"Allentown" (Columbia 03413)
  by Billy Joel (1983)

"Dead End Street" (Capitol 5869)
  by Lou Rawls (1967)

"Eve Of Destruction" (Dunhill 4009)
  by Barry Mc Guire (1965)

"Get A Job" (Ember 1029)
  by The Silhouettes (1958)

"I Am A Rock" (Columbia 43617)
  by Simon and Garfunkel (1966)

"I Am . . . I Said" (Uni 55278)
  by Neil Diamond (1971)

"I Wish" (Tamla 54274)
  by Stevie Wonder (1977)

"It's Your Thing" (T-Neck 901)
  by The Isley Brothers (1969)

"I've Got A Name" (ABC 11389)
  by Jim Croce (1973)

"I've Gotta Be Me" (Reprise 9779)
  by Sammy Davis, Jr. (1968)

"Just The Way You Are" (Columbia 10646)
  by Billy Joel (1977)

"Mamas Don't Let Your Babies Grow Up To Be Cowboys" (RCA 11198)
  by Willie Nelson (1978)

"Mr. Businessman" (Monument 1083)
  by Ray Stevens (1968)

"My Back Pages" (Columbia 44054)
  by The Byrds (1967)

"My Way" (Reprise 0817)
  by Frank Sinatra (1969)

"Night Moves" (Capitol 4369)
  by Bob Seger and The Silver Bullet Band (1977)

"Ohio" (Atlantic 2740)
  by Crosby, Stills, Nash, and Young (1970)

"Only The Good Die Young" (Columbia 10750)
  by Billy Joel (1978)

"Patches" (Atlantic 2748)
  by Clarence Carter (1970)

"A Place In The Sun" (A&M 1976)
  by Pablo Cruise (1977)

"Please Come To Boston" (Epic 11115)
  by Dave Loggins (1974)

"Question" (Threshold 67004)
  by The Moody Blues (1970)

"Respect Yourself" (Stax 0104)
by The Staple Singers (1971)

"The Right Thing To Do" (Elektra 45843)
by Carly Simon (1973)

"Rock And Roll (I Gave You The Best Years Of My Life)" (Columbia 10070)
by Mac Davis (1975)

"School For Sweet Talk" (Reprise 6752)
by Norman Greenbaum (1968)

"School Of Love" (Ko Ko 2112)
by Tommy Tate (1972)

"So You Want To Be A Rock 'N' Roll Star" (Columbia 43987)
by The Byrds (1967)

"Someone Saved My Life Tonight" (MCA 40421)
by Elton John (1975)

"Son-Of-A Preacher Man" (Atlantic 2580)
by Dusty Springfield (1969)

"Son Of Hickory Holler's Tramp" (Columbia 44425)
by O. C. Smith (1968)

"Spiders And Snakes" (MGM 14648)
by Jim Stafford (1974)

"Still Crazy After All These Years" (Columbia 10332)
by Paul Simon (1976)

"Subterranean Homesick Blues" (Columbia 43242)
by Bob Dylan (1965)

"Take This Job And Shove It" (Epic 50469)
by Johnny Paycheck (1977)

"Taxi" (Elektra 45770)
by Harry Chapin (1972)

"Teach Me Tiger" (Imperial 5626)
by April Stevens (1959)

"Teach Me Tonight" (Abbott 3001)
by The DeCastro Sisters (1954)

"That's Life" (Reprise 0531)
by Frank Sinatra (1966)

"That's The Way I've Always Heard It Should Be" (Elektra 45724)
by Carly Simon (1971)

"$2 + 2 = ?$" (Capitol 2143)
by The Bob Seger System (n.d.)

"Wake Me, Shake Me" (Atco 6168)
by The Coasters (1960)

"We Just Disagree" (Columbia 10575)
by Dave Mason (1977)

"We May Never Pass This Way (Again)" (Warner Brothers 7740)
by Seals and Crofts (1973)

"What Boys Are Made Of" (ABC-Paramount 10401)
by The Percells (1963)

"When The Boys Get Together" (Warner Brothers 5308)
by Joanie Sommers (1962)

"When The Boys Talk About The Girls" (Roulette 4066)
by Valerie Carr (1958)

"Who Are You" (MCA 40948)
by The Who (1978)

"Who Will Answer?" (RCA 9400)
by Ed Ames (1968)

"Why Do Kids Grow Up" (Rust 5073)
by Randy and The Rainbows (1963)

"Won't Get Fooled Again" (Decca 32846)
by The Who (1971)

"Woodstock" (Atlantic 2723)
by Crosby, Stills, Nash, and Young (1970)

"Workin' At The Car Wash Blues" (ABC 1147)
by Jim Croce (1974)

"Yesterday When I Was Young" (Dot 17246)
by Roy Clark (1969)

"You May Be Right" (Columbia 11231)
by Billy Joel (1980)

"You've Got To Pay The Price" (Silver Fox 14)
by Gloria Taylor (1969)

5

Marriage, Family Life, and Divorce

For singers of the 1950s, love and marriage were inevitably linked. Vocalists of both sexes acknowledged this. Frank Sinatra and Dinah Shore depicted the unity of courtship and marital bliss as a horse-and-carriage relationship in their separate renditions of "Love And Marriage" (1955). Two years later Jimmie Rodgers expanded this dualistic theme to include the growth of an extremely large family—all because his sweetheart/wife had "Kisses Sweeter Than Wine" (1957). Beyond mythical tales of happily-ever-after lives for newlyweds, however, there are numerous songs that depict realistic strains that inevitably occur within marital relationships. Jealousy resulting from real or imagined incidents, singular sexual indiscretions, or frequent acts of cheating and infidelity are chronicled in tunes such as "Lyin' Eyes" (1975), "Smoke From A Distant Fire" (1977), and "Take A Letter Maria" (1969). Although spouses often elect to forgive and forget the indiscretions of a mate in order to sustain a marriage, there are numerous songs that describe the pain of permanent separation and the finality of divorce. Many of the same emotions expressed in premarital "lost love" tunes sung by unmarried men and single women are even more deeply echoed in songs describing the end of a marriage, the dissolution of a family, and the loneliness of starting over without a partner.

Marriage is often a highly fantasized event. It is seen as a moment of personal exhilaration that propels a groom "From A Jack To A King" (1962). It can also be the fulfillment of a long-time dream, as in "(Today I Met) The Boy I'm Gonna Marry" (1963), "Hey Paula" (1962), "Betty And Dupree" (1958), and "Band Of Gold" (1955). Yet there are also skeptics and jokers observing the institution of marriage along with the idealistic romantics. Some tunes urge caution in selecting a mate—"Shop Around"

(1960), "If You Wanna Be Happy" (1963), "If I Were A Carpenter" (1966), "Take Time To Know Her" (1968), and "Someone Saved My Life Tonight" (1975); other recordings are openly whimsical toward the marital state—"One Mint Julep" (1952), "It's Gonna Work Out Fine" (1961), "You Never Can Tell" (1964), "I'm Henry VIII, I Am" (1965), and "Let's Pretend We're Married" (1983); and a few songs either balk at marriage in general—"Different Drum" (1967), "That's The Way I've Always Heard It Should Be" (1971), and "The Right Thing To Do" (1973)—or express selfish opposition to an impending wedding—"Wedding Bells (Are Breaking Up That Old Gang Of Mine)" (1954), "Go On With The Wedding" (1956), "(I Cried At) Laura's Wedding" (1963), and "Worst That Could Happen" (1968).

Despite the varying feelings described above, The Dreamlovers' plans for "When We Get Married" (1961) are transformed from a wish into reality once the determination "I'm Gonna Get Married" (1959) is finally secured. Examples of wedding songs abound. Among the most popular during the past three decades are: "(I'm Always Hearing) Wedding Bells" (1955), "Church Bells May Ring" (1956), "Get Me To The Church On Time" (1956), "To The Aisle" (1956), "Big Bopper's Wedding" (1958), "Down The Aisle Of Love" (1958), "Hawaiian Wedding Song" (1959), "Down The Aisle" (1960), "For Me And My Gal" (1961), "Down The Aisle (Wedding Bells)" (1963), "Chapel Of Love" (1964), "The Wedding" (1965), "We've Only Just Begun" (1970), and "The Wedding Song (There Is Love)" (1971). As a footnote, Frank Sinatra comments that although the first encounter with marital bliss may be wonderful, even a return engagement at a chapel steps can be personally fulfilling. He proclaims that love is even lovelier "The Second Time Around" (1961).

Reactions to married life vary in popular songs. Images of wives as lifelong companions, lovers, and selfless friends abound. Examples of such recordings are "Kisses Sweeter Than Wine" (1957), "Little Green Apples" (1968), "Friend, Lover, Woman, Wife" (1969), "My Woman, My Woman, My Wife" (1970), "Good Hearted Woman" (1976), "Devoted To You" (1978), and "Do That To Me One More Time" (1979). Other positive reflections of married life include the melancholy "Honey" (1968) and the anti-materialistic "Ruby Ann" (1962). One highlight of marriage, of course, is the annual celebration of the event as depicted in "Our Anniversary" (1962).

Family life is simple when the unit consists only of a newlywed couple. Once children are added to the domestic scene, parental responsibilities become more complicated. Sly and The Family Stone describe the unity/disunity of sibling rivalry within a household in "Family Affair" (1971). The positive sides of parenting are depicted in terms of fatherly pride in "Mama's Pearl" (1971) and of parents' reflections on the maturing, chaos, and talents of their offspring in "Willie And The Hand Jive" (1958),

"Broomstick Cowboy" (1965), "Watching Scotty Grow" (1970), and "Saturday Morning Confusion" (1971). Of course, there is sadness, too. The blight of poverty in the lives of the young is depicted in "Rag Doll" (1964), "Poor Man's Son" (1965), "In The Ghetto" (1969), and "Patches" (1970).

A husband and wife must adopt new roles—and new names. The "daddy" and "mommy" labels denote not only family responsibilities but also changes in lifestyle. Images of fathers in popular music are sometimes funny— "Yakety Yak" (1958), "Peek-A-Boo" (1958), and "Summertime Blues" (1958), but generally are strong and serious. Tunes illustrating this latter thought include "Oh! My Pa-Pa" (1953), "My Dad" (1962), "Father Knows Best" (1962), "My Daddy Knows Best" (1963), "Daddy Sang Bass" (1968), "Color Him Father" (1969), "Let Me Be The Man My Daddy Was" (1969), "Daddy Could Swear, I Declare" (1973), and "Leader Of The Band" (1981). Sometimes, however, the father's behavior is called into question by youngsters, as in "Papa Was Too" (1966) and "Papa Was A Rolling Stone" (1972). Mothers tend to be described as loving, selfless creatures who are totally devoted to their young ones. Songs stating this conviction are "Mama" (1960), "For Mama" (1965), "Mama" (1966), "Dreams Of The Everyday Housewife" (1968), "Lady Madonna" (1968), "Mama Liked The Roses" (1970), "Mother" (1971), "Mother And Child Reunion" (1972), "I'll Always Love My Mama" (1973), and "Loves Me Like A Rock" (1973).

Parents are also remembered and rated in terms of particular situations. Will they allow frequent dating? Do they acknowledge their child's judgments and opinions as having validity? Are they kind and hospitable to their child's teenage friends? Do they understand key adolescent concerns? Do they set rules fairly? Are they consistent models—or hypocrites—in respect to the behavioral and ethical standards they demand of their children? These issues are explored in numerous recordings such as "Teenager's Mother (Are You Right?)" (1956), "Mama Said" (1961), "Wolverton Mountain" (1962), "Mama Didn't Lie" (1963), "Mama Don't Allow" (1963), "Mrs. Brown You've Got A Lovely Daughter" (1965), "Skip A Rope" (1967), "1432 Franklin Pike Circle Hero" (1968), "Harper Valley P.T.A." (1968), "Mama Told Me (Not To Come)" (1970), "Sylvia's Mother" (1972), "The Free Electric Band" (1973), and "Your Daddy Don't Know" (1982). In musical terms, the indictment by Loggins and Messina—"Your Mama Don't Dance (1972)—is symbolic of the generation gap in both age and parental understanding.

Somewhere between the joy of being a bride and a groom and the sorrow of permanent separation and divorce there lies an unpleasant zone of emotional instability. The path to this area may be lined with imagined acts of unfaithfulness that spark fits of jealousy or with real situations of infidelity that mark the abandonment of crucial marriage vows. In either case, tensions within personal and family relationships can become unbearable. Margo Smith defined the ethical situation clearly in her song "Either You're Married Or You're Single" (1982). For some, temptation to cheat on a spouse can be faced and overcome. This is illustrated in "Almost Persuaded" (1966) and "Family Man" (1983); for others, however, there is strong verbal support from the mate that is designed to ensure fidelity to the marriage and to frighten away would-be sources of alienated affection. These recordings include "Leave My Kitten Alone" (1959), "You'll Lose A Good Thing" (1962), "Don't Mess With Bill" (1966), "Him Or Me—What's It Gonna Be?" (1967), "Foolish Fool" (1969), "Let's Stay Together" (1971), "He Don't Love You (Like I Love You)" (1975), "You Belong To Me" (1978), and "Stop In The Name Of Love" (1983).

Despite pleading from a loving spouse, opportunities for sexual indiscretion seem to be never ending. Waitresses, like the tart at "Smokey Joe's Cafe" (1955), urge men to "Come A Little Bit Closer" (1964). Women who don't mind "Steppin' Out" (1976) on their husbands advertise the fact by keeping their "Backfield In Motion" (1969). Dr Hook notes that domestic life can be particularly tense "When You're In Love With A Beautiful Woman" (1979). Of course, the suspicions spawned by jealousy over extreme physical attractiveness are not always well formed or deserved. Yet they exist. The disruptive power of jealousy is thoroughly articulated in songs such as "Hey! Jealous Lover" (1956), "Silhouettes" (1957), "Chip Chip" (1961), "Suspicion" (1964), "Don't Answer The Door" (1966), "The Chokin' Kind" (1969), "Suspicious Minds" (1969), and "How Long (Betcha' Got A Chick On The Side)" (1975).

Infidelity, the pursuit of forbidden fruit, the desire to have an "Outside Woman" (1974) or a "Back Door Man" (1969), is too strong, too exhilarating for many married people. Cheating occurs. These acts of betrayal are described in varying tones of guilt, pleasure, and suspicion about the behavior of the marriage partner in numerous recordings. Among the most popular illustrations are "Tonight You Belong To Me" (1956), "Lipstick On Your Collar" (1959), "I'm Gonna Move To The Outskirts Of Town" (1961), "I've Got News For You" (1961), "Smokey Places" (1961), "Walk On By" (1961), "Your Cheatin' Heart" (1962), "Frankie And Johnny" (1963), "Steal Away" (1964), "Walk On By" (1964), "The Cheater" (1966), "Somebody Has Been Sleeping In My Bed" (1967), "Woman, Woman," (1967), "Delilah" (1968), "I Heard It Through The Grapevine" (1968), "Midnight Confessions" (1968), "Who's Making Love" (1968), "Ruby, Don't Take Your Love To Town" (1969), "Your Husband—My Wife" (1969), "(If Loving You Is Wrong) I Don't Want To Be Right" (1972), "Me And Mrs. Jones" (1972), "Third Rate Romance" (1975), "Torn Between Two Lovers" (1976), "Lucille" (1977), "Smoke From A Distant Fire" (1977), "Trying To Love Two" (1977), "Man On Your Mind" (1982), "The Other Woman" (1982), "Holding Her And Loving You"

(1983), and "Midnight Fire" (1983). Popular songs even document the varying reactions of those involved in love triangles. Betrayed wives voice reactions in "To The Other Woman (I'm The Other Woman)" (1970) and "Angel In Your Arms" (1977); a betrayed husband reacts in "Take A Letter Maria" (1969); and the objects of extramarital affection even respond in "Clean Up Woman" (1971) and "She's Got The Papers (But I Got The Man)" (1981).

On many occasions, marriages are saved because jealousy subsides and is replaced by renewed trust. Similarly, sexual adventurism ceases to be enjoyable, thrilling, or rewarding and cheating finally stops. The difficulties of marital life remain, but the couple survives intact. But popular songs also address the reality of separation and divorce. Actually, singers and songwriters address two themes. First, they cover the facts of legal separation—"Alimony" (1959), "D-I-V-O-R-C-E" (1968), and "With Pen In Hand" (1968)—or the physical disappearance of a mate and parent—"Hit The Road Jack" (1961), "For Lovin' Me" (1965), "Go Now!" (1965), "By The Time I Get To Phoenix" (1967), "You Better Sit Down Kids" (1967), "Leaving On A Jet Plane" (1969), "Got To See If I Can't Get Mommy (To Come Back Home)" (1970), "Your Daddy Don't Live In Heaven (He's In Houston)" (1981). But more important, they depict the differing emotional reactions to the collapse of a supposed-to-be lifetime relationship. There are appeals for resolution of differences based upon the belief that life without the loved one would be meaningless. These include "Hey, Girl" (1963), "I've Been Loving You Too Long (To Stop Now)" (1965), "Let's Hang On!" (1965), "Ain't Too Proud To Beg" (1966), "I Can't Turn You Loose" (1968), "Breaking Up Is Hard To Do" (1975), and "Break It To Me Gently" (1982). But the die is usually cast by this time. The signs of "Love On The Rocks" (1980) are symbolized in dozens of behavioral and attitudinal shifts. Both members of a dissolving marriage articulate feelings such as those contained in "What's The Reason I'm Not Pleasing" (1957), "So Sad (To Watch Good Love Go Bad)" (1960), "Where Did Our Love Go" (1964), "You've Lost That Lovin' Feelin'"(1964), "You Keep Me Hangin' On" (1966), "Time Was" (1969), "(I Know) I'm Losing You" (1970), and "You Don't Bring Me Flowers" (1978).

Although the final separation might be summed up in objective terms like "We Just Disagree' (1977), deep emotional links sometimes echo "I Can't Stop Loving You" (1962). Attempts to renew contacts or reveries about the former relationship prompt images such as those expressed in "Since I Don't Have You" (1959), "All Alone Am I" (1962), "Memphis" (1964), "Crying Time" (1965), and "One Less Bell To Answer" (1970). However, some feel that enough is enough. Once a relationship has ended in emotional pain, it would be foolish to attempt to fan the flame again. Julie London states this position clearly in "Cry Me A River" (1955), as does Fats Domino in "I Hear You Knocking" (1961).

MARRIAGE, FAMILY LIFE, AND DIVORCE

Marriage

"All American Husband" (Decca 32698)
  by Peggy Sue (1970)

"Band Of Gold" (Columbia 40597)
  by Don Cherry (1955)

"Betty And Dupree" (Atlantic 1168)
  by Chuck Willis (1958)

"Big Bopper's Wedding" (Mercury 71375)
  by The Big Bopper (1958)

"Chapel Of Love" (Red Bird 001)
  by The Dixie Cups (1964)

"The Church Bells May Ring" (Mercury 70835)
  by The Diamonds (1956)

"Devoted To You" (Elektra 45506)
  by Carly Simon and James Taylor (1978)

"Different Drum" (Capitol 2004)
  by Linda Ronstadt and The Stone Poneys (1967)

"Do That To Me One More Time" (Casablanca 2215)
  by Captain and Tennille (1979)

"Down The Aisle" (Ace 583)
  by Ike Clanton (1960)

"Down The Aisle Of Love" (Hunt 321)
  by The Quin-Tones (1958)

"Down The Aisle (Wedding Bells)" (Newton 5777)
  by Patti LaBelle and The Blue Belles (1963)

"For Me And My Gal" (Swan 4083)
  by Freddy Cannon (1961)

"Fortuneteller" (Del-Fi 4177)
  by Bobby Curtola (1962)

"Friend, Lover, Woman, Wife" (Columbia 44859)
  by O. C. Smith (1969)

"From A Jack To A King" (Fabor 114)
  by Ned Miller (1962)

"Get Me To The Church On Time" (RCA 6567)
  by Julius LaRosa (1956)

"Go On With The Wedding" (Mercury 70766)
  by Patti Page (1956)

"Good Hearted Woman" (RCA 10529)
  by Waylon and Willie (1976)

"Hawaiian Wedding Song" (Cadence 1358)
by Andy Williams (1959)

"Hey Paula" (Philips 40084)
by Paul and Paula (1962)

"A House, A Car, And A Wedding Ring" (Checker 906)
by Dale Hawkins (1958)

"(I Cried At) Laura's Wedding" (Jamie 1260)
by Barbara Lynn (1963)

"If I Were A Carpenter" (Atlantic 2350)
by Bobby Darin (1966)

"If You Wanna Be Happy" (S.P.Q.R. 3305)
by Jimmy Soul (1963)

"(I'm Always Hearing) Wedding Bells" (RCA 6015)
by Eddie Fisher (1955)

"I'm Gonna Get Married" (ABC-Paramount 10032)
by Lloyd Price (1959)

"I'm Henry VIII, I Am" (MGM 13367)
by Herman's Hermits (1965)

"It's Gonna Work Out Fine" (Sue 749)
by Ike and Tina Turner (1961)

"Just Married" (Columbia 41143)
by Marty Robbins (1958)

"Kisses Sweeter Than Wine" (Roulette 4031)
by Jimmie Rodgers (1957)

"The Lady Came From Baltimore" (Atlantic 2395)
by Bobby Darin (1967)

"Let's Get Married" (Hi 2262)
by Al Green (1974)

"Let's Pretend We're Married" (Warner Brothers 29548)
by Prince (1983)

"Little Egypt (Ying Yang)" (Atco 6192)
by The Coasters (1961)

"Little Green Apples" (Columbia 44616)
by O. C. Smith (1968)

"Love And Marriage" (RCA 6266)
by Dinah Shore (1955)

"Love And Marriage" (Capitol 3260)
by Frank Sinatra (1955)

"Most People Get Married" (Mercury 71950)
by Patti Page (1962)

"My Woman, My Woman, My Wife" (Columbia 45091)
  by Marty Robbins (1970)

"One Mint Julep" (Atlantic 963)
  by The Clovers (1952)

"Our Anniversary" (Hull 748)
  by Shep and The Limelites (1962)

"Put A Ring On My Finger" (Columbia 41222)
  by Les Paul and Mary Ford (1958)

"The Right Thing To Do" (Elektra 45843)
  by Carly Simon (1973)

"Rock And Roll Wedding" (RCA 6479)
  by Sunny Gale (1956)

"Ruby Ann" (Columbia 42614)
  by Marty Robbins (1962)

"The Second Time Around" (Reprise 20001)
  by Frank Sinatra (1961)

"Shop Around" (Tamla 54034)
  by The Miracles (1960)

"Someone Saved My Life Tonight" (MCA 40421)
  by Elton John (1975)

"Take Time To Know Her" (Atlantic 2490)
  by Percy Sledge (1968)

"That's The Way I've Always Heard It Should Be" (Elektra 45724)
  by Carly Simon (1971)

"Third Finger–Left Hand" (Columbia 40956)
  by Eileen Rodgers (1957)

"To The Aisle" (Ember 1019)
  by The Five Satins (1956)

"(Today I Met) The Boy I'm Gonna Marry" (Philles 111)
  by Darlene Love (1963)

"We Told You Not To Marry" (Glover 201)
  by Titus Turner (1959)

"We've Only Just Begun" (A & M 1217)
  by The Carpenters (1970)

"The Wedding" (Cadence 1273)
  by The Chordettes (1956)

"The Wedding" (Mercury 72332)
  by Julie Rogers (1965)

"Wedding Bell Blues" (Soul City 779)
  by The Fifth Dimension (1969)

"Wedding Bells" (Moonshine 3019)
  by Margo Smith (1983)

"Wedding Bells (Are Breaking Up That Old Gang Of Mine)" (Decca 29123)
by The Four Aces (1954)

"Wedding Boogie" (Savoy 764)
by Johnny Otis (1950)

"Wedding Cake" (MGM 14034)
by Connie Francis (1969)

"The Wedding Song (There Is Love)" (Warner Brothers 7511)
by Paul Stookey (1971)

"Wedlock Is A Padlock" (Hot Wax 7007)
by Laura Lee (1971)

"When We Get Married" (Heritage 102)
by The Dreamlovers (1961)

"Where Were You (On Our Wedding Day)" (ABC-Paramount 9997)
by Lloyd Price (1959)

"White On White" (United Artists 685)
by Danny Williams (1964)

"White Wedding (Part 1)" (Chrysalis 42697)
by Billy Idol (1983)

"Worst That Could Happen" (Buddah 75)
by The Brooklyn Bridge (1968)

"You Never Can Tell" (Chess 1906)
by Chuck Berry (1964)

Family Life

"Broomstick Cowboy" (United Artists 952)
by Bobby Goldsboro (1965)

"Color Him Father" (Metromedia 117)
by The Winstons (1969)

"Daddy Could Swear, I Declare" (Soul 35105)
by Gladys Knight and The Pips (1973)

"Daddy Don't You Walk So Fast" (Chelsea 0100)
by Wayne Newton (1972)

"Daddy Sang Bass" (Columbia 44689)
by Johnny Cash (1968)

"Daddy What If" (RCA 0197)
by Bobby Bare (1974)

"Daddy's Little Girl" (Capitol 5825)
by Al Martino (1967)

"Daddy's Little Man" (Columbia 44948)
by O. C. Smith (1969)

"Dear Dad" (Chess 1926)
by Chuck Berry (1965)

"Don't Cry Daddy" (RCA 47-9768)
  by Elvis Presley (1969)

"Dreams Of The Everyday Housewife" (Capitol 2224)
  by Glen Campbell (1968)

"Dust Got In Daddy's Eyes" (Duke 390)
  by Bobby Bland (1965)

"Family Affair" (Epic 10805)
  by Sly and The Family Stone (1971)

"Father Come On Home" (Columbia 45221)
  by Pacific Gas and Electric (1970)

"Father Knows Best" (Chess 1832)
  by The Radiants (1962)

"Father Of Girls" (RCA 9448)
  by Perry Como (1968)

"For Mama" (MGM 13325)
  by Connie Francis (1965)

"1432 Franklin Pike Circle Hero" (Elf 90020)
  by Bobby Russell (1968)

"The Free Electric Band" (Mums 6018)
  by Albert Hammond (1973)

"Get a Job" (Ember 1029)
  by The Silhouettes (1958)

"Harper Valley P.T.A." (Plantation 3)
  by Jeannie C. Riley (1968)

"Have You Seen Your Mother, Baby, Standing In The Shadow?" (London 903)
  by The Rolling Stones (1966)

"Honey" (United Artists 50283)
  by Bobby Goldsboro (1968)

"Husbands And Wives" (Smash 2024)
  by Roger Miller (1966)

"I Found My Dad" (Spring 130)
  by Joe Simon (1972)

"I Saw A Man And He Danced With His Wife" (MCA 40273)
  by Cher (1974)

"I'll Always Love My Mama (Part 1)" (Gamble 2506)
  by The Intruders (1973)

"(I'm The Girl On) Wolverton Mountain" (Cameo 223)
  by Jo Ann Campbell (1962)

"In The Ghetto" (RCA 47-9741)
  by Elvis Presley (1969)

"Lady Madonna" (Capitol 2138)
  by The Beatles (1968)

"Leader Of The Band" (Full Moon 02647)
by Dan Fogelberg (1981)

"Let Me Be The Man My Daddy Was" (Brunswick 55414)
by The Chi-Lites (1969)

"Little Children" (Imperial 66027)
by Billy J. Kramer and The Dakotas (1964)

"Loves Me Like A Rock" (Columbia 45907)
by Paul Simon (1973)

"Mama" (MGM 12878)
by Connie Francis (1960)

"Mama" (Scepter 12139)
by B. J. Thomas (1966)

"A Mama And A Papa" (Barnaby 2029)
by Ray Stevens (1971)

"Mama Didn't Lie" (Chess 1845)
by Jan Bradley (1963)

"Mama Don't Allow" (Vanguard 35020)
by The Rooftop Singers (1963)

"Mama (He Treats Your Daughter Mean)" (Philips 40056)
by Ruth Brown (1962)

"Mama Liked The Roses" (RCA 47-9835)
by Elvis Presley (1970)

"Mama Said" (Scepter 1217)
by The Shirelles (1961)

"Mama Told Me (Not To Come)" (Dunhill 4239)
by Three Dog Night (1970)

"Mama's Pearl" (Motown 1177)
by The Jackson Five (1971)

"The Man That Turned My Mama On" (Columbia 46047)
by Tanya Tucker (1974)

"Mom And Dad's Waltz" (Mercury 71823)
by Patti Page (1961)

"Moments To Remember" (Columbia 40539)
by The Four Lads (1955)

"Mother" (Apple 1827)
by John Lennon (1971)

"Mother And Child Reunion" (Columbia 45547)
by Paul Simon (1972)

"Mother At Your Feet Is Kneeling" (London 968)
by Bobby Wayne (1951)

"A Mother For My Children" (Janus 231)
by The Whispers (1974)

"Mother, Please!" (Cameo 249)
  by Jo Ann Campbell (1963)
"Mother-In-Law" (Minit 623)
  by Ernie K-Doe (1961)
"Mrs. Brown You've Got A Lovely Daughter" (MGM 13341)
  by Herman's Hermits (1965)
"My Dad" (Colpix 663)
  by Paul Petersen (1962)
"My Daddy Knows Best" (Tamla 54082)
  by The Marvelettes (1963)
"Nag" (7 Arts 709)
  by The Halos (1961)
"Oh! My Pa-Pa" (RCA Victor 5552)
  by Eddie Fisher (1953)
"Our House" (Geffen 29668)
  by Madness (1983)
"Papa Was A Rollin' Stone" (Gordy 7121)
  by The Temptations (1972)
"Papa Was Too" (Dial 4051)
  by Joe Tex (1966)
"Patches" (Atlantic 2748)
  by Clarence Carter (1970)
"Peek-A-Boo" (Josie 846)
  by The Cadillacs (1958)
"Play Me Or Trade Me" (Elektra 47247)
  by Mel Tillis and Nancy Sinatra (1981)
"Please, Daddy" (RCA 0182)
  by John Denver (1973)
"Poor Man's Son" (Golden World 20)
  by The Reflections (1965)
"Rag Doll" (Phillips 40211)
  by The Four Seasons (1964)
"Rhythm 'N' Blues (Mama's Got The Rhythm—Papa's Got the Blues)"
  (Coral 61423)
  by The McGuire Sisters (1955)
"Saturday Morning Confusion" (United Artists 50788)
  by Bobby Russell (1971)
"Skip A Rope" (Monument 1041)
  by Henson Cargill (1967)
"Son-In-Law" (Witch 101)
  by Louise Brown (1961)
"The Son Of Hickory Holler's Tramp" (Columbia 44425)
  by O. C. Smith (1968)

"Son Of My Father" (Epic 10837)
  by Chicory (1972)

"Summertime Blues" (Liberty 55144)
  by Eddie Cochran (1958)

"Sylvia's Mother" (Columbia 45562)
  by Dr. Hook (1972)

"Teenager's Mother (Are You Right?)" (Decca 30028)
  by Bill Haley and His Comets (1956)

"Thank God For Kids" (MCA 52145)
  by The Oak Ridge Boys (1982)

"That's The Way I've Always Heard It Should Be" (Elektra 45724)
  by Carly Simon (1971)

"Wake Up Little Susie" (Warner Brothers 50053)
  by Simon and Garfunkel (1982)

"Watching Scotty Grow" (United Artists 50727)
  by Bobby Goldsboro (1970)

"What Did Daddy Do" (Hull 751)
  by Shep and The Limelites (1962)

"Willie And The Hand Jive" (Capitol 3966)
  by Johnny Otis (1958)

"Wives And Lovers" (Kapp 551)
  by Jack Jones (1963)

"Wolverton Mountain" (Columbia 42352)
  by Claude King (1962)

"Yakety Yak" (Atco 6116)
  by The Coasters (1958)

"Your Daddy Don't Know" (Network 69986)
  by Toronto (1982)

"Your Mama Don't Dance" (Columbia 45719)
  by Loggins and Messina (1972)

Jealousy and Infidelity

"Almost Persuaded" (Epic 10025)
  by David Houston (1966)

"Angel In Your Arms" (Big Tree 16085)
  by Hot (1977)

"Back Door Man" (Bang 566)
  by Derek (1969)

"Backfield In Motion" (Bamboo 107)
  by Mel and Tim (1969)

"The Cheater" (Musicland 20001)
  by Bob Kuban and The In-Men (1966)

"Chip Chip" (Liberty 55405)
by Gene McDaniels (1961)

"The Chokin' Kind" (Sound Stage 2628)
by Joe Simon (1969)

"Cinderella" (Handshake 02442)
by Betty Wright (1971)

"Clean Up Woman" (Alston 4601)
by Betty Wright (1971)

"Come A Little Bit Closer" (United Artists 759)
by Jay and The Americans (1964)

"Delilah" (Parrot 40025)
by Tom Jones (1968)

"Don't Answer The Door" (ABC 10856)
by B. B. King (1966)

"Don't Mess With Bill" (Tamla 54126)
by The Marvelettes (1966)

"Drowning In The Sea Of Love" (Spring 120)
by Joe Simon (1971)

"Either You're Married Or You're Single" (AMI 1304)
by Margo Smith (1982)

"Family Man" (RCA 13507)
by Daryl Hall and John Oates (1983)

"Foolish Fool" (Mercury 72880)
by Dee Dee Warwick (1969)

"Frankie and Johnny" (RCA 8215)
by Sam Cooke (1963)

"He Don't Love You (Like I Love You)" (Elektra 45240)
by Tony Orlando and Dawn (1975)

"He Will Break Your Heart" (Vee-Jay 354)
by Jerry Butler (1960)

"Hey! Jealous Lover" (Capitol 3552)
by Frank Sinatra (1956)

"Him Or Me—What's It Gonna Be?" (Columbia 44094)
by Paul Revere and The Raiders (1967)

"Holding Her And Loving You" (RCA 13596)
by Earl Thomas Conley (1983)

"How Long" (Warner Brothers 50051)
by Rod Stewart (1982)

"How Long (Betcha' Got A Chick On The Side)" (Blue Thumb 265)
by The Pointer Sisters (1975)

"I Heard It Through The Grapevine" (Tamla 54176)
by Marvin Gaye (1968)

"If A Man Answers" (Capitol 4837)
by Bobby Darin (1962)

"If A Woman Answers (Hang Up The Phone)" (Mercury 71926)
by LeRoy Van Dyke (1962)

"(If Loving You Is Wrong) I Don't Want To Be Right" (Koko 2111)
by Luther Ingram (1972)

"If You Talk In Your Sleep" (RCA APBO-0280)
by Elvis Presley (1974)

"I'm Gonna Move To The Outskirts Of Town" (Impulse 202)
by Ray Charles (1961)

"I've Got News For You" (Impulse 202)
by Ray Charles (1961)

"Jealous Heart" (London 500)
by Al Morgan (1949)

"Jealousy" (Columbia 39585)
by Frankie Laine (1951)

"Kiss The Bride" (Geffen 29568)
by Elton John (1983)

"Leave My Kitten Alone" (King 5219)
by Little Willie John (1959)

"Let's Stay Together" (Hi 2202)
by Al Green (1971)

"Lipstick On Your Collar" (MGM 12793)
by Connie Francis (1959)

"Lucille" (United Artists 929)
by Kenny Rogers (1977)

"Lyin' Eyes" (Asylum 45279)
by The Eagles (1975)

"Man On Your Mind" (Capitol 5061)
by The Little River Band (1982)

"Mary Lou" (Roulette 4177)
by Ronnie Hawkins and The Hawks (1959)

"Maybellene" (Chess 1604)
by Chuck Berry (1955)

"Me And Mrs. Jones" (Philadelphia International 3521)
by Billy Paul (1972)

"Midnight Confessions" (Dunhill 4144)
by The Grass Roots (1968)

"Midnight Fire" (RCA 13588)
by Steve Waringer (1983)

"Nadine (Is It You?)" (Chess 1883)
by Chuck Berry (1964)

"The Name Of The Game Is Cheatin' " (Town House 1063)
by Charlie Ross (1983)

"The Night Has A Thousand Eyes" (Liberty 55521)
  by Bobby Vee (1962)

"Now I Lay Me Down To Cheat" (Columbia 02678)
  by David Allan Coe (1982)

"One-Night Fever" (Elektra 47179)
  by Mel Tillis (1981)

"The Other Woman" (Arista 0669)
  by Ray Parker, Jr. (1982)

"Outside Woman" (London 1052)
  by Bloodstone (1974)

"Ruby, Don't Take Your Love To Town" (Reprise 0829)
  by Kenny Rogers (1969)

"Separate Ways (Worlds Apart)" (Columbia 03513)
  by Journey (1983)

"She's Got The Papers (But I Got The Man)" (WMOT 02506)
  by Barbara Mason (1981)

"She's Not Really Cheatin' (She's Just Gettin' Even)" (Columbia 02966)
  by Moe Bandy (1982)

"She's Steppin' Out" (Warner Brothers 49800)
  by Con Hunley (1981)

"Silhouettes" (Cameo 117)
  by The Rays (1957)

"Smoke From A Distant Fire" (Warner Brothers 8370)
  by The Sanford/Townsend Band (1977)

"Smokey Joe's Cafe" (Atco 6059)
  by The Robins (1955)

"Smoky Places" (Tuff 1808)
  by The Corsairs (1961)

"Somebody Had Been Sleeping In My Bed" (Stax 235)
  by Johnnie Taylor (1967)

"Steal Away" (Fame 6401)
  by Jimmy Hughes (1964)

"Step Back" (Epic 03203)
  by Ronnie McDowell (1982)

"Steppin' Out" (Rocket 40582)
  by Neil Sedaka (1976)

"Still Doin' Time" (Epic 02526)
  by George Jones (1981)

"Stop In The Name Of Love" (Atlantic 89819)
  by The Hollies (1983)

"Stranger In My House" (RCA 13470)
  by Ronnie Milsap (1983)

"Suspicion" (Crusader 101)
  by Terry Stafford (1964)

"Suspicious Minds" (RCA 47-9764)
  by Elvis Presley (1969)

"Take A Letter Maria" (Atco 6714)
  by R. B. Greaves (1969)

"Temptation Eyes" (Dunhill 4263)
  by The Grass Roots (1970)

"There's Something On Your Mind" (Fire 1022)
  by Bobby Marchan (1960)

"Third Rate Romance" (ABC 12078)
  by The Amazing Rhythm Aces (1975)

"To The Other Woman (I'm The Other Woman)" (Canyon 28)
  by Doris Duke (1970)

"Tonight You Belong To Me" (Liberty 55022)
  by Patience and Prudence (1956)

"Torn Between Two Lovers" (Ariola America 7638)
  by Mary MacGregor (1976)

"Train Of Thought" (MCA 40245)
  by Cher (1974)

"Trying To Love Two" (Mercury 73839)
  by William Bell (1977)

"Turn The Pencil Over" (Viva 29875)
  by Porter Wagoner (1982)

"Walk On By" (Mercury 71834)
  by Leroy Van Dyke (1961)

"Walk On By" (Scepter 1274)
  by Dionne Warwick (1964)

"When You're In Love With A Beautiful Woman" (Capitol 4705)
  by Dr. Hook (1979)

"Who's Making Love" (Stax 0009)
  by Johnnie Taylor (1968)

"Woman, Woman" (Columbia 44297)
  by Gary Puckett and The Union Gap (1967)

"You Belong To Me" (Elektra 45477)
  by Carly Simon (1978)

"You'll Lose A Good Thing" (Jamie 1220)
  by Barbara Lynn (1962)

"Your Body's Here With Me (But Your Mind's On The Other Side Of Town)"
  (Philadelphia International 03009)
  - by The O'Jays (1982)

"Your Cheatin' Heart" (ABC-Paramount 10375)
  by Ray Charles (1962)

"Your Husband—My Wife" (Buddah 126)
by The Brooklyn Bridge (1969)

Separation and Divorce

"Ain't Too Proud To Beg" (Gordy 7054)
by The Temptations (1966)

"Alimony" (Ace 566)
by Frankie Ford (1959)

"All Alone Am I" (Decca 31424)
by Brenda Lee (1962)

"Break It To Me Gently" (Capitol 5148)
by Juice Newton (1982)

"Breaking Up Is Hard to Do" (Rocket 40500)
by Neil Sedaka (1975)

"By The Time I Get To Phoenix" (Capitol 2015)
by Glen Campbell (1967)

"Cry Me A River" (Liberty 55006)
by Julie London (1955)

"Crying Time" (ABC-Paramount 10739)
by Ray Charles (1965)

"D-I-V-O-R-C-E" (Epic 10315)
by Tammy Wynette (1968)

"Don't Leave Me This Way" (Tamla 54278)
by Thelma Houston (1976)

"Either You're Married Or You're Single" (AMI 1304)
by Margo Smith (1982)

"For Lovin' Me" (Warner Brothers 5496)
by Peter, Paul, and Mary (1965)

"Go Now!" (London 9726)
by The Moody Blues (1965)

"Got To See If I Can't Get Mommy (To Come Back Home)" (Mercury 73015)
by Jerry Butler (1970)

"Hey, Girl" (Colpix 692)
by Freddie Scott (1963)

"Hit The Road Jack" (ABC-Paramount 10244)
by Ray Charles (1961)

"I Can't Stop Loving You" (ABC-Paramount 10330)
by Ray Charles (1962)

"I Can't Turn You Loose" (Columbia 44679)
by The Chambers Brothers (1968)

"I Hear You Knocking" (Imperial 5796)
by Fats Domino (1961)

"(I Know) I'm Losing You" (Rare Earth 5017)
  by Rare Earth (1970)

"I'm Sorry" (Decca 31093)
  by Brenda Lee (1960)

"I've Been Loving You Too Long (To Stop Now)" (Volt 126)
  by Otis Redding (1965)

"Leaving On A Jet Plane" (Warner Brothers 7340)
  by Peter, Paul, and Mary (1969)

"Let's Hang On!" (Philips 40317)
  by The Four Seasons (1965)

"Love On The Rocks" (Capitol 4939)
  by Neil Diamond (1980)

"Memphis" (Imperial 66032)
  by Johnny Rivers (1964)

"One Less Bell To Answer" (Bell 940)
  by The Fifth Dimension (1970)

"Operator (That's Not The Way It Feels)" (ABC 11335)
  by Jim Croce (1972)

"Since I Don't Have You" (Calico 103)
  by The Skyliners (1959)

"So Sad (To Watch Good Love Go Bad)" (Warner Brothers 5163)
  by The Everly Brothers (1960)

"(Sweet Sweet Baby) Since You've Been Gone" (Atlantic 2486)
  by Aretha Franklin (1968)

"Time Was" (Liberty 56097)
  by Canned Heat (1969)

"Unchain My Heart" (ABC-Paramount 10266)
  by Ray Charles (1961)

"Walk Right Back" (Warner Brothers 5199)
  by The Everly Brothers (1961)

"We Just Disagree" (Columbia 10575)
  by Dave Mason (1977)

"What's The Reason I'm Not Pleasing" (Imperial 5417)
  by Fats Domino (1957)

"Where Did Our Love Go" (Motown 1060)
  by The Supremes (1964)

"With Pen In Hand" (Atlantic 2526)
  by Billy Vera (1968)

"You Better Sit Down Kids" (Imperial 66261)
  by Cher (1967)

"You Don't Bring Me Flowers" (Columbia 10840)
  by Barbra Streisand and Neil Diamond (1978)

"You Keep Me Hangin' On" (Motown 1101)
   by The Supremes (1966)

"Your Daddy Don't Live In Heaven (He's In Houston)" (Liberty 1437)
   by Michael Ballew (1981)

"Your Good Thing (Is About To End)" (Capitol 2550)
   by Lou Rawls (1969)

"Your Used To Be" (Decca 31454)
   by Brenda Lee (1963)

"You've Lost That Lovin' Feelin' " (Philles 124)
   by The Righteous Brothers (1964)

6

Military Conflicts

The appearance of American popular songs addressing issues related to military conflicts is not a new phenomenon. World War I featured tunes such as "Keep The Home Fires Burning," "My Sweetheart Is Somewhere In France," "It's Time For Every Boy To Be A Soldier," "Goodbye Broadway, Hello France," "Over There," "Oh, How I Hate To Get Up In The Morning," and "Just Like Washington Crossed The Delaware, General Pershing Will Cross The Rhine." The same tradition of lyrical support continued for America's military efforts against Germany and Japan between 1941 and 1945 through songs such as "'Til Reveille," "Remember Pearl Harbor," "Johnny Doughboy Found A Rose In Ireland," "He Wears A Pair Of Silver Wings," "Praise The Lord And Pass the Ammunition," "Comin' In On A Wing And A Prayer," "G. I. Jive," and "White Cliffs Of Dover." The dominate themes in these popular tunes were patriotism, human sacrifices for national honor, and the mutual longing by separated loved ones (mother/son, girlfriend/boyfriend, wife/husband) to be reunited in victory and peace.

The simplicity of popular music perspectives on military conflict ended abruptly during the 1960s. Politely pacificistic folk tunes gave way to openly defiant protest songs as warfare in Vietnam escalated after 1965. It would be inaccurate, though, to imply that patriotic hymns disappeared altogether. What actually happened was that the pluralism of American opinion about war in general and the Southeast Asia conflict in particular prompted a multitude of vinyl spokesmen to profess deep, diverse feelings.

Patriotism was fostered during the 1950s and early 1960s via appeals to American military tradition in Vaughn Monroe's "Sound Off" (1951), Russ Morgan's "Dogface Soldier" (1955), and Johnny Horton's "The Battle Of

New Orleans" (1959) and "Sink The Bismark" (1960). These tunes were supplemented during the Vietnam War period by more direct responses to anti-war attitudes. These post-1965 songs included SSgt. Barry Sadler's "The Ballad Of The Green Berets" (1966) and "The 'A' Team" (1966), Nancy Ames' "He Wore A Green Beret" (1966), Senator Everett McKinley Dirksen's "Gallant Men" (1966), Barbra Streisand's "Stout-Hearted Men" (1967), Bette Midler's "Boogie Woogie Bugle Boy" (1973), and three versions of "Americans" (1974) recorded by Byron MacGregor, Gordon Sinclair, and Tex Ritter. The ultimate flag-wrapped apology tune in this category was C Company's (featuring Terry Nelson) lyrical defense of a soldier's participation in a civilian massacre titled "The Battle Hymn Of Lt. Calley" (1971). One of the most recent rally-'round-the-flag-boys pop single is The Charlie Daniels Band's "In America" (1980).

Anti-military songs stem from a variety of sources. Intellectual pacifism seemed to motivate Donovan's "Universal Soldier" (1965), Coven's "One Tin Soldier" (1971), and John Lennon's "Give Peace A Chance" (1969). Fear of death is the theme in Bo Donaldson and The Heywoods' "Billy Don't Be A Hero" (1974), Creedence Clearwater Revival's "Fortunate Son" (1969), and Phil Ochs' "The Draft Dodger Rag" (n.d.). But beyond philosophy and mortality there are strong elements of cynicism, anger, fear, and mistrust concerning governmental war-making machinations. For example, Edwin Starr defines "War" (1970) as being good for absolutely nothing. He blames military conflicts for the destruction of innocent lives and for robbing mothers of their sons; he decries war for shattering many young men's dreams by leaving them disabled, bitter, and mean. Starr's conclusion is that war is a heartbreaker, with the undertaker as its only benefactor. John Fogerty denounces patriots with star-spangled eyes who gleefully send young men off to war. Bob Seger, in "2 + 2 = ?" (n.d.), is highly reflective in trying to assess the meaning of a friend's death in Vietnam and his own attitude toward military involvement. His conclusion is that the government's rules, not the opposition's soldiers, are his real enemy.

Several songs by Bob Dylan—particularly "Masters Of War" (n.d.) and "With God On Our Side" (n.d.)—emphasize the negative roles of leaders of the military-industrial complex in profiteering from international conflicts and the senselessness of assuming that America is pursuing a divine mission in each military battle it undertakes. Dylan's fear of ultimate nuclear holocaust is contained in "A Hard Rain Is Gonna Fall" (n.d.).

Criticism of military conflict isn't always pronounced in deadly serious tunes, though. There is direct humor in John Fogerty's analysis that some patriotic citizens are born to wave the flag. They're literally red, white, and blue. Though not outwardly funny, Buffy Sainte-Marie's multinational depiction of the "Universal Soldier" (1965) is marvelously effective black humor. The most effective comic, anti-military songs belong to Joe McDonald and Phil Ochs. For Country Joe and The Fish, "The I Feel-Like-

I'm-Fixin'-To-Die Rag" (n.d.) represents the ultimate generation gap put-down to draft-based military combat. McDonald urges both mothers and fathers to send their sons off to war before it's too late so that they can be the first ones on their block to have their boy come home in a box. Phil Ochs' "The Draft Dodger Rag" (n.d.) concludes with a delicious dual comment. First, he wishes the recruiting officer success. Then he adds the restrictive clause concerning his own personal military involvement: if there is ever a war without blood and gore, he'll be the first to go. Ochs also performs a tune titled "I Ain't Marching Anymore" (n.d.). From the view-point of historic American military ventures—the Battle of New Orleans, Little Big Horn, the Mexican War, the Civil War, and two World Wars—he notes how little has been won with a sabre and a gun and asks if it was worth it all. At the end of this tune Ochs responds to his own question by repeating the song's title.

MILITARY CONFLICTS

War

"The Cruel War" (Warner Brothers 5809)
   by Peter, Paul, and Mary (1966)
"War" (Gordy 7101)
   by Edwin Starr (1970)
"The War Song" (Virgin 04638)
   by Culture Club (1984)
"War Song" (Reprise 1099)
   by Neil Young and Graham Nash (1972)

Patriotism and National Honor

"America, Communicate With Me" (Barnaby 2016)
   by Ray Stevens (1970)
"Americans" (Westbound 222)
   by Byron MacGregor (1974)
"Americans (A Canadian's Opinion)" (Capitol 3814)
   by Tex Ritter (1974)
"Americans (A Canadian's Opinion)" (Avco 4628)
   by Gordon Sinclair (1974)
"Ballad Of The Alamo" (Columbia 41809)
   by Marty Robbins (1960)
"The Ballad Of The Green Berets" (RCA 8739)
   by SSgt. Barry Sadler (1966)
"Battle Hymn Of The Republic" (Columbia 41459)
   by The Mormon Tabernacle Choir (1959)

"Battle Hymn Of The Republic" (Columbia 44650)
by Andy Williams (1968)

"Battle Of New Orleans" (Warner Brothers 7223)
by Harpers Bizarre (1968)

"The Battle Of New Orleans" (Columbia 41339)
by Johnny Horton (1959)

"Battle Of New Orleans" (United Artists 544)
by The Nitty Gritty Dirt Band (1974)

"Dawn Of Correction" (Decca 31844)
by The Spokesmen (1965)

"The Declaration" (Bell 860)
by The Fifth Dimension (1970)

"The Fightin' Side Of Me" (Capitol 2719)
by Merle Haggard (1970)

"Gallant Men" (Capitol 5805)
by Senator Everett McKinley Dirksen (1966)

"God Bless America" (MGM 12841)
by Connie Francis (1959)

"God, Country, And My Baby" (Liberty 55379)
by Johnny Burnette (1961)

"He Wore A Green Beret" (Epic 10003)
by Nancy Ames (1966)

"In America" (Epic 50888)
by The Charlie Daniels Band (1980)

"Johnny Freedom" (Columbia 41685)
by Johnny Horton (1960)

"Okie From Muskogee" (Capitol 2626)
by Merle Haggard (1969)

"Pledge Of Allegiance" (Columbia 44798)
by Red Skelton (1969)

"P.T. 109" (Columbia 42338)
by Jimmy Dean (1962)

"Singing In Vietnam Talking Blues" (Columbia 45393)
by Johnny Cash (1971)

"Sink The Bismarck" (Columbia 41568)
by Johnny Horton (1960)

"Sound Off" (RCA Victor 4113)
by Vaughn Monroe (1951)

"The Star-Spangled Banner" (RCA 9665)
by Jose Feliciano (1968)

"Stars And Stripes Forever" (Mercury 5421)
by Frankie Laine (1950)

"Still In Saigon" (Epic 02828)
by The Charlie Daniels Band (1982)

"Stout-Hearted Men" (Columbia 44225)
by Barbra Streisand (1967)

"There's A Star Spangled Banner Waving #2 (The Ballad Of Francis Powers)"
(Savoy 3020)
by Red River Dave (1960)

"This Is My Country" (Curtom 1934)
by The Impressions (1968)

"This Land Is Your Land" (Columbia 42592)
by The New Christy Minstrels (1962)

"Voice Of Freedom" (Capitol 4834)
by Jim Kirk and The TM Singers (1980)

"West Of The Wall" (Big Top 3097)
by Miss Toni Fisher (1962)

Soldiers and the Draft

"The 'A' Team" (RCA 8804)
by SSgt. Barry Sadler (1966)

"Battle Hymn Of Lt. Calley" (Plantation 73)
by Terry Nelson and C Company (1971)

"Billy, Don't Be A Hero" (ABC 11435)
by Bo Donaldson and The Heywoods (1974)

"Boogie Woogie Bugle Boy" (Atlantic 2964)
by Bette Midler (1973)

"Born In The U.S.A." (Columbia 04680)
by Bruce Springsteen (1984)

"Bring The Boys Home" (Invictus 9092)
by Freda Payne (1971)

"Coming Home Soldier" (Epic 10090)
by Bobby Vinton (1967)

"Dogface Soldier" (Decca 29703)
by Russ Morgan (1955)

"Greetings (This Is Uncle Sam)" (V.I.P. 25032)
by The Monitors (1966)

"Greetings (This Is Uncle Sam)" (Miracle 6)
by The Valadiers (1961)

"He Wore A Green Beret" (Epic 10003)
by Nancy Ames (1966)

"In The Navy" (Casablanca 973)
by The Village People (1979)

"Kiss Me Sailor" (20th Century 477)
  by Diane Renay (1964)

"Lonely Soldier" (Atlantic 2339)
  by Mike Williams (1966)

"My Little Marine" (Joy 234)
  by Jamie Horton (1960)

"Navy Blue" (20th Century 456)
  by Diane Renay (1964)

"Old Soldiers Never Die" (RCA Victor 4146)
  by Vaughn Monroe (1951)

"One Tin Soldier" (Warner Brothers 7509)
  by Coven (1971)

"Sailor Boy" (Laurie 3262)
  by The Chiffons (1964)

"Sailor (Your Home Is The Sea)" (Kapp 349)
  by Lolita (1960)

"Soldier Boy" (Scepter 1228)
  by The Shirelles (1962)

"Soldier's Joy" (Columbia 41419)
  by Hawkshaw Hawkins (1959)

"Soldier's Last Letter" (Capitol 3024)
  by Merle Haggard (1971)

"Tin Soldier" (Immediate 5003)
  by Small Faces (1968)

"To A Soldier Boy" (Madison 117)
  by The Tassels (1959)

"To Susan On The West Coast Waiting" (Epic 10434)
  by Donovan (1969)

"Toy Soldier" (Philips 40278)
  by The Four Seasons (1965)

"Universal Soldier" (Hickory 1338)
  by Donovan (1965)

"Universal Soldier" (Vanguard album)
  by Buffy Sainte-Marie (1965)

"The Unknown Soldier" (Elektra 45628)
  by The Doors (1968)

Pacificism

"Friendship Train" (Soul 35068)
  by Gladys Knight and The Pips (1969)

"Give Peace A Chance" (Apple 1809)
  by John Lennon (1969)

"Imagine" (Apple 1840)
  by John Lennon (1971)

"La La Peace Song" (Rocky Road 30200)
  by Al Wilson (1974)

"Lay Down (Candles In The Rain)" (Buddah 167)
  by Melanie (1970)

"Love Train" (Philadelphia International 3524)
  by The O'Jays (1973)

"Peace Brother Peace" (MGM 14000)
  by Bill Medley (1968)

"Peace Train" (A&M 1291)
  by Cat Stevens (1971)

"Peace Will Come (According To Plan)" (Buddah 186)
  by Melanie (1970)

"The Peacemaker" (Mums 6021)
  by Albert Hammond (1973)

"There Will Never Be Peace (Until God Is Seated At The Conference Table)"
  (Brunswick 55512)
  by The Chi-Lites (1974)

Anti-Military Protest, Fear, and Anger

"Are You Ready?" (Columbia 45158)
  by Pacific Gas and Electric (1970)

"Blowin' In The Wind" (Warner Brothers 5368)
  by Peter, Paul, and Mary (1963)

"Draft Dodger Rag" (A & M album)
  by Phil Ochs (n.d.)

"Eve Of Destruction" (Dunhill 4009)
  by Barry McGuire (1965)

"Fortunate Son" (Fantasy 634)
  by Creedence Clearwater Revival (1969)

"Games Without Frontiers" (Mercury 76063)
  by Peter Gabriel (1980)

"Goodnight Saigon" (Columbia 03780)
  by Billy Joel (1983)

"A Hard Rain Is Gonna Fall" (Columbia album)
  by Bob Dylan (n.d.)

"I Ain't Marching Anymore" (A & M album)
  by Phil Ochs (n.d.)

"The I-Feel-Like-I'm-Fixin'-To-Die Rag" (Vanguard album)
  by Country Joe and The Fish (n.d.)

"It's A Mistake" (Columbia 03959)
  by Men at Work (1983)

"Masters Of War" (Columbia Album)
  by Bob Dylan (n.d.)

"Military Madness" (Atlantic 2827)
  by Graham Nash (1971)

"1999" (Warner Brothers 29896)
  by Prince (1982)

"Save The Country" (Bell 895)
  by The Fifth Dimension (1970)

"Stop The War Now" (Gordy 7104)
  by Edwin Starr (1970)

"2 + 2 = ?" (Capitol 2143)
  by The Bob Seger System (n.d.)

"Used To Be" (Motown 1650)
  by Charlene and Stevie Wonder (1982)

"War" (Gordy 7101)
  by Edwin Starr (1970)

"War Games" (Atlantic 89812)
  by Crosby, Stills, and Nash (1983)

"What's Going On" (Tamla 54201)
  by Marvin Gaye (1971)

"Where Have All The Flowers Gone" (Capitol 4671)
  by The Kingston Trio (1962)

"With God On Our Side" (Columbia Album)
  by Bob Dylan (n.d.)

Homefront Thoughts and Civilian Victims of Warfare

"Dear Uncle Sam" (Decca 31893)
  by Loretta Lynn (1966)

"Home Of The Brave" (Capitol 5483)
  by Jody Miller (1965)

"Mary Don't You Weep" (Columbia 41533)
  by Stonewall Jackson (1959)

"An Open Letter To My Teenage Son" (Liberty 55996)
  by Victor Lundberg (1967)

"Ruby, Don't Take Your Love To Town" (Reprise 0829)
  by Kenny Rogers and The First Edition (1969)

"Still In Saigon" (Epic 02828)
  by The Charlie Daniels Band (1982)

"The Unknown Soldier" (Elektra 45628)
  by The Doors (1968)

"War Is Hell On The Homefront, Too" (Curb 29934)
  by T. G. Sheppard (1982)
"Where Have All The Flowers Gone" (Imperial 66133)
  by Johnny Rivers (1965)

7

Occupations, Materialism, and Workplaces

It is difficult to imagine a more stinging indictment of the unethical, impersonal, materialistic practices of many of America's corporate managers than Ray Stevens' statements in "Mr. Businessman" (1968). The goals identified in Stevens' song are without lasting value—bigger cars, bigger houses, term insurance for the spouses—and the personal sacrifices are staggering—ignoring the children growing up and missing the music of their laughter as they play. There are many other popular songs that challenge the morality of business leaders. Among these recordings are Bob Dylan's "Masters Of War" (n.d.) and "Only A Pawn In Their Game" (n.d.). Other tunes criticize the harshness of personnel managers—"9 to 5" (1980) and "Take This Job And Shove It" (1977)—and the failure of middle managers or foremen to acknowledge the humanity of their workers—"Sunshine" (1971), "Big Boss Man" (1961), and "Workin' For The Man" (1962). But none of these songs can match the intensity, hostility, and sense of ethical depravity voiced in "Mr. Businessman."

In the business world there are few managers and numerous workers. Thus, most songs portray the world of work from the vantage point of the employee. Upward mobility appeals to many employees who are "Working In The Coal Mine" (1966) or scrubbing at the "Car Wash" (1976), but most people seem to "Feel Like Number" (1981) in stagnant job situations. For Billy Joel, the big lie of unattainable future success was implanted by hypocritical teachers in "Allentown" (1982). It is hard enough just to "Get A Job" (1958), according to The Silhouettes, let alone to become wealthy and successful. But even though "She Works Hard For The Money" (1983), Donna Summer notes for most employees there are no rainbows at the end of each day. Dolly Parton asserts that workin' "9 to 5" (1980) just ain't no way to make a livin'. The typical employee eyes the factory clock and listens for the plant whistle with eager anticipation. Freedom arrives in the "Five O'Clock World" (1965) after the workplace has been abandoned; individual pursuits dominate weekend activities when secretaries, car wash attendants, miners, stock boys, and assembly line workers can "Rip It Up" (1956), "Dance To The Music" (1968), and (symbolically, if not literally) "Take This Job And Shove It" (1977).

Not unexpectedly, numerous recording industry occupations are mentioned in popular song lyrics. The plight of unsuccessful performers and songwriters is the central message in "Please Come To Boston" (1974), "Rock 'N' Roll (I Gave You The Best Years Of My Life)" (1974), "Tulsa Time" (1980), and "I'm Comin' Home" (1974). The boredom of itinerant rock 'n' roll bands is capsulized in "Homeward Bound" (1966); the exhilaration of stardom (real or imagined) is communicated in "Travelin' Band" (1970), "Guitar Man" (1981), "Keep Playin' That Rock 'N' Roll" (1971), and "Takin' Care Of Business" (1974). While "The Under Assistant West Coast Promotion Man" (1965) continues to hunt for musical talent and many agents tell auditioning bands "Don't Call Us, We'll Call You" (1974), the carrot of fame keeps drawing would-be recording artists. They all dream of seeing their faces on "The Cover Of The 'Rolling Stone'" (1972).

In contrast to the numerous victims of the economic system, a few individuals challenge and defeat the materialistic world. This does not necessarily mean that they gain success, fame, and wealth, though. The young man who runs away from his parents and teachers to join "The Free Electric Band" (1973) is obviously marching to Henry David Thoreau's different drummer. Likewise, the young woman who isn't ready to be tied down in monogamy also hears a "Different Drum" (1968). But Lou Rawls outdoes both Albert Hammond and Linda Ronstadt in making his case against mindless, meaningless employment. The challenge in "A Natural Man" (1971) is anti-authority, anti-materialistic, and pro-humanistic.

A cornerstone of individual development in American society is the expectation of personal success. This goal may be achieved through hard work, formal educational training, luck, or careful professional networking. Whatever the route, though, the assumptions of equal opportunity for advancement and open access to channels of economic development are fundamental to promoting social mobility. The soggy-shoed, would-be executive depicted in Jim Croce's "Workin' At The Car Wash Blues" (1974) epitomizes the plans of many young men who long to be smokin' big cigars and talkin' trash to the secretaries.

Dreams can spawn achievement; so can frustration. Billy Joel provides a vignette about an urban dweller who has to move out of his parent's home in order to move up in society. This departure from one's place of birth in search of wider spaces, more opportunities, bigger challenges, and the achievement of individual identity is not limited to "Movin' Out (Anthony's

Song)" (1978). This theme has been a staple of rock lyrics since Chuck Berry's guitar strumming "Johnny B. Goode" (1958) hit the road, since Elvis Presley's young hero caught a flight to the West Coast's "Promised Land" (1974) and since Lou Rawls abandoned his Chicago area "Dead End Street" (1967) and denounced his "Tobacco Road" (n.d.) roots.

Physical shifts of location by themselves aren't usually sufficient to produce success for either a self-made man or an upwardly mobile woman. Curtis Mayfield capsuled the essence of individual spirit and personal motivation among a minority group when The Impressions urged young blacks to "Keep On Pushin'" (1964). On the distaff side, Helen Reddy offered the same challenge to young and old alike in her 1972 anthem "I Am Woman." The sentiments expressed in Sly Stone's "You Can Make It If You Try" (n.d.), in David Naughton's "Makin' It" (1979), and in Jim Croce's "I Got A Name" (1973) laud strength of character across the boundaries of race, sex, and social class to entice individuals to improve themselves.

If there are logical subsets to the general theme of social mobility, they include varying elements of freedom, ingenuity, enthusiasm, determination, incentive, and access. But there is also risk to setting high goals; the reality of failure is the flipside of success. Not all dreams come true. Jobs that once appeared to be brief, exciting employment steps on an occupational ladder toward financial self-sufficiency can become boring, dead end, emotional traps. Persistence alone may not be sufficient to keep an individual at the top of his or her field forever. What then? The answer for Frank Sinatra in "My Way" (1969), for Sammy Davis, Jr. in "I've Gotta Be Me" (1969), and for Lou Rawls in "A Natural Man" (1971) is maintaining personal integrity. There is no quantitative way to measure the value of character against the goal of mobility.

Although sociologists and psychologists may draw fine distinctions between occupations and vocations or between jobs and professions, there are few clear work-related boundaries found in popular lyrics. Human labor is rarely viewed as ennobling. In fact, work is generally depicted as drudgery performed out of inescapable financial necessity. Craftsmanship and the concern for high-quality, on-the-job performance is rarely mentioned. The money paid for a day's work, a week's work, or even a month's hard labor is never enough. And the five o'clock whistle can never blow soon enough. Although singers may laud their unions, their fellow workers, or the boss's pretty daughter, it is undeniable that the work environment represents a form of wage slavery that denies men and women opportunities for freedom, self-development, leisure, travel, and other forms of personal enjoyment.

Betty Hutton outlined several occupational options in "Doctor, Lawyer, Indian Chief" (1945), while Frank Sinatra preached the life-long volatility of job-related success and failure in "That's Life" (1966). The Silhouettes note the hostile domestic environment of a man who needs to "Get A Job"

(1958), while The Who bemoaned the loss of personal freedom due to working obligations in "Summertime Blues" (1970). The variety of occupations mentioned in popular songs is staggering. Among the positions described are school teachers—"Abigail Beecher" (1964), "Mr. Lee" (1957), "To Sir With Love" (1967), and "Don't Stand So Close To Me" (1981); secretaries—"Take A Letter Maria" (1969) and "9 to 5" (1980); disc jockeys and broadcast journalists—"Agent Double-O-Soul" (1965), "Kansas City Star" (1965), "Dirty Laundry" (1982), and "Clap For The Wolfman" (1974); bartenders—"Smokey Joe's Cafe" (1955) and "Come A Little Bit Closer" (1964); trainmen—"Rock Island Line" (1970); and "The City Of New Orleans" (1972); miners—"Big Bad John" (1961), "Sixteen Tons" (1976), and "Working In The Coal Mine" (1966); truckers—"Convoy" (1975), "Drivin' My Life Away" (1980), and "Phantom 309" (1967); telephone operators—"Memphis" (1964) and "Operator (That's Not The Way It Feels)" (1972); and dozens of other jobs. Not unexpectedly, movie stars and popular music personalities are focal points for job interests. Among the songs examining various motion picture and recording industry occupations are: "Act Naturally" (1965), "Albert Flasher" (1971), "The All American Boy" (1958), "The Cover Of The 'Rolling Stone'" (1972), "The Entertainer" (1974), "Jazzman" (1974), "Keep Playin' That Rock 'N' Roll" (1971), "On The Road Again" (1980), "Piano Man" (1974), "So You Want To Be A Rock 'N' Roll Star" (1967), "Star Baby" (1974), "Travelin' Band" (1970), "The Under Assistant West Coast Promotion Man" (n.d.), and "We're An American Band" (1973).

Unsavory occupations and illegal activities are also surveyed in contemporary lyrics. Men who make their livings with cards, fortune wheels, and dice are featured in "The Gambler" (1978), "Go Down Gamblin'" (1971), "Ramblin' Gamblin' Man" (1969), and "Stagger Lee" (1971). Drug dealers, rum runners, and murderers are also described in "Freddie's Dead" (1972), "Superfly" (1972), "The Ballad Of Thunder Road" (1957), and "Mack The Knife" (1959). The world of striptease, pornography, and prostitution is examined in "Bad Girls" (1979), "Backstreet Ballet" (1983), "Blue Money" (1971), "Lady Marmalade" (1975), "The House Of The Rising Sun" (1981), "Painted Ladies" (1973), "Shake Your Money Maker" (n.d.), and "Sweet Cream Ladies, Forward March" (1968).

In 1933 Ginger Rogers proclaimed "We're In The Money (The Gold Digger's Song)." Although the impact of the Great Depression made this lyric highly ironic, the linkage of material wealth with physical and psychological well-being has been a long-time American assumption. As Joel Grey and Liza Minelli asserted in "The Money Song" from the 1972 film *Cabaret*, it's money that makes the world go around. Who could refute their claim? Even chronic misfortune can supposedly be resolved by "Pennies From Heaven" (1960).

Not everyone feels that money is the solution to all problems, though.

Ray Charles expresses the pain of being "Busted" (1963), while The Beatles assert that money "Can't Buy Me Love" (1964). Even though Bobby Hebb claims that there isn't one rich man in ten with "A Satisfied Mind" (1966), the power of wealth continues to allure. Barrett Strong's unequivocal statement—"Money (That's What I Want)" (1960)—finds varying adherents. Roy Orbison wants to be a woman's "Candy Man" (1961); B. B. King demands respect and obedience because he's working and thereby "Paying The Cost To Be The Boss" (1968); and Gene Watson condemns the selfish materialism of women who contemplate clothes, jewelry, and cash with a "Fourteen Carat Mind" (1981).

The majority of contemporary lyrics are critical of material ends that emphasize the cost of everything while finding lasting value in nothing. Pleas for personal freedom as a better life than dwelling in lonely mansions are heard from Taxxi in "Gold And Chains" (1983) and from Linda Ronstadt in "Silver Threads And Golden Needles" (1974). The Temptations attack the materialistic pillaging of ghetto life in "Masterpiece" (1973), while the O'Jays denounce the act of a woman selling her precious body "For The Love Of Money" (1974). The predatory skills of such dollar-driven ladies are also depicted in "She Only Meant To Use Him" (1982), "Maneater" (1982), and "Fancy" (1969).

Other criticisms focus on the problems of remaining emotionally sensitive to others while living in a materialistic society. These commentaries are often symbolic in tone. Attacks on money-grubbing television evangelists and over-zealous church collections are featured in "The American Dream" (1982) and "Signs" (1971). Stan Freberg even denounces hedonistic yuletide sales campaigns in "Green Chritma" (1958). The materialistic sameness of suburban life is parodied in Pete Seeger's "Little Boxes" (1964) and The Monkees' "Pleasant Valley Sunday" (1967). This critical trend is also notable in "Fortunate Son" (1969), "American Woman" (1970), and "Cheeseburger In Paradise" (1978). Attacks on the immorality or lost innocence of dollar-seeking individuals also illustrates the anti-materialism theme. These recordings include "Goldfinger" (1965) by Shirley Bassey, "Conquistador" (1972) by Procol Harum, and "Rhinestone Cowboy" (1975) by Glen Campbell. Perhaps the best example of a song that encapsules the lost feeling of someone who has gained fame and fortune but lost all direction and meaning in life is Joe Walsh's "Life's Been Good" (1978).

Little Richard lauded both payday and the weekend in his 1956 recording of "Rip It Up." The notion of leaving a frustrating workplace is as popular in work-related tunes as Chuck Berry's descriptions of students joyfully escaping from classes in his school songs. The necessity of daily labor is largely unquestioned; but the love of work—unless it's related to playing in a band, performing as a disc jockey, or serving as a lifeguard—is non-existent in popular lyrics. Loverboy freely admits to "Working For The Weekend" (1982), while both The Easybeats and The Vogues announce they have "Friday On My Mind" (1967) while looking toward a "Five O'Clock World" (1965). Bobby Smith combines staccato audio images of being stuck in traffic, of facing a screaming boss, of getting a headache, and of being indicted on his job for doing everything wrong. His conclusion is "It's Been One Of Those Days" (1982).

Continuing job frustration is even more difficult to resolve than the understandable longing for a regular weekend break. Bob Seger complains that his boss can't even recall his name in "Feel Like A Number" (1981). For Dolly Parton it's not anonymity but lack of formal recognition and thoughtful praise that makes her "9 to 5" (1980) service so upsetting. Bobby Bare views his assembly line job as crushing monotony. He longs to leave "Detroit City" (1963) for a warmer climate, more friendly neighbors, and the cotton fields back home. Reverie and fantasy in the form of "Dreams Of The Everyday Housewife" (1968) also mark a form of dissatisfaction with a domestic job situation.

Work without sufficient time for human pleasure, leisure, and social amenities is truly drudgery. Even top managers need to "Stop And Smell The Roses" (1974) says Mac Davis. But Lou Rawls equates continuous self-sacrifice to job requirements over an entire lifetime as pure foolishness. This is particularly true if the boss can control his own life and leisure at the expense of his workers. Stated succinctly in "A Natural Man" (1971), Rawls says that he doesn't want a gold watch for working forty years from nine to five. One senses that he would prefer to be "Takin' Care Of Business" (1974) on the beach with Bachman-Turner Overdrive. Billy Joel blames an entire community—"Allentown" (1982)—for lying to its youth about the occupational future. Even the frustration of repetitive steel production is preferable to stagnating unemployment brought on by poor planning, inadequate schooling, misleading national myths, and industrial pullouts. The cynicism of this song is matched only by Albert King's personal feelings of isolation in "Angel Of Mercy" (1972). The late 19th- and early 20th-century tunes of working-class anger do have a continuing presence during the 1950–1985 period. Ironically, they are sung by highly successful musicians who are far removed from California waitresses who work hard for their money or blue-collar factory employees who languish in Pennsylvania.

OCCUPATIONS, MATERIALISM, AND WORKPLACES

Social Mobility

"Dead End Street" (Capitol 5868)
  by Lou Rawls (1967)

"Don't Call Us, We'll Call You" (Claridge 402)
  by Sugarloaf (1974)

"Don't Stop Believin' " (Columbia 02567)
  by Journey (1981)

"Don't You Want Me" (A&M 2397)
  by Human League (1982)

"Everybody's Gotta Pay Some Dues" (Tamla 54048)
  by The Miracles (1961)

"Fame" (RCA 10320)
  by David Bowie (1975)

"Fame" (RSO 1034)
  by Irene Cara (1980)

"Fame And Fortune" (RCA 47-7740)
  by Elvis Presley (1966)

"From Levis To Calvin Klein Jeans" (MCA 51230)
  by Brenda Lee (1982)

"Gold" (RSO 931)
  by John Stewart (1979)

"I Am Woman" (Capitol 3350)
  by Helen Reddy (1972)

"I Got A Name" (ABC 11389)
  by Jim Croce (1973)

"I'm Gonna Be A Wheel Some Day" (Imperial 5606)
  by Fats Domino (1959)

"Johnny B. Goode" (Chess 1691)
  by Chuck Berry (1958)

"Johnny B. Goode" (EMI American 8159)
  by Peter Tosh (1983)

"Keep On Pushing" (ABC-Paramount 10555)
  by The Impressions (1964)

"Makin' It" (RSO 916)
  by David Naughton (1979)

"Movin' Out (Anthony's Song)" (Columbia 10708)
  by Billy Joel (1978)

"Oklahoma Crude" (ALFA 7010)
  by The Corbin/Hanner Band (1981)

"On Broadway" (Warner Brothers 8542)
  by George Benson (1978)

"Out Here On My Own" (RSO 1048)
  by Irene Cara (1980)

"Poor Boy" (RCA 13383)
  by Razzy Bailey (1982)

"Promised Land" (RCA PB-10074)
  by Elvis Presley (1974)

"Rag Doll" (Philips 40211)
   by The Four Seasons (1964)

"Say, Has Anybody Seen My Sweet Gypsy Rose" (Bell 45374)
   by Dawn (1973)

"Say It Loud—I'm Black And I'm Proud" (King 6187)
   by James Brown (1968)

"(Sittin' On) The Dock Of The Bay" (Volt 157)
   by Otis Redding (1968)

"Stop And Smell The Roses" (Columbia 10018)
   by Mac Davis (1974)

"Tobacco Road" (London 9689)
   by The Nashville Teens (1964)

"Tobacco Road" (Capitol album)
   by Lou Rawls (n.d.)

"Too Much Monkey Business" (Chess 1635)
   by Chuck Berry (1956)

"Tulsa Time" (ABC 12425)
   by Don Williams (1978)

"You Can Make It If You Try" (Epic album)
   by Sly and the Family Stone (n.d.)

Occupations

"Abigail Beecher" (Warner Brothers 5409)
   by Freddy Cannon (1964)

"Act Naturally" (Capitol 5498)
   by The Beatles (1965)

"Agent Double-O-Soul" (Ric-Tic 103)
   by Edwin Starr (1965)

"Albert Flasher" (RCA 0458)
   by The Guess Who (1971)

"The All American Boy" (Fraternity 835)
   by Bill Parsons (1958)

"Backstreet Ballet" (Mercury 814360)
   by Savannah (1983)

"Bad Girls" (Casablanca 988)
   by Donna Summer (1979)

"The Ballad Of Thunder Road" (Capitol 3986)
   by Robert Mitchum (1958)

"Big Bad John" (Columbia 42175)
   by Jimmy Dean (1961)

"Big In Vegas" (Capitol 2646)
   by Buck Owens (1969)

"Blue Collar" (Mercury 73417)
  by Bachman-Turner Overdrive (1973)

"Blue Collar Man (Long Nights)" (A&M 2087)
  by Styx (1978)

"Blue Money" (Warner Brothers 7462)
  by Van Morrison (1971)

"Car Wash" (MCA 40615)
  by Rose Royce (1976)

"Career Girl" (Solar 12143)
  by Carrie Lucas (1980)

"Chattanooga Shoe Shine Boy" (Swan 4050)
  by Freddy Cannon (1960)

"The City Of New Orleans" (Reprise 1103)
  by Arlo Guthrie (1972)

"Clap For The Wolfman" (RCA 0324
  by The Guess Who (1974)

"Clementine" (Atco 6161)
  by Bobby Darin (1960)

"Coal Miner's Daughter" (Decca 32749)
  by Loretta Lynn (1970)

"Convoy" (MGM 14839)
  by C. W. McCall (1975)

"The Cover Of The 'Rolling Stone' " (Columbia 45732)
  by Dr. Hook (1972)

"Creeque Alley" (Dunhill 4083)
  by The Mamas and The Papas (1967)

"Different Drum" (Capitol 2004)
  by Linda Ronstadt and the Stone Poneys (1968)

"Dirty Laundry" (Asylum 69894)
  by Don Henley (1982)

"Doctor, Lawyer, Indian Chief" (Capitol 220)
  by Betty Hutton (1945)

"Don't Pay The Ferryman" (A&M 2511)
  by Chris DeBurgh (1983)

"Don't Stand So Close To Me" (A&M 2301)
  by The Police (1981)

"Down On The Corner" (Fantasy 634)
  by Creedence Clearwater Revival (1969)

"Dreams Of The Everyday Housewife" (Capitol 2224)
  by Glen Campbell (1968)

"Drivin' My Life Away" (Elektra 46656)
  by Eddie Rabbitt (1980)

"Eleanor Rigby" (Capitol 5715)
  by The Beatles (1966)

"The Entertainer" (Columbia 10064)
  by Billy Joel (1974)

"Fortuneteller" (Del-Fi 4177)
  by Bobby Curtola (1962)

"Freddie's Dead" (Curtom 1975)
  by Curtis Mayfield (1972)

"The Gambler" (United Artists 1250)
  by Kenny Rogers (1978)

"Get A Job" (Ember 1029)
  by The Silhouettes (1958)

"Go Down Gamblin'" (Columbia 45427)
  by Blood, Sweat & Tears (1971)

"The Guitar Man" (Elektra 45803)
  by Bread (1972)

"Guitar Man" (RCA PB-12158
  by Elvis Presley (1981)

"Homeward Bound" (Columbia 43511)
  by Simon and Garfunkel (1966)

"Honky Tonk Man" (Warner Brothers 29847)
  by Marty Robbins (1982)

"The House Of The Rising Sun" (RCA 12282)
  by Dolly Parton (1981)

"Jazzman" (Ode 66101)
  by Carole King (1974)

"Kansas City Star" (Smash 1998)
  by Roger Miller (1965)

"Keep Playin' That Rock 'N' Roll" (Epic 10788)
  by The Edgar Winter Group (1971)

"Killing Me Softly With His Song" (Atlantic 2940)
  by Roberta Flack (1973)

"Lady Marmalade" (Epic 50048)
  by LaBelle (1975)

"Love Potion Number Nine" (King 6385)
  by The Coasters (1971)

"Mack The Knife" (Atco 6147)
  by Bobby Darin (1959)

"Mamas Don't Let Your Babies Grow Up To Be Cowboys" (RCA 11198)
  by Waylon Jennings and Willie Nelson (1978)

"Memphis" (Imperial 66032)
  by Johnny Rivers (1964)

"The Money Song" (ABC album)
by Joel Grey and Liza Minelli (1972)

"Morning Train (Nine to Five)" (EMI America 8071)
by Sheena Easton (1981)

"Mr. Bass Man" (Kapp 503
by Johnny Cymbal (1963)

"Mr. Businessman" (Monument 1083)
by Ray Stevens (1968)

"Mr. Lee" (Atlantic 1144)
by The Bobbettes (1957)

"My Life" (Columbia 10853)
by Billy Joel (1978)

"The Night Chicago Died" (Mercury 73492)
by Paper Lace (1974)

"Night Shift" (Warner Brothers 29932)
by Quarterflash (1982)

"On Broadway" (Atlantic 2182)
by The Drifters (1963)

"On The Road Again" (Columbia 11351)
by Willie Nelson (1980)

"Operator (That's Not The Way It Feels)" (ABC 11335)
by Jim Croce (1972)

"Painted Ladies" (Janus 224)
by Ian Thomas (1973)

"Phantom 309" (Starday 811)
by Red Sovine (1967)

"Piano Man" (Columbia 45963)
by Billy Joel (1974)

"Please Mr. Postman" (Tamla 54046)
by The Marvelettes (1961)

"Proud Mary" (Liberty 56216)
by Ike and Tina Turner (1971)

"Ramblin' Gamblin' Man" (Capitol 2297)
by Bob Seger (1968)

"Ramblin' Man" (Capricorn 0027)
by The Allman Brothers Band (1973)

"Rock Island Line" (Sun 1111)
by Johnny Cash (1970)

"The Rubberband Man" (Atlantic 3355)
by The Spinners (1976)

"Secret Agent Man" (Imperial 66159)
by Johnny Rivers (1966)

"Shake Your Money Maker" (album cut)
by Elmore James (n.d.)

"She Works Hard For The Money" (Mercury 812370)
by Donna Summer (1983)

"Show Biz Kids" (ABC 11382)
by Steely Dan (1973)

"Sixteen Tons" (Atlantic 3323)
by The Don Harrison Band (1976)

"Smoke On The Water" (Warner Brothers 7710)
by Deep Purple (1973)

"Smokey Joe's Cafe" (Atco 6059)
by The Robins (1955)

"So You Want To Be A Rock 'N' Roll Star" (Columbia 43987)
by The Byrds (1967)

"Stagger Lee" (ABC 11307)
by Tommy Roe (1971)

"Star Baby" (RCA 0217)
by The Guess Who (1974)

"Steel Men" (Columbia 42483)
by Jimmy Dean (1962)

"Summertime Blues" (Decca 32708)
by The Who (1970)

"Superfly" (Curtom 1978)
by Curtis Mayfield (1972)

"Sweet Cream Ladies, Forward March" (Mala 12035)
by The Box Tops (1968)

"Take A Letter Maria" (Atco 6714)
by R. B. Greaves (1969)

"That's Life" (Reprise 0531)
by Frank Sinatra (1966)

"To Sir With Love" (Epic 10187)
by Lulu (1967)

"Travelin' Band" (Fantasy 637)
by Creedence Clearwater Revival (1970)

"Waitin' On A Letter/Mr. Postman" (Phase II 5653)
by The Originals (1981)

"We're An American Band" (Capitol 3660)
by Grand Funk Railroad (1973)

"Wichita Lineman" (Capitol 2302)
by Glen Campbell (1968)

"Work To Do" (T-Neck 936)
by The Isley Brothers (1972)

"Working Girl" (RCA 12282)
  by Dolly Parton (1981)
"Working In The Coal Mine" (Amy 958)
  by Lee Dorsey (1966)
"Working Man's Prayer" (Verve 10574)
  by Arthur Prysock (1968)

Materialism

"The American Dream" (Elektra 69960)
  by Hank Williams, Jr. (1982)
"American Woman" (RCA 0325)
  by The Guess Who (1970)
"Baby, You're A Rich Man" (Capital 5964)
  by The Beatles (1967)
"Big Time Spender" (Maske 102)
  by Cornbread and Biscuits (1960)
"Busted" (ABC-Paramount 10481)
  by Ray Charles (1963)
"Candy Man" (MGM 14320)
  by Sammy Davis, Jr. (1972)
"Candy Man" (Monument 447)
  by Roy Orbison (1961)
"Can't Buy Me Love" (Capitol 5150)
  by The Beatles (1964)
"Cheeseburger In Paradise" (ABC 12358)
  by Jimmy Buffett (1978)
"Conquistador" (A&M 1347)
  by Procol Harum (972)
"Dig The Gold" (Cream 7939)
  by Joyce Cobb (1979)
"A Dollar Down" (RCA 7859)
  by The Limeliters (1961)
"Don't Bet Money, Honey" (Canadian American 127)
  by Linda Scott (1961)
"Fancy" (Capitol 2675)
  by Bobbie Gentry (1969)
"For The Love Of Money" (Philadelphia International 3544)
  by The O'Jays (1974)
"Fortunate Son" (Fantasy 634)
  by Creedence Clearwater Revival (1969)
"Fourteen Carat Mind" (MCA 51183)
  by Gene Watson (1981)

"The Free Electric Band" (Mums 6018)
by Albert Hammond (1973)

"Gas Money" (Arwin 111)
by Jan and Arnie (1958)

"Gimme Your Money Please" (Mercury 73843)
by Bachman-Turner Overdrive (1976)

"Gold And Chains" (Fantasy Album)
by Taxxi (1983)

"Goldfinger" (United Artists 790)
by Shirley Bassey (1965)

"Green Chritma" (Capitol 4097)
by Stan Freberg (1958)

"Greenbacks" (Atlantic 1076)
by Ray Charles (1955)

"Hand Me Down World" (RCA 0367)
by The Guess Who (1970)

"Handbags And Gladrags" (Mercury 73031)
by Rod Stewart (1972)

"The House Of The Rising Sun" (MGM 13264)
by The Animals (1964)

"It Takes A Lot Of Money" (Decca 32004)
by Warner Mack (1966)

"Life's Been Good" (Asylum 45493)
by Joe Walsh (1978)

"Little Boxes" (Columbia 42940)
by Pete Seeger (1964)

"Maneater" (RCA 13354)
by Daryl Hall and John Oates (1982)

"Masterpiece" (Gordy 7126)
by The Temptations (1973)

"Masters of War" (Columbia Album)
by Bob Dylan (n.d.)

"Me And The I.R.S." (Epic 50539)
by Johnny Paycheck (1978)

"Money" (Virgin 67003)
by The Flying Lizards (1979)

"Money" (Buddah 487)
by Gladys Knight and The Pips (1975)

"Money" (Kama Sutra 241)
by The Lovin' Spoonful (1968)

"Money" (Harvest 3609)
by Pink Floyd (1973)

"Money Changes Everything" (Portrait 04737)
by Cyndi Lauper (1984)

"Money Honey" (Arista 0170)
by The Bay City Rollers (1976)

"Money Honey" (RCA EPA 821)
by Elvis Presley (1956)

"Money, Money, Money" (Atlantic 3434)
by Abba (1977)

"Money Music" (Spring 106)
by Boys In The Band (1970)

"Money Runner" (Reprise 1062)
by Quincy Jones (1972)

"Money (That's What I Want)" (Wand 150)
by The Kingsmen (1964)

"Money (That's What I Want)" (Anna 1111)
by Barrett Strong (1960)

"The Money Tree" (Capitol 3586)
by Margaret Whiting (1956)

"Money Won't Change You (Part 1)" (King 6048)
by James Brown (1966)

"More Money For You And Me" (Capitol 4599)
by The Four Preps (1961)

"No Money Down" (Chess 1615)
by Chuck Berry (1956)

"Not For All The Money In The World" (Scepter 1248)
by The Shirelles (1963)

"(Oh Lord Won't You Buy Me A) Mercedes Benz" (Capitol 3246)
by The Goose Creek Symphony (1972)

"One For The Money (Part 1)" (Soul Train 10700)
by The Whispers (1976)

"Only A Pawn In Their Game" (Columbia album)
by Bob Dylan (n.d.)

"Paying The Cost To Be The Boss" (Bluesway 61015)
by B. B. King (1968)

"Pennies From Heaven" (Calico 117)
by The Skyliners (1960)

"Plastic Man" (Gordy 7129)
by The Temptations (1973)

"Pleasant Valley Sunday" (Colgems 1007)
by The Monkees (1967)

"Poor Little Rich Girl" (Columbia 42795)
by Steve Lawrence (1963)

"The Price You Have To Pay" (Dionn 512)
by Brenda and The Tabulations (1969)

"Puttin' On The Ritz" (RCA 13574)
 by Taco (1983)

"Rhinestone Cowboy" (Capitol 4095)
 by Glen Campbell (1975)

"Rich Girl" (RCA 10860)
 by Hall and Oates (1977)

"Richest Man (In The World)" (RCA 6290)
 by Eddy Arnold (1955)

"Round The Clock Lovin'" (Warner Brothers 50004)
 by Gail Davies (1982)

"A Satisfied Mind" (Philips 40400)
 by Bobby Hebb (1966)

"She Only Meant To Use Him" (Mercury 76165)
 by Wayne Kemp (1982)

"Signs" (Lionel 3213)
 by The Five Man Electrical Band (1971)

"Silver Threads And Golden Needles" (Asylum 11032)
 by Linda Ronstadt (1974)

"Silver Threads And Golden Needles" (Philips 40038)
 by The Springfields (1962)

"Take The Money And Run" (Capitol 4260)
 by The Steve Miller Band (1976)

"The Under Assistant West Coast Promotion Man" (London 9766)
 by The Rolling Stones (1965)

"Wanted $10,000 Reward" (Minit 623)
 by Ernie K-Doe (1961)

"When You're Hot, You're Hot" (RCA 9976)
 by Jerry Reed (1971)

"Where Did The Money Go" (Jeremiah 1008)
 by Hoyt Axton (1980)

"You're So Vain" (Elektra 45824)
 by Carly Simon (1972)

"Your Cash Ain't Nothin' But Trash" (Capitol 3837)
 by The Steve Miller Band (1974)

Workplaces, Frustration, and Escape

"Allentown" (Columbia 03413)
 by Billy Joel (1982)

"Angel Of Mercy" (Stax 0121)
 by Albert King (1972)

"Big Boss Man" (Vee-Jay 380)
 by Jimmy Reed (1961)

"Country Boy (You Got Your Feet In L.A.)" (Capitol 4155)
by Glen Campbell (1975)

"Cowboy In A Three Piece Business Suit" (Warner Brothers 29968)
by Rex Allen, Jr. (1982)

"Dance To The Music" (Epic 10256)
by Sly and the Family Stone (1968)

"Detroit City" (RCA 8183)
by Bobby Bare (1963)

"Down In The Boondocks" (Columbia 43305)
by Billy Joe Royal (1965)

"Dreams Of The Everyday Housewife" (Capitol 2224)
by Glen Campbell (1968)

"Feel Like A Number" (Capitol 5077)
by Bob Seger and The Silver Bullet Band (1981)

"Five O'Clock World" (CO & CE 232)
by The Vogues (1965)

"Friday On My Mind" (United Artists 50106)
by The Easybeats (1967)

"Get Down Saturday Night" (MCA 52198)
by Oliver Cheatham (1983)

"Get Off Of My Cloud" (London 9792)
by The Rolling Stones (1965)

"A Hard Day's Night" (Capitol 5222)
by The Beatles (1964)

"I Ain't No Fool"(Warner Brothers 8787)
by Big Al Downing (1979)

"I Can't Work No Longer " (Okeh 7221)
by Billy Butler and The Chanters (1965)

"I Know A Place" (Warner Brothers 5612)
by Petula Clark (1965)

"I.O.U." (Casino 052)
by Jimmy Dean (1976)

"I Wish I Had A Job To Shove" (Churchill 94005)
by Rodney Lay and The Wild West (1982)

"I'm Comin' Home" (Atlantic 3027)
by The Spinners (1974)

"I'm Gonna Move To The Outskirts Of Town" (Impulse 202)
by Ray Charles (1961)

"I'm Livin' In Shame" (Motown 1139)
by Diana Ross and The Supremes (1969)

"It's Been One Of Those Days" (Liberty 1480)
by Bobby Smith (1982)

"I've Gotta Be Me" (Reprise 0779)
   by Sammy Davis, Jr. (1969)

"Just Another Day In Paradise" (Kat Family 02839)
   by Bertie Higgins (1982)

"Love On My Mind Tonight" (Gordy 1666)
   by The Temptations (1982)

"My Way" (Reprise 0812)
   by Frank Sinatra (1969)

"A Natural Man" (MGM 14262)
   by Lou Rawls (1971)

"Neutron Dance" (Planet 13951)
   by The Pointer Sisters (1983)

"9 to 5" (RCA 12133)
   by Dolly Parton (1980)

"Playing This Old Working Day Away" (RCA 13208)
   by Dean Dillon (1982)

"Please Come To Boston" (Epic 11115)
   by Dave Loggins (1974)

"Rip It Up" (Specialty 579)
   by Little Richard (1956)

"Rock 'N' Roll (I Gave You The Best Years Of My Life)" (Columbia 10070)
   by Mac Davis (1974)

"She Works Hard For The Money" (Mercury 812370)
   by Donna Summer (1983)

"Stop And Smell The Roses" (Columbia 10018)
   by Mac Davis (1974)

"Sunshine" (Capricorn 8021)
   by Jonathan Edwards (1971)

"Take This Job And Shove It" (Epic 50469)
   by Johnny Paycheck (1977)

"Takin' Care Of Business" (Mercury 73487)
   by Bachman-Turner Overdrive (1974)

"Tulsa Time" (RSO 1039)
   by Eric Clapton (1980)

"Uptown" (Philles 102)
   by The Cyrstals (1962)

"Workin' At The Car Wash Blues" (ABC 11447)
   by Jim Croce (1974)

"Workin For A Livin' " (Chrysalis 2630)
   by Huey Lewis and The News

"Working Class Hero" (MGM SO. 7013)
   by Tommy Roe (1973)

"Workin' For The Man" (Monument 467)
  by Roy Orbison (1962)

"Working For The Weekend" (Columbia 02589)
  by Loverboy (1982)

"Working In The Coal Mine" (Full Moon 47204)
  by Devo (1981)

"Your Cash Ain't Nothin' But Trash" (Atlantic 1035)
  by The Clovers (1954)

8

Personal Relationships, Love, and Sexuality

Throughout the twentieth century, courtship themes have dominated American lyrics. Love songs depict consistent behavioral patterns. Boy meets girl; a special relationship develops; love blooms; sexuality is explored; tensions are noted; rejection occurs; loneliness is felt; and (in a repetition of the pattern) boy meets another girl. Human interaction is never neat. Highly emotional personal involvements are not only less than neat, they are extremely volatile and likely to produce peaks of joy and valleys of depression. It would take an entire book, not just a single chapter, to illustrate accurately the variety of personal relationship themes that exist within the lyrics of popular songs during the past thirty-five years. The following pages examine selected hit recordings that depict the complex nature of male-female interaction.

Prior to the establishment of personal relationships, there is often an ideal mate who is initially conjured in the male or the female mind. Fantasy searches for reality. Actually, fantasy and reality duel in the hearts and minds of romantic dreamers as they seek the "right guy" or the "perfect girl" to make a successful relationship emerge. "This Magic Moment" (1968) is how Jay and The Americans describe such wish fulfillment. Meditation is sometimes a source of inspiration to would-be lovers. Andy Gibb and Victoria Principal declare "All I Have To Do Is Dream" (1981), but their notion simply echoes similar lyrical observations in "Dream Baby (How Long Must I Dream)" (1983), "Everybody's Dream Girl" (1983), "Dreamin'" (1982), and "Dream Lover" (1959). Other individuals appeal to mythical romantic authorities such as "Mister Sandman" (1981) or to voodoo specialists who can whip up "Love Potion No. 9" (1959). The goal remains the same in all cases—to secure "A Sunday Kind Of Love" (1962).

Many young men utilize female traffic on downtown streets to stimulate their romantic imaginations. Recordings illustrating this voyeur behavior include "Standing On The Corner" (1956), "Kansas City" (1959), "Oh, Pretty Woman" (1964), and "Girl Watcher" (1968). Beyond ogling secretaries during lunch breaks or other female strangers, there is the more frustrating situation of being unable to initiate a loving relationship with a known friend. Such situations may arise from shyness, from social class or occupational distinctions, or from the recognition of prior relationships with someone else. Such themes appear in "Guess Who" (1959), "You Don't Know Me" (1962), "Can't Take My Eyes Off Of You" (1967), "If I Were Your Woman" (1970), "My Eyes Adored You" (1974), "Jessie's Girl" (1981), "Somebody's Baby" (1982), "I've Made Love To You A Thousand Times" (1983), and "Scarlet Fever" (1983). Somehow the lonely hope for a beneficent "Cupid" (1961) to transform an "Imaginary Lover" (1978) into an "Angel Baby" (1960) or an "Earth Angel" (1954) doesn't occur too often. Regretably, many folks must echo Stevie Wonder's lament that they've "Never Had A Dream Come True" (1970).

Christopher Cross declared that the best thing you can do is fall in love. This sentiment, expressed in "Arthur's Theme (Best That You Can Do)" (1981), is found in numerous Beatles' recordings including "All My Loving" (1964), "And I Love Her" (1964), "She Loves You" (1964), and "All You Need Is Love" (1967). Even though Paul McCartney acknowledges the universal appeal of "Silly Love Songs" (1976), other singers have described the achievement of loving relationships as games, conquests, mutual agreements, evolutionary patterns, or even accidents. Songs depicting these situations are "It's All In The Game" (1958), "Game Of Love" (1965), "Ten Commandments Of Love" (1958), "Love Is Like An Itching In My Heart" (1966), "To The Aisle" (1957), "Love Is Strange" (1957), "Fooled Around And Fell In Love" (1976), "(Every Time I Turn Around) Back In Love Again" (1977), and "You Make My Dreams" (1981).

Teenage romance often begins with fantasies, but usually shifts from "Cowboys To Girls" (1968) and from dolls to "Boys" (1960). First kisses, first dates, and going steady are noted in numerous recordings that chronicle love among the very young. It is interesting that such songs were particularly prevalent during the 1950s; however, they began to fade from hit charts in the late 1960s and practically disappeared by the late 1970s and early 1980s. Examples of these songs include "I Want You To Be My Girl" (1956), "A Rose And A Baby Ruth" (1956), "Too Young To Go Steady" (1956), "Young Love" (1956), "First Date, First Kiss, First Love" (1957), "Goin' Steady" (1957), "High School Romance" (1957), "Teen-Age Crush" (1957), "Wear My Ring Around Your Neck" (1958), "Sweet Nothin's" (1959), "A Teenager In Love" (1959), "Twixt Twelve And Twenty" (1959), "You're Sixteen" (1960), "Puppy Love" (1960), "Let's Go Steady Again" (1963), "I Saw Her Standing There" (1964), "Puppy Love" (1964), "Hold

Me, Thrill Me, Kiss Me" (1965), "1-2-3" (1965), "I Second That Emotion" (1967), "When You're Young And In Love" (1967), "Put Your Head On My Shoulder" (1978), "Chuck E.'s In Love" (1979), and "P.Y.T. (Pretty Young Thing)" (1983). The immature, irrational erratic behavior of lovers—particularly young and inexperienced romantics—is depicted in numerous songs such as "Fools Fall In Love" (1957), "A Fool In Love" (1960), "Foolish Little Girl" (1963), "Fools Rush In" (1963), and "Why Do Fools Fall In Love" (1981).

The boundless euphoria of love is communicated in music throughout the past thirty-five years. General declarations include "Love Is A Many-Splendored Thing" (1955), "Dedicated To The One I Love" (1959), "I Only Have Eyes For You" (1959), "Every Beat Of My Heart" (1961), "For Your Precious Love" (1963), "Goin' Out Of My Head/Can't Take My Eyes Off You" (1967), "Ain't No Mountain High Enough" (1970), "You're My Best Friend" (1976), "Crazy Little Thing Called Love" (1979), "Cupid I've Loved You For A Long Time" (1980), "The Closer You Get" (1983), and "Words And Music" (1983). Men in love are ecstatic about the virtues of their women. Examples of recordings illustrating this point include "Reet Petite (The Finest Girl You Ever Want To Meet)" (1957), "Portrait Of My Love" (1961), "My Girl" (1965), "This Guy's In Love With You" (1968), "Baby I'm-A Want You" (1971), "Ain't No Woman (Like The One I've Got)" (1973), "How Sweet It Is (To Be Loved By You)" (1975), "Three Times A Lady" (1978), and "You're My Latest, My Greatest Inspiration" (1982). The same enthusiasm for male lovers is demonstrated by female singers in tunes such as "Baby It's You" (1961), "I've Told Every Little Star" (1961), "Baby, I'm Yours" (1965), "My Man" (1965), "Baby I Love You" (1967), "I Never Loved A Man (The Way I Love You)" (1967), "Love Eyes" (1967), "This Girl's In Love With You" (1969), "Best Thing That Ever Happened To Me" (1974), "I Honestly Love You" (1974), "Hopelessly Devoted To You" (1978), "I Only Want To Be With You" (1982), and "My Guy" (1982). Both lyrically and in terms of harmonic declaration, some of the most memorable love songs have been recorded by male and female duos. Some of the most popular romantic tunes performed by singing partners are "True Love" (1956), "Baby (You've Got What It Takes)" (1960), "A Rockin' Good Way (To Mess Around And Fall in Love)" (1960), "I Need Your Loving" (1962), "Let It Be Me" (1964), "River Deep—Mountain High" (1966), "If I Could Build My Whole World Around You" (1967), "It Takes Two" (1967), "Ain't Nothing Like The Real Thing" (1968), "You're All I Need To Get By" (1968), "Never Ending Song Of Love" (1971), "Only You Know And I Know" (1971), "Love Will Keep Us Together" (1975), "You Don't Have To Be A Star (To Be In My Show)" (1976), "Devoted To You" (1958), "You're The One That I Want" (1978), "Reunited" (1979), "My Guy/My Girl" (1980), "Endless Love" (1981), "Friends In Love" (1982), and "Islands In The Stream" (1983).

Although Wilson Pickett accurately observes "Everybody Needs Somebody To Love" (1967), there are numerous songs that illustrate the insecurity of romantic relationships. These tunes feature warnings to those seeking to break up an ongoing love affair, including "Bird Dog" (1958), "Don't Mess With Bill" (1966), and "Potential New Boyfriend" (1983) and complaints or fears about a partner's infidelity, such as "Butterfly" (1957), "Lipstick On Your Collar" (1959), "Mr. Blue" (1959), "Butterfly Baby" (1963), "Mama Didn't Lie" (1963), "Johnny One Time" (1969), "I've Got To Use My Imagination" (1973), "Don't Go Breaking My Heart" (1976), and "Let's Hang On" (1982). Feelings of helplessness in the wake of unfaithful behavior by a friend or lover are also communicated in "Cathy's Clown" (1960) and "Mama Said" (1961).

If the number of recordings describing "going steady/puppy love" relationships declined dramatically during the late 1960s and throughout the 1970s, it should be noted that songs describing sexual encounters increased dramatically during the same decades. The reasons are obvious. Prior taboos about overt references to intimate relations between the sexes were challenged during the 1960s and overthrown by the Woodstock generation. Similarly, the success of women's liberation contributed to greater social independence for females and generated more candid commentaries about working and playing interactions between men and women. Scientific advancements in birth control devices also liberalized sexual encounters by decreasing fears of unwanted pregnancies. It is particularly interesting to note that earthy lyrics from R&B music sources, once subject to sanitizing, sterilizing, and bowdlerizing in respect to sexual descriptions and innuendoes, are now translated directly as "crossover hits" into the pop, country and rock realms. Finally, heavy metal bands, which often present bizarre sexual fantasies in their lyrics, have become a staple of the 1980s youth culture.

The majority of sexual activity references in fifties songs were oblique, metaphorical, and only mildly suggestive. This trend extended into the sixties until The Rolling Stones, The Animals, and a variety of extremely popular black soul singers began to launch more overt sexual images. Typical commentaries on imagined or intended interactions in the more restrained pre-1965 period include "After The Lights Go Down Low" (1956), "Blueberry Hill" (1956), "Party Doll" (1957), "Chantilly Lace" (1958), "One Night" (1958), "Wiggle Wiggle" (1958), "You Got What It Takes" (1959), "Multiplication" (1961), "Lipstick Traces (On A Cigarette)" (1962), and "Let's Lock The Door (And Throw Away The Key)" (1964). The minority of overtly sexual recordings during the same period can be illustrated by tunes such as "Sixty Minute Man" (1951), "Sexy Ways" (1954), "Shake, Rattle And Roll" (1954), "Such A Night" (1954), "TV Mama" (1954), and "Work With Me Annie" (1954).

Post–British invasion lyrics demystified sex. Olivia Newton-John condemned small talk in favor of getting "Physical" (1981); Maria Muldaur shamelessly described her wild exploits in "Midnight At The Oasis" (1974); AC/DC proclaimed, in mock sexual exhaustion, "You Shook Me All Night Long" (1980); Marvin Gaye pledged "Let's Get It On" (1973) and requested "Sexual Healing" (1982); and while Tony Tennille proclaimed "You Never Done It Like That" (1978), The Rolling Stones challenged girls to "Start Me Up" (1981) and Bob Seger extolled the unabashed joy of "The Horizontal Bop" (1980). Other highly suggestive recordings of the past twenty years include "In The Midnight Hour" (1965), "Something You Got" (1965), "Let's Spend The Night Together" (1967), "Light My Fire" (1967), "Love Me Two Times" (1967), "Sunshine Of Your Love" (1968), "Touch Me" (1968), "Tonight I'll Be Staying Here With You" (1969), "Whole Lotta Love" (1969), "Make It With You" (1970), "Love Her Madly" (1971), "Reelin' And Rockin'" (1972), "Pillow Talk" (1973), "Can't Get Enough" (1974), "Love To Love You Baby" (1975), "You Sexy Thing" (1975), "Tonight's The Night (Gonna Be Alright)" (1976), "Fire" (1978), "Sharing The Night Together" (1978), "Do That To Me One More Time" (1979), "Ring My Bell" (1979), "Urgent" (1981), "Jack And Diane" (1982), "Make A Move On Me" (1982), "Action" (1983), "Cold Blooded" (1983), "Get It Right" (1983), and "Love Don't Know A Lady (From A Honky Tonk Girl)" (1983).

If there was Olympic competition to determine champions of sexual prowess, physical attractiveness, and social self-confidence, contemporary songs could suggest a huge field of lyrical male and female participants. The women who are depicted as erogenous dynamos in modern recordings are "Long Tall Sally" (1956), "Good Golly, Miss Molly" (1958), "Big Leg Woman (With A Short, Short Mini Skirt)" (1970), "Maggie May" (1971), "Hot Legs" (1978), "My Sharona" (1979), "She's A Bad Mama Jama (She's Built, She's Stacked)" (1981), "Super Freak" (1981), "Ms. Fine Brown Frame" (1982), "Gloria" (1983), "Ms. Got-The-Body" (1983), "(She's) Sexy + 17" (1983), and "Swing That Sexy Thang" (1983). The male counterparts of these sexy mamas are described in "Handy Man" (1959), "Lee Cross" (1967), "Steamroller Blues" (1973), "Da Ya Think I'm Sexy?" (1978), "Hot Blooded" (1978), "Hot Stuff" (1979), "Slow Hand" (1981), and "Candy Man" (1983).

Although the sexual Olympic competition idea may seem absurd, there is a strong strain of impersonalized sexual athletics depicted in modern lyrics. In several songs, it appears that sex has very little to do with establishing or sustaining personal relationships. These casual sex scenarios are depicted in "Son-Of-A-Preacher Man" (1968), "All Right Now" (1970), "One Night Stand" (1971), "Spiders And Snakes" (1973), "Chevy Van" (1975), "Afternoon Delight" (1976), "Night Moves" (1976), "Paradise By The Dashboard Light" (1978), "We've Got Tonight" (1978), "Shakedown Cruise" (1979), "A Different Woman Every Night" (1983), and "Private Party" (1983). Of course, there must be mutual agreement to allow this kind of noncommital sexual activity. That is, since it is neither rape nor prostitution, the persistence of random sexual encounters demands the kind of cooperation conveyed in "You Don't Have To Say You Love Me"(1966), "Angel Of The Morning" (1968), "Until It's Time For You To Go" (1970), "Help Me Make It Through The Night" (1971), "Only The Good Die Young" (1978), "Do You Wanna Touch Me (Oh Yeah)" (1982), "Should I Do It" (1982), "The Woman In Me" (1982), and "Girls Just Want To Have Fun" (1983). There are a few songs that openly proclaim "It's Your Thing" (1969) so do what you want to do, but there are seldom recordings that respond "No" (1972) to proposals such as "Let's Spend The Night Together" (1967) or "Let's Pretend We're Married" (1983). Some authentically independent responses include "Will You Love Me Tomorrow" (1960), "Don't Touch Me" (1969), and the desire not to become just "Another Motel Memory" (1983).

Other recordings address more complex aspects of human sexual behavior. Extramarital relations are examined in "Ruby, Don't Take Your Love To Town" (1969), "Steppin' Out" (1976), "The Other Woman" (1982), "Don't Cheat In Your Hometown" (1983), "The Name Of The Game Is Cheating" (1983), and "Stranger In My House" (1983); prostitution (examined elsewhere in this book) is illustrated recently in "Backstreet Ballet" (1983) and "I'm Alive" (1983); fear of contracting venereal disease is depicted in "You Ain't Seen Nothing Yet" (1974); birth control is the theme in "The Pill" (1975); and children born out of wedlock are mentioned in "Love Child" (1968), "Gypsies, Tramps, and Thieves" (1971), "(You're) Having My Baby" (1974), and "Unwed Fathers" (1983). Clearly, the sexual revolution of the past quarter century is mirrored in popular lyrics.

Earlier in this section the pattern of fantasizing, establishing, enriching, and terminating male-female relationships was described as a recurring behavioral cycle. This is obviously an oversimplified approach to human interaction. In many cases, of course, dating leads to engagement, marriage, and family life. But for those who lose loved ones, there are deeply emotional periods of loneliness and feelings of personal rejection. Just as popular songs celebrate the development of personal relations, they also document the sadness of dissolving them.

The process of terminating a relationship is described from varying perspectives in popular recordings. Tommy Edwards noted that vacillating personal feelings are common; "It's All In The Game" (1958), he observes. Similar attitudes are voiced in "Build Me Up Buttercup" (1969) and "Break Up To Make Up" (1973). Sometimes one member of a couple sense unspoken tensions and elects to confront the problem directly. This approach appears in "Break-Up" (1958), "Breaking Up Is Hard To Do" (1962), "You Don't Bring Me Flowers" (1978), "Any Day Now" (1982), and "Break It To Me Gently" (1982). Rather than seeking to sustain a failing relationship, though, some individuals feel trapped by an overpossessive lover and simply want their freedom. This attitude is expressed in "Let Me Go Lover" (1954), "Take These Chains From My Heart" (1963), and "Release Me (And Let Me Love Again)" (1967). Unfortunately, honesty doesn't always prevail when personal relationships begin to collapse. While one partner may bemoan the dishonesty of the other, lying, cheating, sneaking around, and emotional hardening often typify the behavior of a disenchanted partner. Recordings that provide examples of these activities are "Hearts Of Stone" (1954), "It's Only Make Believe" (1958), "I Know (You Don't Love Me No More)" (1961), "It's My Party" (1963), "Lies" (1965) "(I Know) I'm Losing You" (1966), "Head Games" (1979), "Stop Draggin' My Heart Around" (1981), "Don't You Want Me" (1982), "Lies" (1983), and "Stop In The Name Of Love" (1983). In spite of this type of behavior, some individuals continue to vow allegiance to even a wandering loved one. They beg their partner "Don't Be Cruel" (1956) to a heart that's true and declare that they "Ain't Too Proud To Beg" (1974) to retain a loving relationship. Other recordings that illustrate this situation are "The Great Pretender" (1955), "Love Me" (1956), "I Can't Stop Loving You" (1958), "Forty Days" (1959), "He'll Have To Go" (1959), "Mr. Blue" (1959), "He Will Break Your Heart" (1960), "So Sad (To Watch Good Love Go Bad)" (1960), "I'm A Fool To Care" (1961), "Too Bad" (1962), "You've Lost That Lovin' Feelin'" (1964), "If You've Got A Heart" (1965), "The Thrill Is Gone" (1969), "Don't Pull Your Love/Then You Can Tell Me Goodbye" (1976), "Piece Of My Heart" (1982), and "I Still Can't Get Over Loving You" (1983).

Heartbreak and loneliness over a lost lover is a universal theme in contemporary music. The recordings illustrating this situation are too numerous to mention here. Selected examples include "Heartbreak Hotel" (1956), "I Was The One" (1956), "Gone" (1957), "Since I Don't Have You" (1959), "Lonely Weekends" (1960), "Don't Get Around Much Anymore" (1961), "You Don't Know What You've Got (Until You Lose It)" (1961), "All Alone Am I" (1962), "Lover Please" (1962), "Hurt So Bad" (1965), "Yesterday" (1965), "Bang Bang (My Baby Shot Me Down)" (1966), "Cry Like A Baby" (1968), "I'll Never Fall In Love Again" (1969), "Yester-Me, Yester-You, Yesterday" (1969), "Can't Get Over Losing You" (1970), "Ain't No Sunshine" (1971), "I Can't Stand The Rain" (1978), "Ain't That A Shame" (1979), "Crying" (1981), "96 Tears" (1981), "Tryin' To Live My Life Without You" (1981), "I Fall To Pieces" (1982), "Always Something There To Remind Me" (1983), "Cuts Like A Knife" (1983), and "Singing The Blues" (1983).

Those who have suffered heartaches seem to be divided into two polarized categories. One group seems dejected and self-deprecating; the other remains self-confident and angry over the thoughtless behavior of a former friend and lover. Recordings that chronicle the feelings of depressed individuals include "Are You Lonesome Tonight?" (1960), "I Want To Be

Wanted" (1960), "Born To Lose" (1962), "(I Was) Born To Cry" (1962), "I'm So Lonesome I Could Cry" (1962), "Another Saturday Night" (1963), "Whoever Finds This, I Love You" (1970), and "When Will I Be Loved" (1975). But the dominant—and occasionally cynical or vindictive—position of a person who refuses to blame himself or herself for the collapse of a romance is much more intriguing. Songs depicting this position include "I Hear You Knocking" (1955), "Gonna Get Along Without You Now" (1956), "Goody Goody" (1957), "Who's Sorry Now" (1958), "I Wanna Be Around" (1963), "Tired Of Waiting For You" (1965), "You Can Have Her" (1965), "Cry Me A River" (1970), "Solitary Man" (1970), "Funny How Time Slips Away" (1982), and "What's New" (1983).

PERSONAL RELATIONSHIPS, LOVE, AND SEXUALITY

Dreams and Fantasy Relationships

"All I Have To Do Is Dream" (RSO 1065)
    by Andy Gibb and Victoria Principal (1981)

"Angel Baby" (Highland 1011)
    by Rosie and The Originals (1960)

"Angels In The Sky" (Mercury 70741)
    by The Crew-Cuts (1955)

"Be My Lady" (Grunt 13350)
    by Jefferson Starship (1982)

"Can't Take My Eyes Off You" (Philips 40446)
    by Frankie Valli (1967)

"Church Bells May Ring" (Melba 102)
    by The Willows (1956)

"Confidential" (Dot 15507)
    by Sonny Knight (1956)

"Crimson and Clover" (Boardwalk 144)
    by Joan Jett and The Blackhearts (1982)

"Cupid" (RCA 7883)
    by Sam Cooke (1961)

"Daydream Believer" (Capitol 4813)
    by Anne Murray (1979)

"Diana" (ABC-Paramount 9831)
    by Paul Anka (1957)

"Did You Ever Have To Make Up Your Mind?" (Kama Sutra 209)
    by The Lovin' Spoonful (1966)

"Don't Stand So Close To Me" (A&M 2301)
    by The Police (1981)

"Dream Baby (How Long Must I Dream)" (Columbia 03926)
  by Lacy J. Dalton (1983)

"Dreamin' " (Scotti Brothers 02889)
  by John Schneider (1982)

"Dream Lover" (Atco 6140)
  by Bobby Darin (1959)

"Dream Maker" (AMI 1314)
  by Tommy Overstreet (1983)

"Earth Angel" (Dootone 348)
  by The Penguins (1954)

"Every Breath You Take" (A&M 2542)
  by The Police (1983)

"Every Little Thing She Does Is Magic" (A&M 2371)
  by The Police (1981)

"Everybody's Dream Girl" (Liberty 1496)
  by Dan Seals (1983)

"Fever" (King 4935)
  by Little Willie John (1956)

"The Girl From Ipanema" (Verve 10323)
  by Stan Getz and Astrud Gilberto (1964)

"Girl Watcher" (ABC 11094)
  by The O'Kaysions (1968)

"Goin' Out Of My Head" (DCP 1119)
  by Little Anthony and The Imperials (1964)

"Guess Who" (RCA 7469)
  by Jesse Belvin (1959)

"Gypsy Woman" (Umi 55240)
  by Brian Hyland (1970)

"I Get Ideas" (RCA Victor 4141)
  by Tony Martin (1951)

"I Want To Know What Love Is" (Atlantic 89596)
  by Foreigner (1984)

"If I Were Your Woman" (Soul 35078)
  by Gladys Knight and The Pips (1970)

"Imaginary Lover" (Polydor 14459)
  by The Atlanta Rhythm Section (1978)

"It's Raining Men" (Columbia 03354)
  by The Weather Girls (1983)

"I've Made Love To You A Thousand Times" (Tamla 1655)
  by Smokey Robinson (1983)

"Jessie's Girl" (RCA 12201)
  by Rick Springfield (1981)

"Just A Dream" (Ace 546)
by Jimmy Clanton (1958)

"Kansas City" (Fury 1023)
by Wilbert Harrison (1959)

"(Love Is Like A) Baseball Game" (Gamble 217)
by The Intruders (1968)

"Love Potion No. 9" (United Artists 180)
by The Clovers (1959)

"Mister Sandman" (Warner Brothers 49684)
by Emmylou Harris (1981)

"My Eyes Adored You" (Private Stock 45003)
by Frankie Valli (1974)

"Never Had A Dream Come True" (Tamla 54191)
by Stevie Wonder (1970)

"Oh, Pretty Woman" (Monument 851)
by Roy Orbison (1964)

"Our Day Will Come" (Kapp 501)
by Ruby and The Romantics (1963)

"Pictures Of Lily" (Decca 32156)
by The Who (1967)

"Scarlet Fever" (Liberty 1503)
by Kenny Rogers (1983)

"Sea Of Love" (Mercury 71465)
by Phil Phillips (1959)

"Somebody's Baby" (Asylum 69982)
by Jackson Browne (1982)

"Standing On The Corner" (Columbia 40674)
by The Four Lads (1956)

"State Of Shock" (Epic 04503)
by The Jacksons (1984)

"A Sunday Kind Of Love" (Liberty 55397)
by Jan and Dean (1962)

"Sweet Dreams" (RCA 13533)
by The Eurythmics (1983)

"This Time" (A&M 2574)
by Bryan Adams (1983)

"Tonight" (Solar 69842)
by The Whispers (1983)

"The Way You Do The Things You Do" (Gordy 7028)
by The Temptations (1964)

"When You Wish Upon A Star" (Laurie 3052)
by Dion and The Belmonts (1960)

"You Are The One" (Mercury 812117)
by Con Funk Shun (1983)

"You Don't Know Me" (ABC-Paramount 10345)
by Ray Charles (1962)

Dating and Going Steady

"The ABC's Of Love" (Gee 1022)
by Frankie Lymon and The Teenagers (1956)

"Ain't No Mountain High Enough" (Motown 1169)
by Diana Ross (1970)

"Ain't No Woman (Like The One I've Got)" (Dunhill 4339)
by The Four Tops (1973)

"Ain't Nothing Like The Real Thing" (Tamla 54163)
by Marvin Gaye and Tammi Terrell (1968)

"All I Have To Do Is Dream" (Cadence 1348)
by The Everly Brothers (1958)

"All My Loving" (Capitol 72144)
by The Beatles (1964)

"All Night Long (All Night)" (Motown 1998)
by Lionel Richie (1983)

"All Shook Up" (RCA 47-6870)
by Elvis Presley (1957)

"All You Need Is Love" (Capitol 5964)
by The Beatles (1967)

"American Made" (MCA 52179)
by The Oak Ridge Boys (1983)

"And I Love Her" (Capitol 5235)
by The Beatles (1964)

"April Love" (Dot 15660)
by Pat Boone (1957)

"Arthur's Theme (Best That You Can Do)" (Warner Brothers 49787)
by Christopher Cross (1981)

"At My Front Door" (Vee-Jay 147)
by The El Dorados (1955)

"Baby Don't Get Hooked On Me" (Columbia 45618)
by Mac Davis (1972)

"Baby I Love You" (Atlantic 2427)
by Aretha Franklin (1967)

"Baby I'm-A Want You" (Elektra 45751)
by Bread (1971)

"Baby, I'm Yours" (Atlantic 2283)
by Barbara Lewis (1965)

"Baby It's Cold Outside" (ABC–Paramount 10298)
  by Ray Charles (1962)

"Baby It's You" (Scepter 1227)
  by The Shirelles (1961)

"Baby (You've Got What It Takes)" (Mercury 71565)
  by Brook Benton and Dinah Washington (1960)

"Back In My Arms Again" (Motown 1075)
  by The Supremes (1965)

"Bad Case Of Loving You (Doctor, Doctor)" (Island 49016)
  by Robert Palmer (1979)

"Barbara-Ann" (Gee 1065)
  by The Regents (1961)

"Be My Baby" (Philles 116)
  by The Ronettes (1963)

"Be Bop A Lula" (Capitol 3450)
  by Gene Vincent (1956)

"Be-Bop Baby" (Imperial 5463)
  by Ricky Nelson (1957)

"Beechwood 4-5789" (Tamla 54065)
  by The Marvelettes (1962)

"Best Of My Love" (Asylum 45218)
  by The Eagles (1974)

"Best Thing That Ever Happened To Me" (Buddah 403)
  by Gladys Knight and The Pips (1974)

"Bird Dog" (Cadence 1350)
  by The Everly Brothers (1958)

"Blue Velvet" (Epic 9614)
  by Bobby Vinton (1963)

"Bobbie Sue" (MCA 51231)
  by The Oak Ridge Boys (1982)

"Bony Moronie" (Specialty 615)
  by Larry Williams (1957)

"Boys" (Scepter 1211)
  by The Shirelles (1960)

"Brown Eyed Girl" (Bang 545)
  by Van Morrison (1967)

"Brown Eyed Woman" (MGM 13959)
  by Bill Medley (1968)

"Burning Love" (RCA 47-0769)
  by Elvis Presley (1972)

"But You Know I Love You" (Reprise 0799)
  by Kenny Rogers and The First Edition (1969)

"Butterfly" (Cameo 105)
  by Charlie Gracie (1957)

"Butterfly Baby" (Cameo 242)
  by Bobby Rydell (1963)

"Calendar Girl" (RCA 7829)
  by Neil Sedaka (1960)

"Can't You Hear My Heartbeat" (MGM 13310)
  by Herman's Hermits (1965)

"Chains" (Dimension 1002)
  by The Cookies (1962)

"Cherish" (Valiant 747)
  by The Association (1966)

"Chuck E.'s In Love" (Warner Brothers 8825)
  by Rickie Lee Jones (1979)

"Cindy, Oh Cindy" (Glory 247)
  by Vince Martin, with The Tarriers (1956)

"The Closer You Get" (RCA 13524)
  by Alabama (1983)

"Come Go With Me" (Dot 15538)
  by The Dell-Vikings (1957)

"Come Rain Or Come Shine" (Atlantic 2084)
  by Ray Charles (1960)

"Come Softly To Me" (Dolphin 1)
  by The Fleetwoods (1959)

"Could It Be I'm Falling In Love" (Atlantic 2927)
  by The Spinners (1972)

"Count Me In" (Liberty 55778)
  by Gary Lewis and The Playboys (1965)

"Cowboys To Girls" (Gamble 214)
  by The Intruders (1968)

"Crazy Little Thing Called Love" (Elektra 46579)
  by Queen (1979)

"Cupid" (Imperial 66087)
  by Johnny Rivers (1965)

"Cupid/I've Loved You For A Long Time" (Atlantic 3664)
  by The Spinners (1980)

"Da Doo Ron Ron (When He Walked Me Home)" (Philles 112)
  by The Crystals (1963)

"Dawn (Go Away)" (Philips 40166)
  by The Four Seasons (1964)

"Dede Dinah" (Chancellor 1011)
  by Frankie Avalon (1958)

"Dedicated To The One I Love" (Scepter 1203)
  by The Shirelles (1959)

"Devoted To You " (Cadence 1350)
  by The Everly Brothers (1958)

"Diamonds And Pearls" (Milestone 2003)
  by The Paradons (1960)

"Dim, Dim The Lights (I Want Some Atmosphere)" (Decca 29317)
  by Bill Haley and His Comets (1954)

"Do I Do" (Tamla 1612)
  by Stevie Wonder (1982)

"Donna" (Del-Fi 4110)
  by Ritchie Valens (1958)

"Don't Go Breaking My Heart" (Rocket 40585)
  by Elton John and Kiki Dee (1976)

"Don't Mess With Bill" (Tamla 54126)
  by The Marvelettes (1966)

"Don't Pull Your Love" (Dunhill 4276)
  by Hamilton, Joe Frank and Reynolds (1971)

"Don't You Know" (RCA 7591)
  by Della Reese (1959)

"Dream Baby (How Long Must I Dream)" (Monument 456)
  by Roy Orbison (1962)

"Dreamin' " (Liberty 55258)
  by Johnny Burnette (1960)

"Eddie My Love" (Cadence 1284)
  by The Chordettes (1956)

"Elvira" (MCA 51084)
  by The Oak Ridge Boys (1981)

"Endless Love" (Motown 1519)
  by Diana Ross and Lionel Richie (1981)

"Even Now" (Capitol 5213)
  by Bob Seger and The Silver Bullet Band (1983)

"Evergreen" (Columbia 10450)
  by Barbra Streisand (1976)

"Every Beat Of My Heart" (Vee-Jay 386)
  by Gladys Knight and The Pips (1961)

"Every Girl (Wants My Guy)" (Arista 9095)
  by Aretha Franklin (1983)

"(Every Time I Turn Around) Back In Love Again" (A&M 1974)
  by L.T.D. (1977)

"Everybody Needs Somebody To Love" (Atlantic 2381)
  by Wilson Pickett (1967)

"Fire And Ice" (Chrysalis 2529)
  by Pat Benatar (1981)

"First Date, First Kiss, First Love" (Capitol 3674)
  by Sonny James (1957)

"First Quarrel" (Philips 40114)
  by Paul and Paula (1963)

"The First Time Ever I Saw Your Face" (Atlantic 2864)
  by Roberta Flack (1972)

"A Fool In Love" (Sue 730)
  by Ike and Tina Turner (1960)

"Fooled Around And Fell In Love" (Capricorn 0252)
  by Elvin Bishop (1976)

"Foolish Little Girl" (Scepter 1248)
  by The Shirelles (1963)

"Fools Fall In Love" (Atlantic 1123)
  by The Drifters (1957)

"Fools Rush In" (Decca 31533)
  by Ricky Nelson (1963)

"For Once In My Life" (Tamla 54174)
  by Stevie Wonder (1968)

"For Your Precious Love" (United Artists 658)
  by Garnet Mims and The Enchanters (1963)

"Friendly Persuasion (Thee I Love)" (Dot 15490)
  by Pat Boone (1956)

"Friends In Love" (Arista 0672)
  by Johnny Mathis and Dionne Warwick (1982)

"Game Of Love" (Fontana 1509)
  by The Mindbenders (1965)

"Gentle On My Mind" (Capitol 5939)
  by Glen Campbell (1967)

"Gimme Little Sign" (Double Shot 116)
  by Brenton Wood (1967)

"Girl, You'll Be A Woman Soon" (Bang 542)
  by Neil Diamond (1967)

"Girls Girls Girls" (Atco 6204)
  by The Coasters (1961)

"Go Away Little Girl" (Columbia 42601)
  by Steve Lawrence (1962)

"Goin' Out Of My Head/Can't Take My Eyes Off You" (Capitol 2054)
  by The Lettermen (1967)

"Goin' Steady" (Capitol 3723)
  by Tommy Sands (1957)

"Got To Get You Into My Life" (Capitol 4274)
  by The Beatles (1976)

"Hang On Sloopy" (Bang 506)
  by The McCoys (1965)

"Hanky Panky" (Roulette 4686)
  by Tommy James and The Shondells (1966)

"Happy Birthday, Sweet Sixteen" (RCA 7957)
  by Neil Sedaka (1961)

"Happy Together" (White Whale 244)
  by The Turtles (1967)

"Hello Mary Lou" (Imperial 5741)
  by Ricky Nelson (1961)

"Help Me Rhonda" (Epic 50121)
  by Johnny Rivers (1975)

"He's Sure The Boy I Love" (Philles 109)
  by The Crystals (1962)

"Hey, Girl" (Colpix 692)
  by Freddie Scott (1963)

"Hey Little Girl" (Abner 1029)
  by Dee Clark (1959)

"High School Romance" (ABC-Paramount 9838)
  by George Hamilton IV (1957)

"Hold Me, Thrill Me, Kiss Me" (Imperial 66113)
  by Mel Carter (1965)

"Hold On, I'm Coming" (RCA 13580)
  by Waylon Jennings and Jerry Reed (1983)

"Honest I Do" (Vee-Day 253)
  by Jimmy Reed (1957)

"Honeycomb" (Roulette 4015)
  by Jimmie Rodgers (1957)

"Hopelessly Devoted To You" (RSO 903)
  by Olivia Newton-John (1978)

"How Do You Do It?" (Laurie 3261)
  by Gerry and The Pacemakers (1964)

"How Sweet It Is (To Be Loved By You)" (Warner Brothers 8109)
  by James Taylor (1975)

"A Hundred Pounds Of Clay" (Liberty 55308)
  by Gene McDaniels (1961)

"The Hunter Gets Captured By The Game" (Tamla 54143)
  by The Marvelettes (1967)

"I Can't Help Myself" (Motown 1076)
  by The Four Tops (1965)

"I Do'wanna Know" (Epic 04659)
by REO Speedwagon (1984)

"I Don't Know How To Love Him" (Decca 32785)
by Yvonne Elliman (1971)

"I Gotta Woman" (ABC-Paramount 10649)
by Ray Charles (1965)

"I Honestly Love You" (MCA 40280)
by Olivia Newton-John (1974)

"I Just Called To Say I Love You" (Motown 1745)
by Stevie Wonder (1984)

"I Just Fall In Love Again" (Capitol 4675)
by Anne Murray (1979)

"I Knew You When" (Asylum 69853)
by Linda Ronstadt (1982)

"I Love A Rainy Night" (Elektra 47066)
by Eddie Rabbitt (1980)

"I Love How You Love Me" (Gregmark 6)
by The Paris Sisters (1961)

"I Love My Baby (My Baby Loves Me)" (Columbia 40794)
by Jill Corey (1956)

"I Love The Way You Love" (United Artists 208)
by Marv Johnson (1960)

"I Loves You, Porgy" (Bethlehem 11021)
by Nina Simone (1959)

"I Met Him On A Sunday" (Decca 30588)
by The Shirelles (1958)

"I Need Your Loving" (Fire 508)
by Don Gardner and Dee Dee Ford (1962)

"I Never Loved A Man (The Way I Love You)" (Atlantic 2386)
by Aretha Franklin (1967)

"I Only Have Eyes For You" (End 1046)
by The Flamingos (1959)

"I Only Want To Be With You" (Warner Brothers 29948)
by Nicolette Larson (1982)

"I Really Don't Want To Know" (MGM 12890)
by Tommy Edwards (1960)

"I Saw Her Standing There" (Capitol 5112)
by The Beatles (1964)

"I Second That Emotion" (Tamla 54159)
by Smokey Robinson and The Miracles (1967)

"I Think I Love You" (Bell 910)
by The Partridge Family (1970)

"I Think We're Alone Now" (Roulette 4720)
by Tommy James and The Shondells (1967)

"I Want To Walk You Home" (Imperial 5606)
by Fats Domino (1959)

"I Want You, I Need You, I Love You" (RCA 47-6540)
by Elvis Presley (1956)

"I Want You To Be My Girl" (Gee 1012)
by Frankie Lymon and The Teenagers (1956)

"I Want You To Want Me" (Epic 50680)
by Cheap Trick (1979)

"I Was Made To Love Her" (Tamla 54151)
by Stevie Wonder (1967)

"I Wonder What She's Doing Tonite" (A&M 893)
by Tommy Boyce and Bobby Hart (1967)

"If I Could Build My Whole World Around You" (Tamla 54161)
by Marvin Gaye and Tammi Terrell (1967)

"If Not For You" (Uni 55281)
by Oliver Newton-John (1971)

"I'll Have To Say I Love You In A Song" (ABC 11424)
by Jim Croce (1974)

"I'll Never Love This Way Again" (Arista 0419)
by Dionne Warwick (1979)

"I'm A Hog For You" (Atco 6146)
by The Coasters (1959)

"I'm In The Mood For Love" (Tag 445)
by The Chimes (1961)

"I'm Into Something Good" (MGM 13280)
by Herman's Hermits (1964)

"I'm Just Too Shy" (Motown 1525)
by Jermaine Jackson (1981)

"I'm Stickin' With You" (Roulette 4001)
by Jimmy Bowen (1957)

"I've Got Love On My Mind" (Capitol 4360)
by Natalie Cole (1977)

"I've Got To Use My Imagination" (Buddah 393)
by Gladys Knight and The Pips (1973)

"I've Told Every Little Star" (Canadian American 123)
by Linda Scott (1961)

"Irresistable You" (Atco 6214)
by Bobby Darin (1961)

"Islands In The Stream" (RCA 13615)
by Kenny Rogers, with Dolly Parton (1983)

"It Takes Two" (Tamla 54141)
by Marvin Gaye and Kim Weston (1967)

"It's All In The Game" (MGM 12688)
by Tommy Edwards (1958)

"It's Just A Matter Of Time" (Mercury 71394)
by Brook Benton (1959)

"It's Late" (Imperial 5565)
by Ricky Nelson (1959)

"It's So Easy" (Asylum 45438)
by Linda Ronstadt (1977)

"Johnny One Time" (Decca 32428)
by Brenda Lee (1969)

"Judy's Turn To Cry" (Mercury 72143)
by Lesley Gore (1963)

"Juke Box Baby" (RCA 6427)
by Perry Como (1956)

"(Just Like) Romeo And Juliet" (Golden World 9)
by The Reflections (1964)

"Just One Look" (Atlantic 2188)
by Doris Troy (1963)

"Just The Two Of Us" (Elektra 47103)
by Grover Washington, Jr. (1981)

"Ka-Ding-Dong" (Mercury 70934)
by The Diamonds (1956)

"Kiss An Angel Good Morning" (RCA 0550)
by Charley Pride (1971)

"Kissin' On The Phone" (ABC-Paramount 10239)
by Paul Anka (1961)

"Knock Three Times" (Bell 938)
by Dawn (1970)

"Lady (You Bring Me Up)" (Motown 1514)
by The Commodores (1981)

"Last Kiss" (Josie 923)
by J. Frank Wilson and The Cavaliers (1964)

"Let It Be Me" (Vee-Jay 613)
by Jerry Butler and Betty Everett (1964)

"Let My Love Open The Door" (Atco 7217)
by Pete Townshend (1980)

"Let's Go Steady Again" (RCA 8169)
by Neil Sedaka (1963)

"Let's Hang On" (Arista 0675)
by Barry Manilow (1982)

"Let's Stay Together" (Capitol 5322)
  by Tina Turner (1983)

"Lightnin' Strikes" (MGM 13412)
  by Lou Christie (1965)

"Lipstick On Your Collar" (MGM 12793)
  by Connie Francis (1959)

"Little Bitty Pretty One" (Aladdin 3398)
  by Thurston Harris (1957)

"Lollipop" (Cadence 1345)
  by The Chordettes (1958)

"Lonely Teenager" (Laurie 3070)
  by Dion (1960)

"Lotta Lovin' " (Capitol 3763)
  by Gene Vincent (1957)

"Love Came To Me" (Laurie 3145)
  by Dion (1962)

"Love Eyes" (Reprise 0559)
  by Nancy Sinatra (1967)

"Love Is A Many-Splendored Thing" (Decca 29625)
  by The Four Aces (1955)

"Love Is Alive" (Warner Brothers 8143)
  by Gary Wright (1976)

"Love Is Like An Itching In My Heart" (Motown 1094)
  by The Supremes (1966)

"Love Is Strange" (Groove 0175)
  by Mickey and Sylvia (1957)

"(Love Is) The Tender Trap" (Capitol 3290)
  by Frank Sinatra (1955)

"Love Letters In The Sand" (Dot 15570)
  by Pat Boone (1957)

"Love, Love, Love" (Atlantic 1094)
  by The Clovers (1956)

"Love Me Do" (Tollie 9008)
  by The Beatles (1964)

"Love Me Tender" (RCA 47-6643)
  by Elvis Presley (1956)

"Love Will Find A Way" (A&M 2048)
  by Pablo Cruise (1978)

"Love Will Keep Us Together" (A&M 1672)
  by Captain and Tennille (1975)

"Love You So" (Donna 1315)
  by Ron Holden (1960)

"Love's Been A Little Bit Hard On Me" (Capitol 5120)
by Juice Newton (1982)

"A Lover's Concerto" (Dynovoice 209)
by The Toys (1965)

"A Lover's Question" (Atlantic 1199)
by Clyde McPhatter (1958)

"Lovers Never Say Goodbye" (End 1035)
by The Flamingos (1959)

"Lovey Dovey" (Liberty 55290)
by Buddy Knox (1960)

"Loving You" (RCA 47-7000)
by Elvis Presley (1957)

"Luanne" (Atlantic 4072)
by Foreigner (1982)

"Lucille (You Won't Do Your Daddy's Will)" (RCA 13465)
by Waylon Jennings (1983)

"The Main Event/Fight" (Columbia 11008)
by Barbra Streisand (1979)

"Mama Didn't Lie" (Chess 1845)
by Jan Bradley (1963)

"Mama Said" (Scepter 1217)
by The Shirelles (1961)

"Maybe I'm Amazed" (Capitol 4385)
by Paul McCartney (1977)

"Melody Of Love" (Decca 29395)
by The Four Aces (1955)

"Memories Are Made Of This" (Dot 15436)
by Gale Storm (1955)

"Michelle" (Capitol 5563)
by David and Jonathan (1966)

"Mickey" (Chrysalis 2638)
by Toni Basil (1982)

"Mission Bell" (Era 3018)
by Donnie Brooks (1960)

"Mixed-Up, Shook-Up Girl" (Herald 590)
by Patty and The Emblems (1964)

"More Love" (Tamla 54152)
by Smokey Robinson and The Miracles (1967)

"Mountain Of Love" (Imperial 66075)
by Johnny Rivers (1964)

"Mr. Blue" (Dolton 5)
by The Fleetwoods (1959)

"Mrs. Brown You've Got A Lovely Daughter" (MGM 13341)
   by Herman's Hermits (1965)

"My Babe" (Moonglow 223)
   by The Righteous Brothers (1963)

"My Bonnie Lassie" (RCA 6208)
   by The Ames Brothers (1955)

"My Cherie Amour" (Tamla 54180)
   by Stevie Wonder (1969)

"My Girl" (Gordy 7038)
   by The Temptations (1965)

"My Guy" (Cotillion 47000)
   by Sister Sledge (1982)

"My Guy/My Girl" (Handshake 5300)
   by Amii Stewart and Johnny Bristol (1980)

"My Heart Belongs To Only You" (Epic 9662)
   by Bobby Vinton (1964)

"My Love Song" (Capitol 3690)
   by Tommy Sands (1957)

"My Man" (Columbia 43323)
   by Barbra Streisand (1965)

"My Pledge Of Love" (Wand 11200)
   by The Joe Jeffrey Group (1969)

"My Special Angel" (Decca 30423)
   by Bobby Helms (1957)

"My True Love" (Carlton 462)
   by Jack Scott (1958)

"Never Ending Song Of Love" (Atco 6804)
   by Delaney and Bonnie (1971)

"Never Knew Love Like This Before" (20th Century 2460)
   by Stephanie Mills (1980)

"Never My Love" (Warner Brothers 7074)
   by The Association (1967)

"The New Girl In School" (Liberty 55672)
   by Jan and Dean (1964)

"Next Door To An Angel" (RCA 8086)
   by Neil Sedaka (1962)

"Nice To Be With You" (Sussex 232)
   by Gallery (1972)

"No, Not Much" (Columbia 40629)
   by The Four Lads (1956)

"Nobody But You" (Abner 1019)
   by Dee Clark (1958)

"Oh Julie" (Nasco 6005)
by The Crescendos (1958)

"(Oh) Pretty Woman" (Warner Brothers 50003)
by Van Halen (1982)

"One Of A Kind (Love Affair)" (Atlantic 2962)
by The Spinners (1973)

"One Of These Nights" (Asylum 45257)
by The Eagles (1975)

"One To One" (Atlantic 4026)
by Carole King (1982)

"1-2-3" (Decca 31827)
by Len Barry (1965)

"The One Who Really Loves You" (Motown 1024)
by Mary Wells (1962)

"Only Sixteen" (Keen 2022)
by Sam Cooke (1959)

"Only You" (Apple 1876)
by Ringo Starr (1974)

"Only You Know And I Know" (Atco 6838)
by Delaney and Bonnie (1971)

"Peaceful Easy Feeling" (Asylum 11013)
by The Eagles (1972)

"Playboy" (Tamla 54060)
by The Marvelettes (1962)

"Pledging My Love" (Duke 136)
by Johnny Ace (1955)

"Poetry In Motion" (Cadence 1384)
by Johnny Tillotson (1960)

"Poor Little Fool" (Imperial 5528)
by Ricky Nelson (1958)

"Portrait Of My Love" (United Artists 291)
by Steve Lawrence (1961)

"Potential New Boyfriend" (RCA 13514)
by Dolly Parton (1983)

"Pride and Joy" (Tamla 54079)
by Marvin Gaye (1963)

"Problems" (Cadence 1355)
by The Everly Brothers (1958)

"P.S. I Love You" (Tollie 9008)
by The Beatles (1964)

"Puppy Love" (ABC-Paramount 10082)
by Paul Anka (1960)

"Puppy Love" (Atlantic 2214)
by Barbara Lewis (1964)

"Push Push" (Laurie 3067)
by Austin Taylor (1960)

"Put Your Head On My Shoulder" (Atlantic 3466)
by Leif Garrett (1978)

"P.Y.T. (Pretty Young Thing)" (Epic 04165)
by Michael Jackson (1983)

"Rama Lama Ding Dong" (Twin 700)
by The Edsels (1961)

"Reach Out (I'll Be There)" (Atlantic 89858)
by Narada Michael Walden (1983)

"Reet Petite (The Finest Girl You Ever Want To Meet)" (Brunswick 55024)
by Jackie Wilson (1957)

"Reunited" (Polydor 14547)
by Peaches and Herb (1979)

"Rich Girl" (RCA 10860)
by Daryl Hall and John Oates (1977)

"River Deep—Mountain High" (Philles 131)
by Ike and Tina Turner (1966)

"A Rockin' Good Way (To Mess Around And Fall In Love)" (Mercury 71629)
by Brook Benton and Dinah Washington (1960)

"Rosanna" (Columbia 02811)
by Toto (1982)

"A Rose And A Baby Ruth" (ABC-Paramount 9765)
by George Hamilton IV (1956)

"Roses Are Red (My Love)" (Epic 9509)
by Bobby Vinton (1962)

"Running Bear" (Mercury 71474)
by Johnny Preston (1959)

"Saturday Night At The Movies" (Atlantic 2260)
by The Drifters (1964)

"Save The Last Dance For Me" (RCA 13703)
by Dolly Parton (1983)

"Say You Do" (A&M 2545)
by Janet Jackson (1983)

"Sea Cruise" (Ace 554)
by Frankie Ford (1959)

"Sea Of Love" (Esparanza 99701)
by The Honeydrippers (1984)

"She Loves You" (Swan 4152)
by The Beatles (1964)

"She Was Only Seventeen (He Was One Year More)" (Columbia 41208)
  by Marty Robbins (1958)

"She's Got Everything" (Roulette 4530)
  by Essex (1963)

"Sherry" (Vee-Jay 456)
  by The Four Seasons (1962)

"The Shoop Shoop Song (It's In His Kiss)" (Vee-Jay 585)
  by Betty Everett (1964)

"Shot Full Of Love" (Liberty 1499)
  by The Nitty Gritty Dirt Band (1983)

"Should I Do It" (Planet 47960)
  by The Pointer Sisters (1982)

"Should I Stay Or Should I Go?" (Epic 03547)
  by The Clash (1983)

"Signed, Sealed, Delivered I'm Yours" (Tamla 54196)
  by Stevie Wonder (1970)

"Silly Love Songs" (Capitol 4256)
  by Paul McCartney (1976)

"Since I Met You Baby" (Atlantic 1111)
  by Ivory Joe Hunter (1956)

"Sittin' In The Balcony" (Liberty 55056)
  by Eddie Cochran (1957)

"16 Candles" (Coed 506)
  by The Crests (1958)

"Skinny Minnie" (Decca 30592)
  by Bill Haley and His Comets (1958)

"So Fine" (Old Town 1062)
  by The Fiestas (1959)

"So Much In Love" (Parkway 871)
  by The Tymes (1963)

"So Tough" (Challenge 1013)
  by The Kuf-Linx (1958)

"Somebody To Love" (RCA 9140)
  by Jefferson Airplane (1967)

"Someday Soon" (Elektra 45649)
  by Judy Collins (1969)

"Someday We'll Be Together" (Motown 1156)
  by Diana Ross and The Supremes (1969)

"Someone Could Lose A Heart Tonight" (Elektra 47239)
  by Eddie Rabbitt (1981)

"Somethin' 'Bout You Baby I Like" (Capitol 4865)
  by Glen Campbell and Rita Coolidge (1980)

"Somethin' Else" (Liberty 55203)
  by Eddie Cochran (1959)

"Something" (Apple 2654)
  by The Beatles (1969)

"Sometimes When We Touch" (20th Century 2355)
  by Dan Hill (1977)

"Southern Nights" (Capitol 4376)
  by Glen Campbell (1977)

"Spiders and Snakes" (MGM 14648)
  by Jim Stafford (1973)

"Stairway To Heaven" (RCA 7709)
  by Neil Sedaka (1960)

"Start Movin' (In My Direction)" (Epic 9216)
  by Sal Mineo (1957)

"Still" (Motown 1474)
  by The Commodores (1979)

"Still The One" (Asylum 45336)
  by Orleans (1976)

"Stop Doggin' Me Around" (MCA 52250)
  by Klique (1983)

"Stop! In The Name Of Love" (Motown 1074)
  by The Supremes (1965)

"String Along" (Decca 31495)
  by Ricky Nelson (1963)

"Sunny" (Philips 40365)
  by Bobby Hebb (1966)

"Sweet Caroline (Good Times Never Seemed So Good)" (Uni 55136)
  by Neil Diamond (1969)

"Sweet Little Sixteen" (Chess 1683)
  by Chuck Berry (1958)

"Sweet Nothin's" (Decca 30967)
  by Brenda Lee (1959)

"Sylvia's Mother" (Columbia 45562)
  by Dr. Hook (1972)

"Take Me To Heart" (Geffen 29603)
  by Quarterflash (1983)

"Take Me To The River" (Sire 1032)
  by Talking Heads (1978)

"Tall Paul" (Disneyland 118)
  by Annette (1959)

"Tallahassee Lassie" (Swan 4031)
  by Freddy Cannon (1959)

"Teen-Age Crush" (Capitol 3639)
by Tommy Sands (1957)

"Teen-Age Doll" (Capitol 3953)
by Tommy Sands (1958)

"Teen Age Goodnight" (Cadence 1299)
by The Chordettes (1956)

"Teen Age Prayer" (Dot 15436)
by Gale Storm (1955)

"Teen Angel" (MGM 12845)
by Mark Dinning (1959)

"A Teenager In Love" (Laurie 3027)
by Dion and The Belmonts (1959)

"A Teenager's Romance" (Verve 10047)
by Ricky Nelson (1957)

"Tell Her No" (Capitol 5265)
by Juice Newton (1983)

"Tell Laura I Love Her" (RCA 7745)
by Ray Peterson (1960)

"Ten Commandments Of Love" (Chess 1705)
by Harvey and The Moonglows (1958)

"That Girl" (Tamla 1602)
by Stevie Wonder (1982)

"That's How Strong My Love Is" (Volt 124)
by Otis Redding (1965)

"Then He Kissed Me" (Philles 115)
by The Crystals (1963)

"Then You Can Tell Me Goodbye" (Fraternity 977)
by The Casinos (1967)

"There! I've Said It Again" (Epic 9638)
by Bobby Vinton (1963)

"There's No Other (Like My Baby)" (Philles 100)
by The Crystals (1961)

"This Girl's In Love With You" (Scepter 12241)
by Dionne Warwick (1969)

"This Guy's In Love With You" (A&M 929)
by Herb Alpert (1968)

"This Magic Moment" (United Artists 50475)
by Jay and The Americans (1968)

"Three Times A Lady" (Motown 1443)
by The Commodores (1978)

"('Til) I Kissed You" (Cadence 1369)
by The Everly Brothers (1959)

"To Be Loved" (Brunswick 55052)
by Jackie Wilson (1958)

"To Be Loved (Forever)" (Donna 1337)
by The Pentagons (1961)

"To Know Him, Is To Love Him" (Dore 503)
by The Teddy Bears (1958)

"To The Aisle" (Ember 1019)
by The Five Satins (1957)

"Tonight, I Celebrate My Love" (Capitol 5242)
by Peabo Bryson and Roberta Flack (1983)

"Tonight's The Night" (Scepter 1208)
by The Shirelles (1960)

"Tonite, Tonite" (Herald 502)
by The Mello-Kings (1957)

"Too Busy Thinking About My Baby" (Tamla 54181)
by Marvin Gaye (1969)

"Too Many Fish In The Sea" (Tamla 54105)
by The Marvelettes (1964)

"Too Much" (RCA 47-6800)
by Elvis Presley (1957)

"Too Young To Go Steady" (Mercury 70820)
by Patti Page (1956)

"Treasure Of Love" (Atlantic 1092)
by Clyde McPhatter (1956)

"True Love" (Capitol 3507)
by Bing Crosby and Grace Kelly (1956)

"Twixt Twelve and Twenty" (Dot 15955)
by Pat Boone (1959)

"Two Faces Have I" (Roulette 4481)
by Lou Christie (1963)

"Two Hearts" (Dot 15338)
by Pat Boone (1955)

"Two Lovers" (Motown 1035)
by Mary Wells (1962)

"Under The Moon Of Love" (Dunes 2008)
by Curtis Lee (1961)

"Up Front" (RCA 13624)
by Diana Ross (1983)

"Up On The Roof" (Atlantic 2162)
by The Drifters (1963)

"Upside Down" (Motown 1494)
by Diana Ross (1980)

"Venus" (Chancellor 1031)
 by Frankie Avalon (1959)

"Waitin' In School" (Imperial 5483)
 by Ricky Nelson (1957)

"Waiting For A Girl Like You" (Atlantic 3868)
 by Foreigner (1981)

"Wake Up Little Susie" (Cadence 1337)
 by The Everly Brothers (1957)

"Walk Right Back" (Warner Brothers 5199)
 by The Everly Brothers (1961)

"We Belong Together" (Old Town 1047)
 by Robert and Johnny (1958)

"We Got Love" (Cameo 169)
 by Bobby Rydell (1959)

"Wear My Ring" (Capitol 3763)
 by Gene Vincent (1957)

"Wear My Ring Around Your Neck" (RCA 47-7240)
 by Elvis Presley (1958)

"We're Doing Fine" (Blue Rock 4027)
 by Dee Dee Warwick (1965)

"What A Sweet Thing That Was" (Scepter 1220)
 by The Shirelles (1961)

"(What A) Wonderful World" (Columbia 10676)
 by Art Garfunkel, with James Taylor and Paul Simon (1978)

"What You Won't Do For Love" (Capitol 4826)
 by Natalie Cole and Peabo Bryson (1980)

"When I Fall In Love" (Capitol 4658)
 by The Lettermen (1961)

"When You're Young And In Love" (Tamla 54150)
 by The Marvelettes (1967)

"Where Or When" (Laurie 3044)
 by Dion and The Belmonts (1959)

"Where The Boys Are" (MGM 12971)
 by Connie Francis (1961)

"A White Sport Coat (And A Pink Carnation)" (Columbia 40864)
 by Marty Robbins (1957)

"Whole Lotta Loving" (Imperial 5553)
 by Fats Domino (1958)

"Why Do Fools Fall In Love" (RCA 12349)
 by Diana Ross (1981)

"Wild Thing" (Fontana 1548)
 by The Troggs (1966)

"Will You Love Me Tomorrow" (Scepter 1211)
   by The Shirelles (1960)

"Wisdom Of A Fool" (Capitol 3597)
   by The Five Keys (1956)

"Without Love (There Is Nothing)" (Atlantic 1117)
   by Clyde McPhatter (1957)

"Words And Music" (RCA 13684)
   by Tavares (1983)

"Working My Way Back To You" (Philips 40350)
   by The Four Seasons (1966)

"You And Me Against The World" (Capitol 3897)
   by Helen Reddy (1974)

"You Are The Sunshine Of My Life" (Tamla 54232)
   by Stevie Wonder (1973)

"You Belong To Me" (Warner Brothers 29552)
   by The Doobie Brothers (1983)

"You Can't Hurry Love" (Atlantic 89933)
   by Phil Collins (1982)

"You Don't Have To Be A Star (To Be In My Show)" (ABC 12208)
   by Marilyn McCoo and Billy Davis, Jr. (1976)

"You Got What It Takes" (United Artists 185)
   by Marv Johnson (1959)

"You Make My Dreams" (RCA 12217)
   by Daryl Hall and John Oates (1981)

"You Needed Me" (Capitol 4574)
   by Anne Murray (1978)

"You Really Got Me" (Reprise 0306)
   by The Kinks (1964)

"You Send Me" (Keen 34013)
   by Sam Cooke (1957)

"You're All I Need To Get By" (Tamla 54169)
   by Marvin Gaye and Tammi Terrell (1968)

"You're My Best Friend" (Elektra 45318)
   by Queen (1976)

"You're My Latest, My Greatest Inspiration" (Philadelphia International 02619)
   by Teddy Pendergrass (1982)

"(You're My) Soul And Inspiration" (Verve 10383)
   by The Righteous Brothers (1966)

"You're Sixteen" (Liberty 55285)
   by Johnny Burnette (1960)

"You're So Fine" (Unart 2013)
   by The Falcons (1959)

"You're The One That I Want" (RSO 891)
by Olivia Newton-John and John Travolta (1978)

"You're The Reason I'm Living" (Capitol 4897)
by Bobby Darin (1963)

"Young Love" (Capitol 3602)
by Sonny James (1956)

"Young World" (Imperial 5805)
by Ricky Nelson (1962)

"Younger Girl" (Kapp 752)
by The Critters (1966)

"(Your Love Has Lifted Me) Higher And Higher" (A&M 1922)
by Rita Coolidge (1977)

"Your Smiling Face" (Columbia 10602)
by James Taylor (1977)

"Your Song" (Uni 55265)
by Elton John (1970)

"You've Got A Friend" (Atlantic 2808)
by Roberta Flack and Donny Hathaway (1971)

"Yummy Yummy Yummy" (Buddah 38)
by The Ohio Express (1968)

Sexual Activity

"Action" (RCA 13682)
by Evelyn "Champagne" King (1983)

"After The Lights Go Down Low" (Decca 29982)
by Al Hibbler (1956)

"After The Lovin' " (Epic 50270)
by Engelbert Humperdinck (1976)

"Afternoon Delight" (Windsong 10588)
by The Starland Vocal Band (1976)

"All Day And All Of The Night" (Reprise 0334)
by The Kinks (1964)

"All Night Long" (Gordy 1690)
by The Mary Jane Girls (1983)

"All Right Now" (A&M 1206)
by Free (1970)

"Angel Of The Morning" (Bell 705)
by Merrilee Rush and The Turnabouts (1968)

"Another Motel Memory" (Viva 29461)
by Shelly West (1983)

"Baby Scratch My Back" (Excello 2273)
by Slim Harpo (1966)

"Back Door Man" (Bang 566)
   by Derek (1969)

"Backstreet Ballet" (Mercury 814360)
   by Savannah (1983)

"Bad Motor Scooter" (Larc 81023)
   by The Chi-Lites (1983)

"Big Leg Woman (With A Short Short Mini Skirt)" (Warren 106)
   by Isreal "Popper Stopper" Tolbert (1970)

"Blueberry Hill" (Imperial 5407)
   by Fats Domino (1956)

"Body Language" (Elektra 47452)
   by Queen (1982)

"Bread And Butter" (Motown 1664)
   by Robert John (1983)

"Calling All Girls" (Elektra 69981)
   by Queen (1982)

"Can't Get Enough" (Swan Song 70015)
   by Bad Company (1974)

"Candy Man" (Gordy 1670)
   by The Mary Jane Girls (1983)

"Chantilly Lace" (Mercury 71343)
   by The Big Bopper (1958)

"Cherry Hill Park" (Columbia 44902)
   by Billy Joe Royal (1969)

"Chevy Van" (GRC 2046)
   by Sammy Johns (1975)

"Cold Blooded" (Gordy 1687)
   by Rick James (1983)

"Come On Eileen" (Mercury 76189)
   by Dexys Midnight Runners (1983)

"Da Ya Think I'm Sexy?" (Warner Brothers 8724)
   by Rod Stewart (1978)

"December, 1963 (Oh, What A Night)" (Warner Brothers 8168)
   by The Four Seasons (1975)

"A Different Woman Every Night" (Kat Family 03562)
   by Bobby Springfield (1983)

"Dixieland Delight" (RCA 13446)
   by Alabama (1983)

"Do That To Me One More Time" (Casablanca 2215)
   by Captain and Tennille (1979)

"Do You Wanna Touch Me (Oh Yeah)" (Boardwalk 150)
   by Joan Jett and The Blackhearts (1982)

"Don't Cheat In Your Hometown" (Epic 04245)
by Ricky Scaggs (1983)

"Don't Stop Me Baby (I'm On Fire)" (Elektra 47406)
by The Boys Band (1982)

"Don't Touch Me" (Capitol 2382)
by Bettye Swann (1969)

"Double Shot (Of My Baby's Love)" (Smash 2033)
by The Swingin' Medallions (1966)

"Easy Lover" (Columbia 04679)
by Philip Bailey (1984)

"Feels Like The First Time" (Atlantic 3394)
by Foreigner (1977)

"Fire" (Planet 45901)
by The Pointer Sisters (1978)

"Foxy Lady (Funky Lady)" (Cotillion 45011)
by Slave (1980)

"Freak-A-Zoid" (Solar 69828)
by Midnight Star (1983)

"Get Closer" (Asylum 69948)
by Linda Ronstadt (1982)

"Get It Right" (Arista 9043)
by Aretha Franklin (1983)

"Gimme All Your Lovin' " (Warner Brothers 29683)
by Z Z Top (1983)

"Gimme Gimme Good Lovin' " (Bell 763)
by Crazy Elephant (1969)

"Girls Just Want To Have Fun" (Portrait 04120)
by Cyndi Lauper (1983)

"Gloria" (Elektra 69770)
by The Doors (1983)

"Gonna Go Huntin' Tonight" (Elektra 69846)
by Hank Williams, Jr. (1983)

"Good Girls Don't" (Capitol 4771)
by The Knack (1979)

"Good Golly, Miss Molly" (Specialty 624)
by Little Richard (1958)

"Gypsys, Tramps, and Thieves" (Kapp 2146)
by Cher (1971)

"Handy Man" (Cub 9049)
by Jimmy Jones (1959)

"Help Me Make It Through The Night" (Mega 0015)
by Sammi Smith (1971)

"He's A Heartache (Lookin' For A Place To Happen)" (Columbia 03899)
by Janie Fricke (1983)

"He's A Pretender" (Gordy 1662)
by High Inergy (1983)

"The Horizontal Bop" (Capitol 4951)
by Bob Seger and The Silver Bullet Band (1980)

"Hot Blooded" (Atlantic 3488)
by Foreigner (1978)

"Hot Girls In Love" (Columbia 03941)
by Loverboy (1983)

"Hot Legs" (Warner Brothers 8535)
by Rod Stewart (1978)

"Hot Stuff" (Casablanca 978)
by Donna Summer (1979)

"The House Of The Rising Sun" (RCA 12282)
by Dolly Parton (1981)

"Human Touch" (RCA 13576)
by Rick Springfield (1983)

"Hurts So Good" (Riva 209)
by John Cougar (1982)

"(I Am Ready) Sexual Healing" (Catawba 8000)
by Eleanor Grant (1983)

"(I Can't Get No) Satisfaction" (London 904)
by The Rolling Stones (1965)

"I Can't Turn You Loose" (Columbia 44679)
by The Chambers Brothers (1968)

"I Never Knew The Devil's Eyes Were Blue" (Handshake 02736)
by Terry Gregory (1982)

"I Recall A Gypsy Woman" (MCA 51151)
by B. J. Thomas (1981)

"I Thank The Lord For The Night Time" (Bang 547)
by Neil Diamond (1967)

"If You Love Me (Let Me Know)" (MCA 40209)
by Olivia Newton-John (1974)

"I'm Alive" (Columbia 03503)
by Neil Diamond (1983)

"I'm So Excited" (Planet 13327)
by The Pointer Sisters (1982)

"In The Midnight Hour" (Atlantic 2289)
by Wilson Pickett (1965)

"It's Your Thing" (T-Neck 901)
by The Isley Brothers (1969)

"Jack And Diane" (Riva 210)
  by John Cougar (1982)

"Jeans On" (Chrysalis 2094)
  by David Dundas (1977)

"Lay Down Sally" (RSO 886)
  by Eric Clapton (1978)

"Lay Lady Lay" (Columbia 44926)
  by Bob Dylan (1969)

"Leather And Lace" (Modern 7341)
  by Stevie Nicks, with Don Henley (1981)

"Lee Cross" (Columbia 44181)
  by Aretha Franklin (1967)

"Let's Get It On" (Tamla 54234)
  by Marvin Gaye (1973)

"Let's Lock The Door (And Throw Away The Key)" (United Artists 805)
  by Jay and The Americans (1964)

"Let's Pretend We're Married" (Warner Brothers 29548)
  by Prince (1983)

"Let's Spend The Night Together" (London 904)
  by The Rolling Stones (1967)

"Life In The Fast Lane" (Asylum 45403)
  by The Eagles (1977)

"Light My Fire" (Elektra 45615)
  by The Doors (1967)

"Like A Virgin" (Sire 29210)
  by Madonna (1984)

"Lipstick Traces (On A Cigarette)" (Minit 644)
  by Benny Spellman (1962)

"Long Tall Sally" (Specialty 572)
  by Little Richard (1956)

"Love Child" (Motown 1135)
  by Diana Ross and The Supremes (1968)

"Love Don't Know A Lady (From A Honky Tonk Girl)" (Soundwaves 4708)
  by Billy Parker and Friends (1983)

"Love Her Madly" (Elektra 45726)
  by The Doors (1971)

"Love Is In Control (Finger On The Trigger)" (Geffen 29982)
  by Donna Summer (1982)

"Love Me Tonight" (Parrot 40038)
  by Tom Jones (1969)

"Love Me Two Times" (Elektra 45624)
  by The Doors (1967)

"Love The One You're With" (T-Neck 930)
by The Isley Brothers (1971)

"Love The One You're With" (Atlantic 2778)
by Stephen Stills (1970)

"Love To Love You Baby" (Oasis 401)
by Donna Summer (1975)

"Lovin' Machine" (Little Darlin' 008)
by Johnny Paycheck (1966)

"Lovin', Touchin', Squeezin' " (Columbia 11036)
by Journey (1979)

"Maggie May" (Mercury 73224)
by Rod Stewart (1971)

"Make A Move On Me" (MCA 52000)
by Olivia Newton-John (1982)

"Make It With You" (Elektra 45686)
by Bread (1970)

"Makin' Love In The Fast Lane" (Larc 81014)
by Mellaa (1983)

"Midnight At The Oasis" (Reprise 1183)
by Maria Muldaur (1974)

"Ms. Fine Brown Frame" (Boardwalk 99904)
by Syl Johnson (1982)

"Ms. Got-The-Body" (Mercury 76198)
by Con Funk Shun (1983)

"Multiplication" (Atco 6214)
by Bobby Darin (1961)

"My Sharona" (Capitol 4731)
by The Knack (1979)

"The Name Of The Game Is Cheating" (Town House 1063)
by Charlie Ross (1983)

"Nasty Girl" (Warner Brothers 29908)
by Vanity 6 (1982)

"Nice Girls" (Arista 1045)
by Melissa Manchester (1983)

"The Night Dolly Parton Was Almost Mine" (CBS 03549)
by The Pump Boys and Dinettes (1983)

"Night Moves" (Capitol 4369)
by Bob Seger and The Silver Bullet Band (1976)

"No" (Decca 32996)
by Bulldog (1972)

"Now I'm A Woman" (Capitol 2934)
by Nancy Wilson (1971)

"On Target" (RCA 13619)
by The Jones Girls (1983)

"One Night" (RCA 47-7410)
by Elvis Presley (1958)

"One Night Stand" (Big Tree 109)
by The Magic Lanterns (1971)

"Only The Good Die Young" (Columbia 10750)
by Billy Joel (1978)

"The Other Woman" (Arista 0669)
by Ray Parker, Jr. (1982)

"Paradise By The Dashboard Light" (Epic 50588)
by Meatloaf (1978)

"Party Doll" (Roulette 4002)
by Buddy Knox (1957)

"The People Next Door" (Arista 1051)
by Ray Parker, Jr. (1983)

"Physical" (MCA 51182)
by Olivia Newton-John (1981)

"The Pill" (MCA 40358)
by Loretta Lynn (1975)

"Pillow Talk" (Vibration 521)
by Sylvia (1973)

"Private Party" (Motown 1695)
by Bobby Nunn (1983)

"Red Neckin', Love Makin' Night" (MCA 51019)
by Conway Twitty (1981)

"Reelin' and Rockin' " (Chess 2136)
by Chuck Berry (1972)

"Right Time Of The Night" (Arista 0223)
by Jennifer Warnes (1977)

"Ring My Bell" (Juana 3422)
by Anita Ward (1979)

"Road Runner" (Checker 942)
by Bo Diddley (1960)

"Ruby, Don't Take Your Love To Town" (Reprise 0829)
by Kenny Rogers (1969)

"Run To You" (A&M 2686)
by Bryan Adams (1984)

"Sexual Healing" (Columbia 03302)
by Marvin Gaye (1982)

"Sexy Mama" (Stang 5052)
by The Moments (1974)

"Sexy Ways" (Federal 12185)
   by The Midnighters (1954)

"Shake, Rattle And Roll" (Atlantic 1026)
   by Joe Turner (1954)

"Shakedown Cruise" (Asylum 46041)
   by Jay Ferguson (1979)

"Sharing The Night Together" (Capitol 4621)
   by Dr. Hook (1978)

"She Talks To Me With Her Body" (Mercury 810435)
   by The Bar-Kays (1983)

"She's A Bad Mama Jama (She's Built, She's Stacked)" (20th Century 2488)
   by Carl Carlton (1981)

"(She's) Sexy + 17" (EMI America 8168)
   by Stray Cats (1983)

"She's Tight" (Epic 03233)
   by Cheap Trick (1982)

"Should I Do It" (Planet 47960)
   by The Pointer Sisters (1982)

"Sixty Minute Man" (Federal 12022)
   by The Dominoes (1951)

"Slow Hand" (Planet 47929)
   by The Pointer Sisters (1981)

"Sneakin' Around" (Liberty 1427)
   by Kin Vassy (1981)

"Somebody's Knockin' " (MCA 41309)
   by Terri Gibbs (1981)

"Someone To Lay Down Beside Me" (Asylum 45361)
   by Linda Ronstadt (1976)

"Something You Got" (Wand 181)
   by Chuck Jackson and Maxine Brown (1965)

"Sometimes When We Touch" (Curb 49753)
   by Stephanie Winslow (1981)

"Son-Of-A-Preacher Man" (Atlantic 2580)
   by Dusty Springfield (1968)

"Southern Women" (Audiograph 470)
   by The Owen Brothers (1983)

"Spiders and Snakes" (MGM 14648)
   by Jim Stafford (1973)

"Start Me Up" (Rolling Stone 21003)
   by The Rolling Stones (1981)

"Steamroller Blues" (RCA 74-0815)
   by Elvis Presley (1973)

"Steppin' Out" (Rocket 40582)
 by Neil Sedaka (1976)

"Stranger In Her Bed" (RCA 13608)
 by Randy Parton (1983)

"Stranger In My House" (RCA 13470)
 by Ronnie Milsap (1983)

"Such A Night" (Atlantic 1019)
 by The Drifters (1954)

"Sunshine Of Your Love" (Atco 6544)
 by Cream (1968)

"Super Freak" (Gordy 7205)
 by Rick James (1981)

"Swing That Sexy Thang" (RCA 13406)
 by Carl Carlton (1983)

"Take It Easy" (Asylum 11005)
 by The Eagles (1972)

"Tell Me When I'm Hot" (Cee Cee 5400)
 by Billy "Crash" Craddock (1983)

"Third Rate Romance" (ABC 12078)
 by The Amazing Rhythm Aces (1975)

"This Girl Is A Woman Now" (Columbia 44967)
 by Gary Puckett and The Union Gap (1969)

"Tonight I'll Be Staying Here With You" (Columbia 45004)
 by Bob Dylan (1969)

"Tonight's The Night (Gonna Be Alright)" (Warner Brothers 8262)
 by Rod Stewart (1976)

"Touch Me" (Elektra 45646)
 by The Doors (1968)

"TV Mama" (Atlantic 1016)
 by Joe Turner (1954)

"Until It's Time For You To Go" (Uni 55204)
 by Neil Diamond (1970)

"Unwed Fathers" (Epic 03971)
 by Tammy Wynette (1983)

"Urgent" (Atlantic 3831)
 by Foreigner (1981)

"The Wanderer" (Laurie 3115)
 by Dion (1961)

"The Way He Makes Me Feel" (Columbia 04177)
 by Barbra Streisand (1983)

"Wet My Whistle" (Solar 69790)
 by Midnight Star (1983)

"We've Got Tonight" (Liberty 1492)
   by Kenny Rogers and Sheena Easton (1983)

"We've Got Tonight" (Capitol 4653)
   by Bob Seger and The Silver Bullet Band (1978)

"Whole Lotta Love" (Atlantic 2690)
   by Led Zeppelin (1969)

"Wiggle Wiggle" (Brunswick 55100)
   by The Accents (1958)

"Wild Girls" (Solar 69955)
   by Klymaxx (1982)

"Will You Love Me Tomorrow" (Scepter 1211)
   by The Shirelles (1960)

"The Woman In Me" (Geffen 29805)
   by Donna Summer (1982)

"The Woman In You" (RSO 813173)
   by The Bee Gees (1983)

"Work With Me Annie" (Federal 12169)
   by The Midnighters (1954)

"You Ain't Seen Nothing Yet" (Mercury 73622)
   by Bachman-Turner Overdrive (1974)

"You Don't Have To Say You Love Me" (Philips 40371)
   by Dusty Springfield (1966)

"You Got What It Takes" (United Artists 185)
   by Marv Johnson (1959)

"You Make Loving Fun" (Warner Brothers 8483)
   by Fleetwood Mac (1977)

"You Never Done It Like That" (A&M 2063)
   by Captain and Tennille (1978)

"You Sexy Thing" (Big Tree 16047)
   by Hot Chocolate (1975)

"You Shook Me All Night Long" (Atlantic 3761)
   by AC/DC (1980)

"(You're) Having My Baby" (United Artists 454)
   by Paul Anka and Odia Coates (1974)

Loneliness, Rejection, and Lost Love

"Ain't No Sunshine" (Sussex 219)
   by Bill Withers (1971)

"Ain't That A Shame" (Epic 50743)
   by Cheap Trick (1979)

"Ain't Too Proud To Beg" (Rolling Stone 19302)
   by The Rolling Stones (1974)

"All Alone Am I" (Decca 31424)
  by Brenda Lee (1962)

"Alone Again (Naturally)" (MAM 3619)
  by Gilbert O'Sullivan (1972)

"Always Something There to Remind Me" (EMI America 8155)
  by Naked Eyes (1983)

"Another Saturday Night" (RCA 8164)
  by Sam Cooke (1963)

"Any Day Now" (RCA 13216)
  by Ronnie Milsap (1982)

"Are You Lonesome To-Night?" (RCA 47-7810)
  by Elvis Presley (1960)

"As Tears Go By" (London 9697)
  by Marianne Faithful (1964)

"Bang Bang (My Baby Shot Me Down)" (Imperial 66160)
  by Cher (1966)

"Before The Next Teardrop Falls" (ABC/Dot 17540)
  by Freddy Fender (1975)

"Big Girls Don't Cry" (Vee-Jay 465)
  by The Four Seasons (1962)

"Blue Moon" (Colpix 186)
  by The Marcels (1961)

"Blue On Blue" (Epic 9593)
  by Bobby Vinton (1963)

"Born To Lose" (ABC-Paramount 10330)
  by Ray Charles (1962)

"Break It To Me Gently" (Capitol 5148)
  by Juice Newton (1982)

"Break-Up" (Sun 303)
  by Jerry Lee Lewis (1958)

"Break Up To Make Up" (Avco 4611)
  by The Stylistics (1973)

"Breaking Up Is Hard To Do" (RCA 8046)
  by Neil Sedaka (1962)

"Build Me Up Buttercup" (55101)
  by The Foundations (1969)

"Buzz Buzz A-Diddle-It" (Swan 4071)
  by Freddy Cannon (1961)

"Bye Bye Love" (Cadence 1315)
  by The Everly Brothers (1957)

"Can't Get Over Losing You" (Rare Bullett 101)
  by Donnie Elbert (1970)

"Cathy's Clown" (Warner Brothers 5151)
  by The Everly Brothers (1960)

"Chain Of Fools" (Atlantic 2464)
  by Aretha Franklin (1967)

"Cold As Ice" (Atlantic 3410)
  by Foreigner (1977)

"Cry Baby" (United Artists 629)
  by Garnet Mimms and The Enchanters (1963)

"Cry Like A Baby" (Mala 593)
  by The Box Tops (1968)

"Cry Me A River" (A&M 1200)
  by Joe Cocker (1970)

"Crying" (Millenium 119799)
  by Don McLean (1981)

"Crying Time" (ABC-Paramount 10739)
  by Ray Charles (1965)

"Cuts Like A Knife" (A&M 2553)
  by Bryan Adams (1983)

"Darling Be Home Soon" (Kama Sutra 220)
  by The Lovin' Spoonful (1967)

"Deep Purple" (Liberty 55099)
  by Billy Ward and His Dominoes (1957)

"Different Drum" (Capitol 2004)
  by Linda Ronstadt and The Stone Poneys (1967)

"Don't Be Cruel" (RCA 47-6604)
  by Elvis Presley (1956)

"Don't Get Around Much Anymore" (Sabrina 501)
  by The Belmonts (1961)

"Don't Let Me Be Lonely Tonight" (Warner Brothers 7655)
  by James Taylor (1972)

"Don't Play That Song (You Lied)" (Atco 6222)
  by Ben E. King (1962)

"Don't Pull Your Love/Then You Can Tell Me Goodbye" (Capitol 4245)
  by Glen Campbell (1976)

"Don't Worry" (Columbia 41922)
  by Marty Robbins (1961)

"Don't You Want Me" (A&M 2397)
  by Human League (1982)

"Drip Drop" (Columbia 42917)
  by Dion (1963)

"Eleanor Rigby" (Capitol 5715)
  by The Beatles (1966)

"Everybody's Somebody's Fool" (MGM 12899)
  by Connie Francis (1960)

"Face It Girl, It's Over" (Capitol 2136)
  by Nancy Wilson (1968)

"Feel So Bad" (Checker 1162)
  by Little Milton (1967)

"50 Ways To Leave Your Lover" (Columbia 10270)
  by Paul Simon (1975)

"Fool #1" (Decca 31309)
  by Brenda Lee (1961)

"Forty Days" (Roulette 4154)
  by Ronnie Hawkins and The Hawks (1959)

"Funny How Time Slips Away" (Atlantic 89922)
  by The Spinners (1982)

"Gone" (Capitol 3628)
  by Ferlin Husky (1957)

"Gonna Get Along Without You Now" (Liberty 55040)
  by Patience and Prudence (1956)

"Goodbye Cruel World" (Colpix 609)
  by James Darren (1961)

"Goody Goody" (Gee 1039)
  by Frankie Lymon and The Teenagers (1957)

"The Great Pretender" (Mercury 70753)
  by The Platters (1955)

"Handy Man" (Columbia 10557)
  by James Taylor (1977)

"Happy, Happy Birthday Baby" (Checker 872)
  by The Tune Weavers (1957)

"Harbor Lights" (Mercury 71563)
  by The Platters (1960)

"Hard Habit To Break" (Fool Moon 29214)
  by Chicago (1984)

"He Will Break Your Heart" (Vee-Jay 354)
  by Jerry Butler (1960)

"He'll Have To Go" (RCA 7643)
  by Jim Reeves (1959)

"Head Games" (Atlantic 3633)
  by Foreigner (1979)

"Heartache Tonight" (Asylum 46545)
  by The Eagles (1979)

"Heartaches" (Colpix 612)
  by The Marcels (1961)

"Heartbreak Hotel" (RCA 47-6420)
by Elvis Presley (1956)

"Heartbreak (It's Hurtin' Me)" (King 5356)
by Little Willie John (1960)

"Hearts Of Stone" (DeLuxe 6062)
by The Charms (1954)

"Hello Stranger" (Atlantic 2184)
by Barbara Lewis (1963)

"Help Me Rhonda" (Capitol 5395)
by The Beach Boys (1965)

"Here You Come Again" (RCA 11123)
by Dolly Parton (1977)

"How Am I Supposed To Live Without You" (Atlantic 89805)
by Laura Branigan (1983)

"How Can You Mend A Broken Heart" (Atco 6824)
by The Bee Gees (1971)

"Hungry Heart" (Columbia 11391)
by Bruce Springsteen (1980)

"Hurt" (Liberty 55343)
by Timi Yuro (1961)

"Hurt So Bad" (DCP 1128)
by Little Anthony and The Imperials (1965)

"I Can Help" (Monument 8621)
by Billy Swan (1974)

"I Can See For Miles" (Decca 32206)
by The Who (1967)

"I Can't Get Next To You" (Gordy 7092)
by The Temptations (1969)

"I Can't Help It (If I'm Still In Love With You)" (Cadence 1432)
by Johnny Tillotson (1962)

"I Can't Stand The Rain" (Ariola 7686)
by Eruption (1978)

"I Can't Stop Loving You" (RCA 7133)
by Don Gibson (1958)

"I Fall To Pieces" (MCA 52052)
by Patsy Cline and Jim Reeves (1982)

"I Hear You Knocking" (Dot 15412)
by Gale Storm (1955)

"(I Know) I'm Losing You" (Gordy 7057)
by The Temptations (1966)

"I Know (You Don't Love Me No More)" (A.F.O. 302)
by Barbara George (1961)

"I Still Can't Get Over Loving You" (Arista 9116)
    by Ray Parker, Jr. (1983)

"I Wanna Be Around" (Columbia 42634)
    by Tony Bennett (1963)

"I Want To Be Wanted" (Decca 31149)
    by Brenda Lee (1960)

"(I Was) Born To Cry" (Laurie 3123)
    by Dion (1962)

"I Was The One" (RCA 47-6420)
    by Elvis Presley (1956)

"I (Who Have Nothing)" (Atco 6267)
    by Ben E. King (1963)

"I Wish It Would Rain" (Gordy 7068)
    by The Temptations (1968)

"I Wonder Who's Kissing Her Now" (Capitol 5126)
    by Bobby Darin (1964)

"If You've Got A Heart" (United Artists 908)
    by Bobby Goldsboro (1965)

"I'll Never Fall In Love Again" (Scepter 12273)
    by Dionne Warwick (1969)

"I'm A Fool To Care" (Smash 1702)
    by Joe Barry (1961)

"I'm Movin' On" (Warner Brothers 29729)
    by Emmylou Harris (1983)

"I'm So Lonesome I Could Cry" (Cadence 1432)
    by Johnny Tillotson (1962)

"I'm Sorry" (Decca 31093)
    by Brenda Lee (1960)

"I've Done Everything For You" (RCA 12166)
    by Rick Springfield (1981)

"It Ain't Me Babe" (White Whale 222)
    by The Turtles (1965)

"It Keeps Right On A-Hurtin' " (Cadence 1418)
    by Johnny Tillotson (1962)

"It's A Heartache" (RCA 11249)
    by Bonnie Tyler (1978)

"It's All In The Game" (MGM 12688)
    by Tommy Edwards (1958)

"It's My Party" (Mercury 72119)
    by Lesley Gore (1963)

"It's Only Make Believe" (MGM 12677)
    by Conway Twitty (1958)

"Ivory Tower" (Dot 15458)
  by Gale Storm (1956)

"The Joker Went Wild" (Philips 40377)
  by Brian Hyland (1966)

"Last Time I Saw Him" (Motown (1278)
  by Diana Ross (1974)

"Leaving On A Jet Plane" (Warner Brothers 7340)
  by Peter, Paul, and Mary (1969)

"Let Me Go Lover" (Columbia 40366)
  by Joan Weber (1954)

"The Letter" (Mala 565)
  by The Box Tops (1967)

"Lies" (Challenge 59321)
  by The Knickerbockers (1965)

"Lies" (Arista 1024)
  by The Thompson Twins (1983)

"Little Darlin' " (Mercury 71060)
  by The Diamonds (1957)

"(Loneliness Made Me Realize) It's You That I Need" (Gordy 7065)
  by The Temptations (1967)

"Lonely Blue Boy" (MGM 12857)
  by Conway Twitty (1959)

"Lonely But Only For You" (Atlantic 99847)
  by Sissy Spacek (1983)

"Lonely Teardrops" (Brunswick 55105)
  by Jackie Wilson (1958)

"Lonely Weekends" (Phillips 3552)
  by Charlie Rich (1960)

"Lonely Women Make Good Lovers" (RCA 13691)
  by Steve Wariner (1983)

"Lookin' For Love" (Full Moon 47004)
  by Johnny Lee (1980)

"Love Hurts" (A&M 1671)
  by Nazareth (1976)

"Love Is A Hurtin' Thing" (Capitol 5709)
  by Lou Rawls (1966)

"Love Is Like An Itching In My Heart" (Motown 1094)
  by The Supremes (1966)

"Love Letters" (Era 3068)
  by Ketty Lester (1962)

"Love Me" (RCA EPA 992)
  by Elvis Presley (1956)

"Lover Please" (Mercury 71941)
by Clyde McPhatter (1962)

"Lovers Who Wander" (Laurie 3123)
by Dion (1962)

"Lovesick Blues" (Vee-Jay 477)
by Frank Ifield (1962)

"(Marie's The Name) His Latest Flame" (RCA 47-7908)
by Elvis Presley (1961)

"Memphis" (Scotti Brothers 02434)
by Fred Knoblock (1981)

"Miss You" (Rolling Stone 19307)
by The Rolling Stones (1978)

"Mona Lisa" (Phillips 3539)
by Carl Mann (1959)

"Mountain Of Love" (Rita 1003)
by Harold Dorman (1960)

"Mr. Blue" (Dolton 5)
by The Fleetwoods (1959)

"Mr. Lonely" (Epic 9730)
by Bobby Vinton (1964)

"My True Story" (Beltone 1006)
by The Jive Five (1961)

"My World Is Empty Without You" (Motown 1089)
by The Supremes (1966)

"Never Going Back" (Kama Sutra 250)
by The Lovin' Spoonful (1968)

"New York Mining Disaster 1941—Have You Seen My Wife, Mr. Jones"
(Atco 6487)
by The Bee Gees (1967)

"96 Tears" (Epic 51008)
by Garland Jeffreys (1981)

"Nothing But Heartaches" (Motown 1081)
by The Supremes (1965)

"Oh Lonesome Me" (RCA 7133)
by Don Gibson (1958)

"One Fine Day" (A&M 2169)
by Rita Coolidge (1979)

"Only The Lonely (Know How I Feel)" (Monument 421)
by Roy Orbison (1960)

"Penny Lover" (Motown 1762)
by Lionel Richie (1984)

"Piece Of My Heart" (Geffen 50059)
by Sammy Hagar (1982)

"Please Come Home For Christmas" (Asylum 45555)
by The Eagles (1978)

"Poison Arrow" (Mercury 811329)
by ABC (1983)

"Private Eyes" (RCA 12296)
by Daryl Hall and John Oates (1981)

"Queen Of My Heart" (Warner Brothers 29500)
by Hank Williams, Jr. (1983)

"Release Me (And Let Me Love Again)" (Parrot 40011)
by Engelbert Humperdinck (1967)

"Rescue Me" (Checker 1120)
by Fontella Bass (1965)

"Return To Sender" (RCA 47-8100)
by Elvis Presley (1962)

"Ruby Baby" (Columbia 42662)
by Dion (1963)

"Runaround Sue" (Laurie 3110)
by Dion (1961)

"Sad Songs (Say So Much)" (Geffen 29292)
by Elton John (1984)

"Sealed With A Kiss" (ABC-Paramount 10336)
by Brian Hyland (1962)

"Second Hand Rose" (Columbia 43469)
by Barbra Streisand (1965)

"See The Funny Little Clown" (United Artists 672)
by Bobby Goldsboro (1964)

"See You In September" (B.T. Puppy 520)
by The Happenings (1966)

"Send Me Some Lovin' " (Specialty 598)
by Little Richard (1957)

"She's A Runner" (Capitol 5202)
by Billy Squier (1983)

"Silver Threads And Golden Needles" (Asylum 11032)
by Linda Ronstadt (1974)

"Since I Don't Have You" (Calico 103)
by The Skyliners (1959)

"Since I Lost My Baby" (Epic 03487)
by Luther Vandross (1983)

"Singing The Blues" (Warner Brothers 29726)
by Gail Davies (1983)

"Smoke Gets In Your Eyes" (Mercury 71383)
by The Platters (1958)

"So Sad (To Watch Good Love Go Bad)" (Warner Brothers 5163)
by The Everly Brothers (1960)

"Solitary Man" (Bang 578)
by Neil Diamond (1970)

"Sorry (I Ran All The Way Home)" (Cub 9022)
by The Impalas (1959)

"Still Crazy After All These Years" (Columbia 10332)
by Paul Simon (1976)

"Stop Doggin' Me Around" (MCA 52250)
by Klique (1983)

"Stop Draggin' My Heart Around" (Modern 7336)
by Stevie Nicks, with Tom Petty and The Heartbreakers (1981)

"Stop In The Name Of Love" (Atlantic 89819)
by The Hollies (1983)

"Strangers In The Night" (Reprise 0470)
by Frank Sinatra (1966)

"(Sweet Sweet Baby) Since You've Been Gone" (Atlantic 2486)
by Aretha Franklin (1968)

"Take Good Care Of My Baby" (Liberty 55354)
by Bobby Vee (1961)

"Take The L" (Capitol 5149)
by The Motels (1982)

"Take These Chains From My Heart" (ABC-Paramount 10435)
by Ray Charles (1963)

"Talk Back Trembling Lips" (MGM 13181)
by Johnny Tillotson (1963)

"Taxi" (Elektra 45770)
by Harry Chapin (1972)

"The Tears Of A Clown" (Tamla 54199)
by The Miracles (1970)

"Tears On My Pillow" (End 1027)
by Little Anthony and The Imperials (1958)

"That Stranger Used To Be My Girl" (Coed 570)
by Trade Martin (1962)

"That'll Be The Day" (Brunswick 55009)
by The Crickets (1957)

"That's When Your Heartaches Begin" (RCA 47-6870)
by Elvis Presley (1957)

"There Goes My Baby" (Geffen 29291)
by Donna Summer (1984)

"There Goes My Everything" (RCA 47-9960)
by Elvis Presley (1970)

"These Boots Are Made For Walkin' " (Reprise 0432)
   by Nancy Sinatra (1966)

"These Eyes" (RCA 0102)
   by The Guess Who (1969)

"This Is Just The First Day" (RCA 13630)
   by Razzy Bailey (1983)

"This Old Heart Of Mine (Is Weak For You)" (Tamla 54128)
   by The Isley Brothers (1966)

"Those Oldies But Goodies (Remind Me Of You)" (Del-Fi 4158)
   by Little Caesar and The Romans (1961)

"Those Were The Days" (Apple 1801)
   by Mary Hopkin (1968)

"The Thrill Is Gone" (Bluesway 61032)
   by B. B. King (1969)

"Ticket To Ride" (Capitol 5407)
   by The Beatles (1965)

"Tired Of Waiting For You" (Reprise 0347)
   by The Kinks (1965)

"Together Again" (ABC-Paramount 10785)
   by Ray Charles (1966)

"Too Bad" (Atco 6231)
   by Ben E. King (1962)

"The Tracks Of My Tears" (Tamla 54118)
   by The Miracles (1965)

"Tragedy" (Dolton 40)
   by The Fleetwoods (1961)

"Tryin' To Live My Life Without You" (Capitol 5042)
   by Bob Seger and The Silver Bullet Band (1981)

"Turn Around, Look At Me" (Reprise 0686)
   by The Vogues (1968)

"Unchained Melody" (Philles 129)
   by The Righteous Brothers (1965)

"Walk Like A Man" (Vee-Jay 485)
   by The Four Seasons (1963)

"The Way We Were" (Columbia 45944)
   by Barbra Streisand (1973)

"The Wayward Wind" (RCA 13441)
   by James Galway, with Sylvia (1983)

"What In The World's Come Over You" (Top Rank 2028)
   by Jack Scott (1960)

"What's New" (Asylum 69780)
   by Linda Ronstadt (1983)

"When She Was My Girl" (Casablanca 2338)
by The Four Tops (1981)

"When Will I Be Loved" (Capitol 4050)
by Linda Ronstadt (1975)

"Where Did Our Love Go" (Motown 1060)
by The Supremes (1964)

"A White Sport Coat (And A Pink Carnation)" (Columbia 40864)
by Marty Robbins (1957)

"Whoever Finds This, I Love You" (Columbia 45117)
by Mac Davis (1970)

"Who's Sorry Now" (MGM 12588)
by Connie Francis (1958)

"Win Your Love For Me" (Keen 2006)
by Sam Cooke (1958)

"Working My Way Back To You/Forgive Me, Girl" (Atlantic 3637)
by The Spinners (1979)

"Yester-Me, Yester-You, Yesterday" (Tamla 54188)
by Stevie Wonder (1969)

"Yesterday" (Capitol 5498)
by The Beatles (1965)

"You Beat Me To The Punch" (Motown 1032)
by Mary Wells (1962)

"You Can Have Her" (Moonglow 239)
by The Righteous Brothers (1965)

"You Cheated" (Domino 500)
by The Slades (1958)

"You Don't Bring Me Flowers" (Columbia 10840)
by Barbra Streisand and Neil Diamond (1978)

"You Don't Know What You've Got (Until You Lose It)" (Gone 5108)
by Ral Donner (1961)

"You'll Never Never Know" (Mercury 70948)
by The Platters (1956)

"You're No Good" (Capitol 3990)
by Linda Ronstadt (1974)

"You're The Reason" (Crest 1075)
by Bobby Edwards (1961)

"You've Lost That Lovin' Feelin' " (Philles 124)
by The Righteous Brothers (1964)

9

Political Protest and Social Criticism

During the first half of the twentieth century it was commonplace to encounter statements of political protest in folk songs. Similarly, social criticism frequently appeared in many forms of underground music from 1919
until 1950. During the past thirty-five years, though, lyrics from popular
songs have also provided strong ideological statements on a variety of
controversial topics. Some of these songs are philosophical, examining such
universal concerns as war, justice, and freedom. But most popular protest
songs are directly related to specific historical events or intense social problems that motivate strong public interest and attention. The launching of
satellites ("Telstar"—1962) and other forms of intercontinental rocketry
("Jupiter C"—1959) were originally treated in a very neutral musical fashion, but from the mid-1960s until the present day the realities of missiles,
nuclear energy, and atomic warfare have become focal points of popular
protest music. However, it was the assassination of John F. Kennedy
("Abraham, Martin, And John") in 1963, the American military involvement in Southeast Asia after 1965, the struggle for black civil rights throughout the sixties and seventies, and the political cynicism of the Nixon
presidency that prompted increasing numbers of chart-topping anthems
calling for more love, more peace, more brotherhood, and more rapid social
and political change (see Table 1). Powerful nationwide issues invariably
filter down to become intense personal concerns. Even such overriding
movements as women's liberation, ecological balancing, and labor unrest
are represented musically by a variety of tunes.

In 1983 three popular songs—"Undercover (Of The Night)," "Synchronicity II," and "Crumblin' Down"—presented serious commentaries on the
nature and meaning of American society. The Rolling Stones urged listeners

Table 1.

A Chronological List of Events and Songs That Illustrate Themes of Political Protest and Social Criticism, 1960–1985

Date(s)	Events, Activities, or Trends	Song Title (Date)
1960–1969	Public demands for individual conformity in respect of race relations, sexual behavior, religious belief, and oral expression	"Town Without Pity" (1961) "Little Boxes" (1964) "A Well-Respected Man" (1965) "Home Of The Brave" (1965) "Society's Child (Baby, I've Been Thinking)" (1967) "Dedicated Follower of Fashion" (1966) "Pleasant Valley Sunday" (1967) "Harper Valley P.T.A." (1968) "The Son Of Hickory Holler's Tramp" (1968)
1960–1969	Individual cynicism toward positions of social or political authority	"Eve Of Destruction" (1965) "Subterranean Homesick Blues" (1965) "For What It's Worth (Stop, Hey What's That Sound)" (1967) "Give A Damn" (1968) "Mr. Business Man" (1968) "Revolution" (1968) "Games People Play" (1969) "Monster" (1969)
1960–1985	Concerns for the civil rights of women, minorities, and the poor	"If I Had A Hammer" (1962) "Blowin' In The Wind" (1963) "We Shall Overcome" (1963) "Keep On Pushing" (1964) "Ninety-Nine And A Half (Won't Do)" (1966) "Dead End Street" (1967) "We're A Winner" (1967) "We're Rolling On (Part 1)" (1968) "Everyday People" (1969) "Get Together" (1969) "Why I Sing The Blues" (1969) "I Am Woman" (1972) "Why Can't We Live Together" (1972)

Date(s)	Events, Activities, or Trends	Song Title (Date)
		"Woman Is The Nigger Of The World" (1972)
		"Half-Breed" (1973)
		"Indian Reservation" (1971)
		"Living For The City" (1973)
		"Ebony And Ivory" (1982)
1961	Construction of the Berlin Wall	"West Of The Wall" (1962)
1962	Right-wing political ideologies	"The John Birch Society" (1962)
1963	Assassination of President John F. Kennedy	"Abraham, Martin, And John" (1968)
		"Six White Horses" (1969)
1965–1973	Criticism of American military involvement in the war in Southeast Asia	"The Universal Soldier" (1965)
		"The Cruel War" (1966)
		"The Unknown Soldier" (1968)
		"Fortunate Son" (1969)
		"Give Peace A Chance" (1969)
		"Stop The War Now" (1970)
		"War" (1970)
		"Bring The Boys Home" (1971)
		"Military Madness" (1971)
		"War Song" (1972)
1965–1973	Support for American military participation in the Southeast Asian conflict	"Ballad Of The Green Berets" (1966)
		"Gallant Men" (1967)
		"Battle Hymn Of Lt. Calley" (1971)
1965–1980	Reaction against political protesters and social critics by Americans who champion patriotism and nationalism	"Dawn Of Correction" (1965)
		"Open Letter To My Teenage Son" (1967)
		"Okie From Muskogee" (1969)
		"The Fightin' Side Of Me" (1970)
		"Americans (A Canadian's Opinion)" (1974)
		"Sweet Home Alabama" (1974)
		"In America" (1980)
1967–1970	Campus protests against the Vietnam War	"On Campus" (1969)
		"Ohio" (1970)

Date(s)	Events, Activities, or Trends	Song Title (Date)
1968	Assassination of Rev. Martin Luther King, Jr.	"Abraham, Martin, And John" (1968) "I Have A Dream" (1968)
1968	Assassination of Senator Robert F. Kennedy	"Abraham, Martin, And John (1968)
1968	Trial of the Chicago Seven for political subversion at the democratic national convention	"Chicago" (1971)
1969	Peace movement activities of John Lennon and Yoko Ono	"The Ballad Of John And Yoko" (1969)
1970–1979	Cynicism toward positions of social or political authority	"America, Communicate With Me" (1970) "American Woman" (1970) "Ball of Confusion (That's What The World Is Today)" (1970) "Compared to What" (1970) "Heaven Help Us All" (1970) "(For God's Sake) Give More Power To The People" (1971) "Hey Big Brother" (1971) "Power To The People" (1971) "What's Going On" (1971) "Won't Get Fooled Again" (1971) "Dialogue" (1972) "Elected" (1972) "You're The Man" (1972) "You Haven't Done Nothin' " (1974) "At Seventeen" (1975) "My Little Town" (1975) "Another Brick In The Wall" (1980) "The Logical Song" (1979)
1970–1985	Concern for ecological balance and control of pollution and nuclear proliferation	"Big Yellow Taxi" (1970) "Mercy Mercy Me (The Ecology)" (1971) "Signs" (1971) "Solution For Pollution" (1971) "The Family Of Man" (1972) "Power" (1980)

Date(s)	Events, Activities, or Trends	Song Title (Date)
1972	Political espionage and coverup during the Nixon administration	"Watergate" (1973)
1973	Canadian radio broadcaster praises the American government's acts on international goodwill	"The Americans (A Canadian's Opinion)" (1974)
1974	Gasoline shortage	"Energy Crisis '74" (1974)
1980–1985	Economic instability, unemployment, and automation	"Allentown" (1982) "Industrial Disease" (1983) "Mr. Roboto" (1983)
1980–1985	Cynicism toward positions of social or political authority	"Power" (1980) "Controversy" (1981) "Love Is Like A Rock" (1981) "Allentown" (1982) "Dirty Laundry" (1982) "Spirits In The Material World" (1982) "Still In Saigon" (1982) "Used To Be" (1982) "The American Dream" (1982) "1999" (1983) "Synchronicity II" (1983) "Undercover (Of The Night)" (1983) "The Authority Song" (1984)

to keep out of sight in order to avoid being victimized by South American death squads, by the race militia, by propaganda merchants, and by American militarists who want to station troops throughout the world to ensure political control. "Undercover" indicted the foreign policy of the Reagan administration while puzzling over the inability of American citizens to recognize, react to, and revolt against the inhumanity inherent in the government's actions toward South Africa, Cuba, and El Salvador. The Police shifted their lyrical focus from the international scene to the domestic front. "Synchronicity II" describes the suicidal tendencies of a bored, frustrated housewife, the ugly mornings created by industrial factories that belch filth into the sky, and the rush-hour traffic where the human beings driving powerful automobiles resemble lemmings packed into shiny metal boxes.

Finally, in "Crumblin' Down," John Cougar Mellencamp shifts from both international and domestic issues to deeply personal concerns. Questions of independence, interpersonal perceptions, and identity are presented in an intense fashion. These three songs typify the three decades of political protest and social criticism found in contemporary popular music.

Commentaries on American overseas imbroglios and foreign policies are invariably cast in extreme terms. That is, there are few examples of tunes that express both sides of any particular activity or that suspend judgment on a specific issue. Members of popular music's most famous quartet contributed songs addressing worldwide issues with "The Ballad Of John And Yoko" (1969), "Bangla-Desh" (1971), and "Give Ireland Back To The Irish" (1972). Barry McGuire challenged several decades of American policies in "Eve of Destruction" (1965). But it was the Southeast Asian conflict of the 1960s and 1970s that generated the most broadly based lyrical criticisms. These anti-war songs included "Bring The Boys Home" (1971), "The Cruel War" (1966), "Fortunate Son" (1969), "Give Peace A Chance" (1969), "Military Madness" (1971), "Still In Saigon" (1982), "Stop The War Now" (1970), "The Universal Soldier" (1965), "The Unknown Soldier" (1968), and "War" (1970). It would be wrong to assume that these antimilitary tunes were accepted without responses from patriotic singers. In fact, the sentiments opposing criticisms of American military activities, supporting the honor and bravery of soliders, and condemning all who would minimize America's ideals and democratic processes are numerous. These pro-U.S. tunes include: "Americans (A Canadian's Opinion)" (1974), "Ballad Of The Green Berets" (1966), "Battle Hymn Of Lt. Calley" (1971), "Dawn Of Correction" (1965), "The Fightin' Side Of Me" (1970), and "Gallant Men" (1967).

Beyond the realm of international political commentary, American music offers a variety of observations and criticisms on domestic concerns. The topics examined include such diverse, complex social issues as racial discrimination, political chicanery, urban decay, and women's liberation. Songs exploring domestic issues include "Ebony And Ivory" (1982), "Half-Breed" (1973), "Immigration Man" (1972), "Why Can't We Live Together" (1972), "Big Yellow Taxi" (1970), "Johnny Can't Read" (1982), "For The Love Of Money" (1974), "Mr. Businessman" (1968), "Dirty Laundry" (1982), "Hey Big Brother" (1971), "Power" (1980), "Spirits In The Material World" (1982), "In The Ghetto" (1969), and "Woman Is The Nigger Of The World" (1972). These lyrics cry for social change. This sense of seeking a better, more humane world without identifying specific causes for social problems is found in "A Change Is Gonna Come/People Gotta Be Free" (1970), "Imagine" (1971), and "Woodstock" (1970). Unlike these general statements, science fiction–like projections of the logical results of current wrongs can be found in "Future Shock" (1973), "In The Year 2525 (Exordium And Terminus)" (1969), and "Shape Of Things To Come" (1968).

Finally, the individual frustrations of being a just person in an unjust society, of being denied the right to express opinions or artistic talents due to demands for social conformity, or of being alienated from work, loved ones, and material possessions lead to an outcry of personal pain. Such feelings can occur to youngsters "At Seventeen" (1975) or as a mid-life crisis to a forty-year-old "Mrs. Robinson" (1968). Close friends often don't even realize that it's "Easy To Be Hard" (1969), that an individual can readily become an "Alien" (1981), that a person can object violently to the "Games People Play" (1969), that many folks can believe "People Are Strange" (1967), and that "Smiling Faces Sometimes" (1971) lie. Social pressure and demands for conformity are depicted in "Dedicated Follower Of Fashion" (1966), "Harper Valley P.T.A." (1968), "Little Boxes" (1964), "Pleasant Valley Sunday" (1967), "Society's Child (Baby, I've Been Thinking)" (1967), and "A Well-Respected Man" (1965). Unemployment and worker frustration only serve to complicate the sense of personal alienation. Songs that demonstrate powerful feelings about occupation-related difficulties are "Allentown" (1982), "Detroit City" (1963), "Industrial Disease" (1983), "Mr. Roboto" (1983), "A Natural Man" (1971), "9 to 5" (1980), "Sixteen Tons" (1955), "Take This Job And Shove It" (1977), and "Workin' At The Car Wash Blues" (1974).

POLITICAL PROTEST AND SOCIAL CRITICISM

General Statements of Protest and Criticism

"America" (Columbia 45663)
    by Simon and Garfunkel (1972)

"America, Communicate With Me" (Barnaby 2016)
    by Ray Stevens (1970)

"The American Dream" (Elektra 69960)
    by Hank Williams, Jr. (1982)

"An American Trilogy" (RCA 74-0672)
    by Elvis Presley (1972)

"American Woman" (RCA 0325)
    by Guess Who (1970)

"The Authority Song" (Riva 216)
    by John Cougar Mellencamp (1984)

"Bad Moon Rising" (Fantasy 622)
    by Creedence Clearwater Revival (1969)

"Ball Of Confusion (That's What The World Is Today)" (Gordy 7099)
    by The Temptations (1970)

"Compared To What" (Atlantic 2694)
    by Les McCann and Eddie Harris (1970)

"Controversy" (Warner Brothers 49808)
by Prince (1981)

"Dialogue (Part I and II) (Columbia 45717)
by Chicago (1972)

"Don't Think Twice, It's All Right" (Warner Brothers 5385)
by Peter, Paul, and Mary (1963)

"Give A Damn" (Mercury 72831)
by Spanky and Our Gang (1968)

"Hair" (MGM 14026)
by The Cowsills (1969)

"Heaven Help Us All" (Tamla 54200)
by Stevie Wonder (1970)

"If I Had A Hammer" (Warner Brothers 5296)
by Peter, Paul, and Mary (1962)

"Let Me Be" (White Whale 224)
by The Turtles (1965)

"Love Is Like A Rock" (MCA 51112)
by Donnie Iris (1981)

"My Little Town" (Columbia 10230)
by Simon and Garfunkel (1975)

"1999" (Warner Brothers 29892)
by Prince (1983)

"Revolution" (Apple 2276)
by The Beatles (1968)

"Rock The Casbah" (Epic 03245)
by The Clash (1982)

"San Francisco (Be Sure To Wear Flowers In Your Hair)" (Ode 103)
by Scott McKenzie (1967)

"Simple Song Of Freedom (Columbia 44920)
by Tim Hardin (1969)

"Sky Pilot" (MGM 13939)
by The Animals (1968)

"Subterranean Homesick Blues" (Columbia 43242)
by Bob Dylan (1965)

"Synchronicity II" (A&M 2571)
by The Police (1983)

"Taxi" (Elektra 45770)
by Harry Chapin (1972)

"Used To Be" (Motown 1650)
by Charlene and Stevie Wonder (1982)

"The Weight" (Capitol 2269)
by The Band (1968)

"You Haven't Done Nothin' " (Tamla 54252)
by Stevie Wonder (1974)

Historical Events Prompting Social Unrest

"Abraham, Martin And John" (Laurie 3464)
by Dion (1968)

"An American Trilogy" (Elektra 45750)
by Mickey Newbury (1971)

"Blowin' In The Wind" (Warner Brothers 5368)
by Peter, Paul, and Mary (1963)

"Chicago" (Atlantic 2804)
by Graham Nash (1971)

"Do They Know It's Christmas?" (Columbia 04749)
by Band Aid (1984)

"Energy Crisis '74" (Rainy Wednesday 206)
by Dickie Goodman (1974)

"George Jackson" (Columbia 45516)
by Bob Dylan (1971)

"Hurricane" (Columbia 10245)
by Bob Dylan (1975)

"I Have A Dream" (Gordy 7023)
by Rev. Martin Luther King (1968)

"The John Birch Society" (Kapp 457)
by The Chad Mitchell Trio (1962)

"Mr. President" (Rainy Wednesday 207)
by Dickie Goodman (1974)

"Ohio" (Atlantic 2740)
by Crosby, Stills, Nash and Young (1970)

"The Old Payola Roll Blues" (Capitol 4329)
by Stan Freberg (1960)

"On Campus" (Cotique 158)
by Dickie Goodman (1969)

"Six White Horses" (Epic 10540)
by Tommy Cash (1969)

"Watergate" (Rainy Wednesday 202)
by Dickie Goodman (1973)

"We Shall Overcome" (Vanguard 35023)
by Joan Baez (1963)

"West of the Wall" (Big Top 3097)
by Miss Toni Fisher (1962)

Alienation

"Alien" (Columbia 02471)
  by Atlanta Rhythm Section (1981)
"At Seventeen" (Columbia 10154)
  by Janis Ian (1975)
"Crumblin' Down" (Riva 214)
  by John Cougar Mellencamp (1983)
"Easy To Be Hard" (Dunhill 4203)
  by Three Dog Night (1969)
"Games People Play" (Capitol 2248)
  by Joe South (1969)
"Jive Talkin' " (RSO 510)
  by The Bee Gees (1975)
"Mrs. Robinson" (Columbia 44511)
  by Simon and Garfunkel (1968)
"People Are Strange" (Elektra 45621)
  by The Doors (1967)
"Smiling Faces Sometimes" (Gordy 7108)
  by Undisputed Truth (1971)
"Sticks And Stones" (ABC-Paramount 10118)
  by Ray Charles (1960)
"Subterranean Homesick Blues" (Columbia 43242)
  by Bob Dylan (1965)
"Trouble In Mind" (Colpix 175)
  by Nina Simone (1961)
"Walk A Mile In My Shoes" (Capitol 2704)
  by Joe South (1970)

Anti-War Sentiments and Reactions

"The Ballad Of John And Yoko" (Apple 2531)
  by The Beatles (1969)
"Bangla-Desh" (Apple 1836)
  by George Harrison (1971)
"Bring The Boys Home" (Invictus 9092)
  by Freda Payne (1971)
"The Cruel War" (Warner Brothers 5809)
  by Peter, Paul, and Mary (1966)
"Eve Of Destruction" (Dunhill 4009)
  by Barry McGuire (1965)
"Fortunate Son" (Fantasy 634)
  by Creedence Clearwater Revival (1969)

"Give Ireland Back To The Irish" (Apple 1847)
   by Paul McCartney (1972)

"Give Peace A Chance" (Apple 1809)
   by John Lennon (1969)

"Home Of The Brave (Capitol 5483)
   by Jody Miller (1965)

"Life During Wartime" (Sire 49075)
   by Talking Heads (1979)

"Military Madness" (Atlantic 2827)
   by Graham Nash (1971)

"Peace Train" (A&M 1291)
   by Cat Stevens (1971)

"Peace Will Come (According To Plan)" (Buddah 186)
   by Melanie (1970)

"Still In Saigon" (Epic 02828)
   by The Charlie Daniels Band (1982)

"Stop The War Now" (Gordy 7104)
   by Edwin Starr (1970)

"There Will Never Be Peace (Until God Is Seated At The Conference Table)"
   (Brunswick 55512)
   by The Chi-Lites (1974)

"The Universal Soldier" (Capitol 5504)
   by Glen Campbell (1965)

"The Unknown Soldier" (Elektra 45628)
   by The Doors (1968)

"War" (Gordy 7101)
   by Edwin Starr (1970)

"War Games" (Atlantic 89812)
   by Crosby, Stills and Nash (1983)

"War Song" (Reprise 1099)
   by Neil Young and Graham Nash (1972)

"Where Have All The Flowers Gone" (Capitol 4671)
   by The Kingston Trio (1962)

Discrimination and Prejudice

"Choice Of Colors" (Curtom 1943)
   by The Impressions (1969)

"Dead End Street" (Capitol 5869)
   by Lou Rawls (1967)

"Deep In The Heart Of Harlem" (Mercury 72220)
   by Clyde McPhatter (1964)

"Ebony And Ivory" (Columbia 02860)
  by Paul McCartney and Stevie Wonder (1982)

"Everyday People" (Epic 10407)
  by Sly and the Family Stone (1968)

"The Family Of Man" (Dunhill 4306)
  by Three Dog Night (1972)

"Get Together" (RCA 9752)
  by The Youngbloods (1969)

"Half-Breed" (MCA 40102)
  by Cher (1973)

"Help The Poor" (ABC-Paramount 10552)
  by B. B. King (1964)

"Immigration Man" (Atlantic 2873)
  by David Crosby and Graham Nash (1972)

"Indian Reservation (The Lament Of The Cherokee Reservation Indian)"
  (Columbia 45332)
  by The Raiders (1971)

"Keep On Pushing" (ABC-Paramount 10554)
  by The Impressions (1964)

"Living For The City" (Tamla 54242)
  by Stevie Wonder (1973)

"Ninety-Nine And A Half (Won't Do)" (Atlantic 2334)
  by Wilson Pickett (1966)

"Pink Houses" (Riva 215)
  by John Cougar Mellencamp (1983)

"Spanish Harlem" (Atco 6185)
  by Ben E. King (1960)

"We're Rolling On (Part 1)" (ABC 11071)
  by The Impressions (1968)

"We're A Winner" (ABC 11022)
  by The Impressions (1967)

"Why Can't We Live Together" (Glades 1703)
  by Timmy Thomas (1972)

"Why I Sing The Blues" (Bluesway 61024)
  by B. B. King (1969)

"The World Is A Ghetto" (United Artists 50975)
  by War (1972)

Ecological Concerns

"Big Yellow Taxi" (Reprise 0906)
  by Joni Mitchell (1970)

"The Crude Oil Blues" (RCA 0224)
  by Jerry Reed (1974)

"Mercy Mercy Me (The Ecology)" (Tamla 54207)
  by Marvin Gaye (1971)

"Solution For Pollution" (Warner Brothers 7451)
  by Charles Wright and The Watts 103rd St. Rhythm Band (1971)

Education

"Another Brick In The Wall" (Part II)" (Columbia 11187)
  by Pink Floyd (1980)

"Johnny Can't Read" (Asylum 69971)
  by Don Henley (1982)

"The Logical Song" (A&M 2128)
  by Supertramp (1979)

"Teach Your Children" (Atlantic 2735)
  by Crosby, Stills, Nash and Young (1970)

Materialism

"For The Love Of Money" (Philadelphia International 3544)
  by The O'Jays (1974)

"Money" (Virgin 67003)
  by The Flying Lizards (1979)

"Mr. Businessman" (Monument 1083)
  by Ray Stevens (1968)

"Signs" (Lionel 3213)
  by The Five Man Electrical Band (1971)

Media Excesses

"Dirty Laundry" (Asylum 69894)
  by Don Henley (1982)

"It's Good News Week" (Parrot 9800)
  by The Hedgehoppers Anonymous (1965)

"A Little Good News" (Capitol 5264)
  by Anne Murray (1983)

Nuclear Uncertainty

"Power" (Gordy 7183)
  by The Temptations (1980)

Patriotic Reactions to Social Criticism

"Americans" (Westbound 222)
  by Byron MacGregor (1974)

"Americans (A Canadian's Opinion)" (Capitol 3814)
  by Tex Ritter (1974)

"Americans (A Canadian's Opinion)" (Atco 4628)
  by Gordon Sinclair (1974)

"Ballad Of The Green Berets" (RCA 8739)
  by SSgt. Barry Sadler (1966)

"Battle Hymn Of Lt. Calley" (Plantation 73)
  by Terry Nelson and C Company (1971)

"Dawn Of Correction" (Decca 31844)
  by The Spokesmen (1965)

"The Fightin' Side Of Me" (Capitol 2719)
  by Merle Haggard (1970)

"Gallant Men" (Capitol 5805)
  by Senator Everett McKinley Dirksen (1967)

"In America" (Epic 50888)
  by The Charlie Daniels Band (1980)

"Made In The U.S.A." (Warner Brothers 29926)
  by The Wright Brothers (1982)

"Okie From Muskogee" (Capitol 2626)
  by Merle Haggard (1969)

"Open Letter To My Teenage Son" (Liberty 55996)
  by Victor Lundberg (1967)

"Philadelphia Freedom" (MCA 40364)
  by Elton John (1975)

"Son Of The South" (Southern Tracks 1021)
  by Bill Anderson (1983)

"Sweet Home Alabama" (MCA 40258)
  by Lynyrd Skynrd (1974)

"This Is My Country" (Curtom 1934)
  by The Impressions (1968)

Political Cynicism and Fear of Government Authority

"Der Kommissar" (Epic 03559)
  by After The Fire (1983)

"Elected" (Warner Brothers 7631)
  by Alice Cooper (1972)

"(For God's Sake) Give More Power To The People" (Brunswick 55450)
  by The Chi-Lites (1971)

"For What It's Worth (Stop, Hey What's That Sound)" (Atco 6459)
  by The Buffalo Springfield (1967)

"Hey Big Brother" (Rare Earth 5038)
  by Rare Earth (1971)

"The Jam Was Moving" (Chrysalis 2554)
  by Debbie Harry (1981)

"Monster" (Dunhill 4221)
  by Steppenwolf (1969)

"Power" (Gordy 7183)
  by The Temptations (1980)

"Power To The People" (Apple 1830)
  by John Lennon (1971)

"So Wrong" (Elektra 69839)
  by Patrick Simmons (1983)

"Spirits In The Material World" (A&M 2390)
  by The Police (1982)

"Undercover Of The Night" (Rolling Stone 99813)
  by The Rolling Stones (1983)

"What's Going On" (Tamla 54201)
  by Marvin Gaye (1971)

"Won't Get Fooled Again" (Decca 32846)
  by The Who (1971)

"You're The Man" (Tamla 54221)
  by Marvin Gaye (1972)

Social Pressure for Conformity

"Dedicated Follower Of Fashion" (Reprise 0471)
  by The Kinks (1966)

"Harper Valley P.T.A." (Plantation 3)
  by Jeannie C. Riley (1968)

"Little Boxes" (Columbia 42940)
  by Pete Seeger (1964)

"Mr. Businessman" (Monument 1083)
  by Ray Stevens (1968)

"Pleasant Valley Sunday" (Colgems 1007)
  by The Monkees (1967)

"Signs" (Lionel 3213)
  by The Five Man Electrical Band (1971)

"Society's Child (Baby, I've Been Thinking)" (Verve 5027)
  by Janis Ian (1967)

"The Son Of Hickory Holler's Tramp" (Columbia 44425)
  by O. C. Smith (1968)

"Town Without Pity" (Musicor 1009)
by Gene Pitney (1961)

"The Universal Soldier" (Capitol 5504)
by Glen Campbell (1965)

"A Well-Respected Man" (Reprise 0420)
by The Kinks (1965)

Speculations on Social Change

"A Change Is Gonna Come/People Gotta Be Free" (Bell 860)
by The Fifth Dimension (1970)

"Future Shock" (Curtom 1987)
by Curtis Mayfield (1973)

"Imagine" (Apple 1840)
by John Lennon (1971)

"In The Year 2525 (Exordium And Terminus)" (RCA 0174)
by Zager and Evans (1969)

"People Got To Be Free" (Atlantic 2537)
by The Rascals (1968)

"Shape Of Things To Come" (Tower 419)
by Max Frost and The Troopers (1968)

"Woodstock" (Atlantic 2723)
by Crosby, Stills, Nash and Young (1970)

Unemployment, Automation, and Worker Frustration

"Allentown" (Columbia 03413)
by Billy Joel (1982)

"Detroit City" (RCA 8183)
by Bobby Bare (1963)

"I Wish I Had A Job To Shove" (Churchill 94005)
by Rodney Lay and The Wild West (1982)

"Industrial Disease" (Warner Brothers 29880)
by Dire Straits (1983)

"Mr. Roboto" (A&M 2525)
by Styx (1983)

"A Natural Man" (MGM 14262)
by Lou Rawls (1971)

"9 to 5" (RCA 12133)
by Dolly Parton (1980)

"Sixteen Tons" (Capitol 3262)
by Tennessee Ernie Ford (1955)

"Steel Men" (Columbia 42483)
  by Jimmy Dean (1962)
"Stormy Monday Blues" (Duke 355)
  by Bobby Bland (1962)
"Take This Job And Shove It" (Epic 50469)
  by Johnny Paycheck (1979)
"Workin' At The Car Wash Blues" (ABC 11447)
  by Jim Croce (1974)
"Working In The Coal Mine" (Amy 958)
  by Lee Dorsey (1966)

Urban Unrest

"Baker Street" (United Artists 1192)
  by Gerry Rafferty (1978)
"Dead End Street" (Capitol 5869)
  by Lou Rawls (1967)
"In The Ghetto" (RCA 47-9741)
  by Elvis Presley (1969)
"Inner City Blues (Make Me Wanna Holler)" (Tamla 54209)
  by Marvin Gaye (1971)
"Living For The City" (Crossover 981)
  by Ray Charles (1975)
"Masterpiece" (Gordy 7126)
  by The Temptations (1973)
"My City Was Gone" (Sire 29840)
  by The Pretenders (1982)
"Takin' It To The Streets" (Warner Brothers 8196)
  by The Doobie Brothers (1976)

Women's Liberation

"I Am Woman" (Capitol 3350)
  by Helen Reddy (1972)
"Woman Is The Nigger Of The World" (Apple 1848)
  by John Lennon (1972)

10

Poverty and Unemployment

All poor people are not unemployed and all unemployed people are not poor. Earning a salary does not guarantee suitable living conditions, personal satisfaction, hope for the future, or many other desirable goals. The continuing existence of ghettos, both urban and rural, based upon either race or nationality demonstrates that securing employment alone cannot alleviate all social problems. It is ironic that being unemployed is not necessarily a sign of poverty. Short-term layoffs and wildcat strikes may take workers off assembly lines for abbreviated periods of time, but their incomes may be maintained through union fund support or by federal unemployment insurance. The retired also constitute a growing class of unemployed but not necessarily impoverished Americans. Whether from the military with healthy federal pensions, from industry with a package of union benefits, from teaching with long-term TIAA-CREF investment support, or from private business with personal nest eggs, there are many nonworking folks today who are still financially stable.

Most contemporary songs that address themes of poverty and unemployment ignore the complexities of the American economic environment. Lyrical commentary is inevitably simplified and personalized. Although there are a few notable exceptions—"Masterpiece" (1973), "For The Love Of Money" (1974), and "Living For The City" (1975)—most songs survey the impact of poverty and unemployment on individuals rather than groups. For example, Jim Croce's would-be business executive is totally discontented while singing the "Workin' At The Car Wash Blues" (1974); Albert King pleads for an "Angel Of Mercy" (1972) to help him maintain his job so that his children can eat properly and his family won't be evicted from their apartment; and Ray Charles enumerates dozens of needs that he can't meet because he's "Busted" (1963). Elvis Presley notes that both landlords and female companions express the same kind of materialistic concern—you've got to have "Money Honey" (1956) if you want to get along with them. This individualizing tendency, so typical of most popular media, frequently disguises broader social implications of serious financial problems.

The most caustic commentary about the contemporary American economy is contained in Billy Joel's "Allentown" (1982). Some might feel that this song echoes the anti-capitalistic sentiments of folk singers from the 1930s and 1940s; others might view the tune as a logical extension of the criticism of the company store system found in Tennessee Ernie Ford's "Sixteen Tons" (1955); and a few might contend that Joel's statements merely echo ideas contained in other anti-bossism songs recorded by Jimmy Reed, Johnny Cash, Bobby Bare, Roy Orbison, and Johnny Paycheck. Whatever the motivation, though, Billy Joel strikes numerous chords of social discontent in "Allentown." First, he identifies the immediate impact of declining levels of mining activities and the termination of steel production in a particular Pennsylvania city. As the factories close, former workers simply kill time by standing in lines, filling out unemployment forms. Next, he shifts his commentary to the upward mobility desired by Americans who participated in the Second World War. Joel's sympathies rest with the men and women, former soldiers, and USO volunteers who settled in Allentown to raise families, mine coal, and make steel. The real target in this lyrical diatribe of lost dreams and found hypocrisy is the American social and economic system as misrepresented by public school educators. Teachers emphasized, according to the singer, the values of hard work, good behavior, and general learning. They omitted what was real—iron and coke, chromium steel. That is, neither industrial automation nor energy obsolescence were discussed; neither job insecurity nor the probability of geographical dislocation were considered. Middle-class myths of eternal upward mobility and unquestioned patriotism masked the cruel reality of plant conversions and mine closings, of times when all of the coal would be taken from the ground and the union people would crawl away. The song concludes with a statement mixing dream and reality. Joel says that he's still living in Allentown. He declares that it's hard to keep a good man down; but he regrets that he won't be getting up today.

Poverty results from a variety of circumstances. Sometimes, lack of interest in contributing to the family income, failure to follow the work ethic, or just individual laziness, ignorance, or nonmotivation render a person financially poor. Although they may not be particularly unhappy—as in the instances of the "Good-Hearted Woman" (1976) by Waylon Jennings and Willie Nelson, the "King Of The Road" (1965) by Roger Miller, and "Mr. Bojangles" (1968) by Jerry Jeff Walker—they tend to envy the workless, irresponsible way of "That Lucky Old Sun" (1963). Ray Charles is frequently a spokesman for the poor, but his messages are often delivered with humor in his lyric and a twinkle in his tone. If you ain't got no money, you just ain't no good, he theorizes in "Hit The Road Jack" (1961). He also contributes images of moneyless predicaments in "Busted" (1963) and "Them That Got" (1961). Additional examples of poverty depicted in humorous situations include The Goose Creek Symphony's "(Oh Lord Won't You Buy Me A) Mercedes Benz" (1972), Leo Sayer's "Long Tall Glasses (I Can Dance)" (1975), and Guy Drake's "Welfare Cadillac" (1970).

Too often it is forgotten that poverty is generally a problem that exceeds individual ability to explain or to overcome. Circumstances of race, nationality, religion, sex, and social class both create and prolong personal financial strife. Contemporary lyrics address these issues. Desires to escape from areas of rural and urban poverty are common as expressed in The Nashville Teens' "Tobacco Road" (1964), Chuck Berry's "Johnny B. Goode" (1958), and Lou Rawls' "Dead End Street" (1967). There is a force at work in the ghetto, however, that seems to undermine efforts to escape. This undertow exists in the form of poor education, lack of peer support for upward mobility, few constructive mentors for economic success, and the mixed negative elements of crime, racism, and sexism. Recordings that identify the social class conflicts and economic depression found in isolated pockets of poverty include Billy Joe Royal's "Down In The Boondocks" (1965), B. B. King's "Ghetto Woman" (1971), The McCoys' "Hang On Sloopy" (1965), Ray Charles' "Living For The City" (1975), The Temptations' "Masterpiece" (1973), Johnny Rivers' "Poor Side Of Town" (1966), The Four Seasons' "Rag Doll" (1964), The Animals' "We Gotta Get Out Of This Place" (1965), and B. B. King's "Why I Sing The Blues" (1969).

It is understandable that the frustration of living in a closed social system, in an unforgiving, harsh economic environment could spark strong responses for independence. One such reaction is criminal activity. This approach to acquiring money without any scruples includes a wide gamut of undertakings. Robbery and murder, chicanery and trickery, drug dealing, pornography, rum running, gambling, and prostitution are among the roads to fast money depicted in Robert Mitchum's "The Ballad Of Thunder Road" (1962), Donna Summer's "Bad Girls" (1979), Van Morrison's "Blue Money" (1971), The O'Jays' "For The Love Of Money" (1974), Curtis Mayfield's "Freddie's Dead" (1972), Cher's "Gypsys, Tramps, And Thieves" (1971), Tony Joe White's "Polk Salad Annie" (1969), Tommy Roe's "Stagger Lee" (1971), and The Steve Miller Band's "Take The Money And Run" (1976). The second response to escaping from poverty is to heighten one's self-image and to raise one's self-esteem as the principle for personal behavior. This does not necessarily rule out illegal activity, as described by Bobbie Gentry's "Fancy" (1969) and O. C. Smith's "The Son Of Hickory Holler's Tramp" (1968). There is also overt recognition that one's level of income directly affects the behavior of others in Nina Simone's "Nobody Knows You When You're Down And Out" (1960) and Richard Fields'

"People Treat You Funky (When Ya Ain't Got No Money)" (1982). Whether portrayed humorously by The Big Bopper in "Chantilly Lace" (1958) or more defensively by John Anderson in "Black Sheep" (1983) and Sammy Johns in "Common Man" (1981), there are several songs that decry using money as the only barometer of individual success. Aggressive stances by less-than-wealthy individuals who value self-esteem and integrity more than selling out to others for cash are featured in Creedence Clearwater Revival's "Fortunate Son" (1969), Tom Jones' "I (Who Have Nothing)" (1970), Marty Robbins' "Ruby Ann" (1962), Donna Summer's "She Works Hard For The Money" (1983), Linda Ronstadt's "Silver Threads And Golden Needles" (1974), and Otis Redding and Carla Thomas' "Tramp" (1967).

Unemployment is often the result of an accumulating process of job dissatisfaction. An individual may be earning a decent wage but still be upset with his or her day-to-day workplace. Hatred of the boss, feelings of anonymity in the hourly operation of a plant, disagreements with fellow workers, and other job-related problems may create an unhappy employee. The drag of the required Monday-through-Friday, nine-to-five presence is chronicled in Fats Domino's "Blue Monday" (1957), Albert King's "Cadillac Assembly Line" (1976), Bobby Bare's "Detroit City" (1963), The Vogues' "Five O'Clock World" (1965), The Easybeats' "Friday On My Mind" (1967), Bobby Bland's "Stormy Monday Blues" (1962), and Mel McDaniel's "Take Me To The Country" (1982). Anger with the boss, the foreman, or some other supervisor is expressed in Elvis Presley's "Big Boss Man" (1967), Billy Joe Royal's "Down In The Boondocks" (1965), Dolly Parton's "9 To 5" (1980), Roy Orbison's "Workin' For The Man" (1962), and Johnny Paycheck's "Take This Job And Shove It" (1977). Other forms of personal alienation and frustration are illustrated in Bob Seger's "Feel Like A Number" (1981), McGuffey Lane's "Making A Living's Been Killing Me" (1982), Eddie Cochran's "Summertime Blues" (1958), The Coasters' "Wake Me, Shake Me" (1960), Huey Lewis and The News' "Workin' For A Livin' " (1982), and Devo's "Working In A Coal Mine" (1981).

Unemployment means that an individual must search for a new workplace. Rodney Lay's "I Wish I Had A Job To Shove" (1982) and The Silhouettes' "Get A Job" (1958) illustrate the personal and family-related tensions involved in an ongoing job search. The action of being released from even an unwanted work position is embarrassing and frustrating. Heatwave's "Lettin' It Loose" (1982) and Bill Anderson's "Laid Off" (1982) illustrate this feeling. Although Billy Joel's "Allentown" (1982) speaks more broadly to industrial change and worker relocation as reasons for reducing work forces, Albert King's impending dismissal described in "Angel Of Mercy" (1972) is much more demoralizing. Of course, the ultimate commentary of suspended hiring judgment to a would-be employee is found in the title of Sugarloaf's 1974 hit—"Don't Call Us, We'll Call You."

All job terminations are not unhappy. Retirements, shifts from one company to another, and decisions of employees not to continue in dead-end positions are self-determined acts of workplace change. Taking advantage of opportunities for new jobs are the central themes of Billy Joel's "Movin' Out (Anthony's Song)" (1978), The Lovin' Spoonful's "Nashville Cats" (1966), Jay and The Americans' "Only In America" (1963), Irene Cara's "Out Here On My Own" (1980), Dave Loggins' "Please Come To Boston" (1974), Chuck Berry's "Promised Land" (1965), and Don Williams' "Tulsa Time" (1978). Although Mac Davis expresses some frustration about his career in "Rock 'N' Roll (I Gave You The Best Years Of My Life)" (1974), it is Lou Rawls who states the ultimate position of independence in "A Natural Man" (1971). Rawls encapsules the feeling of many workers in saying that his commitment to forty-hours-per-week employment is not total and that unequal pay and opportunities among employees and supervisors make him seek genuine freedom beyond the nine-to-five existence. The natural man works only for the convenience of an income and reserves his personal life for his ultimate enjoyment.

POVERTY AND UNEMPLOYMENT

Poverty and Social Class

"Ain't No Money" (Columbia 02937)
   by Rosanne Cash (1982)
"Are The Good Times Really Over (I Wish A Buck Was Still Silver)"
   (Epic 02894)
   by Merle Haggard (1982)
"Backstreet Ballet" (Mercury 814360)
   by Savannah (1983)
"Bad Girls" (Casablanca 988)
   by Donna Summer (1979)
"The Ballad Of Thunder Road" (Capitol 3986)
   by Robert Mitchum (1962)
"Black Sheep" (Warner Brothers 29497)
   by John Anderson (1983)
"Blue Money" (Warner Brothers 7462)
   by Van Morrison (1971)
"Chantilly Lace" (Mercury 71343)
   by Big Bopper (1958)
"Common Man" (MCA 52178)
   by John Conlee (1983)
"Common Man" (Elektra 47192)
   by Sammy Johns (1981)
"Dead End Street" (Capitol 5869)
   by Lou Rawls (1967)

"Down On The Corner" (Fantasy 634)
  by Creedence Clearwater Revival (1969)

"Fancy" (Capitol 2675)
  by Bobbie Gentry (1969)

"For The Love Of Money" (Philadelphia International 3544)
  by The O'Jays (1974)

"Fortunate Son" (Fantasy 634)
  by Creedence Clearwater Revival (1969)

"Freddie's Dead" (Curtom 1975)
  by Curtis Mayfield (1972)

"The Ghetto" (Atco 6719)
  by Donny Hathaway (1970)

"Ghetto Child" (Atlantic 2973)
  by The Spinners (1973)

"Ghetto Woman" (ABC 11310)
  by B. B. King (1971)

"Goin' Downhill" (Warner Brothers 29485)
  by John Anderson (1983)

"Good Hearted Woman" (RCA 10529)
  by Waylon Jennings and Willie Nelson (1976)

"Gotta Get My Hands On Some (Money)" (Spring 3008)
  by Fatback (1980)

"Greenback Dollar" (Capitol 4898)
  by The Kingston Trio (1963)

"Gypsys, Tramps, and Thieves" (Kapp 2146)
  by Cher (1971)

"Hang On Sloopy" (Bang 506)
  by The McCoys (1965)

"Hit The Road Jack" (ABC-Paramount 10244)
  by Ray Charles (1961)

"The House Of The Rising Sun" (Parrot 341)
  by Frijid Pink (1970)

"I (Who Have Nothing)" (Parrot 40051)
  by Tom Jones (1970)

"I'm Livin' In Shame" (Motown 1139)
  by Diana Ross and The Supremes (1969)

"If I Were A Carpenter" (Atlantic 2350)
  by Bobby Darin (1966)

"If You Ain't Got No Money" (Motown 1287)
  by Willie Hutch (1974)

"If You Ain't Got Nothin' (You Ain't Got Nothin' To Lose)" (Columbia 02895)
  by Bobby Bare (1982)

"If You've Got The Money (I've Got The Time)" (Columbia 20739)
  by Lefty Frizzell (1950)

"In The Ghetto" (Fame 91000)
  by Candi Staton (1972)

"I've Got Five Dollars" (Capitol 13369)
  by Faron Young (1956)

"I've Got Five Dollars And It's Saturday Night" (Musicor 1066)
  by George and Gene (1965)

"Johnny B. Goode" (Chess 1691)
  by Chuck Berry (1958)

"King Of The Road" (Smash 1965)
  by Roger Miller (1965)

"Lady Madonna" (Capitol 2138)
  by The Beatles (1968)

"Last Time I Saw Him" (Motown 1278)
  by Diana Ross (1974)

"Let's Clean Up The Ghetto" (Philadelphia International 3627)
  by The Philadelphia International All Stars (1977)

"Living For The City" (Crossover 981)
  by Ray Charles (1975)

"Long Tall Glasses (I Can Dance)" (Warner Brothers 8043)
  by Leo Sayer (1975)

"Love Child" (Motown 1135)
  by Diana Ross and The Supremes (1968)

"Lucille" (United Artists 929)
  by Kenny Rogers (1977)

"Masterpiece" (Gordy 7126)
  by The Temptations (1973)

"Maximum Security (To Minimum Wage)" (Epic 03155)
  by Don King (1982)

"Me And The I.R.S." (Epic 50539)
  by Johnny Paycheck (1978)

"Money Honey" (Atlantic 1006)
  by The Drifters (1953)

"Money Honey" (RCA EPA-821)
  by Elvis Presley (1956)

"Money's Too Tight" (Bridge 1982)
  by The Valentine Brothers (1982)

"Mr. Bojangles" (Atco 6594)
  by Jerry Jeff Walker (1968)

"Mr. Bojangles" (Liberty 56197)
  by The Nitty Gritty Dirt Band (1970)

"Nobody Knows You When You're Down And Out" (Colpix 158)
by Nina Simone (1960)

"(Oh Lord Won't You Buy Me A) Mercedes Benz" (Capitol 3246)
by The Goose Creek Symphony (1972)

"Patches" (Atlantic 2748)
by Clarence Carter (1970)

"People Treat You Funky (When Ya Ain't Got No Money)" (Boardwalk 164)
by Richard "Dimples" Fields (1982)

"Polk Salad Annie" (Monument 1104)
by Tony Joe White (1969)

"Poor Boy" (Elektra 45804)
by Casey Kelly (1972)

"Poor Boy" (RCA EPA-4006)
by Elvis Presley (1956)

"Poor Boy" (RCA 13383)
by Razzy Bailey (1982)

"Poor Boy" (Jubilee 5338)
by The Royaltones (1958)

"Poor Man" (Checker 1221)
by Little Milton (1969)

"A Poor Man's Roses" (Plantation 201)
by Patti Page (1981)

"Poor Man's Son" (Golden World 20)
by The Reflections (1965)

"Poor Man's Son" (Scotti Brothers 02560)
by Survivor (1981)

"Poor Side Of Town" (Imperial 66175)
by Johnny Rivers (1966)

"Poverty" (Duke 407)
by Bobby Bland (1966)

"Rag Doll" (Phillips 40211)
by The Four Seasons (1964)

"Rags To Riches" (RCA 47-9980)
by Elvis Presley (1971)

"Ruby Ann" (Columbia 42614)
by Marty Robbins (1962)

"She Got The Goldmine (I Got The Shaft)" (RCA 13268)
by Jerry Reed (1982)

"She Works Hard For The Money" (Mercury 812370)
by Donna Summer (1983)

"Silver Threads And Golden Needles" (Asylum 11032)
by Linda Ronstadt (1974)

"Sittin' On A Poor Man's Throne" (ABC 12330)
   by Bobby Bland (1978)

"The Son of Hickory Holler's Tramp" (Columbia 44425)
   by O. C. Smith (1968)

"Song Of The South" (Columbia 03033)
   by Tom T. Hall and Earl Scruggs (1982)

"Stagger Lee" (ABC 11307)
   by Tommy Roe (1971)

"Stoney End" (Columbia 45236)
   by Barbra Streisand (1970)

"Sugar Shack" (Dot 16487)
   by Jimmy Gilmer and The Fireballs (1963)

"Synchronicity II" (A&M 2571)
   by The Police (1983)

"Take The Money And Run" (Capitol 4260)
   by The Steve Miller Band (1976)

"That Lucky Old Sun" (ABC-Paramount 10509)
   by Ray Charles (1963)

"That's What The Blues Is All About" (Stax 0189)
   by Albert King (1974)

"Them That Got" (ABC-Paramount 10141)
   by Ray Charles (1961)

"Tobacco Road" (London 9689)
   by The Nashville Teens (1964)

"Tramp" (Stax 216)
   by Otis Redding and Carla Thomas (1967)

"Uptown Girl" (Columbia 04149)
   by Billy Joel (1983)

"Waitin' In Your Welfare Line" (Capitol 5566)
   by Buck Owens and His Buckaroos (1966)

"We Gotta Get Out Of This Place" (MGM 13382)
   by The Animals (1965)

"Welfare Cadillac" (Royal American 1)
   by Guy Drake (1970)

"We're Gonna Make It" (Checker 1105)
   by Little Milton (1965)

"Why I Sing The Blues" (Bluesway 61024)
   by B. B. King (1969)

Job Dissatisfaction

"Big Boss Man" (RCA 47-9341)
   by Elvis Presley (1967)

"Blue Collar Blues" (Excelsior 1005)
  by Mundo Earwood (1981)

"Blue Monday" (Imperial 5417)
  by Fats Domino (1957)

"Cadillac Assembly Line" (Utopia 10544)
  by Albert King (1976)

"Coal Miner's Daughter" (Decca 32749)
  by Loretta Lynn (1970)

"Detroit City" (RCA 8183)
  by Bobby Bare (1963)

"Do You Know The Way To San Jose" (Scepter 12216)
  by Dionne Warwick (1968)

"Don't You Want Me" (A&M 2397)
  by Human League (1982)

"Down In The Boondocks" (Columbia 43305)
  by Billy Joe Royal (1965)

"Feel Like A Number" (Capitol 5077)
  by Bob Seger and The Silver Bullet Band (1981)

"Five O'Clock World" (CO & CE 232)
  by The Vogues (1965)

"Friday On My Mind" (United Artists 50106)
  by The Easybeats (1967)

"Making A Living's Been Killing Me" (Atco 99959)
  by McGuffey Lane (1982)

"Mr. Roboto" (A&M 2525)
  by Styx (1983)

"9 To 5" (RCA 12133)
  by Dolly Parton (1980)

"Play This Old Working Day Away" (RCA 13208)
  by Dean Dillon (1982)

"Sixteen Tons" (Parrot 40016)
  by Tom Jones (1967)

"Stayin' Alive" (RSO 885)
  by The Bee Gees (1977)

"Stormy Monday Blues" (Duke 355)
  by Bobby Bland (1962)

"Summertime Blues" (Liberty 55144)
  by Eddie Cochran (1958)

"Take Me To The Country" (Capitol 5095)
  by Mel McDaniel (1982)

"Take This Job And Shove It" (Epic 50469)
  by Johnny Paycheck (1977)

"Taxi" (Elektra 56770)
  by Harry Chapin (1972)

"Wake Me, Shake Me" (Atco 6168)
  by The Coasters (1960)

"Workin' At The Car Wash Blues" (ABC 11447)
  by Jim Croce (1974)

"Workin' For A Livin' " (Chrysalis 2630)
  by Huey Lewis and The News (1982)

"Workin' For The Man" (Monument 467)
  by Roy Orbison (1962)

"Working In A Coal Mine" (Full Moon 47204)
  by Devo (1981)

Unemployment

"Allentown" (Columbia 03413)
  by Billy Joel (1982)

"Angel Of Mercy" (Stax 0121)
  by Albert King (1972)

"Busted" (ABC-Paramount 10481)
  by Ray Charles (1963)

"Don't Call Us, We'll Call You" (Claridge 402)
  by Sugarloaf (1974)

"Get A Job" (Ember 1029)
  by The Silhouettes (1958)

"I Wish I Had A Job To Shove" (Churchill 94005)
  by Rodney Lay and The Wild West (1982)

"I'm Comin' Home" (Atlantic 3027)
  by The Spinners (1974)

"Laid Off" (Southern Tracks 1011)
  by Bill Anderson (1982)

"Lettin' It Loose" (Epic 02904)
  by Heatwave (1982)

"Lido Shuffle" (Columbia 10491)
  by Boz Scaggs (1977)

"Movin' Out (Anthony's Song)" (Columbia 10708)
  by Billy Joel (1978)

"Nashville Cats" (Kama Sutra 219)
  by The Lovin' Spoonful (1966)

"A Natural Man" (MGM 14262)
  by Lou Rawls (1971)

"On Broadway" (Warner Brothers 8542)
  by George Benson (1978)

"One Piece At A Time" (Columbia 10321)
by Johnny Cash (1976)

"Only In America" (United Artists 626)
by Jay and The Americans (1963)

"Out Here On My Own" (RSO 1048)
by Irene Cara (1980)

"Out Of Work" (EMI America 8117)
by Gary "U.S." Bonds (1982)

"Paperback Writer" (Capitol 5651)
by The Beatles (1966)

"Please Come To Boston" (Epic 11115)
by Dave Loggins (1974)

"Promised Land" (Chess 1916)
by Chuck Berry (1964)

"Proud Mary" (Fantasy 619)
by Creedence Clearwater Revival (1969)

"Rock 'N' Roll (I Gave You The Best Years Of My Life)" (Columbia 10070)
by Mac Davis (1974)

"Tulsa Time" (ABC 12425)
by Don Williams (1978)

11

Race Relations

Although several popular songs during the past thirty-five years have addressed social issues such as the women's movement—"I Am Woman" (1972), the living standards of native Americans—"Indian Reservation" (1971), and the plight of Hispanic immigrants—"Immigration Man" (1972), relations among black and white Americans remain a key lyrical concern. Sociologist Gunnar Myrdal's description of America's racial dilemma remains as relevant today as it was fifty years ago. Of course, the civil rights movement of the 1960s secured voting rights and increased opportunities for political leadership among blacks; the Supreme Court directly attacked the practice of "separate but equal" schooling; and liberalization of both educational and economic opportunity has sparked the growth of a black middle class. Yet the chains of ghetto life—poverty, unemployment, drug abuse, prejudice, bigotry, and racism—continue to enslave a significant portion of the people that songwriter Curtis Mayfield describes as "darker than blue."

Are blacks the only ones in American society who suffer when racism thrives? Of course not. James Baldwin, Kenneth Clark, and dozens of other perceptive black writers have echoed the contention that a less-than-free situation for any citizen means injustice, social stagnation, and economic deprivation for all. Freedom means many things to many people, though, particularly in respect to the issue of race relations. How can a just society be established? Should a minority allow itself to be totally assimilated into the majority culture, abandoning its traditional ethnic songs, dances, speech patterns, dress styles, and religious beliefs? Should the majority culture encourage the continuation of ethnic identity and seek to preserve multicultural richness within a genuinely pluralistic society? Should the minority element be removed and isolated from the larger social order? It is interesting to note that various facets of social philosophy, political realism, economic concern, and personal feeling appear in contemporary lyrics. The oral history of America's ongoing race relations dilemma is molded in the vinyl grooves of numerous hit recordings.

Songs depicting the social lives of black Americans often provide only stereotypic perspectives. That is, they describe jolly bumpkins working at the "Car Wash" (1976), joking about "Charlie Brown" (1959), or retelling traditional tales about "Frankie And Johnny" (1963) and "Stagger Lee" (1958), preparing to "Rip It Up" (1956) on Saturday night to some "Rock And Roll Music" (1957), and joshing one another with jive insults—"Say Man, Back Again" (1959)—concerning the sexual inadequacies of mates, mothers, and women with "Skinny Legs And All" (1967). More serious questions of black self-identity are obscured in such light-hearted tunes. Youthful perceptions of interactions with parents and siblings are explored with deeper meaning in "Family Affair" (1971), "Papa Was A Rollin' Stone" (1972), and "I Wish" (1976); coping with formal educational systems is described in "School Day" (1957) and "Don't Be A Drop-Out" (1966); and the search for an independent identity is portrayed in "Almost Grown" (1959), "You Can't Judge A Book By The Cover" (1962), and "You Never Can Tell" (1964).

The economic condition of American blacks is painted in sharp contrast to the swinging, positive images of white life "Downtown" (1964), or in Frank Sinatra's "Chicago" (1957) as "My Kind Of Town" (1968). Urban life for black men and women is wearying and worrisome. "The World Is A Ghetto" (1972) seems to be an appropriate image. Songs that depict the blight and plight of urban living include "Spanish Harlem" (1960), "Funky Broadway" (1967), "The Ghetto" (1970), "Ghetto Woman" (1971), "Inner City Blues (Make Me Wanna Holler)" (1971), "In The Ghetto" (1972), "Living For The City" (1973), and "Masterpiece" (1973). Prostitution, although a source of power over straight white men for the haughty "Lady Marmalade" (1975) of New Orleans, is more accurately described as a depressing, degrading necessity for survival in "For The Love Of Money" (1974) and "Bad Girls" (1979). The drudgery of menial jobs, poor pay, depressed self-images, and transient relationships are featured in "Stormy Monday Blues" (1962), "How Blue Can You Get" (1964), "Love Child" (1968), "I'm Livin' In Shame" (1969), "Why I Sing The Blues" (1969), and "Nobody Knows You (When You're Down And Out)" (1973).

Clearly, interaction between whites and blacks is inhibited by economic conditions, social class differences, and geographical (ghetto housing systems) separation. How can such monumental barriers be breached? What types of social and personal bridges can resolve such racial division? Youthful dating, as depicted in popular recordings, is chock-full of real and imagined conflicts. Interracial social activity is described in varying degrees of intimacy, from pursuing black prostitutes in "Brown Sugar" (1971) to being desperately attracted to a beautiful "Cinnamon Girl" (1970). Yet even if common sense dictates that "Beauty Is Only Skin Deep" (1966), black-white dating is fraught with the personal and social challenges as articulated in "Society's Child (Baby I've Been Thinking)" (1967), "Brown Eyed Woman" (1968), and "Is It Because I'm Black" (1969).

Overcoming discrimination and prejudice may involve achieving sympathetic political support for economic programs and educational needs. Several tunes by black artists have provided strong sentiments of patriotic fervor. These nationalistic songs include "Back In The U.S.A." (1959), "America Is My Home" (1968), "This Is My Country" (1968), and "The Declaration" (1970). A more critical series of comments about the lack of governmental concern for blacks and other powerless people may be found in "War" (1970), "(For God's Sake) Give More Power To The People" (1971), "You're The Man" (1972), and "You Haven't Done Nothin'" (1974). Obviously, there is a sharp lyrical division over the willingness of the political system to respond to black needs and concerns.

During the 1960s and 1970s a new sense of black pride was kindled. This movement found its voice in James Brown, Aretha Franklin, Curtis Mayfield, Nina Simone, and Sly Stone. Actually, the new black image of what life in the United States could and should be was fueled by a variety of protest tunes. These recordings included "Eve Of Destruction" (1965), "I Chose To Sing The Blues" (1966), "A Change Is Gonna Come" (1965), "Dead End Street" (1967), "For What It's Worth" (1967), "Ball Of Confusion (That's What The World Is Today)" (1970), "A Change Is Gonna Come/People Gotta Be Free" (1970), "Compared To What" (1970), "A Natural Man" (1971), and "Back Stabbers" (1972). These tunes, and others like them, sparked significant feelings of courage, independence, freedom, power, and respect among large segments of the black community. Other songs illustrated this zeal for change, too. The best examples of such black pride recordings are: "Keep On Pushing" (1964), "Ninety-Nine And A Half (Won't Do)" (1966), "We're A Winner" (1967), "I've Gotta Be Me" (1968), "Say It Loud—I'm Black And I'm Proud" (1968), "We're Rolling On" (1968), "Choice Of Colors" (1969), "It's Your Thing" (1969), "Stand!" (1969), "Everybody Is A Star" (1970), "Express Yourself" (1970), "Thank You (Falettinme Be Mice Elf Agin)" (1970), and "Respect Yourself" (1971). More than just vacant pride, though, singers like Nina Simone noted the personal and social responsibility related to achievement by blacks in America. "To Be Young, Gifted And Black" (1969) was indeed a challenging status.

The ideal vision of race relations still haunts American society. The notions of scriptural command and social imperative are bound in Martin Luther King, Jr.'s June 23, 1963 speech that was released on record as "I Have A Dream" (1968). Likewise, popular recordings have noted God's will to make all men brothers in a world at peace. Songs illustrating this theme include "He's Got The Whole World In His Hands" (1958), "People Get Ready" (1965), "Oh Happy Day" (1969), "Spirit In The Sky" (1970), "I'll Take You There" (1972), and "There Will Never Be Any Peace (Until God Is Seated At The Conference Table)" (1974). These pop-gospel messages are admittedly idealized. However, numerous songs by black and white artists have challenged the unnatural segregation of Americans by skin color. These tunes form an oral bridge to shift the question from just race relations to human cooperation for the good of all. Songs illustrating this goal include "Everyday People" (1968), "Friendship Train" (1969), "Let's Work Together" (1969), "We Are Neighbors" (1971), "Black And White" (1972), "The Family Of Man" (1972), "Why Can't We Live Together" (1972), "Ebony And Ivory" (1982), and "New Year's Day" (1983).

RACE RELATIONS

"Chicago" (Capitol 3793)
  by Frank Sinatra (1957)

"Downtown" (Warner Brothers 5494)
  by Petula Clark (1964)

"I Am Woman" (Capitol 3350)
  by Helen Reddy (1972)

"Immigration Man" (Atlantic 2873)
  by David Crosby and Graham Nash (1972)

"Indian Reservation (The Lament Of The Cherokee Reservation Indian)"
  (Columbia 45332)
  by The Raiders (1971)

"My Kind Of Town" (Reprise 0702)
  by Frank Sinatra (1968)

Black Pride

"Choice Of Colors" (Curtom 1943)
  by The Impressions (1969)

"Everybody Is A Star" (Epic 10555)
  by Sly and The Family Stone (1970)

"Everyday People" (Epic 10407)
  by Sly and The Family Stone (1968)

"Express Yourself" (Warner Brothers 7417)
  by Charles Wright and the Watts 103rd Street Rhythm Band (1970)

"Keep On Pushing" (ABC-Paramount 10554)
  by The Impressions (1964)

"Ninety-Nine And A Half (Won't Do)" (Atlantic 2334)
   by Wilson Pickett (1966)

"Respect Yourself" (Stax 0104)
   by The Staple Singers (1971)

"Say It Loud—I'm Black And I'm Proud" (King 6187)
   by James Brown (1968)

"Stand!" (Epic 10450)
   by Sly and The Family Stone (1969)

"To Be Young, Gifted And Black" (RCA 0269)
   by Nina Simone (1969)

"We're A Winner" (ABC 11022)
   by The Impressions (1967)

"We're A Winner" (Curtom 1966)
   by Curtis Mayfield (1971)

"We're Rolling On (Part 1)" (ABC 11071)
   by The Impressions (1968)

Brotherhood of Man

"All God's Children Got Soul" (Elektra 45671)
   by Dorothy Morrison (1969)

"Black And White" (Dunhill 4317)
   by Three Dog Night (1972)

"Ebony And Ivory" (Columbia 02860)
   by Paul McCartney and Stevie Wonder (1982)

"Everyday People" (Blackheart 52272)
   by Joan Jett and The Blackhearts (1983)

"The Family Of Man" (Dunhill 4306)
   by Three Dog Night (1972)

"Friendship Train" (Soul 35068)
   by Gladys Knight and The Pips (1969)

"He's Got The Whole World In His Hands" (Columbia 41150)
   by Mahalia Jackson (1958)

"I Have A Dream" (Gordy 7023)
   by The Rev. Martin Luther King, Jr. (1968)

"Let's Work Together" (Sue 11)
   by Wilbert Harrison (1969)

"New Year's Day" (Island 99915)
   by U2 (1983)

"Oh Happy Day" (Pavilion 20001)
   by The Edwin Hawkins Singers (1969)

"People Get Ready" (ABC-Paramount 10622)
   by The Impressions (1965)

"Spirit In The Sky" (Buddah 196)
by Dorothy Morrison (1970)

"There Will Never Be Any Peace (Until God Is Seated At The Conference Table)" (Brunswick 55512)
by The Chi-Lites (1974)

"We Are Neighbors" (Brunswick 55455)
by the Chi-Lites (1971)

"Why Can't We Live Together" (Glades 1703)
by Timmy Thomas (1972)

Personal Concerns

"Almost Grown" (Chess 1722)
by Chuck Berry (1959)

"Back Stabbers" (Philadelphia International 3517)
by The O'Jays (1972)

"Beauty Is Only Skin Deep" (Gordy 7055)
by The Temptations (1966)

"Black Pearl" (A&M 1053)
by Sonny Charles and The Checkmates, Ltd. (1969)

"Brown Eyed Woman" (MGM 13959)
by Bill Medley (1968)

"Brown Sugar" (Rolling Stone 19100)
by The Rolling Stones (1971)

"A Change Is Gonna Come/People Gotta Be Free" (Bell 860)
by The Fifth Dimension (1970)

"Charlie Brown" (Atco 6132)
by The Coasters (1959)

"Cinnamon Girl" (Reprise 0911)
by Neil Young (1970)

"Compared To What" (Atlantic 2694)
by Les McCann and Eddie Harris (1970)

"Dead End Street" (Capitol 5869)
by Lou Rawls (1967)

"The Declaration" (Bell 860)
by The Fifth Dimension (1970)

"Don't Be A Drop-Out" (King 6056)
by James Brown (1966)

"Fame" (RSO 1034)
by Irene Cara (1980)

"Family Affair" (Epic 10805)
by Sly and The Family Stone (1971)

"Frankie And Johnny" (RCA 8215)
by Sam Cooke (1963)

"Ghetto Woman" (ABC 11310)
by B. B. King (1971)

"Hold What You've Got" (Dial 4001)
by Joe Tex (1964)

"How Blue Can You Get" (ABC-Paramount 10527)
by B. B. King (1964)

"Hunter Gets Captured By The Game" (Island 49531)
by Grace Jones (1980)

"I Gotcha" (Dial 1010)
by Joe Tex (1972)

"I Wish" (Tamla 54274)
by Stevie Wonder (1976)

"I'll Take You There" (Stax 0125)
by The Staple Singers (1972)

"I'm A Man" (Checker 814)
by Bo Diddley (1955)

"I'm Livin' In Shame" (Motown 1139)
by Diana Ross and The Supremes (1969)

"I'm So Excited" (Planet 13857)
by The Pointer Sisters (1982)

"Is It Because I'm Black" (Twinight 125)
by Syl Johnson (1969)

"It's A Man's Man's Man's World" (King 6035)
by James Brown (1966)

"It's Your Thing" (T-Neck 901)
by The Isley Brothers (1969)

"I've Gotta Be Me" (Reprise 0779)
by Sammy Davis, Jr. (1968)

"Johnny B. Goode" (Chess 1691)
by Chuck Berry (1958)

"Lady Marmalade" (Epic 50048)
by LaBelle (1975)

"Little Queenie" (Chess 1722)
by Chuck Berry (1959)

"Long Live Soul Music" (Atlantic 3814)
by The Spinners (1981)

"Love Child" (Motown 1135)
by Diana Ross and The Supremes (1968)

"Love The One You're With" (T-Neck 930)
by The Isley Brothers (1971)

"A Man And A Half" (Atlantic 2575)
by Wilson Pickett (1968)

"Midnight Train To Georgia" (Buddah 383)
by Gladys Knight and The Pips (1973)

"Missing You" (RCA 13966)
by Dianna Ross (1984)

"Nobody Knows You When You're Down And Out" (Colpix 158)
by Nina Simone (1960)

"Papa Was A Rollin' Stone" (Gordy 7121)
by The Temptations (1972)

"Promised Land" (Chess 1916)
by Chuck Berry (1964)

"Rock And Roll Music" (Chess 1671)
by Chuck Berry (1957)

"Say Man" (Checker 931)
by Bo Diddley (1959)

"Say Man, Back Again" (Checker 936)
by Bo Diddley (1959)

"School Day" (Chess 1653)
by Chuck Berry (1957)

"Skinny Legs And All" (Dial 4063)
by Joe Tex (1967)

"Society's Child (Baby I've Been Thinking)" (Verve 5027)
by Janis Ian (1967)

"Spanish Harlem" (Atco 6185)
by Ben E. King (1960)

"Stagger Lee" (ABC-Paramount 9972)
by Lloyd Price (1958)

"Stag-O-Lee" (Atlantic 2448)
by Wilson Pickett (1967)

"Stand By Me" (Atco 6194)
by Ben E. King (1961)

"Superstition" (Tamla 54226)
by Stevie Wonder (1972)

"Sweet Little Sixteen" (Chess 1683)
by Chuck Berry (1958)

"Thank You (Falettinme Be Mice Elf Agin)" (Epic 10555)
by Sly and The Family Stone (1970)

"This Is My Country" (Curtom 1934)
by The Impressions (1968)

"Trouble In Mind" (Colpix 175)
by Nina Simone (1961)

"Trouble Man" (Tamla 54228)
  by Marvin Gaye (1972)

"U Bring The Freak Out" (Gordy 1703)
  by Rick James (1983)

"You Can't Judge A Book By The Cover" (Checker 1019)
  by Bo Diddley (1962)

"You Never Can Tell" (Chess 1906)
  by Chuck Berry (1964)

Social and Economic Conditions

"America Is My Home" (King 6112)
  by James Brown (1968)

"Back In The U.S.A." (Chess 1729)
  by Chuck Berry (1959)

"Bad Girls" (Casablanca 988)
  by Donna Summer (1979)

"Ball Of Confusion (That's What The World Is Today)" (Gordy 7099)
  by The Temptations (1970)

"Big Boss Man" (Vee-Jay 380)
  by Jimmy Reed (1961)

"Blowin' In The Wind" (Warner Brothers 5368)
  by Peter, Paul, and Mary (1963)

"Bright Lights, Big City" (Vee-Jay 398)
  by Jimmy Reed (1961)

"Car Wash" (MCA 40615)
  by Rose Royce (1976)

"Chain Gang" (RCA 7783)
  by Sam Cooke (1960)

"A Change Is Gonna Come" (RCA 8486)
  by Sam Cooke (1965)

"Eve Of Destruction" (Dunhill 4009)
  by Barry McGuire (1965)

"(For God's Sake) Give More Power To The People" (Brunswick 55450)
  by The Chi-Lites (1971)

"For The Love Of Money" (Philadelphia International 3544)
  by The O'Jays (1974)

"For What It's Worth" (Epic 10220)
  by The Staple Singers (1967)

"Funky Broadway" (Atlantic 2430)
  by Wilson Pickett (1967)

"The Ghetto" (Atco 6719)
  by Donny Hathaway (1970)

"Higher Ground" (Tamla 54235)
  by Stevie Wonder (1973)

"I Chose To Sing The Blues" (ABC 10840)
  by Ray Charles (1966)

"In The Ghetto" (Fame 91000)
  by Candi Staton (1972)

"Inner City Blues (Make Me Wanna Holler)" (Tamla 54209)
  by Marvin Gaye (1971)

"Livin' In The Life" (T-Neck 2264)
  by The Isley Brothers (1977)

"Living For The City" (Tamla 54242)
  by Stevie Wonder (1973)

"Masterpiece" (Gordy 7126)
  by The Temptations (1973)

"A Natural Man" (MGM 14262)
  by Lou Rawls (1971)

"Nobody Knows You (When You're Down And Out)" (United Artists 255)
  by Bobby Womack (1973)

"Rip It Up" (Specialty 579)
  by Little Richard (1956)

"Stormy Monday Blues" (Duke 355)
  by Bobby Bland (1962)

"Superfly" (Curtom 1978)
  by Curtis Mayfield (1972)

"That Lucky Old Sun" (ABC 10509)
  by Ray Charles (1963)

"War" (Gordy 7101)
  by Edwin Starr (1970)

"Why I Sing The Blues" (Bluesway 61024)
  by B. B. King (1969)

"The World Is A Ghetto" (United Artists 50975)
  by War (1972)

"You Haven't Done Nothin' " (Tamla 54252)
  by Stevie Wonder (1974)

"You're The Man" (Tamla 54221)
  by Marvin Gaye (1972)

12

Religion

Religion defies singular categorization as either a personal, a social, or a political theme in contemporary American music. It is a multi-dimensional experience. Personal religious feelings have been documented in songs throughout history. Group musical activities related to organized religion, ranging from traditional hymn singing during Protestant revival meetings to modern folk masses performed with acoustic guitars in Catholic churches, are common events today. Finally, latent elements of a nonsectarian civic religion in the United States are visible through inscriptions on coins, in frequent references to divine guidance and prayers by American politicians, and in political protest tunes that chide narrow-minded nationalists who believe that their military adventures will succeed because they are launched "With God On Our Side" (n.d.). Bob Dylan, the composer of the afore-mentioned tune, along with fellow folk singers Joan Baez and Judy Collins, have provided numerous lyrical examples of songs that touch all three aspects—personal, social, and political—of modern American religious experience.

Traditional religious beliefs, as communicated in Bible verses, well-known hymns, prayers, or popular gospel tunes, provide rich lyrical resources for contemporary performers. Folk singer and composer Pete Seeger adapted the spiritual message contained in Ecclesiastes III: 1-8 to create the popular song "Turn! Turn! Turn!". The Bible-based idea that for everything there is a season, and a time to every purpose under heaven yielded a 1965 hit tune for The Byrds. The list of traditionally based popular songs includes Judy Collins' "Amazing Grace" (1970), Sister Janet Mead's "Lord's Prayer" (1974), Perry Como's "Ave Maria" (1949), The Electric Prunes' "Kyrie Eleison" (n.d.), and The Edwin Hawkins Singers' gospel classic "Oh Happy

Day" (1969). In addition, there are a variety of popular songs that acknowl-
edge sacred ceremonies, religious holidays, or other spiritual activities.
Among these recordings are: Bing Crosby's "Adeste Fideles" (1960), The
Dixie Cups' "Chapel Of Love" (1964), The Diamonds' "Church Bells May
Ring" (1956), Johnny Cash's "The Little Drummer Boy" (1959), Mahalia
Jackson's "Silent Night, Holy Night" (1962), and Bing Crosby's "White
Christmas" (1955).

Beyond the realm of hymns, Bible verses, and spirituals, though, there
is another bastion of religious tunes. These songs, usually crafted by contemporary tunesmiths, continue to utilize universally acknowledged religious imagery, Biblical names, and Christian symbols, but with generous
interjections of contemporary issues, ideas, and terminology. To Lawrence
Reynolds, for instance, the force of good that lives in his heart tells him
that "Jesus Is A Soul Man" (1969). And when The Beatles attempt to
describe the peace that passeth all understanding, they depict Mother Mary
whispering words of wisdom in "Let It Be" (1970). The "born again" and
fundamentalist element of Christianity is also well represented in tunes such
as Neil Diamond's "Brother Love's Travelling Salvation Show" (1969);
Ocean's "Put Your Hand In The Hand" (1971), Don Cornell's "The Bible
Tells Me So" (1955), Laurie London's "He's Got The Whole World (In His
Hands)" (1958), Johnny Cash's "Daddy Sang Bass" (1969), The Righteous
Brothers' "He" (1966), The Bachelors' "I Believe" (1964), Jimmy Rodgers'
"Just A Closer Walk With Thee" (1960), and Elvis Presley's "(There'll Be)
Peace In The Valley (For Me)" (1957) and "You'll Never Walk Alone"
(1968). Traditional gospel sounds also achieve recorded popularity. Peter,
Paul, and Mary released "Tell It On The Mountain" (1964) in the same
year that The Impressions issued their haunting religious chant "Amen."
Substituting a train for a horsedrawn coach, Curtis Mayfield and The
Impressions also updated the spiritual "Swing Low, Sweet Chariot" theme
in their 1965 song "People Get Ready." Finally, in a frequently humorous
vein several singers have depicted the issues of salvation, righteous living,
and the value of Jesus' teachings in some most untraditional religious songs.
Examples of these tunes include Norman Greenbaum's "Spirit In The Sky"
(1971), ZZ Topp's "Jesus Just Left Chicago" (n.d.), The Byrds' "Jesus Is
Just Alright" (1970), Manhattan Transfer's "Operator" (1975), Bobby Bare's
"Dropkick Me, Jesus (Through The Goalposts Of Life)" (1976), Wink
Martindale's "Deck Of Cards" (1959), Murray Head's "Superstar—Jesus
Christ Superstar" (1971), and Bob Dylan's "Gotta Serve Somebody" (1979).

As if these previously identified songs weren't sufficient to illustrate the
broad spectrum of contemporary religious ideas, there are numerous other
songs that ignore Biblical names, hymns, and verses, yet still communicate
the basic Christian ideals of love, brotherhood, and peace. Of course, the
temptation exists to label such songs as simply humanistic rather than religious. However, the undeniable spiritual elements inherent in songs such

as The O'Jays' "Love Train" (1973), Ed Ames' "Who Will Answer?" (1967), and Melanie's "Lay Down (Candles In The Rain)" (1970) tend to support a religious interpretation. Images of universal concern among human beings for one another are echoed in John Lennon's "Imagine" (1971), the Hollies' "He Ain't Heavy, He's My Brother" (1969), The Youngbloods' "Get Together" (1967), James Taylor's "You've Got A Friend" (1971), Simon and Garfunkel's classic tune "Bridge Over Troubled Water" (1970), Gladys Knight and The Pips' "Friendship Train" (1969), John Lennon's "Give Peace A Chance" (1969), and three songs by singer/composer Jackie DeShannon— "Put A Little Love In Your Heart" (1969), "The Weight" (1968), and "What The World Needs Now Is Love" (1965). Within this genre of pop hits featuring nontraditional Christian imagery there are also songs that address the apocalypse (Pacific Gas and Electric's "Are You Ready?" in 1970), tunes that investigate the broadest definitions of love (Helen Reddy's "I Don't Know How To Love Him" (1971) from the rock opera (*Jesus Christ Superstar*), lyrics that assess the materialistic nature of congregational donations (the Five Man Electrical Band's "Signs" in 1971), and tunes that urge socially conscious individuals to stop looking myopically at world issues of political injustice and to express more care for a needy friend (Three Dog Night's "Easy To Be Hard" in 1969).

The final aspect of the religious theme in contemporary music relates to the dark side of man's spiritual life. The twin elements of superstition and evil incarnate are not uncommon in contemporary recordings. It is ironic that in an age of technological advancement, symbolic logic, and scientific breakthroughs human behavior is often dictated by or attributed to such nonrational elements as astrology, biorhythms, and a strange variety of voodoos, jujus, devils, and other cult-like ideas. Everything from cracked mirrors to prowling black cats, from strolling under ladders to stepping on sidewalk cracks is mentioned in Stevie Wonder's satirical, critical tune "Superstition" (1972). Yet many songs equate success in life, effectiveness in business, and prowess in sexual relations with spiritual elixirs, spells, and potions. These include Johnny Otis' "Castin' My Spell" (1959), Bobby Curtola's "Fortuneteller" (1962), Creedence Clearwater Revival's "I Put A Spell On You" (1968), Molly Hatchet's "Lady Luck" (1983), The Clovers' "Love Potion No. 9" (1959), Johnny Rivers' "Seventh Son" (1965), Noel Harrison's "Suzanne" (1967), Atlantic Starr's "Touch A Four Leaf Clover" (1983), and The Sapphires' "Who Do You Love" (1964). Accompanying this type of black-and-white, good-versus-evil dichotomy of mystical notions are songs that attribute problems directly to the influence of dark forces in the world. The Devil is identified directly in many instances; but a general sense of evil or sin pervades the interpretations of individual behavior in all cases. Songs illustrating these elements include Bobby Vee's "Devil Or Angel" (1960), Charlie Daniels' "The Devil Went Down To Georgia" (1979), Mitch Ryders' "Devil With A Blue Dress On/Good Golly

Miss Molly" (1966), Cliff Richard's "Devil Woman" (1976), Marty Robbins' "Devil Woman" (1962), Santana's "Evil Ways" (1970), The Electric Light Orchestra's "Evil Woman" (1975), Crow's "Evil Woman Don't Play Your Games With Me" (1970), The Knickerbockers' "Lies" (1965), and Elvis Presley's "(You're The) Devil In Disguise" (1963).

RELIGION

Traditional Religious Ideas

"Amazing Grace" (Elektra 45709)
   by Judy Collins (1970)
"Amen" (ABC-Paramount 10602)
   by The Impressions (1964)
"Amen" (ATCO 6592)
   by Otis Redding (1968)
"Ave Maria" (RCA Victor 45-0071)
   by Perry Como (1949)
"The Bible Tells Me So" (Coral 61467)
   by Don Cornell (1955)
"Daddy Sang Bass" (Columbia 44689)
   by Johnny Cash (1969)
"Deck Of Cards" (Dot 15968)
   by Wink Martindale (1959)
"Dropkick Me, Jesus (Through The Goalposts Of Life)" (RCA 10790)
   by Bobby Bare (1976)
"God Bless America" (MGM 12841)
   by Connie Francis (1959)
"God Knows" (Warner Brothers 8554)
   by Debby Boone (1978)
"God Only Knows" (Big Three 16105)
   by Marilyn Scott (1978)
"Gotta Serve Somebody" (Columbia 11072)
   by Bob Dylan (1979)
"He" (Verve 10406)
   by The Righteous Brothers (1966)
"He's Got The Whole World (In His Hands)" (Capitol 3891)
   by Laurie London (1958)
"I Believe" (London 9672)
   by The Bachelors (1964)
"I Heard The Voice Of Jesus" (Warner Brothers 7397)
   by Turley Richards (1970)

"I Knew Jesus (Before He Was A Star)" (Capitol 3548)
by Glen Campbell (1973)

"I Know What God Is" (RCA 7670)
by Perry Como (1960)

"Jesus Is A Soul Man" (Warner Brothers 7322)
by Lawrence Reynolds (1969)

"Jesus Is Just Alright" (Columbia 45071)
by The Byrds (1970)

"Jesus Just Left Chicago" (London album)
by ZZ Top (n.d.)

"Jesus Was A Capricorn" (Monument 8558)
by Kris Kristofferson (1973)

"Just A Closer Walk With Thee" (Roulette 4234)
by Jimmie Rodgers (1960)

"Kyrie Eleison" (Dunhill album)
by The Electric Prunes (n.d.)

"The Lord Loves You" (Columbia 11232)
by Neil Diamond (1980)

"Lord's Prayer" (A&M 1491)
by Sister Janet Mead (1974)

"Mary's Boy Child/Oh My Lord" (Sire 1036)
by Boney M (1978)

"Me And Jesus" (Mercury 73278)
by Tom T. Hall (1972)

"My Sweet Lord" (Apple 2995)
by George Harrison (1970)

"Oh Happy Day" (Pavilion 20001)
by The Edwin Hawkins Singers (1969)

"Oh Lord, Why Lord" (Calla 154)
by Los Pop Tops (1968)

"Operator" (Atlantic 3292)
by Manhattan Transfer (1975)

"Put Your Hand In The Hand" (Kama Sutra 519)
by Ocean (1971)

"The Shrine Of St. Cecilia" (Capitol 3696)
by Faron Young (1957)

"Spirit In The Sky" (Reprise 0885)
by Norman Greenbaum (1971)

"Superstar—Jesus Christ Superstar" (Decca 32603)
by Murray Head, with The Trinidad Singers (1971)

"Tell It On The Mountain" (Warner Brothers 5418)
by Peter, Paul, and Mary (1964)

"(There'll Be) Peace In The Valley (For Me)" (RCA EPA-4054)
  by Elvis Presley (1957)

"Think His Name" (United Artists 50822)
  by Johnny Rivers (1971)

"Touch Me Lord Jesus" (Gotham 605)
  by The Angelic Gospel Singers (1949)

"Turn! Turn! Turn!" (Columbia 43424)
  by The Byrds (1965)

"Walk With Faith In Your Heart" (London 20018)
  by The Bachelors (1967)

"Where Did They Go, Lord" (RCA 47-9980)
  by Elvis Presley (1971)

"With God On Our Side" (Columbia album)
  by Bob Dylan (n.d.)

"You'll Never Walk Alone" (RCA 47-9600)
  by Elvis Presley (1968)

Religious Ceremonies and Holidays

"Adeste Fideles" (Decca 23777)
  by Bing Crosby (1960)

"Brother Love's Travelling Salvation Show" (Uni 55109)
  by Neil Diamond (1969)

"Chapel Of Love" (Red Bird 001)
  by The Dixie Cups (1964)

"Church Bells May Ring" (Mercury 70835)
  by The Diamonds (1956)

"Crying In The Chapel" (RCA 447-0643)
  by Elvis Presley (1965)

"Go On With The Wedding" (Mercury 70766)
  by Patti Page (1956)

"Hare Krishna" (Jubilee 5666)
  by The Happenings (1969)

"How Lovely Is Christmas" (Kapp 196)
  by Bing Crosby (1957)

"The Little Drummer Boy" (Columbia 41481)
  by Johnny Cash (1959)

"The Reverend Mr. Black" (Columbia 02669)
  by Johnny Cash (1982)

"Reverend Mr. Black" (Capitol 4951)
  by The Kingston Trio (1963)

"Silent Night" (Decca 23777)
  by Bing Crosby (1957)

"Silent Night, Holy Night" (Apollo 750)
by Mahalia Jackson (1962)

"Three Steps From The Altar" (Hull 747)
by Shep and The Limelites (1961)

"White Christmas" (Decca 29342)
by Bing Crosby (1955)

Brotherhood, Love, and Peace

"All God's Children Got Soul" (Elektra 45671)
by Dorothy Morrison (1969)

"Are You Ready?" (Columbia 45158)
by Pacific Gas and Electric (1970)

"Bridge Over Troubled Water" (Columbia 45079)
by Simon and Garfunkel (1970)

"Day By Day" (Bell 45210)
by Godspell's Original Cast (1972)

"Dust In The Wind" (Kirshner 4274)
by Kansas (1978)

"Easy To Be Hard" (Dunhill 4203)
by Three Dog Night (1969)

"Everyday People" (Epic 10407)
by Sly and The Family Stone (1968)

"Friendship Train" (Soul 35068)
by Gladys Knight and The Pips (1969)

"Get Together" (RCA 9264)
by The Youngbloods (1967)

"Give Peace A Chance" (Apple 1809)
by John Lennon (1969)

"God, Country, And My Baby" (Liberty 55379)
by Johnny Burnette (1961)

"God, Love, And Rock And Roll" (Westbound 170)
by Teegarden and Van Winkle (1970)

"God Only Knows" (Capitol 5706)
by The Beach Boys (1966)

"He Ain't Heavy, He's My Brother" (Epic 10532)
by The Hollies (1969)

"Heaven Help Us All" (Tamla 54200)
by Stevie Wonder (1970)

"I Don't Know How To Love Him" (Capitol 3027)
by Helen Reddy (1971)

"I Saw The Light" (Bearsville 0003)
by Todd Rundgren (1972)

"I Say A Little Prayer" (Scepter 12203)
by Dionne Warwick (1967)

"Imagine" (Apple 1840)
by John Lennon (1971)

"In The Year 2525 (Exordium and Terminus)" (RCA 74-0174)
by Zager and Evans (1969)

"Jesus Is Just Alright" (Warner Brothers 7661)
by The Doobie Brothers (1972)

"Lady Madonna" (Capitol 2138)
by The Beatles (1968)

"Lay Down (Candles In The Rain)" (Buddah 167)
by Melanie (1970)

"Let It Be" (Apple 2654)
by The Beatles (1970)

"Love Train" (Philadelphia International 3524)
by The O'Jays (1973)

"Michael" (United Artists 258)
by The Highwaymen (1961)

"Morning Has Broken" (A&M 1335)
by Cat Stevens (1972)

"Oh, Rock My Soul" (Warner Brothers 5442)
by Peter, Paul and Mary (1964)

"People Get Ready" (ABC-Paramount 10622)
by The Impressions (1965)

"Put A Little Love In Your Heart" (Imperial 66385)
by Jackie DeShannon (1969)

"Rock Me On The Water" (Asylum 11006)
by Jackson Browne (1972)

"Sermonette" (Jubilee 5345)
by Della Reese (1959)

"Signs" (Lionel 3213)
by The Five Man Electrical Band (1971)

"Spirit In The Sky" (Buddah 196)
by Dorothy Morrison (1970)

"Thank God And Greyhound" (Dot 17355)
by Roy Clark (1970)

"Top Forty (Of The Lord)" (Kama Sutra 528)
by Sha Na Na (1971)

"The Weight" (Imperial 66313)
by Jackie DeShannon (1968)

"What The World Needs Now Is Love" (Imperial 66110)
    by Jackie DeShannon (1965)

"Who Will Answer?" (RCA Victor 47-9400)
    by Ed Ames (1967)

"A Wonderful Time Up There" (Dot 15690)
    by Pat Boone (1958)

"Woodstock" (Atlantic 2723)
    by Crosby, Stills, Nash and Young (1970)

"You've Got A Friend" (Warner Brothers 7498)
    by James Taylor (1971)

Superstition

"Castin' My Spell" (Capitol 4168)
    by The Johnny Otis Show (1959)

"Fortune Teller" (World Pacific 77851)
    by The Hardtimes (1967)

"Fortuneteller" (Del-Fi 4177)
    by Bobby Curtola (1962)

"I Put A Spell On You" (Fantasy 617)
    by Creedence Clearwater Revival (1968)

"Lady Luck" (Epic album)
    by Molly Hatchet (1983)

"Love Potion No. 9" (United Artists 180)
    by The Clovers (1959)

"Seventh Son" (Imperial 66112)
    by Johnny Rivers (1965)

"Superstition" (Tamla 54226)
    by Stevie Wonder (1972)

"Suzanne" (Reprise 0615)
    by Noel Harrison (1967)

"Touch A Four Leaf Clover" (A&M 2580)
    by Atlantic Starr (1983)

"Under Your Spell" (Arista 0495)
    by Phyllis Hyman (1980)

"Voo-Doo" (Columbia 03411)
    by Rachel Sweet (1983)

"Voodoo Woman" (United Artists 862)
    by Bobby Goldsboro (1965)

"Who Do You Love" (Swan 4162)
    by The Sapphires (1964)

"With A Little Bit Of Luck" (Columbia 40718)
    by Jo Stafford (1956)

Evil Actions and Sinful Behaviors

"Church Of The Poison Mind" (Epic 04144)
by Culture Club (1983)

"Dealing With The Devil" (MCA 52020)
by Merle Haggard (1982)

"The Devil" (Jeremiah 1011)
by Hoyt Axton (1981)

"Devil Inside" (I.E. 009)
by Wyley McPherson (1982)

"The Devil Is A Woman" (Mr. Music 018)
by David Rogers (1983)

"The Devil Made Me Do It" (21 Records 108)
by Golden Earring (1983)

"Devil Or Angel" (Liberty 55270)
by Bobby Vee (1960)

"The Devil Went Down To Georgia" (Epic 50700)
by The Charlie Daniels Band (1979)

"Devil With A Blue Dress On/Good Golly Miss Molly" (New Voice 817)
by Mitch Ryder and The Detroit Wheels (1966)

"Devil Woman" (Rocket 40574)
by Cliff Richard (1976)

"Devil Woman" (Columbia 42486)
by Marty Robbins (1962)

"Evil Ways" (Columbia 45069)
by Santana (1970)

"Evil Woman" (United Artists 729)
by The Electric Light Orchestra (1975)

"Evil Woman Don't Play Your Games With Me" (Amaret 112)
by Crow (1970)

"Games People Play" (Capitol 2248)
by Joe South and The Believers (1969)

"Heaven's Just A Sin Away" (Ovation 1103)
by The Kendalls (1977)

"I Never Knew The Devil's Eyes Were Blue" (Handshake 02736)
by Terry Gregory (1982)

"I Thank The Lord For The Night Time" (Bang 547)
by Neil Diamond (1967)

"If Heaven Ain't A Lot Like Dixie" (Elektra 69960)
by Hank Williams, Jr. (1982)

"In Heaven There Is No Beer" (Vanguard 35162)
by Clean Living (1972)

"It's A Sin To Tell A Lie" (Epic 9093)
  by Somethin' Smith and The Redheads (1955)

"Last Train To Heaven" (Main Street 953)
  by Boxcar Willie (1982)

"Lies" (Challenge 59321)
  by The Knickerbockers (1965)

"Praise The Lord And Send The Money" (Columbia 03334)
  by Bobby Bare (1982)

"Race With The Devil" (Capitol 3530)
  by Gene Vincent (1956)

"Rock The Casbah" (Epic 03245)
  by The Clash (1982)

"Saved" (Atlantic 2580)
  by Lavern Baker (1961)

"Son-Of-A Preacher Man" (Atlantic 2580)
  by Dusty Springfield (1968)

"(You're The) Devil In Disguise" (RCA 47-8188)
  by Elvis Presley (1963)

"You've Got The Devil In Your Eyes" (Prairie Dust 8004)
  by Ann J. Morton (1981)

13

Transportation Systems

Several historians have adopted the term "transportation revolution" to describe the geographical expansion and economic development of the United States during the nineteenth and twentieth centuries. The notion of transportation—whether as an alteration of geographical position, a shift of financial fortune, a change in emotional or spiritual climate, or a search for loved ones, friends, or family roots—is also a dominant theme in American music. The technology of movement begins with machines rather than personal goals, though. Popular music reflects this fact. Composers and crooners have constructed their roving commentaries around numerous transportation vehicles: bicycles ("Bicycle Race" (1979) by Queen, "Brand New Key" (1971) by Melanie, and "Pushbike Song" (1971) by The Mixtures); skateboards ("Sidewalk Surfin" (1964) by Jan and Dean); subways ("M.T.A." (1959) by The Kingston Trio, "Don't Sleep In The Subway" (1967) by Petula Clark, "Homeward Bound" (1966) by Simon and Garfunkel, and "Sub-Rosa Subway" (1977) by Klaatu); motorcycles ("Bad Motorcycle" (1958) by The Storey Sisters, "The Leader Of The Pack" (1964) by the Shangri-Las, "Motorcycle" (1962) by Tico and The Triumphs, "Motorcycle Mama" (1972) by Sailcat, "Sweet Hitch-Hiker" (1971) by Creedence Clearwater Revival, "Ballad Of Easy Rider" (1969) by The Byrds, and "Uneasy Rider" (1973) by The Charlie Daniels Band); steamrollers ("Steamroller Blues" (1973) by Elvis Presley); airplanes ("Jet Airliner" (1977) by The Steve Miller Band, "Leaving On A Jet Plane" (1969) by Peter, Paul, and Mary, "Travelin' Band" (1970) by Creedence Clearwater Revival, "Ebony Eyes" (1961) by The Everly Brothers, and "Fire And Rain" (1970) by James Taylor); buses ("Thank God And Greyhound" (1970) by Roy Clark and "Magic Bus" (1968) by The Who); ships ("Riverboat" (1960) by

Faron Young, "Proud Mary" (1969) by Solomon Burke, "Sea Cruise" (1959) by Frankie Ford, "Shrimp Boats" (1951) by Jo Stafford, "The Sloop John B" (1960) by Jimmie Rodgers, and "Travelin' Man" (1961) by Rick Nelson); trucks ("Truck Stop" (1969) by Jerry Smith, "Convoy" (1976) by C. W. McCall, "Six Days On The Road" (1963) by Dave Dudley, "Take It Easy" (1972) by The Eagles, and "Take Me Home, Country Roads" (1971) by John Denver); and even rockets and satellites ("Jupiter C" (1959) by Pat and The Satellites and "Telstar" (1962) by The Tornadoes).

The two modes of transportation most frequently mentioned in popular songs, though, are trains and automobiles. This is hardly surprising. But it is interesting to note that railroad songs tend to present a broad array of historic, biographic, metaphoric, economic, and rhythmic themes, while car songs more frequently depict personal images of mobility, success, and sexual prowess. Perhaps the declining scope of railroading activities in American life since 1950 has contributed to this lyrical dichotomy. Obviously, the role of the automobile has increased dramatically during the same period. Even during the heyday of railroading between the First and Second World Wars, however, singers presented sharply divided viewpoints about the nature of America's train culture. On one hand, locomotive transportation was lauded as scenic, cheap, readily available, romantic, individualistic, and a constant source of personal freedom and geographical mobility. On the other hand, the same trains were condemned as noisy and ugly, prone to crashes and untimely delays, physically dangerous to humans and animals, sources of choking smoke and forest fires, and potential vehicles for familial separation and human misery.

Between 1950 and 1985 drastic changes occurred in railroad technology and public involvement with railway transportation. Singers and songwriters reflected these changes in their hit tunes. Hank Snow, Kris Kristofferson, and dozens of other singers have written and performed songs that depict trains as vehicles providing avenues of escape from rural poverty; from nagging parents, bossy wives, or interfering mothers-in-law; from prisons of the mind, body, or spirit; or from the drudgery of a boring job. Although the majority of railroad wanderers reported in popular lyrics tend to be men, it is undeniable that women in search of new lives are also frequent users of stream- or diesel-driven transportation. Movement toward greater personal freedom, a new social status, more income potential, and other positive gains is depicted in tunes like "Me And Bobby McGee" (1971), "I'm Movin' On" (1963), "Folsom Prison Blues" (1968), "Midnight Train" (1956), "The Gambler" (1979), and "Train, Train" (1979).

Heroic images often emerge from the commission of anti-social or illegal activities. In the realm of railroad songs, Buck Owens' tribute to a nineteenth-century outlaw—"Let Jesse Rob The Train" (1979)—illustrates this situation. This kind of salute also has been accorded to Railroad Bill. On the other hand, the two most noted heroic figures of lyrical railroad lore are the brave but doomed engineer Casey Jones and the steam drill–hating powerhouse track liner "John Henry" (1956).

Train metaphors occur in songs that portray escapes to freedom from either physical or spiritual captivity. These songs include: "Midnight Special" (1965), "Folsom Prison Blues" (1968), "Friendship Train" (1969), "Love Train" (1973), and "Peace Train" (1971). Transformations from earthy existence to heavenly afterlife are also illustrated in "People Get Ready" (1965), "This Train" (n.d.), and "Hobo On A Freight Train To Heaven" (1977). The complex nature of human relations is metaphorically depicted in several train songs. Several railroad lyric scholars have noted with particular interest the tendency of musicians to portray both positive (motherhood, loving wife, beautiful bride, stable family center) and negative (flighty female, cheating tramp, prostitute, unfaithful wife, and nagging mother-in-law) female images in railroad songs.

Trains are sound machines. Numerous singers allude to engine bells, whistles, clanging wheels, and other distinctive audio elements. Examples of railroad sounds converted to rhythm sources and audio stimuli for human reactions include: "Wabash Cannonball" (1970), "Folsom Prison Blues" (1968), and "Lonesome Whistle Blues" (1961). The rhythm of a train's drivers helped to shape the guitar-playing style of "Johnny B. Goode" (1958), while the distant screech of a locomotive whistle tempts both men and women to wander and roam.

The energy crisis of the 1970s focused public attention on the indispensability of the automobile in American society. No other form of transportation—railroads, buses, subways, bicycles, or airplanes—rivals the motorcar as a personal mode of mobility. But cars are more than just vehicles. In both life and music, automobiles have images that communicate key points about economics, personal attitudes, culture, sex, and a variety of other subjects. It may seem strange that a single form of transportation technology can so powerfully symbolize the hopes, dreams, and ideals of its users. Yet this is true of automobiles in the United States. As many popular culture analysts have noted, television is used more often and telephones are more numerous, but Americans participate in the most remarkable "car culture" in the world.

Since its initial appearance, the automobile has been a popular subject in song lyrics. From the early twentieth-century tunes—"Automobile Of Life" by Roy Acuff (1938), "In My Merry Oldsmobile" by Jean Goldkette Orchestra (1927), "Terraplane Blues" by Robert Johnson (1936), and "Wreck On The Highway" by Roy Acuff (1952)—to the songs of the 1960s, 1970s, and 1980s, there has been a constant recognition that cars are central to the nature of American existence. Although the norm of automobile tunes is the privately owned, privately operated vehicle, there are several songs that involve the commercial taxi and its operator. These recordings are: "At The Darktown Strutters' Ball" (1954) by Lou Monte, "Big Yellow Taxi"

(1970) by Joni Mitchell, "Cab Driver" (1968) by The Mills Brothers, "Taxi" (1972) by Harry Chapin, and "Tijuana Taxi" (1966) by Herb Alpert and The Tijuana Brass.

Highways are sources of adventure according to Steppenwolf in "Born To Be Wild" (1968); Chuck Berry cites the long freeways as one of the things he missed most until he got "Back In The U.S.A." (1959); and The Rolling Stones affirm that you can get your kicks on "Route 66" (n.d.). The notions of roads serving as pathways to fun, excitement, change, escape, and dozens of other goals are also contained in songs such as "Promised Land" (1964), "Tulsa Time" (1980), "Autobahn" (1975), "Highway To Hell" (1979), "L. A. Freeway" (1973), and "I Got A Name" (1973). Individuals pursuing highway thrills are often eccentric and rebellious creatures. This cross-section of humanity includes bootleggers and thieves ("Ballad Of Thunder Road"—1958 and "Cops And Robbers"—1956), drag racers ("Dead Man's Curve"—1964 and "Drag City"—1964), and young men who just enjoy fast, flashy cars ("I Get Around"—1964 and "Hot Rod Lincoln"—1960). Not to be outdone by their male counterparts, women also enjoy putting the pedal to the metal. Whether young, as in The Beach Boys' "Fun Fun Fun" (1964), or old, as in Jan and Dean's "Little Old Lady (From Pasadena)" (1964), the ladies often make men shout, "Mustang Sally" (1966) won't you slow that Mustang down. It should be noted that excessive speed does not always lead to good times, though. Sometimes the results are fatal. Among the songs that depict the hazards of wreckless driving and drag racing are: "Just Dropped In (To See What Condition My Condition Was In)" (1968) by Kenny Rogers and The First Edition, "Transfusion" (1956) by Nervous Norvus, "Dead Man's Curve" (1964) by Jan and Dean, and "Tell Laura I Love Her" (1960) by Ray Peterson.

America's car culture prompts a great deal of fantasy about using the perfect vehicle to snare the perfect mate. The legion of songs depicting this theme includes "Custom Machine" (1964), "Somethin' Else" (1959), and "Greased Lightin' " (1978). With a new set of wheels, the prospective lover hopes to gain the "Expressway To Your Heart" (1967). But what is the right car? The variety of makes and models is astounding, if not frustrating: "Chevy Van" (1975), "409" (1962), "G.T.O." (1964), "Hey Little Cobra" (1964), "Pontiac Blues" (1951), and "Sting Ray" (1963).

Automobile songs, both implicitly and explicitly, covertly and overtly, illustrate the trials of dating and sex among young Americans. Billy Emerson states emphatically that "Every Woman I Know" (1955) is crazy about automobiles. But some girls are extremely fickle. Chuck Berry's women—"Maybellene" (1955) and "Nadine (Is It You?)" (1964)—are particularly partial to Cadillacs, while he is stuck driving his V-8 Ford. David Lindley notes that his girl has the "Mercury Blues" (n.d.). Many women are satisfied to go along for the ride—"No Particular Place To Go" (1964), "Carol" (1958), "Seven Little Girls" (1959), and "Hot Rod Hearts (1980); while others see the ride only as a prelude to sexual encounters—"Paradise By The Dashboard Light" (1978), "Night Moves" (1976), "The Horizontal Bop" (1980), "Steppin' Out" (1976), and "Bad Girls" (1979). The reputation of the "Chevy Van" as a location for heterosexual recreation was confirmed in 1975 by Sammy Johns.

The car song is also utilized to illustrate general social and economic conditions. These situations may be either national ("Back When Gas Was Thirty Cents A Gallon"—1980 and "Get That Gasoline Blues"—1975) or personal ("No Money Down"—n.d., "Welfare Cadillac"—1970, and "(Oh Lord Won't You Buy Me A) Mercedes Benz"—1972). The tunes depict the drudgery of employment in the automotive industry ("Cadillac Assembly Line"—1976 and "Detroit City"—1963), along with the humor and creativity of individual laborers ("One Piece At A Time"—1976 and "Cheva-Kiser-Olds-MoLaca-Stude-Var-Linco-Baker"—1961). Associated occupations are also illustrated in terms of joy ("Car Wash"—1976), humor ("No Money Down"—n.d.), and frustration ("Too Much Monkey Business"—n.d. and "Workin At The Car Wash Blues"—1974).

It is difficult to conceive how thoroughly transportation systems, particularly automotive and railroad technology, have become integrated into the nation's popular music scheme. Yet the evidence is overwhelming. From drag racing ("Stick Shift"—1961) to freeway cruising ("Ventura Highway"—1972), from heavenly goals ("People Get Ready"—1965) to heavenly girls ("Sweet Hitch-Hiker"—1971), from mechanical disasters ("Dead Man's Curve"—1964) to human disillusionment ("Workin' At The Car Wash Blues"—1974), an entire spectrum of American social, political, and personal issues is mirrored in contemporary lyrics dealing with transportation systems.

Transportation Systems

"Bad Motorcycle" (Cameo 126)
   by the Storey Sisters (1958)
"Ballad Of Easy Rider" (Columbia 44990)
   by The Byrds (1969)
"Bicycle Race" (Elektra 45541)
   by Queen (1979)
"Born To Be Wild" (Dunhill 4138)
   by Steppenwolf (1968)
"Brand New Key" (Neighborhood 4201)
   by Melanie (1971)
"Jupiter C" (Atco 6131)
   by Pat and The Satellites (1959)
"Leader Of The Pack" (Red Bird 014)
   by The Shangri-Las (1964)

"Magic Bus" (Decca 32362)
  by The Who (1968)

"Motorcycle" (Amy 835)
  by Tico and The Triumphs (1962)

"Motorcycle Mama" (Elektra 45782)
  by Sailcat (1972)

"Mr. Bus Driver" (Mala 579)
  by Bruce Channel (1967)

"Proud Mary" (Bell 783)
  by Solomon Burke (1969)

"Pushbike Song" (Sire 350)
  by The Mixtures (1971)

"Riverboat" (Capitol 4291)
  by Faron Young (1960)

"Rockin' Bicycle" (Imperial 5779)
  by Fats Domino (1961)

"Roll Me Away" (Capitol 5235)
  by Bob Seger and The Silver Bullet Band (1983)

"Sea Cruise" (Ace 554)
  by Frankie Ford (1959)

"Shrimp Boats" (Columbia 39581)
  by Jo Stafford (1951)

"Sidewalk Surfin' " (Liberty 55727)
  by Jan and Dean (1964)

"Sloop John B" (Roulette 4260)
  by Jimmie Rodgers (1960)

"Steamroller Blues" (RCA 74-0910)
  by Elvis Presley (1973)

"Sweet Hitch-Hiker" (Fantasy 665)
  by Creedence Clearwater Revival (1971)

"Telstar" (London 9561)
  by The Tornadoes (1962)

"Thank God And Greyhound" (Dot 17355)
  by Roy Clark (1970)

"Trains And Boats And Planes" (Scepter 12153)
  by Dionne Warwick (1966)

"Travelin' Man" (Imperial 5741)
  by Rick Nelson (1961)

"Uneasy Rider" (Kama Sutra 576)
  by The Charlie Daniels Band (1973)

"Wreck Of The Edmund Fitzgerald" (Reprise 1369)
  by Gordon Lightfoot (1976)

Airplanes

"Air Disaster" (Mums 6030)
  by Albert Hammond (1974)

"Airplane Song (My Airplane)" (Laurie 3391)
  by The Royal Guardsmen (1967)

"Back In The U.S.A." (Chess 1729)
  by Chuck Berry (1959)

"Back In The U.S.S.R." (Buddah 100)
  by Chubby Checker (1969)

"Early Morning Rain" (Warner Brothers 5659)
  by Peter, Paul, and Mary (1965)

"Ebony Eyes" (Warner Brothers 5199)
  by The Everly Brothers (1961)

"Fire And Rain" (Warner Brothers 7423)
  by James Taylor (1970)

"Flight 309 To Tennessee" (Viva 29597)
  by Shelly West (1983)

"Jet Airliner" (Capitol 4424)
  by The Steve Miller Band (1977)

"L.A. International Airport" (Capitol 3035)
  by Susan Raye (1971)

"Leaving On A Jet Plane" (Warner Brothers 7340)
  by Peter, Paul, and Mary (1969)

"Next Plane To London" (Atco 6510)
  by Rose Garden (1967)

"Travelin' Band" (Fantasy 637)
  by Creedence Clearwater Revival (1970)

Automobiles and Trucks

"Almost Grown" (Chess 1722)
  by Chuck Berry (1959)

"Arrested For Driving While Blind" (London 251)
  by Z Z Top (1977)

"At The Darktown Strutters' Ball" (RCA Victor 5611)
  by Lou Monte (1954)

"Autobahn" (Vertigo 203)
  by Kraftwerk (1975)

"Back Home Again" (RCA 10065)
  by John Denver (1974)

"Back When Gas Was Thirty Cents A Gallon" (RCA 12066)
  by Tom T. Hall (1980)

"Bad Brakes" (A&M 2109)
by Cat Stevens (1979)

"Bad Girls" (Casablanca 988)
by Donna Summer (1979)

"Ballad Of Thunder Road" (Capitol 3986)
by Robert Mitchum (1958)

"Beep Beep" (Roulette 4155)
by The Playmates (1958)

"Big Yellow Taxi" (Reprise 0906)
by Joni Mitchell (1970)

"Bucket 'T' " (Mala 492)
by Ronny and The Daytonas (1964)

"Buick '59" (Dootone 347)
by The Medallions (1954)

"Cab Driver" (Dot 17041)
by The Mills Brothers (1968)

"Cadillac Assembly Line" (Utopia 10544)
by Albert King (1976)

"Car Wash" (MCA 40615)
by Rose Royce (1976)

"Carefree Highway" (Reprise 1309)
by Gordon Lightfoot (1974)

"Carol" (Chess 1700)
by Chuck Berry (1958)

"Cars" (Atco 7211)
by Gary Numan (1980)

"C.B. Savage" (Plantation 144)
by Rod Hart (1977)

"Cheva-Kiser-Olds-Mo-Laca-Stude-Var-Linco-Baker" (Dot 16183)
by Pete Stamper (1961)

"Chevy Van" (GRC 2046)
by Sammy Johns (1975)

"Convoy" (MGM 14839)
by C. W. McCall (1976)

"Cops And Robbers" (Checker 850)
by Bo Diddley (1956)

"Cruisin'" (Tamla 54306)
by Smokey Robinson (1979)

"Custom Machine" (Columbia 42956)
by Bruce and Terry (1964)

"Dead Man's Curve" (Liberty 55672)
by Jan and Dean (1964)

"Detroit City" (RCA 8183)
  by Bobby Bare (1963)

"Dinah Flo" (Columbia 45670)
  by Boz Scaggs (1972)

"Drag City" (Liberty 55641)
  by Jan and Dean (1964)

"Drive In Show" (Liberty 55087)
  by Eddie Cochran (1957)

"Drive My Car" (P.I.P. 6509)
  by Gary Toms Empire (1975)

"Driver's Seat" (Atlantic 3604)
  by Sniff 'N' The Tears (1979)

"Drivin' Home" (Jamie 1195)
  by Duane Eddy (1961)

"Drivin' My Life Away" (Elektra 46656)
  by Eddie Rabbit (1980)

"Every Woman I Know" (Vee-Jay 219)
  by Billy "The Kid" Emerson (1955)

"Expressway To Your Heart" (Crimson 1010)
  by Soul Survivors (1967)

"409" (Capitol 4777)
  by The Beach Boys (1962)

"Free Wheelin' " (Mercury 73622)
  by Bachman-Turner Overdrive (1974)

"Fun Fun Fun" (Capitol 5118)
  by The Beach Boys (1964)

"Games People Play" (Capitol 2248)
  by Joe South (1969)

"Gas Money" (Arwin III)
  by Jan and Arnie (1958)

"The General Lee" (Scotti Brothers 02803)
  by Johnny Cash (1982)

"Geronimo's Cadillac" (A&M 1368)
  by Michael Murphy (1972)

"Get That Gasoline Blues" (Kama Sutra 586)
  by NRBQ (1975)

"Greased Lightnin' " (RSO 909)
  by John Travolta (1978)

"G.T.O." (Mala 481)
  by Ronny and The Daytonas (1964)

"Hey, Good Lookin' " (Columbia 39570)
  by Jo Stafford and Frankie Laine (1951)

"Hey Little Cobra" (Columbia 42921)
  by The Rip Chords (1964)

"Highway 40 Blues" (Epic 03812)
  by Ricky Scaggs (1983)

"Highway Song" (Atco 7104)
  by Blackfoot (1979)

"Highway To Hell" (Atlantic 3617)
  by AC/DC (1979)

"The Horizontal Bop" (Capitol 4951)
  by Bob Seger (1980)

"Hot Rod Hearts" (Elektra 47005)
  by Robbie Dupree (1980)

"Hot Rod Lincoln" (Republic 2005)
  by Johnny Bond (1960)

"Hot Rod Race" (Mercury 5547)
  by Tiny Hill (1951)

"House, A Car, & A Wedding Ring" (Checker 906)
  by Dale Hawkins (1958)

"I Can't Drive 55" (Geffen 29173)
  by Sammy Hagar (1984)

"I Get Around" (Capitol 5174)
  by The Beach Boys (1964)

"I Got A Name" (ABC 11389)
  by Jim Croce (1973)

"I Love My Truck" (Mirage 3845)
  by Glen Campbell (1981)

"It's A Long Way To Daytona" (Elektra 47412)
  by Mel Tillis (1982)

"It's Late" (Imperial 5565)
  by Ricky Nelson (1959)

"Just Dropped In (To See What Condition My Condition Was In)..."
  (Reprise 0655)
  by Kenny Rogers and The First Edition (1968)

"Kansas City Star" (Smash 1998)
  by Roger Miller (1965)

"L.A. Freeway" (MCA 40054)
  by Jerry Jeff Walker (1973)

"Life In The Fast Lane" (Asylum 45403)
  by The Eagles (1977)

"Little Deuce Coupe" (Capitol 5009)
  by The Beach Boys (1963)

"Little Honda" (Mercury 72324)
  by The Hondells (1964)

"Little Old Lady (From Pasadena)" (Liberty 55703)
    by Jan and Dean (1964)

"Little Red Corvette" (Warner Brothers 29746)
    by Prince (1983)

"Lord, Mr. Ford" (RCA 0960)
    by Jerry Reed (1973)

"Maybellene" (Chess 1604)
    by Chuck Berry (1955)

"Mercury Blues" (Asylum album)
    by David Lindley (n.d.)

"Mr. Limousine Driver" (Capitol 2691)
    by Grand Funk (1969)

"Mrs. Robinson" (Columbia 44511)
    by Simon and Garfunkel (1968)

"Mustang Sally" (Atlantic 2365)
    by Wilson Pickett (1966)

"My Old Car" (Amy 987)
    by Lee Dorsey (1967)

"Nadine (Is It You?)" (Chess 1883)
    by Chuck Berry (1964)

"Night Moves" (Capitol 4369)
    by Bob Seger (1976)

"No Money Down" (Chess album)
    by Chuck Berry (n.d.)

"No Particular Place To Go" (Chess 1898)
    by Chuck Berry (1964)

"(Oh Lord Won't You Buy Me A) Mercedes Benz" (Capitol 3246)
    by Goose Creek Symphony (1972)

"One Piece At A Time" (Columbia 10321)
    by Johnny Cash (1976)

"Paradise By The Dashboard Light" (Epic 50588)
    by Meatloaf (1978)

"Pontiac Blues" (Trumpet 145)
    by Sonny Boy Williamson (1951)

"Promised Land" (Chess 1916)
    by Chuck Berry (1964)

"Pushbutton Automobile" (Dooto 400)
    by The Medallions (1956)

"Ridin' My Thumb To Mexico" (Mercury 73416)
    by Johnny Rodriguez (1973)

"Rocket '88'" (Chess 1458)
    by Jackie Brenston (1951)

"Rolene" (Capitol 4765)
  by Moon Martin (1979)

"Roll On Down The Highway" (Mercury 73656)
  by Bachman-Turner Overdrive (1975)

"Route 66" (London album)
  by The Rolling Stones (n.d.)

"Running On Empty" (Asylum 45460)
  by Jackson Browne (1978)

"Sequel" (Boardwalk 5700)
  by Harry Chapin (1980)

"Seven Little Girls Sitting In The Back Seat" (Guaranteed 200)
  by Paul Evans (1959)

"Shut Down" (Capitol 4932)
  by The Beach Boys (1963)

"Six Days On The Road" (Golden World 3020)
  by Dave Dudley (1963)

"Somethin' Else" (Liberty 55203)
  by Eddie Cochran (1959)

"Star Baby" (RCA 0217)
  by The Guess Who (1974)

"Steppin' Out" (Rocket 40582)
  by Neil Sedaka (1976)

"Stick Shift" (Sue 745)
  by The Duals (1961)

"Sting Ray" (Warner Brothers 5349)
  by The Routers (1963)

"Summertime Blues" (Liberty 55144)
  by Eddie Cochran (1958)

"Super Highway" (Columbia 45312)
  by Ballin' Jack (1971)

"Take It Easy" (Asylum 11005)
  by The Eagles (1972)

"Take Me Home, Country Roads" (RCA 0445)
  by John Denver (1971)

"Taxi" (Elektra 45770)
  by Harry Chapin (1972)

"Tell Laura I Love Her" (RCA 7745)
  by Ray Peterson (1960)

"Texas In My Rear View Mirror" (Casablanca 2305)
  by Mac Davis (1980)

"Three Window Coupe" (Columbia 43035)
  by The Rip Chords (1964)

"Tijuana Taxi" (A&M 787)
   by Herb Alpert and The Tijuana Brass (1966)

"Too Much Monkey Business" (Chess album)
   by Chuck Berry (n.d.)

"Transfusion" (Dot 15470)
   by Nervous Norvus (1956)

"Truck Stop" (ABS 11162)
   by Jerry Smith (1969)

"Tulsa Time" (RSO 1039)
   by Eric Clapton (1980)

"Two Car Garage" (Cleveland International 04237)
   by B. J. Thomas (1983)

"Two Lane Highway" (RCA 10302)
   by Pure Prairie League (1975)

"Under My Wheels" (Warner Brothers 7529)
   by Alice Cooper (1972)

"Vehicle" (Warner Brothers 7378)
   by Ides of March (1970)

"Ventura Highway" (Warner Brothers 7641)
   by America (1972)

"Wake Up Little Susie" (Cadence 1337)
   by The Everly Brothers (1957)

"Welfare Cadillac" (Royal American 1)
   by Guy Drake (1970)

"Workin' At The Car Wash Blues" (ABC 11447)
   by Jim Croce (1974)

"Wreck On The Highway" (Hickory album)
   by Roy Acuff (1952)

"You Don't Mess Around With Jim" (ABC 11328)
   by Jim Croce (1972)

"You Got What It Takes" (United Artists 185)
   by Marv Johnson (1960)

"You Never Can Tell" (Chess 1906)
   by Chuck Berry (1964)

"You're My Driving Wheel" (Motown 1407)
   by The Supremes (1976)

Railroads, Transit Trains, and Subways

"Back Up Train" (Hot Line 15000)
   by Al Green and The Soul Mates (1967)

"Blue Train (Of The Heartbreak Line)" (RCA 8308)
   by John D. Loudermilk (1964)

"C.C. Rider" (Atlantic 1130)
by Chuck Willis (1957)

"Chattanooga Choo Choo" (Butterfly 1205)
by Tuxedo Junction (1978)

"Choo-Choo Train" (Mala 12005)
by The Box Tops (1968)

"The City Of New Orleans" (Reprise 1103)
by Arlo Guthrie (1972)

"Click-Clack" (Swan 4001)
by Dickey Doo and The Don'ts (1958)

"Disco Train" (AVI 131)
by Jerry Rix (1977)

"Don't Sleep In The Subway" (Warner Brothers 7049)
by Petula Clark (1967)

"Down By The Station" (Capitol 4312)
by The Four Preps (1960)

"Down Home Special" (Checker 850)
by Bo Diddley (1957)

"Engine Engine #9" (Smash 1983)
by Roger Miller (1965)

"Engine Number 9" (Atlantic 2765)
by Wilson Pickett (1970)

"Folsom Prison Blues" (Columbia 44513)
by Johnny Cash (1968)

"Freight Train" (Mercury 71102)
by Rusty Draper (1957)

"Freight Train Blues" (Hickory 1291)
by Roy Acuff (1965)

"Friendship Train" (Soul 35068)
by Gladys Knight and The Pips (1969)

"The Gambler" (United Artists 1250)
by Kenny Rogers (1979)

"Green, Green Grass Of Home" (Parrot 40009)
by Tom Jones (1967)

"Hey Porter" (Sun 221)
by Johnny Cash (1955)

"Hitchcock Railway" (RCA 9641)
by Jose Feliciano (1968)

"Hobo On A Freight Train To Heaven" (MCA 40769)
by Kenny Starr (1977)

"Homeward Bound" (Columbia 43511)
by Simon and Garfunkel (1966)

"Honky Train" (Hi 2038)
  by Bill Black's Combo (1961)

"I Been To Georgia On A Fast Train" (Columbia 03058)
  by Johnny Cash (1982)

"I'm A Train" (Mums 6026)
  by Albert Hammond (1974)

"I'm Coming Home" (Atlantic 3027)
  by The Spinners (1974)

"I'm Leaving On That Late, Late Train" (Chess 2159)
  by Solomon Burke (1975)

"I'm Movin' On" (Smash 1813)
  by Matt Lucas (1963)

"John Henry" (London 1650)
  by Lonnie Donegan (1956)

"Johnny B. Goode" (Chess 1691)
  by Chuck Berry (1958)

"Keep This Train-A-Rollin' " (Warner Brothers 49670)
  by The Doobie Brothers (1981)

"King Of The Road" (Smash 1965)
  by Roger Miller (1965)

"King's Special" (ABC 11280)
  by B. B. King (1970)

"Last Train To Clarksville" (Colgems 1001)
  by The Monkees (1966)

"Last Train To London" (Jet 5067)
  by The Electric Light Orchestra (1979)

"Let Jesse Rob The Train" (Warner Brothers 49118)
  by Buck Owens (1979)

"Little Train" (Mercury 71286)
  by Marianne Vasel and Erich Storz (1958)

"Locomotive Breath" (Chrysalis 2110)
  by Jethro Tull (1976)

"Lonesome Train" (Modern 888)
  by Johnny Moore's Three Blazers (1951)

"Lonesome Whistle Blues" (Federal 12415)
  by Freddie King (1961)

"Long Train Runnin' " (Warner Brothers 7698)
  by The Doobie Brothers (1973)

"Long Twin Silver Line" (Capitol 4836)
  by Bob Seger (1980)

"Loose Caboose" (Dial 2800)
  by Joe Tex (1978)

"Love Train" (Philadelphia International 3524)
by The O'Jays (1973)

"Lover Please" (Mercury 71941)
by Clyde McPhatter (1962)

"Mama From The Train (A Kiss, A Kiss)" (Mercury 70971)
by Patti Page (1956)

"Marrakesh Express" (Atlantic 2652)
by Crosby, Stills, Nash and Young (1969)

"Me And Bobby McGee" (Columbia 45314)
by Janis Joplin (1971)

"Mean Old Train" (Gotham 515)
by John Lee Hooker (1953)

"Memphis Train" (Mercury 72945)
by Buddy Miles (1969)

"The Metro" (Geffen 29638)
by Berlin (1983)

"Midnight Cannonball" (Atlantic 1069)
by Joe Turner (1955)

"Midnight Flyer" (Capitol 4248)
by Nat King Cole (1959)

"Midnight Rider" (Capricorn 0035)
by Gregg Allman (1974)

"Midnight Special" (Imperial 66087)
by Johnny Rivers (1965)

"Midnight Train" (Coral 61675)
by The Johnny Burnette Trio (1956)

"Midnight Train To Georgia" (Buddah 383)
by Gladys Knight and The Pips (1973)

"Milk Train" (Warner Brothers 7226)
by The Everly Brothers (1969)

"Morning Train (Nine To Five)" (EMI American 8071)
by Sheena Easton (1981)

"Movin' Train" (Mercury 814195)
by The Kendalls (1983)

"M.T.A." (Capitol 4221)
by The Kingston Trio (1959)

"My Baby Thinks He's A Train" (Columbia 02463)
by Rosanne Cash (1981)

"Mystery Train" (Sun 223)
by Elvis Presley (1955)

"New River Train" (Decca 30831)
by Bobby Helms (1959)

"Night Train" (King 5614)
by James Brown (1962)

"Nine Pound Steel" (Sound Stage 72589)
by Joe Simon (1967)

"Orange Blossom Special" (Dot 16174)
by Billy Vaughn (1961)

"Peace Train" (A&M 1291)
by Cat Stevens (1971)

"People Get Ready" (ABC-Paramount 10622)
by The Impressions (1965)

"The Promised Land" (Chess 1916)
by Chuck Berry (1965)

"Rock Island Line" (London 1650)
by Lonnie Donegan (1956)

"Smokestack Lightnin' " (Chess 1618)
by Howlin' Wolf (1956)

"Somebody's Always Saying Goodbye" (Capitol 5183)
by Anne Murray (1982)

"Soul Train" (Rampage 100)
by The Ramrods (1972)

"Soul Train '75" (Soul Train 10400)
by The Soul Train Gang (1975)

"Southbound Train" (Atlantic 2892)
by Graham Nash and David Crosby (1972)

"S.P. Blues" (MGM 10618)
by Ivory Joe Hunter (1950)

"Stop That Train In Harlem" (Bullet 326)
by Walter Davis (1950)

"Sub-Rosa Subway" (Capitol 4412)
by Klaatu (1977)

"'T' 99 Blues" (RPM 325)
by Jimmy Nelson (1951)

"Tennessee Flat-Top Box" (Columbia 42147)
by Johnny Cash (1961)

"There's A Train Leavin' " (A&M 2309)
by Quincy Jones (1981)

"This Train" (Columbia album)
by Johnny Cash (n.d.)

"Ticket To Ride" (Capitol 5407)
by The Beatles (1965)

"Tomorrow's Train" (Astroscope 114)
by The Ponderosa Twins + One (1973)

"Took The Last Train" (Elektra 45500)
by David Gates (1978)

"Toot, Toot, Tootsie (Good-Bye)" (MGM 10548)
by Art Mooney (1949)

"The Train" (Buddah 130)
by The 1910 Fruitgum Co. (1969)

"Train Called Freedom" (Wand 11294)
by The South Shore Commission (1976)

"Train Medley" (Main Street 954)
by Boxcar Willie (1983)

"Train Of Love" (Vista 359)
by Annette (1960)

"Train Of Thought" (MCA 40345)
by Cher (1974)

"Train, Train" (Atco 7207)
by Blackfoot (1979)

"Train, Train Blues" (Hollywood 1043)
by Johnny Fuller (1955)

"Trains And Boats And Planes" (Imperial 66115)
by Billy J. Kramer, with The Dakotas (1965)

"Trans-Europe Express" (Capitol 4460)
by Kraftwerk (1978)

"Trouble In Mind" (Columbia 42525)
by Aretha Franklin (1962)

"Trouble In Mind" (Colpix 175)
by Nina Simone (1961)

"Tuxedo Junction" (Chancellor 1052)
by Frankie Avalon (1960)

"Wabash Cannonball" (RCA 9785)
by Danny Davis and The Nashville Brass (1970)

"Westbound #9" (Hot Wax 7003)
by Flaming Ember (1970)

"Wreck Of Old 97" (RCA Victor 20-4095)
by Hank Snow (1951)

14

Urban Life

The patriotic hymn "O Beautiful For Spacious Skies" describes the ideal of American urban life. The goal is to create a metropolitan situation where alabaster cities gleam, undimmed by human tears. Few would deny that Los Angeles, Chicago, New York, Dallas, Boston, San Francisco, and St. Louis offer their citizens exceptional opportunities for physical recreation, cultural enrichment, diverse employment, flexible housing, educational development, and many other benefits. Of course, there are several prerequisites to taking advantage of these urban opportunities. Time, training, money, and a variety of social, political, and personal skills separate those who can make city life productive and enjoyable from those who can only eke out an existence within the boundaries of a metropolitan area. For the poor, the unemployed, the dislocated, the illiterate and undereducated, and those unfamiliar with urban protocol, the city can be a concrete and metal jungle. Alternatives to metropolitan living include suburban, rural, or wilderness existences. The sacrifices of symphonies, libraries, universities, museums, parks, business offices, high-rise apartments, and specialized shopping facilities are compensated for in more rustic settings by an abundance of clean air, a more leisurely paced work schedule, greater personal independence, cheaper food costs, the absence of traffic jams, and more natural beauty. This latter type of idyllic existence is eulogized by John Denver in "Rocky Mountain High" (1972) and "Thank God I'm A Country Boy" (1975).

New York and Los Angeles were two cities that attracted Chuck Berry in 1959. Linda Ronstadt echoed these same sentiments twenty years later, adding Detroit, Chicago, Chattanooga, Baton Rouge, and St. Louis to her favorite cities list. Many other male and female singers have lauded urban

life. Beyond the generalized praises proclaimed in "Back In The U.S.A."
(1959, 1978), many songs express both appreciation for or fond memories
about specific big towns. These tunes include "Barefoot In Baltimore"
(1967), "The Lady Came From Baltimore" (1967), "Detroit Rock City"
(1976), "Galveston" (1969), "Monterey" (1967), "Nashville" (1966), "Philadelphia Freedom" (1975), and "Do You Know The Way To San Jose"
(1968). There are certain American cities that feature numerous songs praising their distinctive attributes. Examples of songs about these highly popular
areas are:

Chicago

"Chicago" (1957)
"My Kind Of Town" (1968)
"Only In Chicago" (1980)
"Sweet Home Chicago" (1980)
"Take Me Back To Chicago" (1978)

Hollywood

"Hollywood" (1978)
"Hollywood" (1977)
"Hollywood" (1982)
"Hollywood Nights" (1972)
"Hollywood Swinging" (1974)

New Orleans

"New Orleans" (1960)
"New Orleans" (1976)
"New Orleans Ladies" (1978)
"Walking To New Orleans" (1960)
"Way Down Yonder In New Orleans" (1959)

New York

"A Heart In New York" (1981)
"New York New York" (1983)
"New York You Got Me Dancing" (1977)
"New York's My Home" (1956)
"Theme From New York, New York" (1980)

San Francisco

"I Left My Heart In San Francisco" (1962)
"San Franciscan Nights" (1967)
"San Francisco (Be Sure To Wear Flowers In Your Hair)" (1967)
"San Francisco Girls (Return Of The Native)" (1968)

The enjoyment of urban settings is often described in terms of "Dancin'
In The Street" (1964) and partying with friends after work. Even the op-
pressive heat of "Summer In The City" (1966) becomes bearable when love

can be shared "Under The Boardwalk" (1978) or "Up On The Roof" (1979). Similarly, on-the-job cutting up in downtown service stations can be fun, as depicted in "Car Wash" (1976). Cities are sites of potential personal success, too, as mentioned in "Hollywood City" (1962), "Tulsa Time" (1978), "On Broadway" (1978), "Katmandu" (1975), and "Promised Land" (1964). Of course, the most unbounded statement of urban comradery was sounded in 1964 by Petula Clark. Her recording of "Downtown" broadened earlier pro-city sentiments of Tony Bennett and Frank Sinatra.

Numerous songs provide fascinating character sketches of city dwellers. Some tunes explore the lives of prostitutes—"Bad Girls" (1979); others mark proclamations by jealous husbands that they are going to halt their wives' infidelity by leaving the city—"I'm Gonna Move To The Outskirts of Town" (1961); still others depict the ideas and actions of urban gangs, rock music groups, and inner city teachers—"Bennie And The Jets" (1974), "Cover Of The 'Rolling Stone'" (1972), and "Welcome Back" (1976). Audio images of women and men in urban settings often provide a general sense of confusion, anxiety, and violence. Although some of these city characters have been explored earlier in this text, there are a few examples that deserve repetition. Metropolitan women are variously depicted in "Tallahassee Lassie" (1959), "City Girl Stole My Country Boy" (1961), "Eyes Of A New York Woman" (1968), "Sweet City Woman" (1971), "Big City Miss Ruth Ann" (1973), "Lady Marmalade" (1975), "Native New Yorker" (1977), "Hot Child In The City" (1978), "Big Shot" (1979), and "Uptown Girl" (1983). The urban male is equally intriguing and complex, as illustrated in "Stagger Lee" (1958), "Big Boy Pete" (1960), "Boy From New York City" (1965), "A Natural Man" (1971), "Honky Cat" (1972), "Superfly" (1972), "You Don't Mess Around With Jim" (1972), "Bad, Bad Leroy Brown" (1973), and "Movin' Out (Anthony's Song)" (1978).

Most city dwellers can be described as survivors. That is, they are able to overcome the potentially destructive forces of personal isolation and social alienation that are prevalent in metropolitan settings. Yet even those who thrive in city environments often communicate love-hate feelings about urban life. These ambivalent attitudes are highlighted in "New York's A Lonely Town" (1965), "Funky Broadway" (1967), "Born To Run" (1975), "Country Boy (You Got Your Feet In L.A.)" (1975), "Another Rainy Day In New York City" (1976), "Lido Shuffle" (1977), and "On Broadway" (1978). Beneath those who are successful yet ambivalent are those individuals who feel trapped in urban failure. The unforgiving nature of the day-to-day metropolitan rat race is described in "Uptown" (1962), "Detroit City" (1963), "No Pity (In The Naked City)" (1965), "Twelve Thirty (Young Girls Are Coming To The Canyon)" (1967), "San Francisco Is A Lonely Town" (1969), "Down And Out In New York City" (1973), "Midnight Train To Georgia" (1973), and "Ain't No Love In The Heart Of The City" (1974).

The depression and anxiety that culminates from living in the inner city is encapsuled by B. B. King in lyrical exchanges with helpless, poverty-stricken companions and unresponsive, unsympathetic social workers. "Why I Sing The Blues" (1969) contains themes echoed in several Stevie Wonder and Ray Charles tunes. It is ironic that both of these creative sensitive artists used the same tune—"Living For The City" (1973, 1975)—to express their own frustrations about black life in the urban ghetto. Other forms of dissatisfaction are expressed in relation to personal stagnation—"We Gotta Get Out Of This Place" (1965); in respect to frightening occupations—"The Night Chicago Died" (1974); in reflections about political abuses—"Chicago" (1971). More universal criticisms of urban alienation are featured in "Ball Of Confusion (That's What The World Is Today)" (1970) and "Baker Street" (1978).

The erosion of city life during the past four decades is depicted as an evolutionary decline in several songs. The shift toward dependence on imported metal and away from Pennsylvania steel leading to the economic collapse of "Allentown" (1982) is detailed by Billy Joel; the sterilization of Akron, Ohio as a metropolitan ghetto is derided by Chrissie Hynde of The Pretenders in "My City Was Gone" (1982); and the general paving over of parks, destruction of greenery, and mindless expansion of shopping facilities are condemned in Joni Mitchell's "Big Yellow Taxi" (1970). More personalized feelings about the lack of police protection, the insensitivity of ghetto inhabitants toward each other, the predatory nature of drug dealers, pimps, and mobsters, and the heartless nature of urban politicians are dramatically proclaimed in "M.T.A." (1959), "Dead End Street" (1967), "Ghetto Woman" (1971), "Inner City Blues (Make Me Wanna Holler)" (1971), "In The Ghetto" (1969), "Masterpiece" (1973), "For The Love Of Money" (1974), and "Living For The City" (1975). The often discussed solution—"Let's Clean Up The Ghetto" (1977)—seems to be more of a dream than a reality. The sentiments of patriotic hymns continue to provide unfulfilled hopes.

URBAN LIFE

City Dwellers

"Bad, Bad Leroy Brown" (ABC 11359)
   by Jim Croce (1973)

"Bad Girls" (Casablanca 988)
   by Donna Summer (1979)

"Bennie And The Jets" (MCA 40198)
   by Elton John (1974)

"Big Boy Pete" (Arvee 595)
  by The Olympics (1960)

"Big City Miss Ruth Ann" (Sussex 248)
  by Gallery (1973)

"Big In Vegas" (Capitol 2646)
  by Buck Owens and His Buckaroos (1969)

"Big Shot" (Columbia 10913)
  by Billy Joel (1979)

"Boy From New York City" (Blue Cat 102)
  by The Ad Libs (1965)

"City Girl Stole My Country Boy" (Mercury 71792)
  by Patti Page (1961)

"Country Girl—City Man" (Atlantic 2480)
  by Billy Vera and Judy Clay (1968)

"The Cover Of 'Rolling Stone' " (Columbia 45732)
  by Dr. Hook (1972)

"Dirty Water" (Tower 185)
  by The Standells (1966)

"Don't Go City Girl On Me" (ABC 17697)
  by Tommy Overstreet (1977)

"Eyes Of A New York Woman" (Scepter 12219)
  by B. J. Thomas (1968)

"High Heel Sneakers" (Smash 1930)
  by Jerry Lee Lewis (1964)

"Honky Cat" (Uni 55343)
  by Elton John (1972)

"Hot Child In The City" (Chrysalis 2226)
  by Nick Gilder (1978)

"Hot City" (Elektra 47002)
  by Shadow (1980)

"I'm Gonna Move To The Outskirts Of Town" (Impulse 202)
  by Ray Charles (1961)

"Johnny B. Goode" (Chess 1691)
  by Chuck Berry (1958)

"Junk Food Junkie" (Warner Brothers 8165)
  by Larry Groce (1976)

"Kansas City Star" (Smash 1998)
  by Roger Miller (1965)

"Lady Marmalade" (Epic 50048)
  by LaBelle (1975)

"Movin' Out (Anthony's Song)" (Columbia 10708)
  by Billy Joel (1978)

"Native New Yorker"(RCA 11129)
  by Odyssey (1977)

"A Natural Man" (MGM 14262)
  by Lou Rawls (1971)

"Never Going Back" (Kama Sutra 250)
  by The Lovin' Spoonful (1968)

"New York City" (EMI 8005)
  by Zwol (1978)

"Oh Pretty Woman" (Warner Brothers 50003)
  by Van Halen (1982)

"Only The Good Die Young" (Columbia 10750)
  by Billy Joel (1978)

"Please Come To Boston" (Epic 11115)
  by Dave Loggins (1974)

"Spanish Harlem" (Atco 6185)
  by Ben E. King (1960)

"Stagger Lee" (ABC-Paramount 9972)
  by Lloyd Price (1958)

"Superfly" (Curtom 1978)
  by Curtis Mayfield (1972)

"Sweet City Woman" (Bell 45120)
  by The Stampeders (1971)

"Tallahassee Lassie" (Swan 4031)
  by Freddy Cannon (1959)

"Uptown Girl" (Columbia 04149)
  by Billy Joel (1983)

"Welcome Back" (Reprise 1349)
  by John Sebastian (1976)

"You Don't Mess Around With Jim" (ABC 11328)
  by Jim Croce (1972)

Isolation and Alienation in the City

"Ain't No Love In The Heart Of The City" (Dunhill 15003)
  by Bobby Bland (1974)

"Another Rainy Day In New York City" (Columbia 10360)
  by Chicago (1976)

"Baker Street" (United Artists 1192)
  by Gerry Rafferty (1978)

"Ball Of Confusion (That's What The World Is Today)" (Gordy 7099)
  by The Temptations (1970)

"Big City" (Epic 02686)
  by Merle Haggard (1982)

"Born To Run" (Columbia 10209)
by Bruce Springsteen (1975)

"Bright Lights, Big City" (Vee-Jay 398)
by Jimmy Reed (1961)

"By The Time I Get To Phoenix" (Capitol 2015)
by Glen Campbell (1967)

"Chicago" (Atlantic 2804)
by Crosby, Stills, Nash and Young (1971)

"Chicago Damn" (Blue Note 395)
by Bobbi Humphrey (1974)

"A Country Boy Can Survive" (Elektra 47257)
by Hank Williams, Jr. (1982)

"Country Boy (You Got Your Feet In L.A.)" (Capitol 4155)
by Glen Campbell (1975)

"Deep In The Heart Of Harlem" (Mercury 72220)
by Clyde McPhatter (1964)

"Detroit City" (RCA 8183)
by Bobby Bare (1963)

"Dirty Laundry" (Asylum 69892)
by Don Henley (1982)

"Down And Out In New York City" (Polydor 14168)
by James Brown (1973)

"Down In The Boondocks" (Columbia 43305)
by Billy Joe Royal (1965)

"Funky Broadway" (Atlantic 2430)
by Wilson Pickett (1967)

"House Of The Rising Sun" (Parrot 341)
by Frijid Pink (1970)

"I Am . . . I Said" (Uni 55278)
by Neil Diamond (1971)

"I Guess The Lord Must Be In New York City" (RCA 0261)
by Nilsson (1969)

"Inner City" (Cotillion 47004)
by Mass Production (1982)

"Lido Shuffle" (Columbia 10491)
by Boz Scaggs (1977)

"Little Boxes" (Columbia 42940)
by Pete Seeger (1964)

"Living For The City" (Tamla 54242)
by Stevie Wonder (1973)

"Midnight Train To Georgia" (Buddah 383)
by Gladys Knight and the Pips (1973)

"My Little Town" (Columbia 10230)
  by Simon and Garfunkel (1975)

"New York's A Lonely Town" (Red Bird 020)
  by Trade Winds (1965)

"The Night Chicago Died" (Mercury 73492)
  by Paper Lace (1974)

"No Pity (In The Naked City)" (Brunswick 55280)
  by Jackie Wilson (1965)

"On Broadway" (Warner Brothers 8542)
  by George Benson (1978)

"Pleasant Valley Sunday" (Colgems 1007)
  by The Monkees (1967)

"San Francisco Is A Lonely Town" (Sound Stage 2641)
  by Joe Simon (1969)

"Say Goodbye To Hollywood" (Columbia 02518)
  by Billy Joel (1981)

"Tulsa Time" (ABC 12425)
  by Don Williams (1978)

"Twelve Thirty (Young Girls Are Coming To The Canyon)" (Dunhill 4099)
  by The Mamas and the Papas (1967)

"Uptown" (Philles 102)
  by The Crystals (1962)

"We Gotta Get Out Of This Place" (MGM 13382)
  by The Animals (1965)

"Who Can It Be Now?" (Columbia 02888)
  by Men at Work (1981)

"Why I Sing The Blues" (Bluesway 61024)
  by B. B. King (1969)

Metropolitan Advantages

"Alright In The City" (Capitol 2935)
  by Dunn and McCashen (1970)

"American City Suite" (Dunhill 4324)
  by Cashman and West (1972)

"Back In The U.S.A." (Chess 1729)
  by Chuck Berry (1959)

"Back In The U.S.A." (Asylum 45519)
  by Linda Ronstadt (1978)

"Barefoot In Baltimore" (Uni 55076)
  by Strawberry Alarm Clock (1968)

"Car Wash" (MCA 40615)
  by Rose Royce (1976)

"Chicago" (Capitol 3793)
  by Frank Sinatra (1957)

"Chicago Theme (Love Loop)" (CTI 27)
  by Hubert Laws (1975)

"City In The Sky" (Stax 0215)
  by The Staple Singers (1974)

"City Lights" (Dot 16071))
  by Debbie Reynolds (1960)

"City Of Angels" (Bally 1018)
  by The Highlights (1956)

"Concrete And Clay" (DynoVoice 204)
  by Eddie Rambeau (1965)

"Dancin' In The Street" (Gordy 7033)
  by Martha and The Vandellas (1964)

"Detroit Rock City" (Casablanca 863)
  by Kiss (1976)

"Dirty Water" (Polydor 2032)
  by The Inmates (1979)

"Do You Know The Way To San Jose" (Scepter 12216)
  by Dionne Warwick (1968)

"Downtown" (Warner Brothers 5494)
  by Petula Clark (1964)

"Fool For The City" (Bearsville 0307)
  by Foghat (1976)

"A Friend In The City" (Steed 7 23)
  by Andy Kim (1970)

"Galveston" (Capitol 2428)
  by Glen Campbell (1969)

"A Heart In New York" (Columbia 02307)
  by Art Garfunkel (1981)

"The Heart Of Rock 'N' Roll" (Chrysalis 42782)
  by Huey Lewis and The News (1984)

"The Heat Is On" (MCA 52512)
  by Glenn Frey (1984)

"Hollywood" (MGM 13039)
  by Connie Francis (1961)

"Hollywood" (ABC 12269)
  by Rufus, featuring Chaka Khan (1977)

"Hollywood" (Columbia 10679)
  by Boz Scaggs (1978)

"Hollywood" (Epic 02755)
  by Shooting Star (1982)

"Hollywood City" (Columbia 42405)
  by Carl Perkins (1962)

"Hollywood Hot" (20th Century 2215)
  by Eleventh Hour (1975)

"Hollywood Nights" (Capitol 4618)
  by Bob Seger and The Silver Bullet Band (1978)

"Hollywood Swinging" (De-Lite 561)
  by Kool and The Gang (1974)

"Hot In The City" (Chrysalis 2605)
  by Billy Idol (1982)

"I Left My Heart In San Francisco" (Columbia 42332)
  by Tony Bennett (1962)

"Kansas City" (Reprise 20236)
  by Trini Lopez (1964)

"Katmandu" (Capitol 4116)
  by Bob Seger (1975)

"L.A. Freeway" (MCA 40054)
  by Jerry Jeff Walker (1973)

"L.A. Goodbye" (Warner Brothers 7466)
  by Ides of March (1971)

"L.A. International Airport" (Capitol 3035)
  by Susan Raye (1971)

"The Little Old Lady (From Pasadena)" (Liberty 55704)
  by Jan and Dean (1964)

"Love In The City" (White Whale 326)
  by The Turtles (1969)

"Monterey" (MGM 13868)
  by The Animals (1967)

"My Home Town" (ABC-Paramount 10106)
  by Paul Anka (1960)

"My Kind Of Town" (Reprise 0702)
  by Frank Sinatra (1968)

"Nashville Cats" (Kama Sutra 219)
  by The Lovin' Spoonful (1960)

"New Orleans" (LeGrand 1003)
  by Gary "U.S." Bonds (1960)

"New Orleans" (Curtom 0113)
  by The Staple Singers (1976)

"New Orleans Ladies" (Capitol 4586)
  by Le Roux (1978)

"New York Groove" (Casablanca 941)
  by Ace Frehely (1978)

"New York New York" (Sugar Hill 457)
   by Grandmaster Flash and The Furious Five (1983)

"New York, You Got Me Dancing" (Buddah 564)
   by The Andrea True Connection (1977)

"New York's My Home" (Decca 30111)
   by Sammy Davis, Jr. (1956)

"On Broadway" (Warner Brothers 8542)
   by George Benson (1978)

"Only In Chicago" (Arista AS 0566)
   by Barry Manilow (1980)

"Philadelphia Freedom" (MCA 40364)
   by Elton John (1975)

"Philadelphia, U.S.A." (Carlton 492)
   by Nu Tornados (1958)

"Promised Land" (Chess 1916)
   by Chuck Berry (1964)

"Rip It Up" (Decca 30028)
   by Bill Haley and The Comets (1956)

"Rock This Town" (EMI American 8132)
   by The Stray Cats (1982)

"San Franciscan Nights" (MGM 13769)
   by The Animals (1967)

"San Francisco (Be Sure To Wear Flowers In Your Hair)" (Ode 103)
   by Scott McKenzie (1967)

"San Francisco Girls (Return Of The Native)" (Uni 55060)
   by Fever Tree (1968)

"Spring In Manhattan" (Columbia 42779)
   by Tony Bennett (1963)

"Summer In The City" (Kama Sutra 211)
   by The Lovin' Spoonful (1966)

"Sweet Home Chicago" (Duke 301)
   by Little Junior Parker (1958)

"Take Me Back To Chicago" (Columbia 10737)
   by Chicago (1978)

"Theme From New York, New York" (Reprise 49233)
   by Frank Sinatra (1980)

"Under The Boardwalk" (Private Stock 45192)
   by Billy Joe Royal (1978)

"Up On The Roof" (Columbia 11005)
   by James Taylor (1979)

"Up Town" (Monument 412)
   by Roy Orbison (1960)

"Walking To New Orleans" (Imperial 5675)
  by Fats Domino (1960)

"Way Down Yonder In New Orleans" (Swan 4043)
  by Freddy Cannon (1959)

Rejection of Urban Life

"Rocky Mountain High" (RCA 0829)
  by John Denver (1972)

"Take Me Home, Country Roads" (RCA 0445)
  by John Denver (1971)

"Thank God I'm A Country Boy" (RCA 10239)
  by John Denver (1975)

Urban Erosion

"Allentown" (Columbia 03413)
  by Billy Joel (1982)

"Big Yellow Taxi" (Reprise 0906)
  by Joni Mitchell (1970)

"Dead End Street" (Capitol 5869)
  by Lou Rawls (1967)

"For The Love Of Money" (Philadelphia International 3544)
  by The O'Jays (1974)

"The Ghetto" (Atco 6719)
  by Donny Hathaway (1970)

"Ghetto Woman" (ABC 11310)
  by B. B. King (1971)

"In The Ghetto" (RCA 47-9741)
  by Elvis Presley (1969)

"Inner City Blues (Make Me Wanna Holler)" (Tamla 54209)
  by Marvin Gaye (1971)

"Let's Clean Up The Ghetto" (Philadelphia International 3627)
  by The Philadelphia International All Stars (1977)

"Living For The City" (Crossover 981)
  by Ray Charles (1975)

"Masterpiece" (Gordy 7126)
  by The Temptations (1973)

"M.T.A." (Capitol 4221)
  by The Kingston Trio (1959)

"My City Was Gone" (Sire 29840)
  by The Pretenders (1982)

15

Youth Culture

Popular music is both a reflection of and a defining factor for America's youth culture. With this kind of all-inclusive topical influence, it is extremely difficult to isolate a narrow list of subjects that define youth culture in contemporary song. Previous chapters in this book resolve part of this problem. Key topics such as education, dating/love/sex, automobiles, employment, and social criticism already have been examined. What remains to be explored is a triad of themes that have dominated the thoughts of most young people and nearly everyone who has encountered America's strident youth culture during the past thirty-five years. These issues are leisure activities—alcohol and drug use, clothing styles, dances, music, party times, vacations, fads, and humor; idealism—hopes for a positive future; and self-identity—personal maturity and identity, peer groups, friends, family, authority figures, and generation gaps.

The use and abuse of alcohol and other drugs is neither a new social phenomenon nor a behavioral problem restricted to American youth. However, during the 1950–1985 period there has been a distinctive shift in drug use imagery. Beer drinking was viewed as an acceptable form of rebellious activity throughout the 1950s and early 1960s. Alcoholic beverages continued to be consumed by young people in the post-1965 period, but the introduction of other drugs—marijuana, LSD, cocaine, and heroin—led to heightened levels of public concern. Parents, teachers, politicians, community leaders, and others invoked medical arguments, moral warnings, and legal standards to diminish the use of drugs. Since drugs themselves and even associated smoking paraphenalia became more and more associated with a general countercultural movement, the debate about the pros and cons of drug use frequently emerged in the lyrics of contemporary songs.

Although no resolution was achieved, the commentaries continued into the late 1970s and early 1980s. Alcohol resumed dominance over heavier drugs, and the public debate over drinking and use of drugs shifted toward automobile safety (drunken driving) and illegal substance trafficking (smuggling and pushing drugs).

The joys of imbibing alcoholic beverages are widely chronicled in contemporary song. These tunes range from individual statements of enjoyment such as "Drinking Wine Spo-Dee O'Dee" (1973), "Scotch And Soda" (1962), and "Margaritaville" (1977) to plans for group activities including "Beer Drinkin' Song" (1982), "Bottle Of Wine" (1967), "Champagne Jam" (1978), "Let's Go Get Stoned" (1966), "Livingston Saturday Night" (1978), and "Sweet Cherry Wine" (1969). Songs also illustrate points of personal liberation—"Escape (The Pina Colada Song)" (1979), and individual depression—"What's Made Milwaukee Famous (Has Made A Loser Out Of Me)" (1968). The humor of alcohol-influenced misbehavior is illustrated in "Chug-A-Lug" (1964), "Dang Me" (1964), "D. W. Washburn" (1968), "One Mint Julep" (1952), and "White Lightning" (1959).

Much of the music that has been defined as drug oriented or drug-use stimulating is couched in a symbolic or metaphoric format. "Magic Carpet Ride" (1968), "Magic Bus" (1968), "Psychedelic Shack" (1970), "Eight Miles High" (1966), and "Lucy In The Sky With Diamonds" (1975) are examples of this type of music. Humorous approaches are presented in "Wildwood Weed" (1974) and in "Mama Told Me (Not To Come)" (1972). Other songs that seem unbelievably straightforward in their acknowledgment of drug use are "Along Comes Mary" (1966), "Cocaine" (1980), "Purple Haze" (1967), and "White Rabbit" (1967).

If the preceding songs seem to be pro-drug, then there is a lyrical antidote available in a variety of tunes that describe the negative effects of amphetamines, heroin, and other drugs. The loss of reality depicted in "Lookin' Out My Back Door" (1970) and "I Had Too Much To Dream (Last Night)" (1966) is expanded in the deadly delusion described in "Mother's Little Helper" (1966). A more pointed warning is offered in "Kicks" (1966). But the most horrifying anti-drug songs are " Amphetamine Annie" (n.d.), "Dolly Dagger" (1971), "Freddie's Dead" (1972), "The Pusher" (n.d.), and "Snow Blind Friend" (1971). Whether as warnings or as invitations, music describing alcohol and drugs within the youth culture is broad based and enthusiastic.

Although the universal clothing item worn by the American youth culture is jeans (followed closely by tennis shoes), the lyrics of the past thirty-five years allude to all kinds of fads and fancies of dress. Z Z Topp declared in 1983 that every girl is crazy about a "Sharp Dressed Man." The male response to well-dressed females is similar. It is unclear, though, which specific articles of clothing are most satisfying. The choices include "Betty In Bermudas" (1963), "Big Leg Woman (With A Short Short Mini Skirt)"

(1970), "Black Denim Trousers" (1955), "Black Slacks" (1957), "Chantilly Lace" (1958), "No Chemise, Please" (1958), "Pink Pedal Pushers" (1958), "Short Shorts" (1958), and "A White Sport Coat (And A Pink Carnation)" (1957). Undeniably, males would flock to see either an "Itsy Bitsy Teenie Weenie Yellow Polkadot Bikini" (1960) or a "One Piece Topless Bathing Suit" (1964). But slacks, shirts, and sport coats take second place in lyrical interest to jeans and footwear. The recordings lauding levis include "Baby Makes Her Blue Jeans Talk" (1982), "Be Bop A Lulu" (1956) in her red blue jeans, "Bell Bottom Blues" (1971), "Bluejean Bop" (1956), "Designer Jeans" (1982), "Dungaree Doll" (1955), "Forever In Blue Jeans" (1979), "From Levis To Calvin Klein Jeans" (1982), "Jeans On" (1977), "Tight Fittin' Jeans" (1981), and "Venus In Blue Jeans" (1962). On the footwear front, the variety of shoe songs illustrate the utility as well as the beauty of fancy pads. These tunes include "Betty Lou Got A New Pair Of Shoes" (1958), "Blue Suede Shoes" (1956), "Boogie Shoes" (1978), "Cowboy Boots" (1963), "Hang Up My Rock 'N' Roll Shoes" (1958), "Hi-Heel Sneakers" (1964), "Penny Loafers And Bobby Socks" (1957), "Pointed Toe Shoes" (1959), "Rockin' Shoes" (1957), "Slip-In Mules (No High Heel Sneakers)" (1964), "Travelin' Shoes" (1974), and "White Bucks And Saddle Shoes" (1958).

On the more exotic (and sometimes kinky) side, Steve Miller describes a young woman's attire as silk and satin, leather and lace, and black panties in "Abracadabra" (1982). Peter and Gordon sang of opposite extremes of dress in "Knight In Rusty Armour" (1966) and the totally uncovered "Lady Godiva" (1966). Bob Dylan described an outlandish "Leopard-Skin Pill-Box Hat" (1967), while The Coasters raved about a scantily dressed dancer named "Little Egypt" (1961). The most outrageous dress, in terms of voo-doo-oriented clothing, is lauded by The Sapphires in "Who Do You Love" (1964). Attention to clothing detail is provided in the lyrics of hundreds of other songs, too.

If it is anything, rock era music is a blaring, insistent invitation to dance. There are innumerable examples of songs that describe specific dance styles, that urge individuals to abandon their self-conscious feelings and to get out on the floor, that equate hip-shaking movements with sexual activities and desires, and that praise the acrobatic beauty and startling athleticism of a "Fancy Dancer" (1977) or a "Dancin' Fool" (1974).

Invitations to dance are consistently emphatic as in "At The Hop" (1957), "Dance To The Music" (1968), and "You Should Be Dancing" (1976). The infectious nature of the foot-stomping activity is described in "(We're Gonna) Rock Around The Clock" (1955), "Quarter To Three" (1961), "Let Me In" (1962), and "You Can't Sit Down" (1963). But individual egos (rather than just boy-meets-girl on the dance floor themes) are dominant in the realm of youth culture music. The positions range from "Do You Love Me" (1962) to "Nobody But Me"(1967), where skills in the upper levels

Table 2.
Selected Dances and Dancing Styles as Illustrated in Popular Songs, 1950–1985

Specific Dance or Dancing Style	Song Title (Date)
Polka	"Too Fat Polka" (1947) "Hop-Scotch Polka" (1949) "Merry Christmas Polka" (1949) "Metro Polka" (1951)
Waltz	"Blue Skirt Waltz" (1949) "Merry-Go-Round Waltz" (1949) "Petite Waltz" (1950) "Tennessee Waltz" (1950) "Till I Waltz Again With You" (1952) "The Teen-Ager's Waltz" (1955) "Rock And Roll Waltz" (1956)
Tango	"Blue Tango" (1952) "Takes Two To Tango" (1952)
Mambo	"Mambo Italiano" (1954) "Papa Loves Mambo" (1954) "St. Louis Blues Mambo" (1954) "Mambo Rock" (1955) "They Were Doin' The Mambo" (1955)
Stroll	"The Stroll" (1957)
Freeze	"The Freeze" (1958)
Walk	"The Walk" (1958)
Cha-Cha	"I Want To Be Happy Cha Cha" (1958) "Tea For Two (Cha Cha)" (1958) "Everybody Loves To Cha Cha Cha" (1959) "The Cha-Cha-Cha" (1962)
Bunny Hop	"The Bunny Hop" (1959)
Shag	"Shag (Is Totally Cool)" (1959)
Shimmy	"Shimmy, Shimmy, Ko-Ko-Bop" (1959) "(I Do The) Shimmy Shimmy" (1960) "Shimmy Like Kate" (1960) "Shout And Shimmy" (1962) "Shimmy Shimmy" (1964)
Hucklebuck	"The Hucklebuck" (1960)
Madison	"The Madison" (1960) "Madison Time" (1960)

Specific Dance or Dancing Style	Song Title (Date)
Hully Gully	"(Baby) Hully Gully" (1960) "Hully Gully Again" (1961) "Hully Gully Baby" (1962)
Mashed Potatoes	"(Do The) Mashed Potatoes" (1960) "Gravy (For My Mashed Potatoes)" (1962) "Mashed Potato Time" (1962) "Mashed Potatoes" (1962) "Mashed Potatoes U.S.A." (1962) "Hot Pastrami With Mashed Potatoes" (1963)
Twist	"The Twist" (1960) "Twistin' Bells" (1960) "Twistin' U.S.A." (1960) "Dear Lady Twist" (1961) "Let's Twist Again" (1961) "Peppermint Twist" (1961) "Twistin' U.S.A." (1961) "Bristol Twistin' Annie" (1962) "Hey, Let's Twist" (1962) "La Paloma Twist" (1962) "Slow Twistin' " (1962) "Soul Twist" (1962) "Twist And Shout" (1962) "Twist, Twist Senora" (1962) "Twist-Her" (1962) "Twistin' All Night Long" (1962) "Twistin' Matilda" (1962) "Twistin' Postman" (1962) "Twistin' The Night Away" (1962) "Twistin' With Linda" (1962) "Twist It Up" (1963)
Bristol Stomp	"Bristol Stomp" (1961)
Fly	"The Fly" (1961)
Mess Around	"Dance The Mess Around" (1961) "The Mess Around" (1961)
Continental	"Continental Walk" (1961) "Do The New Continental" (1962) "Doin' The Continental Walk" (1962)
Pony	"Pony Time" (1961) "Let's Go (Pony)" (1962)
Locomotion	"The Loco-Motion" (1962)

Specific Dance or Dancing Style	Song Title (Date)
Hitch Hike	"Popeye The Hitchhiker" (1962) "Hitch Hike" (1963)
Limbo	"Limbo" (1962) "Limbo Rock" (1962) "Let's Limbo Some More" (1963) "Oo-La-La-Limbo" (1963)
Popeye	"Pop Pop Pop-Pie" (1962) "Pop-Eye" (1962) "Popeye The Hitchhiker" (1962) "The Popeye Waddle" (1963)
Watusi	"Wah Watusi" (1962) "El Watusi" (1963)
Bossa Nova	"The (Bossa Nova) Bird" (1962) "Blame It On The Bossa Nova" (1963) "Can't Get Over (The Bossa Nova)" (1964)
Jerk	"Can You Jerk Like Me" (1962) "Come On Do The Jerk" (1964) 'The Jerk" (1964) "Jerk And Twine" (1965) "Cool Jerk" (1966)
Bounce	"The Bounce" (1963)
Monkey	"Do The Monkey" (1963) "Everybody Monkey" (1963) "Mickey's Monkey" (1963) "The Monkey Time" (1963)
Stomp	"Let's Stomp" (1963)
Bird	"Do The Bird" (1963) "Surfin' Bird" (1963) "Bird Dance Beat" (1964)
Dog	"The Dog" (1963) "Walkin' The Dog" (1963) "Can Your Monkey Do The Dog" (1964) "Baby, Do The Philly Dog" (1966) "Philly Dog" (1966)
Swim	"C'mon And Swim" (1964) "She Wants T' Swim" (1964) "S-W-I-M" (1964)
Freddie	"Do The Freddie" (1965) "Let's Do The Freddie" (1965)

Specific Dance or Dancing Style	Song Title (Date)
Boogaloo	"Boo-Ga-Loo" (1965) "Alvin's Boo-Ga-Loo" (1966) "The Boogaloo Party" (1966) "Hey You! Little Boo-Ga-Loo" (1966) "Aligator Boogaloo" (1967) "Boogaloo Down Broadway" (1967) "Karate-Boo-Ga-Loo" (1967)
Horse	"The Horse" (1968) "Horse Fever" (1968)
Popcorn	"Let A Man Come In And Do The Popcorn" (1969) "Lowdown Popcorn" (1969) "Mother Popcorn" (1969) "The Popcorn" (1969)
Funky Chicken	"Do The Funky Chicken" (1970) "Funky Chicken" (1970)
Funky Penguin	"Do The Funky Penguin" (1971)
Hustle	"The Hustle" (1975)
Disco	"Disco Queen" (1975) "Disco Duck" (1976) "Disco Lady" (1976) "Disco 9000" (1976) "Disco Sax" (1976) "Disco Lucy (I Love Lucy Theme)" (1977) "Discomania" (1977) "Let's Go Down To The Disco" (1977) "Dance (Disco Heat)" (1978) "Disco Inferno" (1978) "Disco Rufus" (1978) "I Love The Nightlife (Disco 'Round)" (1978) "Disco Nights (Rock-Freak)" (1979) "Do You Think I'm Disco?" (1979) "It's A Disco Night (Rock Don't Stop)" (1979)
Breakdance	"Breakdance" (1984)

of boppin' movements are depicted in "Go, Jimmy, Go" (1959), "Dancing Machine" (1974), and "Maniac" (1983). The recent popularity of "Break-dance" (1983), "Footloose" (1984), and "Flashdance . . . What A Feeling" (1983) illustrate that America remains the "Land Of 1000 Dances" (1965).

In many ways, the youth culture tends to divide life into two unequal periods during each calendar year. From September through May, both high school and college work demand physical presence and varying com-mitments of daily time, thought, energy, and involvement. However, June, July, and August are universally perceived by young people as times for personal leisure activities. Vacation is a three-month period of open options, even if a part-time job occasionally interferes with total relaxation and absolute freedom. Many popular songs illustrate the annual cycle of youthful summertime joy. The onset of the three-month respite is heralded in "Here Comes Summer" (1959), "See You In September" (1959), "School Is Out" (1961), and "Almost Summer" (1978). The activities of the vacation time vary from "Hangin' Out At The Mall" (1983) to travelling to "Palisades Park" (1962) or "Surf City" (1963), with occasional bouts of the "Sum-mertime Blues" (1958) caused by parental insensitivity or occupational de-mands. Still, the joys are chronicled over the years in "Summertime, Summertime" (1958/1962), "Seven Day Weekend" (1962), "Vacation" (1962), "Those Lazy-Hazy-Crazy Days Of Summer" (1963), "Summer-time" (1966), "In The Summertime" (1970), and "Summer Nights" (1978). The inevitable termination of joyful vacation time is somewhat sadly la-mented in "Summer's Gone" (1960) and "Back To School Again" (1982).

If blue jeans are the symbolic attire of America's youth culture, then *Mad* magazine is the chief literary resource of teenage humor. Parody, satire, and nonsense are also staples of recordings from 1950 to the present. The popularity of cut-and-paste recordings manufactured from small segments of hit songs began with Buchanan and Goodman's "Flying Saucer" (1956, 1957) tunes and continued through anti-Nixon audio collages "Watergate" (1973) and "Mr. President" (1974). But novelty records are more creative than simply borrowing the words from other tunes. Many singers have attempted to formulate lyrical responses to questions either directly asked or inferred in other hit songs. Examples of these "answer songs" include Rufus Thomas' "Bear Cat" (1953) as a rejoinder to Big Mama Thornton's "Hound Dog" (1953) and Damita Jo's "I'll Save The Last Dance For You" (1960) reaction to The Drifter's request of the same year. Another form of response to the ideas stated in a hit song is found in the parody. This form of humorous recording was mastered by Spike Jones—"Chinese Mule Train" (1950) and "Tennessee Waltz" (1951); by Stan Freberg—"The Yellow Rose Of Texas" (1955), "Heartbreak Hotel" (1956), and "The Banana Boat Song" (1957); and most recently by Weird Al Yankovic—"Ricky" (1983), "I Love Rocky Road" (1983), and "Eat It" (1984).

Novelty songs are obviously funny. But there are also elements of social criticism and political cynicism in many of these tunes. Examples of re-cordings that satirize social fads or political events include "The Old Payola Roll Blues" (1960), "Little Boxes" (1964), "On Campus" (1969), "Junk Food Junkie" (1976), and "Dirty Laundry" (1982). Social trends are also chronicled in novelty recordings. These songs include salutes to singing stars—"Dear Elvis (Pages 1 & 2)" (1956), "My Boyfriend Got A Beatle Haircut" (1964), and "We Love You Beatles" (1964); commentaries on fads or crazes—"The Hula Hoop Song" (1958), "Sidewalk Surfin' " (1964), "Do You Think I'm Disco?" (1979), and "Work That Body" (1982); and illus-trations of the popularity of television programs and motion pictures—"The Creature (Parts 1 & 2)" (1957), "Ben Crazy" (1962), "Mr. Jaws" (1975), and "General Hospi-tale" (1981). Finally, there are many recordings that range from raucous comedy to outrageous nonsense. Songs that are examples of this zany genre include "Aba Daba Honeymoon" (1951), "Ape Call" (1956), "The Bird's The Word" (1963), "My Ding-A-Ling" (1972), "Short People" (1977), and "Rappin' Rodney" (1983).

Although idealism cannot be assigned to any single age group, there is an undeniable tendency for young people to be less controlled by past failures and more animated toward potential successes. During the teenage years the future seems to be forever. Change to create a better society is an undercurrent in song, along with pleas for brotherhood, peace, love, and patriotism—both regional and national. The idealism seems to begin with the assumption that "Only In America" (1963) can the battle against in-justices be launched, fought, and won. In terms of civil rights and racial equality, this theme is echoed in "We Shall Overcome" (1963), "America Is My Home" (1968), "Let's Work Together" (1969), "Black And White" (1972), and "Ebony And Ivory" (1982). If "A Change Is Gonna Come" (1965), then musical responses that set the general tone over the past two decades are "Everyday People" (1968), "People Got To Be Free" (1968), "Aquarius/Let The Sunshine In" (1969), and "I'd Like To Teach The World To Sing (In Perfect Harmony)" (1972). The peace issue continues to be evoked in "If I Had A Hammer" (1962), "People Get Ready" (1965), "Friendship Train" (1969), "Give Peace A Chance" (1969), "Lay Down (Candles In The Rain)" (1970), "Peace Train" (1971), and "Love Train" (1973). Beyond peace, the willingness to assist others who are in need of aid is widely articulated in "What The World Needs Now Is Love" (1965), "Give A Damn" (1968), "He Ain't Heavy, He's My Brother" (1969), "Bridge Over Troubled Water" (1970), and "Lean On Me" (1972). The bottom line of this idealism is the acceptance of human equality and personal worth. This is voiced in "A Place In The Sun" (1966), "Stand!" (1969), "Everything Is Beautiful" (1970), "Stand Tall" (1976), "Every One's A Winner" (1978), and "Up Where We Belong" (1982).

Self-identity is a function of personal maturity and social independence. "Who Are You" (1978) is a youth anthem. The evolution from teenage

Table 3.
Recordings Illustrating Humor, Parody, Satire, and Nonsense in Popular Music, 1950–1985

Answer Songs	
Original Recording	Response Recording
"Hound Dog" (1953)	"Bear Cat" (1953)
"He'll Have To Go" (1959)	"He'll Have To Stay" (1960)
"Are You Lonesome To-Night?" (1960)	"Yes, I'm Lonesome Tonight" (1961)
"Please Help Me I'm Falling" (1960)	"(I Can't Help You) I'm Falling Too" (1960)
"Shop Around" (1960)	"Don't Let Him Shop Around" (1961)
"Mother-In-Law" (1961)	"Son-In-Law" (1961)
"Stand By Me" (1961)	"I'll Be There" (1961)
"Tower Of Strength" (1961)	"You Don't Have To Be A Tower Of Strength" (1961)
"Bring It On Home To Me" (1962)	"I'll Bring It On Home To You" (1962)
'The Duke of Earl" (1962)	"Duchess of Earl" (1962)
"Wolverton Mountain" (1962)	"I'm The Girl From Wolverton Mountain" (1962)
"My Boyfriend's Back" (1963)	"Your Boyfriend's Back" (1963)
"Walk Like A Man" (1963)	"He Walks Like A Man" (1964)
"King Of The Road" (1965)	"Queen Of The House" (1965)
"An Open Letter To My Teenage Son" (1967)	"Letter To Dad" (1967)
"If I Were Your Woman" (1971)	"From His Woman To You" (1975)
"The Logical Song" (1979)	"The Topical Song" (1979)
"Take This Job And Shove It" (1977)	"I Wish I Had A Job To Shove" (1982)

Parody Songs	
Original Recording	Response Recording
"Jingle Bells" (n.d.)	"Yingle Bells" (1949)
"Mule Train" (1949)	"Chinese Mule Train" (1950)
"The Tennessee Waltz" (1951)	"Tennessee Waltz" (1951)
"The Yellow Rose Of Texas" (1955)	"The Yellow Rose Of Texas" (1955)
"Heartbreak Hotel" (1956)	"Heartbreak Hotel" (1956)
"Banana Boat (Day-O)" (1957)	"The Banana Boat Song" (1957)
"Wonderful! Wonderful!" (1957)	"Wun'erful Wun'erful (Parts 1 & 2)" (1957)
"The Battle Of New Orleans" (1959)	"The Battle Of Kookamonga" (1959)
"Big Bad John" (1961)	"Small Sad Sam" (1961)
"Detroit City" (1963)	"Detroit City No. 2" (1963)
"Downtown" (1964)	"Crazy Downtown" (1965)
"Leader Of The Pack" (1964)	"Leader Of The Laundromat" (1964)
"Eve Of Destruction" (1965)	"Dawn Of Correction" (1965)

Answer Songs

Original Recording	Response Recording
"Uptight (Everything's Alright)" (1965)	"Little Ole Man (Uptight—Everything's Alright)" (1967)
"Almost Persuaded" (1966)	"Almost Persuaded No. 2" (1966)
"Wild Thing" (1966)	"Wild Thing" (1967)
"Mellow Yellow" (1966)	"Mellow Yellow" (1967)
"Harper Valley P.T.A." (1968)	"Harper Valley P.T.A. (Later That Same Day)" (1968)
"The Ballad Of Easy Rider" (1969)	"Uneasy Rider" (1973)
"Desiderata" (1971)	"Deteriorata" (1972)
"Dueling Banjos" (1973)	"Dueling Tubas" (1973)
"The Logical Song" (1979)	"The Topical Song" (1979)
"Mickey" (1982)	"Ricky" (1983)
"I Love Rock 'N' Roll" (1982)	"I Love Rocky Road" (1983)
"Beat It" (1983)	"Eat It" (1984)

Satirical Songs

Historical Events or Social Situations	Humorous Recording
Legal challenge to copyright infringement activities	"Buchannan And Goodman On Trial" (1956)
Drafting of Elvis Presley into the U.S. Army	"The All American Boy" (1958)
Motion pictures and television programs depicting hero versus villain plots	"Along Came Jones" (1959)
Image of public school system	"Charlie Brown" (1959)
Transit system strike in Boston	"M.T.A." (1959)
Defeat of General George Custer at the Battle of Little Big Horn	"Mr. Custer" (1960)
Recording company practices of paying disc jockeys to promote particular recordings	"The Old Payola Roll Blues" (1960)
Insect plague among cotton growers	"The Boll Weevil Song" (1961)
Impact of individual poverty	"Hit The Road Jack" (1961)
Rise of ultra-conservative rightwing political organizations	"The John Birch Society" (1962)
Summer camp experiences of urban children	"Hello Mudduh, Hello Fadduh (a Letter from Camp)" (1963)
Plastic nature of suburban living conditions	"Little Boxes" (1964)
Life of a disc jockey in an urban setting	"Kansas City Star" (1965)
Reaction to the military draft system	"The Draft Dodger Rag" (n.d.)
Development of a rock band	"Gitarzan" (1969)
Political and social unrest at American colleges in the late 1960s	"On Campus" (1969)

Answer Songs	
Original Recording	**Response Recording**
Political chicanery of President Richard Nixon and his advisors	"Watergate" (1973) "Mr. President" (1974)
Upward mobility dreams of a common laborer	"Workin' At The Car Wash Blues" (1974)
Popularity of health foods and natural diets	"Junk Food Junkie" (1976)
Triumph of an assemblyline worker	"One Piece At A Time" (1976)
Night club and dancing lifestyle of the late 1970s	"Do You Think I'm Disco?" (1979)
Romantic desire to resolve personal problems through music	"I Need Your Help Barry Manilow" (1979)
Television news manipulation	"Dirty Laundry" (1982)

Songs Illustrating Social Trends	
Fad, Fashion, or Craze	**Illustration Recording**
Popular hair style	"My Boy—Flat Top" (1955)
Emergence of Elvis Presley	"Dear Elvis (Pages 1 & 2)" (1956)
Radio and television detectives	"Searchin' " (1956)
Slang phrase	"See You Later, Alligator" (1956)
Motion picture titled "The Creature from the Black Lagoon"	"The Creature (Parts 1 & 2)" (1957)
Plastic toy	"Hoopa Hoola" (1958) "The Hula Hoop Song" (1958)
California vacation spot	"26 Miles (Santa Catalina)" (1958)
Television cowboy programs	"Western Movies" (1958)
TV series "77 Sunset Strip"	"Kookie Kookie (Lend Me Your Comb)" (1959)
1960 presidential campaign	"Alvin For President" (1960)
Manned space flight	"The Astronaut (Parts 1 & 2)" (1961)
Television series "The Untouchables"	"Santa And The Touchables" (1961) "The Touchables" (1961) "The Touchables In Brooklyn" (1961)
Popular singing style	"Who Put the Bomp (In The Bomp, Bomp, Bomp)" (1961) "Mr. Bass Man" (1963)
Dance craze	"The Alvin Twist" (1962)
TV series "Ben Casey"	"Ben Crazy" (1962) "Callin' Doctor Casey" (1962) "Dr. Ben Basey" (1962)
Popularity of Caroline, President John F. Kennedy's daughter	"My Daddy Is President" (1962)
Popularity of watersport activity	"Surfin' Hootenanny" (1963)
Rise of skateboard activity	"Sidewalk Surfin' " (1964)
Emergence of The Beatles	"My Boyfriend Got A Beatle Haircut" (1964)

Original Recording	Answer Songs Response Recording
	"We Love You Beatles" (1964)
Motion picture series featuring Ian Fleming's superspy James Bond	"Agent Double-O-Soul" (1965) "Double-O-Seven" (1965)
1968 presidential campaign	"Snoopy For President" (1968)
Popular music style	"Bubble Gum Music" (1969)
1972 presidential campaign	"Convention '72" (1972)
Popularity of a rock culture magazine	"The Cover Of 'Rolling Stone' " (1972)
Emergence of films featuring black stars	"Super Fly Meets Shaft" (1973)
Political corruption in the Nixon administration	"Watergate" (1973)
Energy crisis caused by petroleum shortage	"Energy Crisis '74" (1974)
Nostalgia for heroes of cowboy movies (Hopalong Cassidy, Gene Autry, and others)	"Hoppy, Gene, And Me" (1974)
Nude running craze	"The Streak" (1974)
Citizen's band radio broadcasting craze	"Convoy" (1975) "Breaker-Breaker" (1976) "C. B. Savage" (1976)
Motion picture featuring a giant white shark	"Mr. Jaws" (1975)
Motion picture remake of classic horror film featuring a giant ape	"King Kong (Part 1)" "Kong" (1977)
Popularity of dance craze and lifestyle	"Disco Duck" (1976) "Discomania" (1977) "Dis-gorilla (Part 1)" (1977) "Do You Think I'm Disco" (1979)
World tour of Egyptian art exhibition	"King Tut" (1978)
Roller skating craze	"Bounce, Rock, Skate, Roll" (1980) "Roller Skate" (1980)
Rise of computer games	"Computer Game" (1980) "Pac-Man Fever" (1983)
Popularity of television program "Dallas" and villain J. R. Ewing	"Who Shot J.R.?" (1980)
Popular jump rope game	"Double Dutch Bus" (1981)
Popularity of television soap opera "General Hospital"	"General Hospi-Tale" (1981)
Interest in physical fitness and aerobic dancing	"(Aerobic Dancin') Keep Dancin' " (1982) "Muscles" (1982) "Work That Body" (1982) "Monday Night Football" (1982)

| | Answer Songs |
Original Recording	Response Recording
Speech and lifestyle of Southern California teenagers	"Valley Girl" (1982)
Nostalgic interest in the Three Stooges—Larry, Curly, and Moe	"The Curly Shuffle" (1983)
Street dancing	"Breakdance" (1984)

Comedy and Nonsense Songs

"Bibbidi-Bobbidi-Boo" (1950)
"I've Got A Lovely Bunch of Coconuts" (1950)
"Rag Mop" (1950)
"Aba Daba Honeymoon" (1951)
"I Saw Mommy Kissing Santa Claus" (1952)
"Santa Baby" (1953)
"Hernando's Hideaway" (1954)
"Sh-Boom" (1954)
"Skokiaan" (1954)
"Ko Ko Mo" (1955)
"Nuttin' For Christmas" (1955)
"Oh! Susanna" (1955)
"Ain't Got No Home" (1956)
"Ape Call" (1956)
"Green Door" (1956)
"I Put A Spell On You" (1956)
"The Old Philosopher" (1956)
"Stranded In The Jungle" (1956)
"Transfusion" (1956)
"The Trouble With Harry" (1956)
"Rocking Pneumonia And The Boogie Woogie Flu" (1957)
"Beep Beep" (1958)
"Chantilly Lace" (1958)
"The Chipmunk Song" (1958)
"Dinner With Drac (Part 1)" (1958)
"Naughty Lady Of Shady Lane" (1958)
"Nee Nee Na Na Na Na Nu Nu" (1958)
"The Purple People Eater" (1958)
"Real Wild Child" (1958)
"Witch Doctor" (1958)
"Alvin's Harmonica" (1959)
"Ambrose (Part 5)" (1959)
"The Clouds" (1959)
"Love Potion No. 9" (1959)
"Peek-A-Boo" (1959)
"Say Man" (1959)
"Seven Little Girls (Sitting In The Back Seat)" (1959)

Answer Songs

"White Lightning" (1959)

"Alley-Oop" (1960)

"Hot Rod Lincoln" (1960)

"Itsy Bitsy Teenie Weenie Yellow Polkadot Bikini" (1960)

"Baby Sittin' Boogie" (1961)

"Does Your Chewing Gum Lose Its Flavor (On The Bedpost Over Night)" (1961)

"Jeremiah Peabody's Poly-Unsaturated Quick Dissolving Fast Acting Pleasant Tasting Green and Purple Pills" (1961)

"Little Egypt (Ying-Yang)" (1961)

"Mother-In-Law" (1961)

"Nag" (1961)

"Rama Lama Ding Dong" (1961)

"Ahab The Arab" (1962)

"Papa-Oom-Mow-Mow" (1962)

"Santa Claus Is Watching You" (1962)

"You Can't Judge A Book By The Cover" (1962)

"The Bird's The Word" (1963)

"Long Tall Texan" (1963)

"The Marvelous Toy" (1963)

"Surfin' Bird" (1963)

"Chug-A-Lug" (1963)

"Dang Me" (1964)

'The Haunted House" (1964)

"The Name Game" (1964)

"The Jolley Green Giant" (1965)

"Makin' Whoopee" (1965)

"May The Bird Of Paradise Fly Up Your Nose" (1965)

"Super-Cali-Fragil-Istic-Expi-Ali-Docious" (1965)

"Wooly Bully" (1965)

"Downtown" (1966)

"The Eggplant That Ate Chicago" (1966)

"Snoopy Vs. The Red Baron" (1966)

"They're Coming To Take Me Away, Ha-Haaa!" (1966)

"The Little Black Egg" (1967)

"Skinny Legs And All" (1967)

"Tramp" (1967)

"Here Comes The Judge" (1968)

"Along Came Jones" (1969)

"A Boy Named Sue" (1969)

"Rubber Duckie" (1970)

"Welfare Cadillac" (1970)

"Chick-A-Boom (Don't Ya Jes' Love It)" (1971)

"Saturday Morning Confusion" (1971)

Original Recording	Answer Songs Response Recording

"When You're Hot, You're Hot" (1971)
"Coconut" (1972)
"I Gotcha" (1972)
"My Ding-A-Ling" (1972)
"No" (1972)
"Troglodyte" (1972)
"Basketball Jones, Featuring Tyrone Shoelaces" (1973)
"Dead Skunk" (1973)
"Lord, Mr. Ford" (1973)
"Don't Eat The Yellow Snow" (1974)
"Wildwood Weed" (1974)
"The Bertha Butt Boogie (Part 1)" (1975)
"The Biggest Parakeets In Town" (1975)
"Kentucky Moonrunner" (1976)
"In The Mood" (1977)
"Short People" (1977)
"Up Your Nose" (1977)
"Werewolves Of London" (1978)
"Merry Christmas In The N.F.L." (1980)
"What Can You Get A Wookie For Christmas (When He Already Owns A Comb?)" (1980)
"Shaddap You Face" (1981)
"Attack Of The Name Game" (1982)
"Rappin' Rodney" (1983)
"Swingin' " (1983)

childhood to adult status begins with halting steps and conflicts as described in "Sweet Little Sixteen" (1958), "Yakety Yak" (1958), "When I Grow Up (To Be A Man)" (1964), "Society's Child (Baby I've Been Thinking)" (1967), "Summertime Blues" (1968), "I Wish" (1976), "Jack And Diane" (1982), and "Bang The Drum All Day" (1983). The transition is further acknowledged in "Almost Grown" (1959) and "Eighteen" (1971). As in any case where real freedom exists, individual perceptions of achieving personal goals vary greatly. Some young people seize the moment by exclaiming "It's My Life" (1965) and by declaring "We Gotta Get Out Of This Place" (1965); others proclaim their desire to march to a "Different

Drum" (1967). There are also examples of adults who wish to note the need for continuing personal change in order to maintain independence and to avoid stereotyping. These attitudes are expressed in "I Am, I Said" (1971) and "Garden Party" (1972). Ultimate recognitions of individuality are provided in a variety of recordings such as "Go Where You Wanna Go" (1967), "It's Your Thing" (1969), "Make Your Own Kind Of Music" (1969), "Stand!" (1970), "Thank You (Falettinme Be Mice Elf Agin)" (1970), "Just The Way You Are" (1977), and "I'm Still Standing" (1983).

There are several groups and individuals who exert influence on all aspects of youthful thrusts for self-identity. Many individuals function as models for constructive character development, but there are also persons who contribute to continuing dependency, to isolation, or to subservience. Each of these significant others is acknowledged in contemporary lyrics. Parents are depicted in mixed terms. Some are dramatically positive as in "Harper Valley P.T.A." (1968), "Color Him Father" (1969), "Daddy Sang Bass" (1969), "Patches" (1970), and "Mother And Child Reunion" (1972); others exert either questionable or negative influences as in "Peek-A-Boo" (1958), "Skip A Rope" (1967), "A Boy Named Sue" (1969), "Your Mama Don't Dance" (1972), "The Free Electric Band" (1973), and "Cat's In The Cradle" (1974). As Sly Stone declares in "Family Affair" (1971), each child is different and demands different forms of parental attention. In the classroom, teachers are either heroes, as in "Abigail Beecher" (1964), "To Sir With Love" (1967), and "Welcome Back" (1976), or villains, as in "The Logical Song" (1979) or "Another Brick In The Wall" (1980). In yet another polar circumstance, employers tend to be perceived in negative ways, while most peers are viewed as understanding and sympathetic toward the development of individual identity. This latter support chain is illustrated in "Don't Worry Baby" (1964), "The 'In' Crowd" (1965), "You've Got A Friend" (1971), "Still Crazy After All These Years" (1976), "You're My Best Friend" (1976), "With A Little Help From My Friends" (1978), and "Street Kids" (1983).

YOUTH CULTURE

Alcohol and Drug Use

"Ain't Gonna Drink No More" (Decca 31314)
   by Clyde Beavers (1961)

"Along Comes Mary" (Valiant 741)
   by The Association (1966)

"Amphetamine Annie" (Dunhill Album)
   by Steppenwolf (n.d.)

"Arrested For Driving While Blind" (London 251)
  by Z Z Top (1977)
"The Beer Drinkin' Song" (Casablanca 2355)
  by Mac Davis (1982)
"Bombed, Boozed, and Busted" (Ovation 1152)
  by Joe Sun (1980)
"Bottle Of Wine" (Atco 6491)
  by Jimmy Gilmer and The Fireballs (1967)
"Caffein, Nicotine, Benzedrine (And Wish Me Luck)" (RCA 12157)
  by Jerry Reed (1981)
"Champagne Jam" (Polydor 14504)
  by Atlanta Rhythm Section (1978)
"Cherry Berry Wine" (Cadence 1390)
  by Charlie McCoy (1961)
"Chug-A-Lug" (Smash 1926)
  by Roger Miller (1964)
"Cloud Nine" (Gordy 7081)
  by The Temptations (1968)
"Cocaine" (RSO 1039)
  by Eric Clapton (1980)
"Cold Turkey" (Apple 1813)
  by John Lennon (1969)
"Crown Prince Of The Barroom" (Master Music 012)
  by David Rogers (1982)
"Dang Me" (Smash 1881)
  by Roger Miller (1964)
"Devil In The Bottle" (Melodyland 6002)
  by T. G. Shephard (1975)
"D. O. A. (Drunk On Arrival)" (Epic 03052)
  by Johnny Paycheck (1982)
"Dolly Dagger" (Reprise 1044)
  by Jimi Hendrix (1971)
"Drinkin' And Drivin' " (Epic 50818)
  by Johnny Paycheck (1979)
"Drinkin' My Way Back Home" (MCA 52309)
  by Gene Watson and His Farewell Party Band (1983)
"Drinking Man's Diet" (Warner Brothers 5672)
  by Allan Sherman
"Drinking Wine Spo-Dee O'Dee" (Mercury 73374)
  by Jerry Lee Lewis (1973)
"D. W. Washburn" (Colgems 1023)
  by The Monkees (1968)

"Eight Miles High" (Columbia 43578)
  by The Byrds (1966)

"Escape (The Pina Colada Song)" (Infinity 50035)
  by Rupert Holmes (1979)

"Freddie's Dead" (Curtom 1975)
  by Curtis Mayfield (1972)

"Hey Bartender" (Full Moon 29605)
  by Johnny Lee (1983)

"I Got Stoned And I Missed It" (MGM 14819)
  by Jim Stafford (1975)

"I Had Too Much To Dream (Last Night)" (Reprise 0532)
  by The Electric Prunes (1966)

"I'll Drink To That" (Soundwaves 4643)
  by Billy Parker (1981)

"I'll Drink To You" (Coast to Coast 02801)
  by Duke Jupiter (1982)

"In Heaven There Is No Beer" (Vanguard 35162)
  by Clean Living (1972)

"The Joker" (Capitol 3732)
  by The Steve Miller Band (1973)

"Kicks" (Columbia 43556)
  by Paul Revere and The Raiders (1966)

"King Heroin" (Polydor 14116)
  by James Brown (1972)

"Let's Go Get Stoned" (ABC 10808)
  by Ray Charles (1966)

"Livingston Saturday Night" (ABC 12391)
  by Jimmy Buffett (1978)

"Long Haired Country Boy" (Kama Sutra 601)
  by The Charlie Daniels Band (1975)

"Lookin' Out My Back Door" (Fantasy 645)
  by Creedence Clearwater Revival (1970)

"Lucy In The Sky With Diamonds" (MCA 40344)
  by Elton John (1975)

"Magic Bus" (Decca 32362)
  by The Who (1968)

"Magic Carpet Ride" (Dunhill 4161)
  by Steppenwolf (1968)

"Mama Told Me Not To Come" (Atlantic 2909)
  by Wilson Pickett (1972)

"Margaritaville" (ABC 12254)
  by Jimmy Buffett (1977)

"Mother's Little Helper" (London 902)
  by The Rolling Stones (1966)

"Mountain Dew" (RCA 12328)
  by Willie Nelson (1981)

"Mr. Tambourine Man" (Columbia 43271)
  by The Byrds (1965)

"Okie From Muskogee" (Capital 2626)
  by Merle Haggard (1969)

"One For My Baby (And One More For The Road)" (Columbia 40907)
  by Tony Bennett (1957)

"One Mint Julep" (Impulse 200)
  by Ray Charles (1961)

"One Mint Julep" (Atlantic 963)
  by The Clovers (1952)

"Please Don't Sell My Daddy No More Wine" (Kapp 742)
  by The Greenwoods (1966)

"Psychedelic Shack" (Gordy 7096)
  by The Temptations (1970)

"(The Puppet Song) Whiskey On A Sunday" (Decca 32333)
  by The Irish Rovers (1968)

"Purple Haze" (Reprise 0597)
  by Jimi Hendrix

"The Pusher" (Dunhill album)
  by Steppenwolf (n.d.)

"Reasons To Quit" (Epic 03494)
  by Merle Haggard and Willie Nelson (1983)

"Red Red Wine" (Bang 556)
  by Neil Diamond (1968)

"Scotch And Soda" (Capital 4740)
  by The Kingston Trio (1962)

"Sloe Gin And Fast Women" (Mercury 76139)
  by Wayne Kemp (1982)

"Snow Blind Friend" (Dunhill 4269)
  by Steppenwolf (1971)

"Spill The Wine" (MGM 14118)
  by Eric Burdon and War (1970)

"Stoned Out Of My Mind" (Brunswick 55500)
  by The Chi-Lites (1973)

"Stoned Soul Picnic" (Soul City 766)
  by The Fifth Dimension (1968)

"Street Corner" (Capital 5109)
  by Ashford and Simpson (1982)

"Sunday Mornin' Comin' Down" (Columbia 45211)
by Johnny Cash (1970)

"Sunshine Superman" (Epic 10045)
by Donovan (1966)

"Sweet Cherry Wine" (Roulette 7039)
by Tommy James and The Shondells (1969)

"Tennessee Whiskey" (Epic 04082)
by George Jones (1983)

"Tequila Sunrise" (Asylum 11017)
by The Eagles (1973)

"Two More Bottles Of Wine" (Warner Brothers 8553)
by Emmylou Harris (1978)

"Wasn't That A Party" (Epic 51007)
by The Rovers (1981)

"What's Made Milwaukee Famous (Has Made A Loser Out Of Me)"
by Jerry Lee Lewis (1968)

"Whiskey Made Me Stumble (The Devil Made Me Fall)" (MCA 51204)
by Bill Anderson (1981)

"Whiskey River" (Columbia 10877)
by Willie Nelson (1978)

"White Lightning" (Mercury 71406)
by George Jones (1959)

"White Rabbit" (RCA 9248)
by The Jefferson Airplane (1967)

"Wildwood Weed" (MGM 14737)
by Jim Stafford (1974)

"Witchy Woman" (Asylum 11008)
by The Eagles (1972)

"The Wreck Of The 'John B' " (Roulette 4260)
by Jimmie Rodgers (1960)

Clothing Styles

"Abracadabra" (Capitol 5126)
by The Steve Miller Band (1982)

"Baby Makes Her Blue Jeans Talk" (Casablanca 2347)
by Dr. Hook (1982)

"Be Bop A Lula" (Capitol 3450)
by Gene Vincent (1956)

"Bell Bottom Blues" (Atco 6803)
by Derek and The Dominos (1971)

"Betty In Bermudas" (Parkway 882)
by The Dovells (1963)

"Betty Lou Got A New Pair Of Shoes" (Josie 841)
  by Bobby Freeman (1958)

"Big Leg Woman (With A Short Short Mini Skirt)" (Warren 106)
  by Isreal "Popper Stopper" Tolbert (1970)

"Black Denim Trousers" (Capitol 3219)
  by The Cheers (1955)

"Black Slacks" (ABC-Paramount 9837)
  by Joe Bennett and The Sparkletones (1957)

"Blue Jeans" (RCA 12335)
  by Chocolate Milk (1981)

"Blue Suede Shoes" (Sun 234)
  by Carl Perkins (1956)

"Bluejean Bop" (Capitol 3558)
  by Gene Vincent and His Blue Caps (1956)

"Bobby Sox To Stockings" (Chancellor 1036)
  by Frankie Avalon (1959)

"Boogie Shoes" (T. K. 1025)
  by KC and The Sunshine Band (1978)

"Brass Buttons" (Warwick 625)
  by The String-A-Longs (1961)

"Buttons And Bows" (Columbia 38284)
  By Dinah Shore (1948)

"Chantilly Lace" (Mercury 71343)
  by The Big Bopper (1958)

"Cowboy Boots" (Golden Ring 3030)
  by Dave Dudley (1963)

"Designer Jeans" (Yatahey 3024)
  by Glen Bailey (1982)

"Dungaree Doll" (RCA 6337)
  by Eddie Fisher (1955)

"Forever In Blue Jeans" (Columbia 10897)
  by Neil Diamond (1979)

"From Levis To Calvin Klein Jeans" (MCA 51230)
  by Brenda Lee (1982)

"Hang Up My Rock 'N' Roll Shoes" (Atlantic 1179)
  by Chuck Willis (1958)

"Hi-Heel Sneakers" (Checker 1067)
  by Tommy Tucker (1964)

"Itsy Bitsy Teenie Weenie Yellow Polkadot Bikini" (Leader 805)
  by Brian Hyland (1960)

"Jeans On" (Chrysalis 2094)
  by David Dundas (1977)

"Knight In Rusty Armour" (Capitol 5808)
   by Peter and Gordon (1966)

"Lady Godiva" (Capitol 5740)
   by Peter and Gordon (1966)

"Lavender-Blue" (Big Top 3016)
   by Sammy Turner (1959)

"Leopard-Skin Pill-Box Hat" (Columbia 44069)
   by Bob Dylan (1967)

"Little Egypt (Ying-Yang)" (Atco 6192)
   by The Coasters (1961)

"My Boy—Flat Top" (King 1494)
   by Boyd Bennett and His Rockets (1955)

"No Chemise, Please" (Sunbeam 102)
   by Gerry Granahan (1958)

"One Piece Topless Bathing Suit" (Columbia 43093)
   by The Rip Chords (1964)

"Penny Loafers And Bobby Socks" (ABC-Paramount 9867)
   by Joe Bennett and The Sparkletones (1957)

"Pink Chiffon" (Guyden 2034)
   by Mitchell Torok (1960)

"Pink Pedal Pushers" (Columbia 41131)
   by Carl Perkins (1958)

"Pointed Toe Shoes" (Columbia 41379)
   by Carl Perkins (1959)

"Rockin' Shoes" (RCA 6930)
   by The Ames Brothers (1957)

"Sadie's Shawl" (London 1661)
   by Bob Sharples and His Music (1956)

"Sam, You Made The Pants Too Long" (Columbia 43612)
   by Barbra Streisand (1966)

"Satin Red And Black Velvet Woman" (Blue Thumb 7117)
   by Dave Mason (1970)

"Scarlet Ribbons (For Her Hair)" (RCA 7614)
   by The Browns (1959)

"Seventeen" (King 1470)
   by Boyd Bennett and His Rockets (1955)

"Sharp Dressed Man" (Warner Brothers 29576)
   by Z Z Top (1983)

"Shoppin' For Clothes" (Atco 6178)
   by The Coasters (1960)

"Short Shorts" (ABC-Paramount 9882)
   by The Royal Teens (1958)

"Slip-In Mules (No High Heel Sneakers)" (Checker 1073)
   by Sugar Pie DeSanto (1964)

"Sweet Little Sixteen" (Chess 1683)
   by Chuck Berry (1958)

"Tight Fittin' Jeans" (MCA 51137)
   by Conway Twitty (1981)

"Travelin' Shoes" (Capricorn 0202)
   by Elvin Bishop (1974)

"Venus In Blue Jeans" (Ace 8001)
   by Jimmy Clanton (1962)

"White Bucks And Saddle Shoes" (Big Top 3004)
   by Bobby Pedrick, Jr. (1958)

"White On White" (United Artists 685)
   by Danny Williams (1964)

"A White Sport Coat (And A Pink Carnation)" (Columbia 40864)
   by Marty Robbins (1957)

"Who Do You Love" (Swan 4162)
   by The Sapphires (1964)

"Young Blood" (Atco 6087)
   by The Coasters (1957)

"You're So Vain" (Elektra 45824)
   by Carly Simon (1972)

"A Zoot Suit" (Columbia 36517)
   by Kay Kyser (1942)

Dances, Music, and Party Times

"After The Dance" (Tamla 54273)
   by Marvin Gaye (1976)

"Alligator Boogaloo" (Blue Note 1934)
   by Lou Donaldson (1967)

"Alvin's Boo-Ga-Loo" (Mar-V-Lus 6014)
   by Alvin Cash and The Registers (1966)

"American Music" (Planet 13254)
   by The Pointer Sisters (1982)

"Annie Get Your Yo-Yo" (Duke 345)
   by Little Junior Parker (1962)

"At The Club" (Atlantic 2268)
   by The Drifters (1965)

"At The Darktown Strutters' Ball" (RCA Victor 5611)
   by Lou Monte (1954)

"At The Hop" (ABC-Paramount 9871)
   by Danny and The Juniors (1957)

"Baby, Do The Philly Dog" (Mirwood 5523)
by The Olympics (1966)

"(Baby) Hully Gully" (Arvee 562)
by The Olympics (1960)

"Baby Workout" (Brunswick 55239)
by Jackie Wilson (1963)

"Back Off Boogaloo" (Apple 1849)
by Ringo Starr (1972)

"Back To The Hop" (Swan 4082)
by Danny and The Juniors (1961)

"Barefootin' " (Nola 721)
by Robert Parker (1966)

"The Barracuda" (Mar-V-Lus 6005)
by Alvin Cash and The Crawlers (1965)

"The Beat Goes On" (Atco 6461)
by Sonny and Cher (1967)

"Bird Dance Beat" (Garrett 4003)
by The Trashmen (1964)

"Birdland" (Parkway 873)
by Chubby Checker (1963)

"Blame It On The Boogie" (Epic 50595)
by The Jackson Five (1978)

"Blame It On The Bossa Nova" (Columbia 42661)
by Eydie Gorme (1963)

"Blue Skirt Waltz" (Columbia 12394)
by Frankie Yankovic and The Marlin Sisters (1949)

"Blue Tango" (Capitol 1966)
by Les Baxter (1952)

"Blue Tango" (Hi 2027)
by Bill Black's Combo (1960)

"Bongo Rock" (Original Sound 4)
by Preston Epps (1959)

"Bongo Stomp" (Joy 262)
by Little Joey and The Flips (1962)

"Boo-Ga-Loo" (ABC-Paramount 10638)
by Tom and Jerrio (1965)

"Boogaloo Down Broadway" (Phil. L. A. of Soul 305)
by Fantastic Johnny C (1967)

"The Boogaloo Party" (Philips 40347)
by The Flamingos (1966)

"Boogie Child" (RSO 867)
by The Bee Gees (1977)

"Boogie Down" (Tamla 54243)
by Eddie Kendricks (1974)

"Boogie Oogie Oogie" (Capitol 4565)
by Taste of Honey (1978)

"Boogie Woogie Dancin' Shoes" (Chrysalis 2313)
by Claudja Barry (1979)

"Boppin' The Blues" (Sun 243)
by Carl Perkins (1956)

"The (Bossa Nova) Bird" (Argo 5428)
by The Dells (1962)

"The Bounce" (Tri Disc 106)
by The Olympics (1963)

"Break Dancin'—Electric Boogie" (Sugar Hill 460)
by The West Street Mob (1983)

"Breakdance" (Geffen 29328)
by Irene Cara (1983)

"The Breakdown (Part 1)" (Stax 0098)
by Rufus Thomas (1971)

"Bristol Stomp" (Parkway 827)
by The Dovells (1961)

"Bristol Twistin' Annie" (Parkway 838)
by The Dovells (1962)

"Bump Me Baby (Part 1)" (Cotton 636)
by Dooley Silverspoon (1975)

"The Bunny Hop" (Cameo 158)
by The Applejacks (1959)

"Can You Jerk Like Me" (Gordy 7037)
by The Contours (1962)

"Can Your Monkey Do The Dog" (Stax 144)
by Rufus Thomas (1964)

"Can't Get Over (The Bossa Nova)" (Columbia 43082)
by Eydie Gorme (1964)

"Can't Stop Dancin' " (A&M 1912)
by Captain and Tennille (1977)

"Celebration" (De-Lite 807)
by Kool and The Gang (1981)

"The Cha-Cha-Cha" (Cameo 228)
by Bobby Rydell (1962)

"Chance To Dance" (Erect 114)
by The Wrecking Crew (1983)

"Cheek To Cheek" (Motown 1676)
by The Dazz Band (1983)

"Chicken Strut" (Josie 1018)
  by The Meters (1970)

"Cincinnati Dancing Pig" (Decca 46261)
  by Red Foley (1950)

"Cinnamon Cinder (It's A Very Nice Dance)" (Zen 102)
  by The Pastel Six (1963)

"Cissy Strut" (Josie 1005)
  by The Meters (1969)

"C'mon And Swim" (Autumn 2)
  by Bobby Freeman (1964)

" 'C'mon Everybody" (Liberty 55166)
  by Eddie Cochran (1958)

"Come Dancing" (Arista 1054)
  by The Kinks (1983)

"Come On Do The Jerk" (Tamla 54109)
  by The Miracles (1964)

"Continental Walk" (King 5491)
  by Hank Ballard and The Midnighters (1961)

"Cool Jerk" (Karen 1524)
  by The Capitols (1966)

"Dance" (SRI 00009)
  by Silver Platinum (1980)

"Dance Across The Floor" (Sunshine Superman 1003)
  by Jimmy "Bo" Horne (1978)

"Dance And Shake Your Tambourine" (Red Greg 207)
  by The Universal Robot Band (1977)

"Dance Away" (Atco 7100)
  by Roxy Music (1979)

"Dance By The Light Of The Moon" (Arvee 5020)
  by The Olympics (1960)

"Dance, Dance, Dance" (Capitol 5306)
  by The Beach Boys (1964)

"Dance, Dance, Dance" (Roulette 4503)
  By Joey Dee and The Starliters (1963)

"Dance, Dance, Dance" (Elektra 45805)
  by The New Seekers (1972)

"Dance, Dance, Dance All Night" (Phase II 5651)
  by Hamilton Bohannon (1980)

"Dance, Dance, Dance (Yowsah, Yowsah, Yowsah)" (Atlantic 3435)
  by Chi (1978)

"Dance (Disco Heat)" (Fantasy 827)
  by Sylvester (1978)

"Dance, Everybody, Dance" (Dot 16502)
  by The Dartells (1963)

"Dance Everyone Dance" (Coral 62007)
  by Betty Madigan (1958)

"Dance Floor" (Warner Brothers 29961)
  by Zapp (1982)

"Dance Like Crazy" (MCA 52035)
  by Klique (1982)

"Dance Little Jean" (Liberty 1507)
  by The Nitty Gritty Dirt Band (1983)

"Dance Little Lady Dance" (RCR 19765)
  by Danny White (1977)

"Dance Master" (Playboy 50057)
  by Willie Henderson (1974)

"Dance Me Loose" (Columbia 39632)
  by Arthur Godfrey (1951)

"Dance Of Destiny" (RCA Victor 5008)
  by Tony Martin (1952)

"Dance On Little Girl" (ABC-Paramount 10220)
  by Paul Anka (1961)

"Dance Only With Me" (RCA 7202)
  by Perry Como (1958)

"Dance Sister" (Island 90094)
  by The New York Citi Peech Boys (1983)

"Dance The Kung Fu" (20th Century 2168)
  by Carl Douglas (1975)

"Dance The Mess Around" (Parkway 822)
  by Chubby Checker (1961)

"Dance The Night Away" (Warner Brothers 8823)
  by Van Halen (1979)

"Dance To The Bop" (Capitol 3839)
  by Gene Vincent (1958)

"Dance To The Music" (Vanguard 65)
  by Junior Byron (1983)

"Dance To The Music" (Epic 10256)
  by Sly and The Family Stone (1968)

"Dance Turned Into Romance" (Philadelphia International 3111)
  by The Jones Girls (1980)

"Dance Wit Me" (ABC 12179)
  by Rufus, featuring Chaka Khan (1976)

"Dance Wit' Me—Part One" (Gordy 1619)
  by Rick James (1982)

"Dance With Me" (Drive 6269)
  by Peter Brown (1978)

"Dance With Me" (Atlantic 2040)
  by The Drifters (1959)

"Dance With Me" (Autumn 19)
  by The Mojo Men (1965)

"Dance With Me" (Asylum 45261)
  by Orleans (1975)

"Dance With Me Georgie" (Triplex-X 106)
  by The Bobbettes (1960)

"Dance With Me Henry" (Mercury 70572)
  by Georgia Gibbs (1955)

"Dance With Mr. Domino" (Imperial 5863)
  by Fats Domino (1962)

"Dance With The Devil" (Chrysalis 2029)
  by Cozy Powell (1974)

"(Dance With The) Guitar Man" (RCA 8087)
  by Duane Eddy (1962)

"Dance With You" (Solar 11482)
  by Carrie Lucas (1979)

"Dancer" (RFC 8757)
  by Gino Soccio (1979)

"Dancin' " (RCA 6991)
  by Perry Como (1957)

"Dancin' " (De-Lite 1588)
  by Crown Heights Affair (1977)

"Dancin' " (RCA 11460)
  by Grey and Hanks (1979)

"Dancin' Fever" (Salsoul 2058)
  by Claudja Barry (1978)

"Dancin' Fool" (RCA 10075)
  by The Guess Who (1974)

"Dancin' Holiday" (Tri Disc 107)
  by The Olympics (1963)

"Dancin' In The Streets" (Casablanca 2278)
  by Teri DeSario with K.C. (1980)

"Dancin' Kid" (Chelsea 3045)
  by Disco Tex and The Sex-O-Lettes (1976)

"Dancin' Like Lovers" (RSO 1025)
  by Mary MacGregor (1980)

"Dancin' Man" (Epic 50335)
  by Q (1977)

"Dancin' (On A Saturday Night)" (Epic 11102)
by Flash Cadillac and The Continental Kids (1974)

"Dancin' Out Of My Heart" (Diamond 233)
by Ronnie Dove (1967)

"Dancin' Party" (Parkway 842)
by Chubby Checker (1962)

"Dancin' 'Round And 'Round" (MCA 41074)
by Olivia Newton-John (1979)

"Dancin' Shoes" (Bang 740)
by Nigel Olsson (1979)

"Dancin' The Strand" (Landa 689)
by Maureen Gray (1962)

"Dancin' Your Memory Away" (Epic 02975)
by Charly McClain (1982)

"Dancing Bear" (Dunhill 4113)
by The Mamas and the Papas (1968)

"Dancing Chandelier" (Decca 30143)
by Sylvia Syms (1957)

"Dancing In Heaven (Orbital Be-Bop)" (Jive 2001)
by Q-Feel (1983)

"Dancing In Paradise" (AVI 203)
by El Coco (1978)

"Dancing In The City" (Harvest 4648)
by Marshall Hain (1979)

"Dancing In The Moonlight" (Perception 515)
by King Harvest (1973)

"Dancing In The Shadows" (Epic 03908)
by After the Fire (1983)

"Dancing In The Street" (Warner Brothers 29986)
by Van Halen (1982)

"Dancing Machine" (Motown 1286)
by The Jackson Five (1974)

"Dancing On The Floor (Hooked On Love)" (Columbia 02170)
by Third World (1981)

"Dancing Queen" (Atlantic 3372)
by Abba (1977)

"Dancing To Your Music" (Glades 1707)
by Archie Bell and The Drells (1973)

"Dancing With My Shadow" (Columbia 41076)
by The Four Voices (1958)

"Dancing With Myself" (Chrysalis 42723)
by Billy Idol (1982)

"Dancing With The Mountains" (RCA 12017)
by John Denver (1980)

"Dear Lady Twist" (Legrand 1015)
by Gary "U.S." Bonds (1961)

"Did You Boogie (With Your Baby)" (Private Stock 45079)
by Flash Cadillac and The Continental Kids (1976)

"Disco Inferno" (Atlantic 3389)
by The Trammps (1978)

"Disco Lady" (Columbia 10281)
by Johnnie Taylor (1976)

"Disco Lucy (I Love Lucy Theme)" (Island 078)
by Wilton Place Street Band (1977)

"Disco Nights (Rock-Freak)" (Arista 0388)
by GQ (1979)

"Disco 9000" (Columbia 10610)
by Johnnie Taylor (1976)

"Disco Queen" (Big Tree 16038)
by Hot Chocolate (1975)

"Disco Rufus" (MCA 40825)
by Stargard (1978)

"Disco Sax" (Westbound 5015)
by Houston Person (1976)

"Discomania" (Marlin 3313)
by The Lovers (1977)

"Dizzy, Miss Lizzy" (Specialty 626)
by Larry Williams (1958)

"Do The Bird" (Cameo 244)
by Dee Dee Sharp (1963)

"Do The Boomerang" (Soul 35012)
by Jr. Walker and The All Stars (1965)

"Do The Choo Choo" (Atlantic 2559)
By Archie Bell and The Drells (1968)

"Do The Clam" (RCA 47–8500)
by Elvis Presley (1965)

"Do The Freddie" (Mercury 72428)
by Freddie and The Dreamers (1965)

"Do The Funky Chicken" (Stax 0059)
by Rufus Thomas (1970)

"Do The Funky Penguin" (Stax 0112)
by Rufus Thomas (1971)

"(Do The) Mashed Potatoes (Part 1)" (Dade 1804)
by Nat Kendrik and The Swans (1960)

"Do The Monkey" (Capitol 4998)
by King Curtis (1963)

"Do The New Continental" (Parkway 833)
by The Dovells (1962)

"(Do The) Push And Pull—Part 1" (Stax 0079)
by Rufus Thomas (1970)

"Do You Love Me" (Gordy 7005)
by The Contours (1962)

"Do You Want To Dance" (Josie 835)
by Bobby Freeman (1958)

"Do You Want To Dance?" (Atlantic 2928)
by Bette Midler (1972)

"Do Your Dance—Part 1" (Whitfield 8440)
by Rose Royce (1977)

"Does She Do It Like She Dances" (Buddah 579)
by The Addrisi Brothers (1977)

"The Dog" (Stax 130)
by Rufus Thomas (1963)

"Doin' The Continental Walk" (Swan 4100)
by Danny and The Juniors (1962)

"Don't Forget To Dance" (Arista 9075)
by The Kinks (1983)

"Don't It Make You Wanna Dance?" (20th Century 2219)
by Rusty Wier (1975)

"El Watusi" (Tico 419)
by Ray Barretto (1963)

"Electric Avenue" (Portrait 03793)
by Eddy Grant (1983)

"Everybody Be Dancin' " (Private Stock 45144)
by Starbuck (1977)

"Everybody Dance" (Atlantic 3469)
by Chic (1978)

"Everybody Loves To Cha Cha Cha" (Keen 2018)
by Sam Cooke (1959)

"Everybody Monkey" (Swan 4149)
by Freddy Cannon (1963)

"Fancy Dancer" (Motown 1408)
by The Commodores (1977)

"Fancy Dancer" (Warner Brothers 8734)
by Frankie Valli (1979)

"The Fish" (Cameo 192)
by Bobby Rydell (1961)

"Flashdance . . . What A Feeling" (Casablanca 811440)
by Irene Cara (1983)

"The Float" (King 5510)
by Hank Ballard and The Midnighters (1961)

"The Fly" (Parkway 830)
by Chubby Checker (1961)

"Foot Stompin' Music" (Dakar 4544)
by Hamilton Bohannon (1975)

"Foot Stomping—Part 1" (Felsted 8624)
by The Flares (1961)

"Footloose" (Columbia 04310)
by Kenny Loggins (1984)

"For A Dancer" (Pye 71045)
by Prelude (1975)

"The Freeze" (Era 1075)
by Tony and Joe (1958)

"Funky Chicken (Part 1)" (Brunswick 55429)
by Willie Henderson (1970)

"The Gandy Dancer's Ball" (Columbia 39665)
by Frankie Laine (1952)

"Get Dancin' " (Chelsea 3064)
by Disco Tex and The Sex-O-Lettes (1974)

"Get Down On It" (De-Lite 818)
by Kool and The Gang (1982)

"Get Up And Boogie (That's Right)" (Midland 10571)
by The Silver Convention (1976)

"Ghost Dancer" (Scotti Brothers 500)
by The Addrisi Brothers (1979)

"Give Up The Funk (Let's Dance)" (Columbia 11249)
by The B. T. Express (1980)

"Go, Jimmy, Go" (Ace 575)
by Jimmy Clanton (1959)

"Going To A Go-Go" (Rolling Stones 21301)
by The Rolling Stones (1982)

"Gravy (For My Mashed Potatoes)" (Cameo 219)
by Dee Dee Sharp (1962)

"Hanky Panky" (Roulette 4686)
by Tommy James and The Shondells (1966)

"Hard Times (The Slop)" (Baton 249)
by Nobel "Thin Man" Watts (1957)

"Harem Dance" (Kapp 181)
by The Armenian Jazz Sextet (1957)

"Harlem Shuffle" (Marc 104)
by Bob and Earl (1963)

"Having A Party" (RCA 8036)
by Sam Cooke (1962)

"The Heart Of Rock 'N' Roll" (Chrysalis 42782)
by Huey Lewis and The News (1984)

"Heat Of The Moment" (Geffen 50040)
by Asia (1982)

"Hey, Let's Twist" (Roulette 4408)
by Joey Dee and The Starliters (1962)

"Hey You! Little Boo-Ga-Loo" (Parkway 989)
by Chubby Checker (1966)

"Hi-Heel Sneakers" (Checker 1067)
by Tommy Tucker (1964)

"Hitch Hike" (Tamla 54075)
by Marvin Gaye (1963)

"Hoochi Coochi Coo" (King 5430)
by Hank Ballard and The Midnighters (1961)

"Hooka Tooka" (Parkway 890)
by Chubby Checker (1963)

"Hop-Scotch Polka" (MGM 10500)
by Art Mooney (1949)

"The Horizontal Bop" (Capitol 4951)
by Bob Seger and The Silver Bullet Band (1980)

"The Horse" (Phil. L.A. 313)
by Cliff Nobles and Company (1968)

"Horse Fever" (Phil. L.A. 318)
by Cliff Nobles and Company (1968)

"Hot Pastrami" (Dot 16453)
by The Dartells (1963)

"Hot Pastrami With Mashed Potatoes" (Roulette 4488)
by Joey Dee and The Starliters (1963)

"The Hucklebuck" (Parkway 813)
by Chubby Checker (1960

"Hully Gully Again" (Del-Fi 4164)
by Little Caesar and The Romans (1961)

"Hully Gully Baby" (Parkway 845)
by The Dovells (1962)

"The Hustle" (Avco 4653)
by Van McCoy (1975)

"I Can Make You Dance (Part 1)" (Warner Brothers 29553)
by Zapp (1983)

"I Can't Dance To The Music You're Playin' "(Gordy 7075)
by Martha and The Vandellas (1968)

"I Can't Stop Dancing" (Atlantic 2534)
by Archie Bell and The Drells (1968)

"I Could Have Danced All Night" (Decca 29903)
by Sylvia Syms (1956)

"(I Do The) Shimmy Shimmy" (King 5373)
by Bobby Freeman (1960)

"I Don't Want Nobody Else (To Dance With You)" (Atlantic 3541)
by Narada Michael Walden (1979)

"I Got Ants In My Pants (And I Want To Dance)" (Polydor 14162)
by James Brown (1973)

"I Gotta Dance To Keep From Crying" (Tamla 54189)
by The Miracles (1963)

"I Gotta Keep Dancin' " (Soul Train 10891)
by Carrie Lucas (1977)

"I Just Came Here To Dance" (Viva 29980)
by David Frizzell and Shelly West (1982)

"I Just Wanna Dance With You" (Chocolate City 3208)
by Starpoint (1980)

"I Love Rock 'N' Roll" (Boardwalk 135)
by Joan Jett and The Blackhearts (1982)

"I Love The Nightlife (Disco 'Round)" (Polydor 14483)
by Alicia Bridges (1978)

"I Saw A Man And He Danced With His Wife" (MCA 40273)
by Cher (1974)

"I Wanna Dance Wit' Choo (Doo Dat Dance), Part 1" (Chelsea 3015)
by Disco Tex and The Sex-O-Lettes (1975)

"(I Wanna) Dance With The Teacher" (Demon 1512)
by The Olympics (1958)

"I Want To Be Happy Cha Cha" (Decca 30790)
by The Tommy Dorsey Orchestra (1958)

"I Was Made For Dancin' " (Scotti Brothers 403)
by Leif Garrett (1978)

"I'll Dance At Your Wedding" (Columbia 37967)
by Ray Noble (1947)

"I'll Never Dance Again" (Cameo 217)
by Bobby Rydell (1962)

"I'll Save The Last Dance For You" (Mercury 71690)
by Damita Jo (1960)

"I'll Take You Where The Music's Playing" (Atlantic 2298)
by The Drifters (1965)

"I'm Dancing For Your Love" (MCA 41230)
    by Rufus and Chaka Khan (1980)

"I'm Just A Dancing Partner" (Mercury 70753)
    by The Platters (1956)

"I'm Your Boogie Man" (T.K. 1022)
    by KC and The Sunshine Band (1977)

"Itchy Twitchy Feeling" (Sue 706)
    by Bobby Hendricks (1958)

"It's A Disco Night (Rock Don't Stop)" (T-Neck 2287)
    by The Isley Brothers (1979)

"I've Got The Next Dance" (ARC 10971)
    by Deniece Williams (1979)

"The Jam—Part 1" (Cotton 1003)
    by Bobby Gregg and His Friends (1962)

"The Jerk" (Money 106)
    by The Larks (1964)

"Jerk And Twine" (Chess 1920)
    by Jackie Ross (1965)

"The Jitterbug" (Parkway 855)
    by The Dovells (1962)

"The Jive Samba" (Riverside 4541)
    by The Cannonball Adderly Quintet (1963)

"Jump" (Warner Brothers 29384)
    by Van Halen (1984)

"Jump Back" (Stax 157)
    by Rufus Thomas (1964)

"Karate-Boo-Ga-Loo" (Shout 217)
    by Jerryo (1967)

"Keep On Dancin' " (Columbia 10884)
    by Gary's Gang (1979)

"Keep On Dancing" (Toddlin' Town III)
    by Alvin Cash (1968)

"Keep On Dancing" (MGM 13379)
    by The Gentrys (1965)

"Keep On Playing That Country Music" (Musicom 52701)
    by Sierra (1983)

"La Paloma Twist" (Parkway 835)
    by Chubby Checker (1962)

"Land Of A Thousand Dances" (EMI America 8156)
    by J. Geils Band (1983)

"Land Of 1000 Dances" (Rampart 642)
    by Cannibal and The Headhunters (1965)

"Last Dance At Danceland" (Warner Brothers 49276)
    by Randy Crawford (1980)

"The Last Waltz" (Parrot 40019)
    by Englebert Humperdinck (1967)

"Let A Man Come In And Do The Popcorn" (King 6255)
    by James Brown (1969)

"Let Me In" (Argo 5405)
    by The Sensations (1962)

"Let The Music Play" (Mirage 99810)
    by Shannon (1983)

"Let's Dance" (EMI America 8158)
    by David Bowie (1983)

"Let's Dance" (GRP 2513)
    by Tom Browne (1981)

"Let's Dance" (Monogram 505)
    by Chris Montez (1962)

"Let's Dance (Make Your Body Move)" (Sugar Hill 763)
    by The West Street Mob (1981)

"Let's Do The Freddie" (Parkway 949)
    by Chubby Checker (1965)

"Let's Go Dancin' (Ooh La, La, La)" (De-Lite 824)
    by Kool and The Gang (1982)

"Let's Go Down To The Disco" (Whitfield 8306)
    by Undisputed Truth (1977)

"Let's Go (Pony)" (Warner Brothers 5283)
    by The Routers (1962)

"Let's Have A Party" (Capitol 4397)
    by Wanda Jackson (1962)

"Let's Limbo Some More" (Parkway 862)
    by Chubby Checker (1963)

"Let's Stomp" (Lawn 202)
    by Bobby Comstock and The Counts (1963)

"Let's Turkey Trot" (Dimension 1006)
    by Little Eva (1963)

"Let's Twist Again" (Parkway 824)
    by Chubby Checker (1961)

"Limbo" (Mr. Peeke 118)
    by The Capris (1962)

"Limbo Rock" (Parkway 849)
    by Chubby Checker (1962)

"The Loco-Motion" (Dimension 1000)
    by Little Eva (1962)

"Long Tall Glasses (I Can Dance)" (Warner Brothers 8043)
by Leo Sayer (1975)

"Lowdown Popcorn" (King 6250)
by James Brown (1969)

"The Madison" (Amy 804)
by Al Brown's Tunetoppers (1960)

"Madison Time" (Columbia 41628)
by Ray Bryant Combo (1960)

"Mama, Teach Me to Dance" (ABC-Paramount 9684)
by Eydie Gorme (1956)

"Mambo Italiano" (Columbia 40361)
by Rosemary Clooney (1954)

"Mambo Rock" (Decca 29418)
by Bill Haley and His Comets (1955)

"Maniac" (Casablanca 812516)
by Michael Sembello (1983)

"Mashed Potato Time" (Cameo 212)
by Dee Dee Sharp (1962)

"Mashed Potatoes" (Checker 1006)
by Steve Alaimo (1962)

"Mashed Potatoes U.S.A." (King 5672)
by James Brown (1962)

"The Mess Around" (Josie 887)
by Bobby Freeman (1961)

"Metro Polka" (Mercury 5581)
by Frankie Laine (1951)

"Mickey's Monkey" (Tamla 54083)
by The Miracles (1963)

"Middle Of A Slow Dance" (MCA 51159)
by Klique (1981)

"Miss Busy Body (Get Your Body Busy)" (Gordy 1707)
by The Temptations (1983)

"Mojo Workout (Dance)" (Tide 006)
by Larry Bright (1960)

"The Monkey Time" (Okeh 7175)
by Major Lance (1963)

"Mother Popcorn" (King 6245)
by James Brown (1969)

"Muskrat Ramble" (Coral 61278)
by The McGuire Sisters (1954)

"My Baby Don't Slow Dance" (Full Moon 29486)
by Johnny Lee (1983)

"Mystery Dancer" (Elektra 47002)
  by Shadow (1980)

"Night Dancin' " (Ariola 7748)
  by Taka Boom (1979)

"Nobody But Me" (Capitol 5990)
  by Human Beinz (1967)

"N.Y., You Got Me Dancing" (Buddah 564)
  by The Andrea True Connection (1977)

"Oh What A Night For Dancing" (20th Century 2365)
  by Barry White (1978)

"On The Dance Floor" (Sugar Hill 797)
  by The New Guys on the Block (1983)

"Oo-La-La-Limbo" (Guyden 2076)
  by Danny and The Juniors (1963)

"Papa Loves Mambo" (RCA Victor 5857)
  by Perry Como (1954)

"Party Animal" (Qwest 29493)
  by James Ingram (1983)

"Party Lights" (Chancellor 1113)
  by Claudine Clark (1962)

"Party Right Here" (Motown 1680)
  by The Dazz Band (1983)

"Party Train" (Total Experience 8209)
  by The Gap Band (1983)

"Patty Baby" (Swan 4139)
  by Freddy Cannon (1963)

"Peppermint Twist—Part 1" (Roulette 4408)
  by Joey Dee and The Starliters (1961)

"Petite Waltz" (Decca 27208)
  by Guy Lombardo (1950)

"Philly Dog" (Stax 185)
  by The Mar-Keys (1966)

"The Philly Freeze" (Mar-V-Lus 6012)
  by Alvin Cash and The Registers (1966)

"The Politics Of Dancing" (Capitol 5301)
  by Re-Flex (1983)

"Pony Express" (Swan 4068)
  by Danny and The Juniors (1961)

"Pony Time" (Parkway 818)
  by Chubby Checker (1961)

"Pop Pop Pop-Pie" (Guyden 2068)
  by The Sherrys (1962)

"The Popcorn" (King 6240)
  by James Brown (1969)

"Pop-Eye" (Ace 649)
  by Huey Smith and The Clowns (1962)

"Pop-Eye Stroll" (Stax 121)
  by The Mar-Keys (1962)

"Popeye The Hitchhiker" (Parkway 849)
  by Chubby Checker (1962)

"The Popeye Waddle" (Cameo 239)
  by Don Covay (1963)

"The Push And Kick" (Swan 4121)
  by Mark Valentino (1962)

"Quarter To Three" (LeGrand 1008)
  by Gary "U.S." Bonds (1961)

"Queen Of The Hop" (Atco 6127)
  by Bobby Darin (1958)

"Rain Dance" (RCA 0522)
  by The Guess Who (1971)

"Record Hop Blues" (Wizz 715)
  by The Quarter Notes (1959)

"Reelin' And Rockin' " (Chess 1683)
  by Chuck Berry (1958)

"Reelin' And Rockin' " (Chess 2136)
  by Chuck Berry (1973)

"Ride!" (Cameo 230)
  by Dee Dee Sharp (1962)

"Rock And Roll Dancin' " (Casablanca 1000)
  by The Beckmeier Brothers (1979)

"Rock And Roll Music" (Chess 1671)
  by Chuck Berry (1957)

"Rock And Roll Waltz" (RCA 6359)
  by Kay Starr (1956)

"Rock 'N' Roll Is King" (Jet 03964)
  by The Electric Light Orchestra (1983)

"Rock Of Ages" (Mercury 812604)
  by Def Leppard (1983)

"Rock This Town" (EMI American 8132)
  by The Stray Cats (1982)

"Rocking Pneumonia And The Boogie Woggie Flu" (Ace 530)
  by Huey (Piano) Smith And The Clowns (1957)

"Sabre Dance" (Columbia 38102)
  by Woody Herman (1948)

"Sabre Dance Boogie" (RCA Victor 2721)
by Freddie Martin (1948)

"The Safety Dance" (Backstreet 52232)
by Men without Hats (1983)

"Save The Last Dance For Me" (RCA 13703)
by Dolly Parton (1983)

"Shadow Dancing" (RSO 893)
by Andy Gibb (1978)

"Shag (Is Totally Cool)" (Monument 401)
by Billy Graves (1959)

"Shake" (RCA 8486)
by Sam Cooke (1965)

"Shake A Tail Feather" (One-Derful! 4815)
by The Five Du-Tones (1963)

"Shake And Dance With Me" (Mercury 74008)
by Con Funk Shun (1978)

"Shake And Fingerpop" (Soul 35013)
by Jr. Walker and the All Stars (1965)

"Shake It Up" (Elektra 47250)
by The Cars (1981)

"Shake! Shake! Shake!" (Brunswick 55246)
by Jackie Wilson (1963)

"(Shake, Shake, Shake) Shake Your Booty" (T.K. 1019)
by KC and The Sunshine Band (1976)

"Shake Sherry" (Gordy 7012)
by The Contours (1962)

"Shake Your Body (Down To The Ground)" (Epic 50656)
by The Jackson Five (1979)

"Shake Your Rump To The Funk" (Mercury 73833)
by The Bar-Kays (1976)

"She Blinded Me With Science" (Capitol 5204)
by Thomas Dolby (1983)

"She Wants T' Swim" (Parkway 922)
by Chubby Checker (1964)

"She's Got To Be (A Dancer)" (A&M 2519)
by Jerry Knight (1983)

"Shimmy Like Kate" (Arvee 5006)
by The Olympics (1960)

"Shimmy Shimmy" (Cameo 295)
by The Orlons (1964)

"Shimmy, Shimmy, Ko-Ko-Bop" (End 1060)
by Little Anthony and The Imperials (1959)

"Shotgun" (Soul 35008)
by Jr. Walker and The All Stars (1965)

"Shout And Shimmy" (King 5657)
by James Brown (1962)

"Sittin' In The Balcony" (Liberty 55056)
by Eddie Cochran (1957)

"Slop Time" (Guyden 2077)
by The Sherrys (1963)

"Slow Dance" (Warner Brothers 49277)
by David Ruffin (1980)

"Slow Dancin' Don't Turn Me On" (Buddah 566)
by The Addrisi Brothers (1977)

"Slow Dancing" (Arista 0209)
by The Funky Kings (1976)

"Slow Dancing (Swayin' To The Music)" (Big Tree 16094)
by Johnny Rivers (1977)

"Slow Twistin' " (Parkway 835)
by Chubby Checker (1962)

"Smokin' In The Rockies" (RCA 13472)
by Gary Stewart and Dean Dillon (1983)

"Somebody Stole My Dog" (Stax 149)
by Rufus Thomas (1964)

"Soul Twist" (Enjoy 1000)
by King Curtis (1962)

"Splish Splash" (Atco 6117)
by Bobby Darin (1958)

"St Louis Blues Mambo" ("X" 0042)
by Ray Maltby (1954)

"Stomp!" (A&M 2216)
by The Brothers Johnson (1980)

"Stop Monkeyin' Aroun' " (Parkway 889)
by The Dovells (1963)

"Stray Cat Strut" (EMI American 8122)
by The Stray Cats (1982)

"Strip Polka" (Decca 18470)
by The Andrews Sisters (1942)

"The Stroll" (Mercury 71242)
by The Diamonds (1957)

"Sultans Of Swing" (Warner Brothers 8736)
by Dire Straits (1979)

"Surfin' Bird" (Garrett 4002)
by The Trashmen (1963)

"S-W-I-M" (Autumn 5)
  by Bobby Freeman (1964)

"The Switch-A-Roo" (King 5510)
  by Hank Ballard and The Midnighters (1961)

"Takes Two To Tango" (Coral 60871)
  by Pearl Bailey (1952)

"Tea For Two Cha Cha" (Decca 30704)
  by The Tommy Dorsey Orchestra (1958)

"The Teen-Ager's Waltz" (Mercury 70700)
  by Eddy Howard and His Orchestra (1955)

"Tennessee Waltz" (Mercury 5534)
  by Patti Page (1950)

"They Can't Take Away Our Music" (MGM 14196)
  by Eric Burdon and War (1970)

"They Were Doin' The Mambo" (RCA Victor 5767)
  by Vaughn Monroe (1954)

"Tighten Up" (Atlantic 2478)
  by Archie Bell and The Drells (1968)

"Till I Waltz Again With You" (Coral 60873)
  by Teresa Brewer (1952)

"Touch Me When We're Dancing" (Free Flight 11629)
  by Bama (1979)

"Twine Time" (Mar-V-Lus 6002)
  by Alvin Cash and The Crawlers (1965)

"The Twist" (Parkway 811)
  by Chubby Checker (1960)

"Twist And Shout" (Wand 124)
  by The Isley Brothers (1962)

"Twist It Up" (Parkway 879)
  by Chubby Checker (1963)

"Twist, Twist Senora" (Legrand 1018)
  by Gary "U.S." Bonds (1962)

"Twist-Her" (Hi 2042)
  by Bill Black's Combo (1962)

"Twistin' All Night Long" (Swan 4092)
  by Danny and The Juniors (1962)

"Twistin' Bells" (Canadian American 120)
  by Santo and Johnny (1960)

"Twistin' Matilda" (S.P.Q.R. 3300)
  by Jimmy Soul (1962)

"Twistin' Postman" (Tamla 54054)
  by The Marvelettes (1962)

"Twistin' The Night Away" (RCA 7983)
by Sam Cooke (1962)

"Twistin' U.S.A." (Parkway 811)
by Chubby Checker (1961)

"Twistin' U.S.A." (Swan 4060)
by Danny and The Juniors (1960)

"Twistin' White Silver Sands" (Hi 2052)
by Bill Black's Combo (1962)

"Twistin' With Linda" (Wand 127)
by The Isley Brothers (1962)

"Voyeur" (EMI American 8127)
by Kim Carnes (1982)

"Wah Watusi" (Cameo 218)
by The Orlons (1962)

"The Walk" (Checker 885)
by Jimmy McCracklin (1958)

"Walkin' With Mr. Lee" (Ember 1027)
by Lee Allen and His Band (1958)

"Walking The Dog" (Stax 140)
by Rufus Thomas (1963)

"The Wallflower" (Modern 947)
by Etta James (1955)

"The Waltz You Saved For Me" (Capitol 4650)
by Ferlin Husky (1962)

"The Wedding Samba" (Decca 24841)
by Carmen Miranda and The Andrews Sisters (1950)

"(We're Gonna) Rock Around The Clock" (Decca 29124)
by Bill Haley and His Comets (1955)

"When She Dances" (Elektra 47201)
by Joey Scarbury (1981)

"When You Dance" (Herald 458)
by The Turbans (1955)

"While You Danced, Danced, Danced" (Mercury 5681)
by Georgia Gibbs (1951)

"Wiggle Wobble" (Everlast 5019)
by Les Cooper and The Soul Rockers (1962)

"Willie And The Hand Jive" (Capitol 3966)
by Johnny Otis (1958)

"You Can't Sit Down" (Parkway 867)
by The Dovells (1963)

"You Make Me Feel Like Dancing" (Warner Brothers 8283)
by Leo Sayer (1977)

"You Should Be Dancing" (RSO 853)
by The Bee Gees (1976)

"You'll Be Dancing All Night" (Capitol 5026)
by Sheree Brown (1981)

"Your Mama Don't Dance" (Columbia 45719)
by Loggins and Messina (1972)

"(You're So Square) Baby, I Don't Care" (Geffen 29849)
by Joni Mitchell (1982)

Novelty Songs

" 'A' You're Adorable" (Capitol 15393)
by Jo Stafford and Gordon MacRae (1949)

"Aba Daba Honeymoon" (MGM 30282)
by Carleton Carpenter and Debbie Reynolds (1951)

"(Aerobic Dancin') Keep Dancing' " (Zoo York 1393)
by R. J.'s Latest Arrival (1982)

"Agent Double-O-Soul" (Ric-Tic 103)
by Edwin Starr (1965)

"Ahab The Arab" (Mercury 71966)
by Ray Stevens (1962)

"Ain't Got No Home" (Argo 5259)
by Clarence "Frog Man" Henry (1956)

"The All American Boy" (Fraternity 835)
by Bill Parsons (1958)

"All I Want For Christmas (Is My Two Front Teeth)" (RCA Victor 2963)
by Spike Jones (1949)

"Alley-Oop" (Lute 5905)
by The Hollywood Argyles (1960)

"Almost Persuaded No. 2" (MGM 13590)
by Ben Colder (1966)

"Along Came Jones" (Atco 6141)
by The Coasters (1959)

"Along Came Jones" (Monument 1150)
by Ray Stevens (1969)

"Alvin For President" (Liberty 55277)
by The Chipmunks with David Seville (1960)

"The Alvin Twist" (Liberty 55424)
by The Chipmunks with David Seville (1962)

"Alvin's Harmonica" (Liberty 55179)
by The Chipmunks with David Seville (1959)

"Alvin's Orchestra" (Liberty 55233)
by The Chipmunks with David Seville (1960)

"Ambrose (Part 5)" (Glory 290)
by Linda Laurie (1959)

"Ape Call" (Dot 15485)
by Nervous Norvus (1956)

"The Astronaut (Parts 1 & 2)" (Kapp 409)
by Jose Jimenez (1961)

"Attack Of The Name Game" (Cotillion 99968)
by Stacy Lattisaw (1982)

"Baby Sittin' Boogie" (Columbia 41876)
by Buzz Clifford (1961)

"Back To The Hop" (Swan 4082)
by Danny and The Juniors (1961)

"The Banana Boat Song" (Capitol 3687)
by Stan Freberg (1957)

"Basketball Jones Featuring Tyrone Shoelaces" (Ode 66038)
by Cheech and Chong (1973)

"Batman And His Grandmother" (Red Bird 10058)
by Dickie Goodman (1966)

"The Battle of Kookamonga" (RCA 7585)
by Homer and Jethro (1959)

"Beans In My Ears" (Philips 40198)
by The Serendipity Singers (1964)

"Bear Cat" (Sun 181)
by Rufus Thomas (1953)

"Beep Beep" (Roulette 4115)
by The Playmates (1958)

"Ben Crazy" (Diamond 119)
by Dickie Goodman (1962)

"The Bertha Butt Boogie (Part 1)" (Atlantic 3232)
by The Jimmy Castor Bunch (1975)

"Bibbidi-Bobbidi-Boo" (RCA Victor 3113)
by Perry Como with The Fontane Sisters (1950)

"Big Bad John" (Columbia 42175)
by Jimmy Dean (1961)

"The Big Bopper's Wedding" (Mercury 71375)
by The Big Bopper (1958)

"The Biggest Parakeets In Town" (Melodyland 6015)
by Jud Strunk (1975)

"The Bird On My Head" (Liberty 55140)
by David Seville (1958)

"The Bird's The Word" (Liberty 55553)
by The Rivingtons (1963)

"The Blob" (Columbia 41250)
   by The Five Blobs (1958)

"The Boll Weevil Song" (Mercury 71820)
   by Brook Benton (1961)

"Bounce, Rock, Skate, Roll" (Brunswick 55548)
   by Vaughan Mason and Crew (1980)

"A Boy Named Sue" (Columbia 44944)
   by Johnny Cash (1969)

"Breaker-Breaker" (Arista 0188)
   by The Outlaws (1976)

"Bridget The Midget (The Queen Of The Blues)" (Barnaby 2024)
   by Ray Stevens (1970)

"Bruce" (Mercury 880405)
   by Rick Springfield (1984)

"Bubble Gum Music" (Buddah 78)
   by The Rock and Roll Dubble Bubble Trading Card Company
   of Philadelphia - 19141 (1969)

"Buchanan And Goodman On Trial" (Luniverse 102)
   by Buchanan and Goodman (1956)

"Busted" (ABC 10481)
   by Ray Charles (1963)

"Callin' Doctor Casey" (RCA 8054)
   by John D. Loudermilk (1962)

"C. B. Savage" (Plantation 144)
   by Rod Hart (1976)

"Cement Mixer (Put-ti Put-ti)" (Capitol 248)
   by Alvino Rey (1946)

"Chantilly Lace" (Mercury 71343)
   by The Big Bopper (1958)

"Charlie Brown" (Atco 6132)
   by The Coasters (1959)

"Chattanoogie Shoe Shine Boy" (RCA Victor 3216)
   by Phil Harris (1950)

"Chick-A-Boom (Don't Ya Jes' Love It)" (Sunflower 105)
   by Daddy Dewdrop (1971)

"Chinese Mule Train" (RCA Victor 3741)
   by Spike Jones (1950)

"The Chipmunk Song" (Liberty 55168)
   by The Chipmunks with David Seville (1958)

"Christmas Dragnet" (Capitol 2671)
   by Stan Freberg (1953)

"Chug-A-Lug" (Smash 1926)
   by Roger Miller (1964)

"The Clapping Song (Clap Pat Clap Slap)" (Congress 234)
by Shirley Ellis (1965)

"Close The Door" (Dot 15381)
by Jim Lowe (1955)

"The Clouds" (Alton 254)
by The Spacemen (1959)

"Cocktails For Two" (Victor 1628)
by Spike Jones (1945)

"Coconut" (RCA 0718)
by Nilsson (1972)

"Computer Game" (Horizon 127)
by The Yellow Magic Orchestra (1980)

"Convention '72" (Mainstream 5525)
by The Delegates (1972)

"Convoy" (MGM 14839)
by C. W. McCall (1975)

"The Cover Of 'Rolling Stone' " (Columbia 45732)
by Dr. Hook (1972)

"Crazy Downtown" (Warner Brothers 5614)
by Allan Sherman (1965)

"The Creature (Parts 1 & 2)" (Flying Saucer 501)
by Buchanan and Ancell (1957)

"The Crude Oil Blues" (RCA 0224)
by Jerry Reed (1974)

"The Crusher" (Parrot 45005)
by The Novas (1965)

"The Curly Shuffle" (Atlantic 89718)
by Jump 'N The Saddle (1983)

"Dang Me" (Smash 1881)
by Roger Miller (1964)

"Dawn Of Correction" (Decca 31844)
by The Spokesmen (1965)

"Dead Skunk" (Columbia 45726)
by Loudon Wainwright III (1973)

"Dear Elvis (Pages 1 & 2)" (Plus 104)
by Audrey (1956)

"Delaware" (RCA 7670)
by Perry Como (1960)

"Deteriorata" (Banana 218)
by National Lampoon (1972)

"Detroit City No. 2" (MGM 13167)
by Ben Colder (1963)

"Diet Song" (Columbia 04092)
  by Bobby Bare (1983)

"Dinner With Drac (Part 1)" (Cameo 130)
  by John Zacherle (1958)

"Dirty Laundry" (Asylum 69894)
  by Don Henley (1982)

"Disco Duck" (RSO 857)
  by Rick Dees and His Cast Of Idiots (1976)

"Discomania" (Marlin 3313)
  by The Lovers (1977)

"Dis-Gorilla (Part 1)" (RSO 866)
  by Rick Dees and His Cast Of Idiots (1977)

"Do-Wacka-Do" (Smash 1947)
  by Roger Miller (1964)

"Do You Think I'm Disco?" (Ovation 1132)
  by Steve Dahl and Teenage Radiation (1979)

"Does Your Chewing Gum Lose Its Flavor (On The Bedpost Over Night)"
  (Dot 15911)
  by Lonnie Donegan (1961)

"Donald Where's Your Trousers?" (Warwick 665)
  by Andy Stewart (1961)

"Don't Eat The Yellow Snow" (Discreet 1312)
  by Frank Zappa (1974)

"Don't Go Near The Eskimos" (MGM 13104)
  by Ben Colder (1962)

"Don't Let Him Shop Around" (Motown 1007)
  by Debbie Dean (1961)

"Double Dutch Bus" (WMOT 5356)
  by Frankie Smith (1981)

"Double-O-Seven" (Roulette 4603)
  by The Detergents (1965)

"Downtown" (Capitol 5640)
  by Mrs. Miller (1966)

"Dr. Ben Basey" (Tuba 8001)
  by Mickey Shorr and The Cutups (1962)

"Duchess Of Earl" (Vee-Jay 435)
  by The Pearlettes (1962)

"Dueling Banjos" (Warner Brothers 7659)
  by Eric Weissberg and Steve Mandell (1973)

"Dueling Tubas" (Capricorn 0019)
  by Martin Mull and Orchestra (1973)

"Eat It" (Rock 'N' Roll 04374)
  by Weird Al Yankovic (1984)

"The Eggplant That Ate Chicago" (Go Go 100)
  by Dr. West's Medicine Show and Junk Band (1966)
"Energy Crisis '74" (Rainy Wednesday 206)
  by Dickie Goodman (1974)
"Feet Up (Pat Him On The Po-Po)" (Columbia 39822)
  by Guy Mitchell (1952)
"First Name Initial" (Vista 349)
  by Annette (1959)
"The Flying Saucer (Parts 1 & 2)" (Luniverse 101)
  by Buchanan and Goodman (1956)
"Flying Saucer The 2nd" (Luniverse 105)
  by Buchanan and Goodman (1957)
"Freddie Feelgood (And His Funky Little Five Piece Band)" (Monument 946)
  by Ray Stevens (1966)
"From His Woman To You" (Buddah 441)
  by Barbara Mason (1975)
"Funky North Philly" (Warner Brothers 7171)
  by Bill Cosby (1968)
"General Hospi-Tale" (MCA 51148)
  by The Afternoon Delights (1981)
"Gitarzan" (Monument 1131)
  by Ray Stevens (1969)
"Got A Match?" (ABC-Paramount 9931)
  by Frank Gallop (1958)
"Gotta Get To Your House" (Liberty 55079)
  by David Seville (1957)
"Green Chritma" (Capitol 4097)
  by Stan Freberg (1958)
"Green Door" (Dot 15486)
  by Jim Lowe (1956)
"Hambone" (Columbia 39672)
  by Jo Stafford and Frankie Laine (1952)
"The Happy Reindeer" (Capitol 4300)
  by Dancer, Prancer, and Nervous (The Singing Reindeer) (1959)
"Harper Valley P.T.A. (Later That Same Day)" (MGM 13997)
  by Ben Colder (1968)
"Harry The Hairy Ape" (Mercury 72125)
  by Ray Stevens (1963)
"The Haunted House" (Hi 2076)
  by Jumpin' Gene Simmons (1964)
"The Haunted House Of Rock" (Jive 9031)
  by Whodini (1983)

"Hawaiian War Chant" (RCA Victor 1893)
   by Spike Jones (1946)

"He Walks Like A Man" (Capitol 5090)
   by Jody Miller (1964)

"Heartbreak Hotel" (Capitol 3480)
   by Stan Freberg (1956)

"He'll Have To Stay" (Capitol 4368)
   by Jeannie Black (1960)

"Hello Muddah, Hello Fadduh (A Letter From Camp)" (Warner Brothers 5378)
   by Allan Sherman (1963)

"Here Comes The Judge" (Soul 35044)
   by Shorty Long (1968)

"Hernando's Hideaway" (Cadence 1241)
   by Archie Bleyer (1954)

"Hey Shirley (This Is Squirrely)" (GRT 054)
   by Shirley and Squirrely (1956)

"High School U.S.A." (Atlantic 51–78)
   by Tommy Facenda (1959)

"Hit The Road Jack" (ABC 10244)
   by Ray Charles (1961)

"The Ho Ho Song" (Columbia 39981)
   by Red Buttons (1953)

"Hoopa Hoola" (Atlantic 2002)
   by Betty Johnson (1958)

"Hooray For The Salvation Army Band" (Warner Brothers 7096)
   by Bill Cosby (1976)

"Hoppy, Gene, And Me" (20th Century 2154)
   by Roy Rogers (1974)

"Hot Rod Lincoln" (Republic 2005)
   by Johnny Bond (1960)

"Hound Dog" (Peacock 1612)
   by Willie Mae "Big Mama" Thornton (1953)

"The Hula Hoop Song" (Roulette 4106)
   by Georgia Gibbs (1958)

"(I Can't Help You) I'm Falling Too" (RCA 7767)
   by Skeeter Davis (1960)

"I Gotcha" (Dial 1010)
   by Joe Tex (1972)

"I Love Rocky Road" (Rock 'N' Roll 03998)
   by Weird Al Yankovic (1983)

"I Need Your Help Barry Manilow" (Warner Brothers 8785)
   by Ray Stevens (1979)

"I Said My Pajamas (And Put On My Prayers)" (Decca 24873)
  by Ray Bolger and Ethel Merman (1950)

"I Saw Mommy Kissing Santa Claus" (Columbia 39871)
  by Jimmy Boyd (1952)

"I Saw Mommy Kissing Santa Claus" (RCA Victor 5067)
  by Spike Jones (1952)

"I Taut I Taw A Puddy Tat" (Capitol 1360)
  by Mel Blanc (1951)

"I Went To Your Wedding" (RCA Victor 5107)
  by Spike Jones (1953)

"I'll Be There" (Mercury 71840)
  by Damita Jo (1961)

"I'll Bring It Home To You" (Atlantic 2163)
  by Carla Thomas (1962)

"I'll Save The Last Dance For You" (Mercury 71760)
  by Damita Jo (1960)

"I'm The Girl On Wolverton Mountain" (Cameo 223)
  by Jo Ann Campbell (1962)

"In The Mood" (Warner Brothers 8301)
  by The Henhouse Five Plus Two (1977)

"Itsy Bitsy Teenie Weenie Yellow Polkadot Bikini" (Leader 805)
  by Brian Hyland (1960)

"I've Got A Lovely Bunch Of Coconuts" (Decca 24784)
  by Danny Kaye (1950)

"I've Got You Under My Skin" (Capitol 1711)
  by Stan Freberg (1951)

"Jeremiah Peabody's Poly-Unsaturated Quick Dissolving Fast Acting Pleasant
  Tasting Green and Purple Pills" (Mercury 71843)
  by Ray Stevens (1961)

"The Jogger" (Columbia 03809)
  by Bobby Bare (1983)

"John And Marsha" (Capitol 1356)
  by Stan Freberg (1951)

"The John Birch Society" (Kapp 457)
  by The Chad Mitchell Trio (1962)

"The Jolly Green Giant" (Wand 172)
  by The Kingsmen (1955)

"Juanita Banana" (Karate 522)
  by The Peels (1966)

"Junk Food Junkie" (Warner Brothers 8165)
  by Larry Groce (1976)

"Kansas City Star" (Smash 1998)
  by Roger Miller (1965)

"Kentucky Moonrunner" (Mercury 73789)
  by Cledus Maggard and The Citizen's Band (1976)

"King Kong (Part 1)" (Atlantic 3295)
  by The Jimmy Castor Bunch (1975)

"King Of The Road" (Smash 1965)
  by Roger Miller (1965)

"King Tut" (Warner Brothers 8577)
  by Steve Martin with The Toot Uncommons (1978)

"Ko Ko Mo" (Mercury 70529)
  by The Crew-Cuts (1955)

"Kong" (Shock 6)
  by Dickie Goodman (1977)

"Kookie Kookie (Lend Me Your Comb)" (Warner Brothers 5047)
  by Edward Byrnes (1959)

"La Dee Dah" (Swan 4002)
  by Billy and Lillie (1958)

"Leader Of The Laundromat" (Roulette 4590)
  by The Detergents (1964)

"Ling, Ting, Tong" (Capitol 2945)
  by The Five Keys (1954)

"The Little Black Egg" (Kapp 709)
  by The Nightcrawlers (1967)

"The Little Blue Man" (Atlantic 1169)
  by Betty Johnson (1958)

"Little Blue Riding Hood" (Capitol 2596)
  by Stan Freberg (1953)

"Little Boxes" (Columbia 42940)
  by Pete Seeger (1964)

"Little Eeefin Annie" (Sound Stage 2511)
  by Joe Perkins (1963)

"Little Egypt (Ying-Yang)" (Atco 6192)
  by The Coasters (1961)

"Little Ole Man (Uptight-Everything's Alright)" (Warner Brothers 7072)
  by Bill Cosby (1967)

"The Little Space Girl" (Carlton 496)
  by Jesse Lee Turner (1959)

"Long Tall Texan" (M.O.C. 653)
  by Murry Kellum (1963)

"Lord, Mr. Ford" (RCA 0960)
  by Jerry Reed (1973)

"Love Potion No. 9" (United Artists 180)
  by The Clovers (1959)

"Luna Trip" (Cotique 173)
by Dickie Goodman (1969)

"Makin' Whoopee" (ABC 10609)
by Ray Charles (1965)

"Martian Hop" (Chairman 4403)
by The Ran-Dells (1963)

"The Marvelous Toy" (Mercury 72197)
by The Chad Mitchell Trio (1963)

"May The Bird Of Paradise Fly Up Your Nose" (Columbia 43388)
by "Little" Jimmy Dickens (1965)

"Mellow Yellow" (Parkway 137)
by Senator Bobby (1967)

"Merry Christmas In The N.F.L." (Handshake 5308)
by Willis "The Guard" and Vigorish (1980)

"Monday Night Football" (Profile 5011)
by Hurt 'Em Bad and The S.C. Band (1982)

"Monster Mash" (Garpax 44167)
by Bobby "Boris" Pickett and The Crypt-Kickers (1962)

"Monster's Holiday" (Garpax 44171)
by Bobby "Boris" Pickett and The Crypt-Kickers (1962)

"Moonlight Special" (Barnaby 604)
by Ray Stevens (1974)

"Mother-In-Law" (Minit 623)
by Ernie K-Doe (1961)

"Mr. Bass Man" (Kapp 503)
by Johnny Cymbal (1963)

"Mr. Custer" (ERA 3024)
by Larry Verne (1960)

"Mr. Jaws" (Cash 451)
by Dickie Goodman (1975)

"Mr. Livingston" (ERA 3034)
by Larry Verne (1960)

"Mr. President" (Rainy Wednesday 207)
by Dickie Goodman (1974)

"M.T.A." (Capitol 4221)
by The Kingston Trio (1959)

"The Mummy" (Brunswick 55140)
by Bob McFadden and Dor (1959)

"Murphy's Law" (Venture 149)
by Cheri (1982)

"Muscles" (RCA 13348)
by Diana Ross (1982)

"My Boomerang Won't Come Back" (United Artists 398)
   by Charlie Drake (1962)

"My Boy—Flat Top" (King 1494)
   by Boyd Bennett and His Rockets (1955)

"My Boyfriend Got A Beatle Haircut" (Capitol 5127)
   by Donna Lynn (1964)

"My Daddy Is President" (Kapp 467)
   by Little Jo Ann (1962)

"My Ding-A-Ling" (Chess 2131)
   by Chuck Berry (1972)

"My Girl Bill" (MGM 14718)
   by Jim Stafford (1974)

"My Uncle Used To Love Me But She Died" (Smash 2055)
   by Roger Miller (1966)

"My Wife, The Dancer" (Ivanhoe 502)
   by Eddie and Dutch (1970)

"Nag" (7 Arts 709)
   by The Halos (1961)

"The Name Game" (Congress 230)
   by Shirley Ellis (1964)

"Naughty Lady of Shady Lane" (RCA 5897)
   by The Ames Brothers (1958)

"Nee Nee Na Na Na Na Nu Nu" (Swan 4006)
   by Dicky Doo and The Don'ts (1958)

"Nick Teen And Al K. Hall" (Epic 9615)
   by Rolf Harris (1963)

"No" (Decca 32996)
   by Bulldog (1972)

"Nuttin' For Christmas" (MGM 12092)
   by Barry Gordon (1955)

"Ob-La-Di, Ob-La-Da" (Capitol 4347)
   by The Beatles (1976)

"Oh! Susanna" (RCA 6344)
   by The Singing Dogs (1955)

"Old Home Filler-Up An' Keep On-A-Truckin' Cafe" (MGM 14738)
   by C. W. McCall (1974)

"The Old Master Painter" (RCA Victor 3114)
   by Phil Harris (1949)

"The Old Payola Roll Blues" (Capitol 4329)
   by Stan Freberg (1960)

"The Old Philosopher" (Coral 61671)
   by Eddie Lawrence (1956)

"On Campus" (Cotique 158)
   by Dickie Goodman (1969)

"On Top Of Spaghetti" (Kapp 526)
   by Tom Glazer and The Do-Re-Mi Children's Chorus (1963)

"One Piece At A Time" (Columbia 10321)
   by Johnny Cash (1976)

"Ooh Poo Pah Doo" (Minit 607)
   by Jessie Hill (1960)

"Open The Door, Richard" (Decca 23841)
   by Louis Jordan (1947)

"Pac-Man Fever" (Columbia 02673)
   by Buckner and Garcia (1982)

"Papa-Oom-Mow-Mow" (Liberty 55427)
   by The Rivingtons (1962)

"Peek-A-Boo" (Josie 846)
   by The Cadillacs (1959)

"Pepino The Italian Mouse" (Reprise 20106)
   by Lou Monte (1962)

"Please, Mr. President" (Westbound 5001)
   by Paula Webb (1975)

"Psycho" (Sue 732)
   by Bobby Hendricks (1960)

"The Purple People Eater" (MGM 12651)
   by Sheb Wooley (1958)

"The Puzzle Song (A Puzzle In Song)" (Congress 238)
   by Shirley Ellis (1965)

"Queen Of The House" (Capitol 5402)
   by Jody Miller (1965)

"Rap Mop" (Coral 60140)
   by The Ames Brothers (1950)

"Ragtime Cowboy Joe" (Liberty 55200)
   by The Chipmunks with David Seville (1959)

"Rama Lama Ding Dong" (Twin 700)
   by The Edsels (1961)

"Rappin' Rodney" (RCA 13656)
   by Rodney Dangerfield (1983)

"Real Wild Child" (Coral 62017)
   by Ivan (1958)

"The Return Of The Red Baron" (Laurie 3379)
   by The Royal Guardsmen (1967)

"Ricky" (Rock 'N' Roll 03849)
   by Weird Al Yankovic (1983)

"Rocking Pneumonia And The Boogie Woogie Flu" (Ace 530)
by Huey (Piano) Smith and The Clowns (1957)

"Roller Skate" (Brunswick 212)
by Vaughn Mason and Crew (1980)

"Roller-Skatin' Mate" (Polydor 2031)
by Peaches and Herb (1979)

"Rubber Duckie" (Columbia 45207)
by Ernie (1970)

"Rudolph The Red-Nosed Reindeer" (Challenge 1010)
by Gene Autry (1957)

"Rudolph The Red Nosed Reindeer" (Liberty 55289)
by The Chipmunks with David Seville (1960)

"Rudolph, The Red Nosed Reindeer" (RCA Victor 3934)
by Spike Jones (1950)

"Santa And The Satellite (Parts 1 & 2)" (Luniverse 107)
by Buchanan and Goodman (1957)

"Santa And The Touchables" (Rori 701)
by Dickie Goodman (1961)

"Santa Baby" (RCA Victor 5502)
by Eartha Kitt (1953)

"Santa Claus Is Watching You" (Mercury 72058)
by Ray Stevens (1962)

"Saturday Morning Confusion" (United Artists 50788)
by Bobby Russell (1971)

"Say Man" (Checker 931)
by Bo Diddley (1959)

"Say Man, Back Again" (Checker 936)
by Bo Diddley (1959)

"Searchin' " (Atco 6087)
by The Coasters (1957)

"See You Later, Alligator" (Decca 29791)
by Bill Haley and The Comets (1956)

"Serutan Yob" (Capitol 15210)
by Red Ingle and The Natural Seven (1948)

"Seven Little Girls Sitting In The Back Seat" (Guaranteed 200)
by Paul Evans (1959)

"Sh-Boom" (Mercury 70404)
by The Crew-Cuts (1954)

"Shaddap You Face" (MCA 51053)
by Joe Dolce (1981)

"She Can't Find Her Keys" (Colpix 620)
by Paul Peterson (1962)

"Shoo-Fly Pie And Apple Pan Dowdy" (Columbia 36943)
by Dinah Shore (1946)

"Shoppin' For Clothes" (Atco 6178)
by The Coasters (1960)

"Short People" (Warner Brothers 8492)
by Randy Newman (1977)

"Sidewalk Surfin' " (Liberty 55727)
by Jan and Dean (1964)

"Skinny Legs And All" (Dial 4063)
by Joe Tex (1967)

"Skokiaan" (Columbia 40306)
by The Four Lads (1954)

"Small Sad Sam" (Versatile 107)
by Phil McLean (1961)

"Snoopy For President" (Laurie 3451)
by The Royal Guardsmen (1968)

"Snoopy Vs. The Red Baron" (Laurie 3366)
by The Royal Guardsmen (1966)

"Society Girl" (Parkway 921)
by The Rag Dolls (1964)

"Somebody Bad Stole De Wedding Bell" (RCA Victor 5610)
by Eartha Kitt (1954)

"Son-In-Law" (Witch 101)
by Louise Brown (1961)

"Speed Ball" (Mercury 72189)
by Ray Stevens (1963)

"Splish Splash" (Atco 6117)
by Bobby Darin (1958)

"St. George And The Dragonet" (Capitol 2596)
by Stan Freberg (1953)

"Stand By Me" (MGM 13617)
by Spyder Turner (1966)

"Stranded In The Jungle" (Flash 109)
by The Jayhawks (1956)

"The Streak" (Barnaby 600)
by Ray Stevens (1974)

"Super-Cali-Fragil-Istic-Expi-Ali-Docious" (Vista 434)
by Julie Andrews, Dick Van Dyke, and The Pearlies (1965)

"Super Fly Meets Shaft" (Rainy Wednesday 201)
by John and Ernest (1973)

"Surfin' Bird" (Garrett 4002)
by The Trashmen (1963)

"Surfin' Hootenanny" (Stacy 962)
  by The Al Casey Combo (1963)

"Surfin' U.S.A." (Capitol 4932)
  by The Beach Boys (1963)

"Swingin' " (Warner Brothers 29788)
  by John Anderson (1983)

"T'ain't Nothin' To Me" (Atco 6287)
  by The Coasters (1964)

"Take Off" (Mercury 76134)
  by Bob and Doug McKenzie (1982)

"Tennessee Waltz" (RCA Victor 4011)
  by Spike Jones (1951)

"They're Coming To Take Me Away, Ha-Haaa!" (Warner Brothers 5831)
  by Napoleon XIV (1966)

"The Thing" (RCA Victor 3968)
  by Phil Harris (1950)

"Tie Me Kangaroo Down, Sport" (Epic 9596)
  by Rolf Harris (1963)

"The Topical Song" (Epic 50755)
  by Barron Knights (1979)

"Touchables" (Mark-X 8009)
  by Dickie Goodman (1961)

"The Touchables In Brooklyn" (Mark-X 8010)
  by Dickie Goodman (1961)

"Tramp" (Stax 216)
  by Otis and Carla (1967)

"Transfusion" (Dot 15470)
  by Nervous Norvus (1956)

"Troglodyte (Cave Man)" (RCA 1029)
  by The Jimmy Castor Bunch (1972)

"The Trouble With Harry" (Liberty 55008)
  by Alfi and Harry (1956)

"Tutti Frutti" (Specialty 561)
  by Little Richard (1956)

"Tweedle Dee" (Mercury 70517)
  by Georgia Gibbs (1955)

"26 Miles (Santa Catalina)" (Capitol 3845)
  by The Four Preps (1958)

"Uh! Oh! (Parts 1 & 2)" (Hanover 4540)
  by The Nutty Squirrels (1959)

"Uneasy Rider" (Kama Sutra 576)
  by The Charlie Daniels Band (1973)

"Up Your Nose" (Elektra 45369)
by Gabriel Kaplan (1977)

"Valley Girl" (Barking Pumpkin 02972)
by Frank and Moon Zappa (1982)

"Watergate" (Rainy Wednesday 202)
by Dickie Goodman (1973)

"We Love You Beatles" (London International 10614)
by The Carefrees (1964)

"We Told You Not To Marry" (Glover 201)
by Titus Turner (1959)

"Welfare Cadillac" (Royal American 1)
by Guy Drake (1970)

"Werewolves Of London" (Asylum 45472)
by Warren Zevon (1978)

"Western Movies" (Demon 1508)
by The Olympics (1958)

"What Can You Get A Wookee For Christmas (When He Already Owns A
Comb?)" (RSO 1058)
by The Star Wars Intergalactic Droid Choir and Chorale (1980)

"What'd I Say" (Atlantic 2031)
by Ray Charles (1959)

"When A Woman Loves A Man" (Atlantic 2335)
by "Little Esther" Phillips (1966)

"When You're Hot, You're Hot" (RCA 9976)
by Jerry Reed (1971)

"The White Knight" (Mercury 73751)
by Cledus Maggard and The Citizen's Band (1975)

"White Lightning" (Mercury 71406)
by George Jones (1959)

"Who Put The Bomp (In The Bomp, Bomp, Bomp)" (ABC-Paramount 10237)
by Barry Mann (1961)

"Who Shot J.R.?" (Ovation 1150)
by Gary Burbank, with Band McNally (1980)

"Wild Thing" (Parkway 127)
by Senator Bobby (1967)

"Wild Thing" (Fontana 1548)
by The Troggs (1966)

"Wildwood Weed" (MGM 14737)
by Jim Stafford (1974)

"Witch Doctor" (Liberty 55132)
by David Seville (1958)

"Wolverton Mountain" (Columbia 42352)
by Claude King (1962)

"Woody Woodpecker" (Capitol 15145)
   by Mel Blanc (1948)

"Wooly Bully" (MGM 13322)
   by Sam The Sham and The Pharaohs (1965)

"Work That Body" (RCA 13201)
   by Diana Ross (1982)

"Workin' At The Car Wash Blues" (ABC 11447)
   by Jim Croce (1974)

"Wun'erful Wun'erful (Parts 1 & 2)" (Capitol 3815)
   by Stan Freberg (1957)

"The Yellow Rose Of Texas" (Capitol 3249)
   by Stan Freberg (1955)

"Yingle Bells" (Capitol 781)
   by Yogi Yorgesson (1949)

"You Can't Judge A Book By The Cover" (Checker 1019)
   by Bo Diddley (1962)

"You Can't Roller Skate In A Buffalo Herd" (Smash 2043)
   by Roger Miller (1966)

"You Don't Have To Be A Tower Of Strength" (Everest 19428)
   by Gloria Lynne (1961)

"Your Boyfriend's Back" (Lawn 219)
   by Bobby Comstock (1963)

"Your Bulldog Drinks Champagne" (MGM 14775)
   by Jim Stafford (1974)

"Zing Zing—Zoom Zoom" (RCA Victor 3997)
   by Perry Como (1951)

Vacation and Leisure Time

"Almost Summer" (MCA 40891)
   by Celebration (1978)

"Back To School Again" (RSO 1069)
   by The Four Tops (1982)

"Cap And Gown" (Columbia 41408)
   by Marty Robbins (1959)

"Hangin' Out At The Mall" (Motown 1711)
   by Bobby Nunn (1983)

"Here Comes Summer" (Kapp 277)
   by Jerry Keller (1959)

"In The Summertime" (Janus 125)
   by Mungo Jerry (1970)

"Let's Go On Vacation" (Cotillion 45020)
   by Sister Sledge (1980)

"Palisades Park" (Swan 4106)
  by Freddy Cannon (1962)

"Queen Of The Senior Prom" (Decca 30299)
  by The Mills Brothers (1957)

"School Is Out" (Legrand 1009)
  by Gary "U.S." Bonds (1961)

"See You In September" (Climax 102)
  by The Tempos (1959)

"Seven Day Weekend" (Legrand 1019)
  by Gary "U.S." Bonds (1962)

"Summer Nights" (RSO 906)
  by Olivia Newton-John and John Travolta (1978)

"Summer's Gone" (ABC-Paramount 10147)
  by Paul Anka (1960)

"Summertime" (Chess 1966)
  by Billy Stewart (1966)

"Summertime Blues" (Liberty 55144)
  by Eddie Cochran (1958)

"Summertime, Summertime" (Epic 9281)
  by The Jamies (1958/1962)

"Surf City" (Liberty 55580)
  by Jan and Dean (1963)

"Surfin' Safari" (Capitol 4777)
  by The Beach Boys (1962)

"Surfin' U.S.A." (Capitol 4932)
  by The Beach Boys (1963)

"Those Lazy-Hazy-Crazy Days Of Summer" (Capitol 4965)
  by Nat King Cole (1963)

"Vacation" (MGM 13087)
  by Connie Francis (1962)

Idealism and Hope for a Positive Future

"America Is My Home" (King 6112)
  by James Brown (1968)

"Aquarius/Let The Sunshine In" (Soul City 772)
  by The Fifth Dimension (1969)

"The Best Of Times" (A&M 2300)
  by Styx (1981)

"Black And White" (Dunhill 4317)
  by Three Dog Night (1972)

"Bridge Over Troubled Water" (Columbia 45079)
  by Simon and Garfunkel (1970)

"California Dreamin' " (Dunhill 4020)
  by The Mamas and the Papas (1966)

"A Change Is Gonna Come" (RCA 8486)
  by Sam Cooke (1965)

"Come Together" (Apple 2654)
  by The Beatles (1969)

"Ebony And Ivory" (Columbia 02860)
  by Paul McCartney and Stevie Wonder (1982)

"Every One's A Winner" (Infinity 50002)
  by Hot Chocolate (1978)

"Everyday People" (Epic 10407)
  by Sly and The Family Stone (1968)

"Everything Is Beautiful" (Barnaby 2011)
  by Ray Stevens (1970)

"Eye Of The Tiger" (Scotti Brothers 02912)
  by Survivor (1982)

"Friendship Train" (Soul 35068)
  by Gladys Knight and The Pips (1969)

"Give A Damn" (Mercury 72831)
  by Spanky and Our Gang (1968)

"Give Peace A Chance" (Apple 1809)
  by John Lennon (1969)

"He Ain't Heavy, He's My Brother" (Epic 10532)
  by The Hollies (1969)

"I'd Like To Teach The World To Sing (In Perfect Harmony)" (Elektra 45762)
  by The New Seekers (1972)

"If I Had A Hammer" (Warner Brothers 5296)
  by Peter, Paul, and Mary (1962)

"I'm Always Chasing Rainbows" (Victor 1788)
  by Perry Como (1946)

"Johnny B. Goode" (EMI America 8159)
  by Peter Tosh (1983)

"Lay Down (Candles In The Rain)" (Buddah 167)
  by Melanie (1970)

"Lean On Me" (Sussex 235)
  by Bill Withers (1972)

"Let's Work Together" (Sue 11)
  by Wilbert Harrison (1969)

"Love Train" (Philadelphia International 3524)
  by The O'Jays (1973)

"Only In America" (United Artists 626)
  by Jay and The Americans (1963)

"Peace Brother Peace" (MGM 14000)
  by Bill Medley (1968)

"Peace Train" (A&M 1291)
  by Cat Stevens (1971)

"People Get Ready" (ABC-Paramount 10622)
  by The Impressions (1965)

"People Got To Be Free" (Atlantic 2537)
  by The Rascals (1968)

"Put A Little Love In Your Heart" (Imperial 66385)
  by Jackie DeShannon (1969)

"Reach Out and Touch (Somebody's Hand)" (Motown 1165)
  by Diana Ross (1970)

"Reach Out I'll Be There" (Motown 1098)
  by The Four Tops (1966)

"Reach Out Of The Darkness" (Verve Forecast 5069)
  by Friend and Lover (1968)

"Reach Out Your Hand" (Deram 85073)
  by Brotherhood of Man (1971)

"The Rose" (Atlantic 3656)
  by Bette Midler (1980)

"Share The Land" (RCA 0388)
  by The Guess Who (1970)

"Stand!" (Epic 10450)
  by Sly and The Family Stone (1969)

"Stand Tall" (Portrait 70001)
  by Burton Cummings (1976)

"Up Where We Belong" (Island 99996)
  by Joe Cocker and Jennifer Warnes (1982)

"We Are The World" (Columbia 04839)
  by USA for Africa (1985)

"We Shall Overcome" (Vanguard 35023)
  by Joan Baez (1963)

"The Wedding Song (There Is Love)" (Ariola 7726)
  by Mary MacGregor (1978)

"What The World Needs Now Is Love" (Imperial 66110)
  by Jackie DeShannon (1965)

"Wonderful World, Beautiful People" (A&M 1146)
  by Jimmy Cliff (1970)

Maturity and Self-Identity

"Against The Wind" (Capitol 4863)
  by Bob Seger and The Silver Bullet Band (1980)

"All Grown Up" (Philles 122)
  by The Crystals (1964)

"All I Really Want To Do" (Imperial 66114)
  by Cher (1965)

"Almost Grown" (Chess 1722)
  by Chuck Berry (1959)

"American Heartbeat" (Scotti Brothers 03213)
  by Survivor (1982)

"At Seventeen" (Columbia 10154)
  by Janis Ian (1975)

"Ballad Of A Teenage Queen" (Sun 283)
  by Johnny Cash (1958)

"Bang The Drum All Day" (Bearsville 29686)
  by Todd Rundgren (1983)

"A Boy Named Sue" (Columbia 44944)
  by Johnny Cash (1969)

"Department Of Youth" (Atlantic 3280)
  by Alice Cooper (1975)

"Did You Ever Have To Make Up Your Mind?" (Kama Sutra 209)
  by The Lovin' Spoonful (1966)

"Different Drum" (Capitol 2004)
  by Linda Ronstadt and The Stone Poneys (1967)

"Edge Of Seventeen (Just Like The White Winged Dove)" (Modern 7401)
  by Stevie Nicks (1982)

"Eighteen" (Warner Brothers 7449)
  by Alice Cooper (1971)

"Friday's Child" (Reprise 0491)
  by Nancy Sinatra (1966)

"Garden Party" (Decca 32980)
  by Rick Nelson (1972)

"Girl, You'll Be A Woman Soon" (Bang 542)
  by Neil Diamond (1969)

"Go Where You Wanna Go" (Soul City 753)
  by The Fifth Dimension (1967)

"I Am . . . I Said" (Uni 55278)
  by Neil Diamond (1971)

"I Wish" (Tamla 54274)
  by Stevie Wonder (1976)

"I'm Still Standing" (Geffen 29639)
  by Elton John (1983)

"It's My Life" (MGM 13414)
  by The Animals (1965)

"It's Still Rock 'N' Roll To Me" (Columbia 11276)
   by Billy Joel (1980)

"It's Your Thing" (T-Neck 901)
   by The Isley Brothers (1969)

"Jack And Diane" (Riva 210)
   by John Cougar (1982)

"Johnny B. Goode" (Chess 1691)
   by Chuck Berry (1958)

"Just The Way You Are" (Columbia 10646)
   by Billy Joel (1977)

"The Kid Is Hot Tonite" (Columbia 02068)
   by Loverboy (1981)

"Kids In America" (EMI America 8110)
   by Kim Wilde (1982)

"Kodachrome" (Columbia 45859)
   by Paul Simon (1973)

"Livin' In The Life" (T-Neck 2264)
   by The Isley Brothers (1977)

"Make Your Own Kind Of Music" (Dunhill 4214)
   by Mama Cass (1969)

"New Kid In Town" (Asylum 45373)
   by The Eagles (1976)

"No" (Decca 32996)
   by Bulldog (1972)

"Only Sixteen" (Capitol 4171)
   by Dr. Hook (1976)

"A Place In The Sun" (A&M 1976)
   by Pablo Cruise (1977)

"Problems" (Cadence 1355)
   by The Everly Brothers (1958)

"Puff The Magic Dragon" (Warner Brothers 5348)
   by Peter, Paul, and Mary (1963)

"Respect" (Atlantic 2403)
   by Aretha Franklin (1968)

"Respect" (Volt 128)
   by Otis Redding (1965)

"Runaway Child, Running Wild" (Gordy 7084)
   by The Temptations (1969)

"Saturday Night's Alright For Fighting" (MCA 40105)
   by Elton John (1973)

"Seventeen" (King 1470)
   by Boyd Bennett and His Rockets (1955)

"She Was Only Seventeen (He Was One Year More)" (Columbia 41208)
by Marty Robbins (1958)

"Smokin' In The Boys' Room" (Big Tree 16011)
by Brownsville Station (1973)

"Society's Child (Baby I've Been Thinking)" (Verve 5027)
by Janis Ian (1967)

"Stand!" (Epic 10450)
by Sly and The Family Stone (1970)

"Stand Tall" (Portrait 70001)
by Burton Cummings (1976)

"Summertime Blues" (Philips 40516)
by Blue Cheer (1968)

"Sweet Little Sixteen" (Chess 1683)
by Chuck Berry (1958)

"Take It Easy" (Asylum 11005)
by The Eagles (1972)

"Thank You (Falettinme Be Mice Elf Agin)" (Epic 10555)
by Sly and The Family Stone (1970)

"Think" (Atlantic 2518)
by Aretha Franklin (1968)

"Those Were The Days" (RCA 13401)
by Gary Stewart and Dean Dillon (1983)

"Unwed Fathers" (Epic 03971)
by Tammy Wynette (1983)

"We Gotta Get Out Of This Place" (MGM 13382)
by The Animals (1965)

"When I Grow Up (To Be A Man)" (Capitol 5245)
by The Beach Boys (1964)

"When You're Young And In Love" (Kapp 615)
by Ruby and The Romantics (1964)

"Who Are You" (MCA 40948)
by The Who (1978)

"Why Don't They Understand" (ABC-Paramount 9862)
by George Hamilton IV (1957)

"With A Little Help From My Friends" (A&M 991)
by Joe Cocker (1968)

"Yakety Yak" (Atco 6116)
by The Coasters (1958)

"You And Me Against The World" (Capitol 3897)
by Helen Reddy (1974)

"You Never Can Tell" (Chess 1906)
by Chuck Berry (1964)

"(You're So Square) Baby I Don't Care" (Geffen 29849)
  by Joni Mitchell (1982)

"You're So Vain" (Elektra 45824)
  by Carly Simon (1972)

"Young Americans" (RCA 10152)
  by David Bowie (1975)

"Young And In Love" (Warner Brothers 5342)
  by Dick and DeeDee (1963)

"Young Blood" (Swan Song 70108)
  by Bad Company (1976)

"Young Blood" (Warner Brothers 49018)
  by Rickie Lee Jones (1979)

"Young Boy" (Renee 5001)
  by Barbara Greene (1968)

"Young Boy Blues" (Atco 6207)
  by Ben E. King (1961)

"Young Emotions" (Imperial 5663)
  by Ricky Nelson (1960)

"A Young Girl" (London 9795)
  by Noel Harrison (1966)

"Young Hearts Run Free" (Warner Brothers 8181)
  by Candi Staton (1976)

"Young Love" (Arista 1005)
  by Air Supply (1982)

"Young Love" (Mercury 72553)
  by Lesley Gore (1966)

"Young Love" (A&M 2440)
  by Janet Jackson (1956)

"Young Love" (Capitol 3602)
  by Sonny James (1956)

"Young Lovers" (Philips 40096)
  by Paul and Paula (1963)

"Young School Girl" (Imperial 5537)
  by Fats Domino (1958)

"Young Turks" (Warner Brothers 49843)
  by Rod Stewart (1981)

"Young Wings Can Fly (Higher Than You Know)" (Kapp 557)
  by Ruby and The Romantics (1963)

"Young World" (Imperial 5805)
  by Ricky Nelson (1962)

"Younger Days" (Millenium 13107)
  by Joe Fagin (1982)

"Younger Girl" (Kapp 752)
   by The Critters (1966)

Peer Groups, Friends, and Family

"Beat It" (Epic 03759)
   by Michael Jackson (1983)

"Billie Jean" (Epic 03509)
   by Michael Jackson (1982)

"Blue Jean" (EMI America 8231)
   by David Bowie (1984)

"Boys" (Gordy 1704)
   by The Mary Jane Girls (1983)

"Charlie Brown" (Atco 6132)
   by The Coasters (1959)

"Chuck E.'s In Love" (Warner Brothers 8825)
   by Rickie Lee Jones (1979)

"Color Him Father" (Metromedia 117)
   by The Winstons (1969)

"Daddy Don't You Walk So Fast" (Chelsea 0100)
   by Wayne Newton (1972)

"Daddy-O" (Dot 15428)
   by The Fontane Sisters (1955)

"Daddy Sang Bass" (Columbia 44689)
   by Johnny Cash (1969)

"Daddy's Home" (EMI America 8103)
   by Cliff Richard (1982)

"Daddy's Little Girl" (Capitol 5825)
   by Al Martino (1967)

"Down On The Corner" (Fantasy 634)
   by Creedence Clearwater Revival (1969)

"Family Affair" (Epic 10805)
   by Sly and The Family Stone (1971)

"Father Come On Home" (Columbia 45221)
   by Pacific Gas and Electric (1970)

"Father Knows Best" (Chess 1832)
   by The Radiants (1962)

"Father Of Girls" (RCA 9448)
   by Perry Como (1968)

"Friend And A Lover" (Bell 45336)
   by The Partridge Family (1973)

"A Friend In The City" (Steed 723)
   by Andy Kim (1970)

"Friend Of Mine" (Sussex 257)
  by Bill Withers (1973)

"Girls Just Want To Have Fun" (Portrait 04120)
  by Cyndi Lauper (1983)

"Handy Man" (Columbia 10557)
  by James Taylor (1977)

"Harper Valley P.T.A." (Plantation 3)
  by Jeannie C. Riley (1968)

"Help!" (Capitol 5476)
  by The Beatles (1965)

"Hey Little Girl" (Abner 1029)
  by Dee Clark (1959)

"High School Dance" (Capitol 4405)
  by The Sylvers (1977)

"I Think We're Alone Now" (Roulette 4720)
  by Tommy James and The Shondells (1967)

"Kids In America" (EMI America 8110)
  by Kim Wilde (1982)

"Lady Madonna" (Capitol 2138)
  by The Beatles (1968)

"The Longest Time" (Columbia 04400)
  by Billy Joel (1983)

"Loves Me Like A Rock" (Columbia 45907)
  by Paul Simon (1973)

"Mother" (Apple 1827)
  by John Lennon (1971)

"Mother And Child Reunion" (Columbia 45547)
  by Paul Simon (1972)

"A Mother For My Children" (Janus 231)
  by The Whispers (1974)

"Mother, Please!" (Cameo 249)
  by Jo Ann Campbell (1963)

"My Girl" (Gordy 7038)
  by The Temptations (1965)

"New Girl In School" (Liberty 55672)
  by Jan and Dean (1964)

"Papa Was A Rollin' Stone" (Gordy 7121)
  by The Temptations (1972)

"Patches" (Atlantic 2748)
  by Clarence Carter (1970)

"Seventeen" (King 1470)
  by Boyd Bennett and His Rockets (1955)

"Still Crazy After All These Years" (Columbia 10332)
  by Paul Simon (1976)

"Street Kids" (De-Lite 825)
  by Kool and The Gang (1983)

"Wake Up Little Susie" (Warner Brothers 50053)
  by Simon and Garfunkel (1982)

"You Bug Me, Baby" (Specialty 615)
  by Larry Williams (1957)

"Your Friends" (Vee-Jay 372)
  by Dee Clark (1961)

"You've Got A Friend" (Warner Brothers 7498)
  by James Taylor (1971)

Authority Figures and Generation Gaps

"Abigail Beecher" (Warner Brothers 5409)
  by Freddy Cannon (1964)

"Albert Flasher" (RCA 0458)
  by The Guess Who (1971)

"Another Brick In The Wall" (Columbia 11187)
  by Pink Floyd (1980)

"The Authority Song" (Riva 216)
  by John Cougar Mellencamp (1984)

"Big Boss Man" (Vee-Jay 380)
  by Jimmy Reed (1961)

"A Boy Named Sue" (Columbia 44944)
  by Johnny Cash (1969)

"Cat's In The Cradle" (Elektra 45203)
  by Harry Chapin (1974)

"Clap For The Wolfman" (RCA 0324)
  by The Guess Who (1974)

"Don't Worry Baby" (Capitol 5174)
  by The Beach Boys (1964)

"Everybody's Talkin' " (RCA 0161)
  by Nilsson (1969)

"The Free Electric Band" (Mums 6018)
  by Albert Hammond (1973)

"Harper Valley P.T.A." (Plantation 3)
  by Jeannie C. Riley (1968)

"Hey Nineteen" (MCA 51036)
  by Steely Dan (1980)

"I Get Around" (Capitol 5174)
  by The Beach Boys (1964)

"I Think We're Alone Now" (Roulette 4720)
by Tommy James and The Shondells (1967)

"The 'In' Crowd" (Charger 105)
by Dobie Gray (1965)

"I've Got A Rock 'N' Roll Heart" (Warner Brothers 29780)
by Eric Clapton (1983)

"Kansas City Star" (Smash 1998)
by Roger Miller (1965)

"Kodachrome" (Columbia 45859)
by Paul Simon (1973)

"The Little Old Lady (From Pasadena)" (Liberty 55704)
by Jan and Dean (1964)

"The Logical Song" (A&M 2128)
by Supertramp (1979)

"Me And Julio Down By The Schoolyard" (Columbia 45585)
by Paul Simon (1972)

"My Generation" (Decca 31877)
by The Who (1966)

"An Open Letter To My Teenage Son" (Liberty 55996)
by Victor Lundberg (1967)

"Peek-A-Boo" (Josie 846)
by The Cadillacs (1958)

"Roll Over Beethoven" (Chess 1626)
by Chuck Berry (1956)

"School Day" (Chess 1653)
by Chuck Berry (1957)

"Skip A Rope" (Monument 1041)
by Henson Cargill (1967)

"Society's Child (Baby, I've Been Thinking)" (Verve 5027)
by Janis Ian (1967)

"Sticks And Stones" (ABC-Paramount 10118)
by Ray Charles (1960)

"Summertime Blues" (Decca 32708)
by The Who (1970)

"Sylvia's Mother" (Columbia 45562)
by Dr. Hook (1972)

"Teach Your Children" (Atlantic 2735)
by Crosby, Stills, Nash and Young (1970)

"To Sir With Love" (Epic 10187)
by Lulu (1967)

"Town Without Pity" (Musicor 1009)
by Gene Pitney (1961)

"Welcome Back" (Reprise 1349)
  by John Sebastian (1976)

"With A Little Help From My Friends" (Capitol 4612)
  by The Beatles (1978)

"Workin' For The Man" (Monument 467)
  by Roy Orbison (1962)

"Yakety Yak" (Atco 6116)
  by The Coasters (1958)

"You Never Can Tell" (Chess 1906)
  by Chuck Berry (1964)

"Young Blood" (Atco 6087)
  by The Coasters (1957)

"You're My Best Friend" (Elektra 45318)
  by Queen (1976)

"Your Mama Don't Dance" (Columbia 45719)
  by Loggins and Messina (1972)

An Audio Profile of the Rock Era, 1950–1985: A Selected Discography

1. The Origins of Rock Music
   A. Country and Western Music
      Bill Haley, *Golden Country Origins* (1977).
         Grass Roots Record (Australia). GR 1001.
      Bill C. Malone (Comp.), *The Smithsonian Collection of Classic Country Music*—Volumes 1–5 (1971).
         Smithsonian Recordings. R 025.
      60 Years of Country Music (1982).
         RCA Records. CPL 2–4351.
      Hank Snow and Jimmie Rodgers, *All About Trains* (1975).
         RCA Records. ANL 1–1052.
      Stars of the Grand Ole Opry, 1926–1974 (1974).
         RCA Records. CPL 2–0466.
      Hank Williams, *24 of Hank Williams' Greatest Hits* (n.d.).
         MGM Records. SE 4755–2.
   B. Early Blues
      The Blues and All That Jazz, 1937–1947 (1982).
         MCA Records. MCA 1353.
      The Blues Are Black (1976).
         Columbia Records. P 13211.
      John Lee Hooker, *This Is Hip* (1981).
         Oxford Records (Italy). OX 3236.
      Howlin' Wolf, *Chester Burnett A.K.A. Howlin' Wolf* (1972).
         Chess/Janus Records. 2CH–60016.
      Elmore James, *The Best of Elmore James* (1982).
         Ace Records (Great Britain). CH 31.
      B. B. King, *The Rarest King* (1981).
         Blues Boy Records (Sweden). BB 301.

The Legacy of the Blues Sampler: Twelve Great Blues (1976).
  G.N.P./Crescendo Records. GNP5 X10010.
Okeh Chicago Blues (1982).
  Epic Records. EG 37318.
Out Came the Blues (1982).
  MCA Records. MCA 1352.
T-Bone Walker, *T-Bone Walker: Classics of Modern Blues* (1975).
  Blue Note Records. BN-LA 533-H2.
Muddy Waters, *Rolling Stone* (1982).
  Chess Records. CH 8202.

C. Rhythm 'n' Blues

Arthur "Big Boy" Crudup, *Arthur "Big Boy" Crudup—The Father of Rock and Roll* (1971).
  RCA Records. LPV 573.
Fats Domino, *The Fats Domino Story—Volume One* (1977).
  United Artists Records (Great Britain). UAS 30067.
History of Rhythm and Blues—Volume One: The Roots, 1947–52 (1968).
  Atlantic Records. SD 8161.
Honkers and Screamers: Roots of Rock 'n' Roll—Volume Six (1979).
  Savoy Records. Savoy 2234.
Louis Jordan and His Tympany Five, *Louis Jordan's Greatest Hits* (n.d.).
  MCA Records. MCA 274.
Meade Lux Lewis, Pete Johnson, and Albert Ammons, *The Original Boogie Woogie Piano Giants: Original Recordings, 1938–1951* (1974).
  Columbia Records. KC 32708.
Smiley Lewis, *The Bells Are Ringing: The Smiley Lewis Story—Volume One* (1978).
  United Artists Records (Great Britain). UAS 30186.
Percy Mayfield, *The Best of Percy Mayfield* (1970).
  Specialty Records. SPS 2126.
Johnny Otis, *The Original Johnny Otis Show* (1978).
  Savoy Records. SJL 2230.
The Ravens, *The Ravens—"The Greatest Group of Them All": Roots of Rock and Roll—Volume Three* (1978).
  Arista Records. Savoy 2227.
The Roots of Rock 'n' Roll (1977).
  Arista Records. SJL 2221.
The Shouters: The Roots of Rock 'n' Roll—Volume Nine (1980).
  Savoy Records. Savoy 2244.
Stars of the Apollo Theatre (1973).
  Columbia Records. KG 30788.
Straighten Up and Fly Right: Rhythm and Blues from the Close of the Swing Era to the Dawn of Rock 'n' Roll (1977).
  New World Records. NW 261.
This Is How It All Began: The Roots of Rock 'n' Roll as Recorded from 1945 to 1955 on Specialty Records—Two Volumes (1969/1970).
  Specialty Records. SPS 2117/8.

D. Gospel Music

Mahalia Jackson, *The Great Mahalia Jackson* (1972).
  Columbia Records. CG 31379.
The Soul Stirrers, *The Original Soul Stirrers, Featuring Sam Cooke, Johnnie Taylor, Paul Foster, and R. H. Harris* (1971).
  Specialty Records. SPS 2137.
E. Pop Music
  The Best of the Gold—5 Volumes (1973).
    Columbia Records. P 13796/7/8/9/800.
  Hoagy Carmichael, *The Stardust Road* (1982).
    MCA Records. MCA 1507.
  The Great Girl Singers (1974).
    Capitol Records. SLB 6952.
  Al Hibbler, *The Best of Al Hibbler* (1976).
    MCA Records. MCA 2–4098.
  The Ink Spots, *The Best of the Ink Spots* (1977).
    MCA Records. MCA 2–4005.
  The Mills Brothers, *The Best of The Mills Brothers* (1980).
    MCA Records. MCA 2–4039.
  Guy Mitchell, *American Legend—16 Greatest Hits* (1977).
    Embassy Records (Holland). Embassy 31459.
  Les Paul and Mary Ford, *The Very Best of Les Paul and Mary Ford* (1974).
    Music for Pleasure Records. MFP 5604.
  The Unforgettable Hits of The '40s and '50s (n.d).
    MCA Records. R214291.
  Your Hit Parade (1975)
    H.R.B. Music P12750.
2. The Revolution in Country Music
  A. Country and Western Music
    Ray Charles, *Modern Sounds in Country and Western Music* (1962).
      ABC-Paramount Records. ABC 410.
    Ray Charles, *Modern Sounds in Country and Western Music—Volume Two* (1962).
      ABC-Paramount Records. ABC 435.
    Patsy Cline, *Patsy Cline's Greatest Hits* (1973).
      MCA Records. MCA 12.
    Bill Haley and His Comets, *Golden Hits* (1972).
      MCA Records. MCA 2–4010.
    Bill Haley and The Comets, *The King of Rock and Roll* (1979).
      Alshire International Records. S 5313.
    Buddy Holly, *The Complete Buddy Holly* (1980).
      MCA Coral Records (London). CDSP 808.
    George Jones, *Anniversary—Ten Years of Hits* (1982).
      Epic Records. KE 2–38324.
    Buddy Knox, *Party Doll* (1979).
      Pye Records (Great Britain). NSPL 28243.
    Brenda Lee, *The Brenda Lee Story: Her Greatest Hits* (1973).
      MCA Records. MCA 2–4012.

Jerry Lee Lewis, *Jerry Lee Lewis Sings the Country Music Hall of Fame—2 Volumes* (1969).
    Mercury Records. SRS 67117/8.
Jerry Lee Lewis, *"Old Tyme Country Music"* (1970).
    Sun International Records. Sun 121.
Bill C. Malone (Comp.), *The Smithsonian Collection of Classic Country Music—Volumes Six and Eight* (1981).
    Smithsonian Recordings. R 025.
Jim Reeves, *The Best of Jim Reeves* (1964).
    RCA Records. AHL 1–2990.
Hank Snow, *Railroad Man* (1963).
    RCA Records. LSP 2705.

B. Rockabilly

The Collins Kids, *The Collins Kids: Introducing Larry and Lorrie* (1983).
    Epic Records. PE 38457.
King-Federal Rockabillys (1978).
    Gusto Records. King 5016X.
Sleepy LaBeef, *Early, Rare, and Rockin' Sides* (n.d.).
    Baron Records. LP 102.
"Let's Have a Party": The Rockabilly Influence, 1950–1960 (1980).
    Capitol Records (Holland). CGB 1008.
Roy Orbison, *Roy Orbison at the Rock House* (1981).
    Sun Records (Great Britain). CRM 2007.
Roy Orbison, *Roy Orbison: The Sun Years* (1984).
    Charly Records (Great Britain). CDX 4.
Carl Perkins, *The Sun Years* (1982).
    Charly Records (Great Britain). Sun Box 101.
Elvis Presley, *Elvis—The Sun Sessions* (1976).
    RCA Records. APM 1–1675.
Rockabilly Rebels (1983).
    Cambra Sound Records (Great Britain). CR 104.
Rockabilly Stars—3 Volumes (1981 and 1982).
    Epic Records. EG 37618/21 and 37984.
Rockabilly: The Roots of Rock and Roll (1982).
    Imperial House Records. WU 3590.
Wild, Wild Young Women (n.d.).
    Rounder Records. RR 1031.

C. Country Rock

The Band, *Anthology* (1978).
    Capitol Records. SKBO 11856.
The Blue Ridge Rangers, *The Blue Ridge Rangers.* (1973).
    Fantasy Records. F 9415.
Creedence Clearwater Revival, *Creedence Country* (1981).
    Fantasy Records. MFP 4509.
The Eagles, *Eagles Greatest Hits—Volume Two* (1982).
    Asylum Records (Canada). 9–602051.
The Eagles, *Hotel California* (1976).
    Asylum Records. Asylum 6E–103.

The Eagles, *Their Greatest Hits, 1971–1975* (1976).
 Asylum Records. Asylum 7E–1052.
Freddy Fender, *The Best of Freddy Fender* (1977).
 ABC Records. DO 2079.
Ronnie Hawkins, *Rockin'* (1978).
 Pye International Records (Great Britain). NSPL 28238.
Waylon Jennings, *Greatest Hits of Waylon* (1979).
 RCA Records. AHL 1–3378.
Waylon Jennings, Willie Nelson, Jessi Colter, and Others, *Wanted! The Outlaws* (1976).
 RCA Records. RCA 1321.
Kris Kristofferson, *Songs of Kristofferson* (1977).
 Columbia Records. PZ 34687.
Willie Nelson, *Willie Nelson's Greatest Hits (and Some That Will Be)* (1981).
 Columbia Records. KC 2–37542.
Dolly Parton, *Greatest Hits* (1982).
 RCA Records. AHL 1–4422.
Elvis Presley, *"Elvis Country"* (1971).
 RCA Records. AFL 1–4460.
Jerry Reed, *The Best of Jerry Reed* (1972).
 RCA Records. AHL 1–4729.
Marty Robbins, *Marty Robbins: A Lifetime of Song, 1951–1982* (1983).
 Columbia Records. C2–38870.
Kenny Rogers, *Greatest Hits* (1980).
 Liberty Records. Loo–1072.
Kenny Rogers, *Ten Years of Gold* (1977).
 United Artists Records. UA-LA 835H.
Linda Ronstadt, *Greatest Hits* (1976).
 Asylum Records. Asylum 7E–1092.
Linda Ronstadt, *Linda Ronstadt Greatest Hits—Volume Two* (1980).
 Asylum Records. Asylum 5E–516.
Hank Williams, Jr., *Whiskey Bent and Hell Bound* (1979).
 Elektra Records. 6E–237.
 D. Southern Rock
 Alabama, *The Closer You Get* (1983).
 RCA Records. AHL 1–4663.
 The Allman Brothers, *The Allman Brothers Band at Fillmore East* (1971).
 Capricorn Records. SD 2–802.
 The Atlanta Rhythm Section, *Champagne Jam* (1978).
 Polydor Records. PD 1–6134.
 The Charlie Daniels Band, *A Decade of Hits* (1983).
 Epic Records. FE 38795.
 Lynyrd Skynyrd Band, *Gold and Platinum* (1979).
 MCA Records. MCA 2–6898.
 E. Rockabilly Revival
 Billy Burnette, *Billy Burnette* (1980).
 Columbia Records. NJC 36792.
 Ray Campi and His Rockabilly Rebels, *Wildcat Shakeout* (1978).

Radar Records. RAD 9.
Charlie Feathers, *Rockabilly Rhythm* (1981).
   Cowboy Carl Records. CCLP 108.
Robert Gordon, *Rock Billy Boogie* (1979).
   RCA Records. AFL 1–3294.
Matchbox, *Rockabilly Rebel* (1979).
   Sire Records. SRK 6087.
Delbert McClinton, *Genuine Cowhide* (1976).
   ABC Records. ABCD 959.
Orion, *Rockabilly* (1980)
   Sun International Records. Sun 1021.
Carl Perkins, *Ol' Blue Suede's Back: Carl Perkins' Tribute to Rock and Roll* (1978).
   Jet Records. KZ 35604.
Billy Lee Riley, *"Vintage"* (1980).
   Cowboy Carl Records. CCLP 105.
Johnny Rivers, *Superpack* (1972).
   United Artists Records. UX5 93.
Shakin' Stevens, *Get Shakin'* (1980).
   Epic Records. FE 37415.
The Stray Cats, *Built for Speed* (1981).
   EMI America. ST 17070.
Neil Young and The Shocking Pinks, *Everybody's Rockin'* (1983).
   Geffen Records. GHS 4013.

3. The Evolution of Rhythm 'n' Rock
   A. Early Rhythm 'n' Blues
      LaVern Baker, *Real Gone Gal* (1984).
         Charly Records (Great Britain). CRB 1072.
      The Blues—5 Volumes (n.d.).
         Cadet Records. LPS 4026/27/34/42/51.
      Ruth Brown, *Rockin' with Ruth* (1984).
         Charly Records (Great Britain). CRB 1069.
      Gene Chandler, *Stroll On with the Duke* (1984).
         Solid Smoke Records. SS 8027.
      Ray Charles, *A Life In Music* (1982).
         Atlantic/DeLuxe Records. AD 5–4700.
      Bobby Day, *The Best of Bobby Day* (1984).
         Rhino Records. RNDF 209.
      Bo Diddley, *Bo Diddley—His Greatest Sides: Volume One* (1983).
         Chess Records. CH 8204.
      El Dorados, *Low Mileage–High Octane: Their Greatest Recordings* (1984).
         Solid Smoke Records. SS 8025.
      14 Golden Recordings from the Historic Vaults of Duke/Peacock Records—2 Volumes (1973).
         ABC Records. ABC 784 and 789.
      14 Golden Recordings from the Historical Vaults of Vee Jay Records (1973).
         ABC Records. ABC 785.
      Gabe's Dirty Blues: Gabe's Archive of Sounds—Rhythm and Blues (1978).

Gabe's Archive of Sounds. GTS 110.

History of Rhythm and Blues—Volumes 2–6 (1968).
Atlantic Records. SD 8162/63/64/93/94.

Etta James, *Etta James: Her Greatest Sides—Volume One* (1984).
Chess Records. CH 9110.

Little Willie John, *Free at Last* (1976).
Gusto Records. KS 1081.

Clyde McPhatter, *Rock and Cry* (1984).
Charly Records (Great Britain). CRB 1073.

Clyde McPhatter, Chuck Jackson, Gene Chandler, and Jimmy Jones,
Treasures of Love (1980).
Hall of Music Records. DD 1017.

Okeh Rhythm and Blues (1982).
Epic Records. EG 37649.

Old King Gold—10 Volumes (1975).
Gusto Records. KS 16001–10.

The Johnny Otis Show, *Rock 'n' Roll Revue* (1982).
Charly Records (Great Britain). CRB 1041.

Rhythm and Rock: The Best of Chess/Checker/Cadet (n.d.).
Chess Records (Great Britain). CXMP 2002.

Joe Turner, *Joe Turner: His Greatest Recordings* (1971).
Atco Records. SD 33–376.

Joe Turner, *Jumpin' with Joe* (1984).
Charlie Records (Great Britain). CRB 1070.

Chuck Willie, *Keep a Drivin'* (1984).
Charly Records (Great Britain). CRB 1074.

Jackie Wilson, *The Jackie Wilson Story* (1983).
Epic Records. EG 38623.

Wizards from the South Side (1982).
Chess Records. CH 8203.

B. New Orleans Sounds

Fats Domino, *Fats Domino: Legendary Masters Series* (1971).
United Artists Records. UAS 9958.

Doug Kershaw, *Alive and Pickin'—Recorded Live in Atlanta* (1975).
Warner Brothers Records. BS 2851.

Dr. John (Mac Rebennack), *Gumbo* (1972).
Atco Records. SD 7006.

The Neville Brothers, *Fiyo on the Bayou* (1981).
A&M Records. SP 4866.

New Orleans Jazz and Heritage Festival (1979).
Flying Fish Records. Fly/Fish 099.

Professor Longhair, *The Last Mardi Gras* (1982).
Atlantic/Deluxe Records. AD 2–4001.

Rockin' to New Orleans (1982).
Aura Records. A 1007.

Rock's World Revolution: The Roots (1979).
Legrand Records. Legrand 1000.

C. Caribbean and Latin Styles

David Lindley, *El Rayo-X* (1981).
  Album Records. Asylum SE–524.
Bob Marley and The Wailers, *Legend: The Best of Bob Marley and The Wailers* (1984).
  Island Records. 7–90169–1.
Ritchie Valens, *The Best of Ritchie Valens* (1981).
  Rhino Records. RNDF 200.

D. Group Harmony

The Coasters, *Young Blood* (1982).
  Atlantic/DeLuxe Records. AD 2–4003.
Dion and The Belmonts, *The Dion Years, 1958–1963* (1975).
  GRT Corporation Records. 2103–7–7.
The Dominoes, *The Dominoes* (1977).
  Gusto Records. King 5005X.
The Drifters, *The Drifters' Golden Hits* (1968)
  Atlantic Records. SD 8153.
The Drifters, *The Drifters—Their Greatest Hits: The Early Years* (1971).
  Atco Records. SD 33–375.
The El Dorados, *Bim Bam Boom* (1981).
  Charly Records (Great Britain). CRB 1022.
The El Dorados, *Low Mileage–High Octane: Their Greatest Recordings* (1984).
  Solid Smoke Records. SS 8025.
Great Hits of R&B (n.d.).
  Columbia Records. G 30503.
"In The Still of the Night": The Doo-Wop Groups, 1951–1962 (1980).
  Capitol Records (Holland): CGB 1004.
Leiber and Stoller—Only In America: The Original Hits (1980).
  WEA International Records (Germany). ATL 99098.
Clyde McPhatter and The Drifters, *Bip Bam* (1984).
  Edsel Records (Great Britain). ED 132.
Manhattan Transfer, *The Best of Manhattan Transfer* (1981).
  Atlantic Records. SD 19319.
The Platters, *Platterama* (1982).
  Mercury Records. SRM 1–4050.
The Spaniels, *Great Googley Moo!* (1981).
  Charly Records (Great Britain). CRB 1021.
The Spaniels, *16 Soulful Serenades* (1984).
  Solid Smoke Records. SS 8028.
Teen Dreams (1981).
  RCA Records (Great Britain). LRSLP 1003.
You Found the Vocal Group Sound: Greatest Hits of the Era—Two Volumes (1984).
  Solid Smoke Records. SS 8031/2.

E. Girl Group Sounds

Diana Ross and The Supremes, *Diana Ross and The Supremes Anthology* (1974).
  Motown Records. M7–794 A3.
Phil Spector's Greatest Hits (1977).
  Warner Brothers Records. 2 SP 9104.

The Shirelles, *The Very Best of The Shirelles* (1975).
  United Artists Records. UA-LA 340E.
Silhouettes (1981).
  Audio Encore Records. AEI 1009.
Super Girls (1979).
  Warner Special Product Records. OP 3507.
Wonder Women: The History of the Girl Group Sound—Volume One, 1961–1964 (1982).
  Rhino Records. RNLP 055.
F. Motown Sounds
The Commodores, *Commodores' Greatest Hits* (1978).
  Motown Records. M7–912 R1.
The Four Tops, *Four Tops Anthology* (1974).
  Motown Records. M9–803 A9.
Marvin Gaye, *Marvin Gaye Anthology* (1974).
  Motown Records. M9–791 A3.
Michael Jackson, *Michael Jackson—Volume Seven* (1980).
  Motown Records. M5–107 V1.
Rick James, *Street Songs* (1981).
  Gordy Records. G8–1002 M1.
Gladys Knight and The Pips, *Gladys Knight and The Pips Anthology* (1973).
  Motown Records. M 792 S2.
The Motown Story: The First Twenty-Five Years (1983).
  Motown Records. 6048 ML5.
Motown's Preferred Stock—3 Volumes (1977).
  Motown Records. M6–881/2/3/ S1.
Smokey Robinson and The Miracles, *Smokey Robinson and The Miracles' Anthology* (1973).
  Motown Records. M 793 R3.
Diana Ross, *All the Great Hits* (1981).
  Motown Records. M13–960 C2.
The Temptations, *The Temptations' Anthology: A Tenth Anniversary Special* (1973).
  Motown Records. M 782 A3.
20/20: Twenty No. 1 Hits from Twenty Years at Motown (1980).
  Motown Records. M9–937 A2.
Stevie Wonder, *Stevie Wonder's Original Musiquarium I* (1982).
  Tamla Records. Ramla 6002 TL2.
G. Dance Music
Dance! Dance! Dance! (n.d.).
  Telehouse Records. CD 2023.
Disco Party (1975).
  Adam VIII Records. A 8021.
Discotech # 1 (1975).
  Motown Records. M6–824 S1.
Let's Twist Again (1981).
  Audio Encore Records. AEI 1004.

A Night at Studio 54 (1979).
  Casablanca Records. NBLP 2–7161.
Donna Summer, *On the Radio: Greatest Hits—Volumes One and Two* (1979).
  Casablanca Records. NBLP 2–7191.
H. Soul Music
Bootsy's Rubber Band, *Ahh . . . The Name is Bootsy, Baby!* (1977).
  Warner Brothers Records. BSK 2972.
James Brown, *Solid Gold: 30 Golden Hits in 21 Golden Years* (1978).
  Polydor Records. Polydor 2679044.
Solomon Burke, *Cry to Me* (1984).
  Charly Records (Great Britain). CRB 1075.
Ray Charles, *A 25th Anniversary in Show Business Salute to Ray Charles: His All-Time Great Performances* (1971).
  ABC Records. ABCH 731.
Roberta Flack, *The Best of Roberta Flack* (1981).
  Atlantic Records. SD 19317.
Aretha Franklin, *Aretha's Greatest Hits* (1971).
  Atlantic Records. SD 8295.
Funkadelic, *One Nation under a Groove* (1978).
  Warner Brothers Records. BSK 3209.
History of Rhythm and Blues—Volumes Seven and Eight (1969).
  Atlantic Records. SD 8208/9.
The Impressions, *The Impressions, Featuring Jerry Butler and Curtis Mayfield: The Vintage Years* (1976).
  Sire Records. Sash 3717–2.
The Isley Brothers, *Go for Your Guns* (1977).
  T-Neck Records. PZ 34432.
Michael Jackson, *Off the Wall* (1979).
  Epic Records. FE 35745.
Ooh Poo Pah Doo: Early Sixties Soul, 1960–1965 (1981).
  Capitol Records (Holland). CGB 1012.
Wilson Pickett, *Wilson Pickett's Greatest Hits* (1973).
  Atlantic Records. SD 2–501.
The Pointer Sisters, *So Excited* (1982).
  Planet Records. BXL 1–4355.
Otis Redding, *The Best of Otis Redding* (1972).
  Atco Records. SD 2–801.
Nina Simone, *The Best of Nina Simone* (1970).
  RCA Records. LSP 4374.
Sly and The Family Stone, *Sly and The Family Stone* (1981).
  Epic Records. E2–37071.
Soul (1981).
  Audio Encore Records. AEI 1005.
The Spinners, *The Best of The Spinners* (1978).
  Atlantic Records. SD 19179.
Donna Summer, *Walk Away: Collector's Edition of the Best of 1977–1980* (1980).

Casablanca Records. NBLP 7244.

Ike and Tina Turner, *Workin' Together* (1970).

Liberty/United Artists Records. LST 7650.

I. Blue-Eyed Soul

Daryl Hall and John Oates, *Rock 'n Soul—Part One* (1983).

RCA Records. CPL 1–4858.

John Hammond, *John Hammond—Live in Greece* (1983).

Anezapthtoi Naparoroi (Greece). CP 931.

The Righteous Brothers, *Right Now!* (1963).

Moonglow Records. Moonglow 1001.

J. Blues Revival

Long John Baldry, *Long John's Blues: 12 Classic Performances by Long John Baldry and The Hoochie Coochie Men Recorded in London, 1964–1966* (1971).

United Artists Records. UAS 5543.

Michael Bloomfield, *Bloomfield: A Retrospective* (1983).

Columbia Records. C2–37578.

Blues DeLuxe (1980).

XRT Records. XRT 9301.

Lonnie Brooks, *Bayou Lightening* (1979).

Alligator Records. AL 4714.

The Paul Butterfield Blues Band, *The Paul Butterfield Blues Band* (1965).

Elektra Records. EKS 7294.

Canned Heat, *The Canned Heat Cook Book* (1969).

Liberty/United Artists Records. LST 11000.

Eric Clapton, *Timepieces: The Best of Eric Clapton* (1982).

R.S.O. Records. RX 1–3099.

Albert Collins, *Ice Pickin'* (1978).

Alligator Records. AL 4713.

Fleetwood Mac, *Fleetwood Mac in Chicago* (1975).

Sire Records. Sash 3715–2.

Great Bluesmen—Recorded Live at the Newport Folk Festivals in Newport, Rhode Island, 1959–1965 (1976).

Vanguard Recording Society. VSD 77/78.

The Heartfixers, *Live at the Moonshadow* (1983).

Landslide Records. LD 1007.

Janis Joplin, *Janis Joplin's Greatest Hits* (1973).

Columbia Records. PC 32169.

Albert King, *Live Wire/Blues Power* (1968).

Stax Records. STS 2003.

B. B. King, *Back in the Alley: The Classic Blues of B. B. King* (1973).

Bluesway/ABC Records. BLS 6050.

John Mayall, with Eric Clapton, *Blues Breakers* (1977).

London Records. LC 50009.

The Nighthawks, *Times Four* (1982).

Adelphi Records. AD 4130/35.

Son Seals, *Bad Axe* (1984).

Alligator Records. AL 4738.

Taj Mahal, *The Natch'l Blues* (1969).
    Columbia Records. CS 9698.
George Thorogood and The Destroyers, *Bad to the Bone* (1982).
    EMI America. ST 17076.

4. The Triumph of Rock
   A. Rock 'n' Roll
    Chuck Berry, *The Great Twenty-Eight* (1982).
       Chess Records. CH 8201.
    Eddie Cochran and Gene Vincent, *Eddie Cochran and Gene Vincent: Their Finest Years, 1958–1956* (1980).
       Capitol Records (Holland). CGB 1007.
    Don "Sugarcane" Harris and Dewey Terry, *Don and Dewey* (1970).
       Specialty Records. SPS 2131.
    Wanda Jackson, *Only Rock 'n' Roll* (1978).
       Capitol Records (France). 2C 150–85334/35.
    Let the Good Times Roll: Early Rock Classics, 1952–1958 (1981).
       Capitol Records (Holland). 046–78020.
    Jerry Lee Lewis, *Good Rocking Tonite: 16 Classics by Jerry Lee Lewis,1956/ 62* (1979).
       Sun Records (Great Britain). Sun 1003.
    Little Richard, *Little Richard!* (1983).
       Cambra Sound Records. CR 102.
    Ricky Nelson, *Rockin' with Ricky* (1983).
       Ace Records (Great Britain). CH 85.
    Carl Perkins, *Dance Album* (1981).
       Sun Records (Great Britain). CRM 2012.
    Rock Begins—2 Volumes (1970).
       Atco Records. SD 33–314/5.
    Shake, Rattle, and Roll: Rock 'n' Roll in the 1950s (1978).
       New World Records. NW 249.
    Gene Vincent and The Blue Caps, *Rock 'n' Roll Legend* (1977).
       Capitol Records (France). 2C 154–85071.
   B. Instrumental Rock
    Duane Eddy, *Duane Eddy—The Vintage Years* (1975).
       Sire Records. Sash 3707–2.
    The Guitar Album (1972).
       Polydor Records (Great Britain). Polydor Super 2659 027.
    The History of Surf Music—Volume One: Original Instrumental Hits, 1961– 1963 (1982).
       Rhino Records. RNLP 051.
    Rockin' and Raunchy (1981).
       Audio Encore Records. AEI 1007.
    The Very Best of the Oldies—Volume Four: The Instrumentals (1975).
       United Artists Records. UA-LA 518E.
   C. British Invasions
    The Beatles, *The Beatles/1962–1966* (1973).
       Apple Records. SKBO 3403.
    The Beatles, *The Beatles/1967–1970* (1973).

Apple Records. SKBO 3404.
The Beatles, *Rock 'n' Roll Music* (1976).
  Capitol Records. SKBO 11537.
The Bee Gees, *Bee Gees Greatest* (1979).
  R.S.O. Records. RS 2–4200.
British Airwaves (1981).
  Audio Encore Records. AEI 1008.
Joe Cocker, *Mad Dogs and Englishmen* (1970).
  A&M Records. SP 6002.
Culture Club, *Colour by Numbers* (1983).
  Virgin Records. QE 39107.
Eurythmics, *Sweet Dreams (Are Made of This)* (1983).
  RCA Records. AFL 1–4681.
Fleetwood Mac, *Fleetwood Mac* (1975).
  Reprise Records. MSK 2281.
Fleetwood Mac, *Rumors* (1977).
  Warner Brothers Records. BSK 3010.
Peter Frampton, *Frampton Comes Alive!* (1976)
  A&M Records. SP 3703.
Herman's Hermits, *The Best of Herman's Hermits* (1965)
  MGM Records. E 4315.
History of British Rock (1975).
  Sire Records. Sash 3702/05/12–2.
Elton John, *Elton John's Greatest Hits—Volume Two* (1977).
  RCA Records. MCA 3027.
Elton John, *Greatest Hits* (1974).
  MCA Records. MCA 2128.
Rock Invasion, 1956–1969 (1978).
  London Records. LC 50012.
The Rolling Stones, *Hot Rocks, 1964–1971* (1972).
  London Records. London.
The Rolling Stones, *Made in the Shade* (1975).
  Rolling Stone Records. COC 79102.
The Rolling Stones, *More Hot Rocks (Big Hits and Fazed Cookies)* (1972).
  London Records. 2 PS 626/7.
The Rolling Stones, *Sucking in the Seventies* (1981).
  Rolling Stone Records. COC 16028.
Rod Stewart, *Rod Stewart Greatest Hits* (1979).
  Warner Brothers Records. HS 3373.
The Who, *Hooligans* (1981).
  MCA Records. MCA 2–12001.
Wings, *Wings over America* (1976).
  Capitol Records. SWCO 11593.
D. San Francisco Sounds
  The Grateful Dead, *What a Long Strange Trip It's Been: The Best of the Grateful Dead* (1977).
    Warner Brothers Records. 2 W 3091.
  The Jefferson Airplane, *Flight Log, 1966–1976* (1977).

Grunt Records. BYL 2–1255.

The Steve Miller Band, *Fly Like an Eagle* (1976).
Capitol Records. ST 11497.

E. Psychedelic/Acid Rock and Other Hybrid Sounds

David Bowie, *Changesonebowie* (1976).
RCA Records. AQL 1–1732.

David Bowie, *Changestwobowie* (1981).
RCA Records. AFL 1–4202.

Genesis, *Duke* (1980).
Atlantic Records. SD 16014.

Journey, *Escape* (1981).
Columbia Records. TC 37408.

Kansas, *Point of Know Return* (1977).
Kirshner Records. JZ 34929.

Nuggets: Original Artyfacts from the First Psychedelic Era, 1965–1968 (1976).
Sire Records. Sash 3716–2.

Steppenwolf, *16 Greatest Hits* (1973).
ABC Records. DSX 50135.

Styx, *Paradise Theatre* (1980).
A&M Records. SP 3719.

F. Hard Rock and Heavy Metal

Axe Attack (1980).
K-Tel International Records (Great Britain). NE 1100.

Axe Attack (1981).
K-Tel International Records (Great Britain). NE 1120.

Bachman-Turnover Overdrive, *Best of B.T.O.* (1976).
Phonogram Records. SRM 1–1101.

Black Sabbath, *Paranoid* (1970).
Warner Brothers Records. WS 1887.

Cheap Trick, *Cheap Trick at Budokan* (1979).
Epic Records. FE 35795.

Creedence Clearwater Revival, *Creedence Gold* (1972).
Fantasy Records. F 9418.

Creedence Clearwater Revival, *More Creedence Gold* (1973).
Fantasy Records. F 9430.

Deep Purple, *When We Rock, We Rock and When We Roll, We Roll* (1978).
Warner Brothers Records. PRK 3223.

Def Leppard, *On through the Night* (1980).
Mercury Records. SRM 1–3828.

The Doobie Brothers, *The Best of The Doobies* (1976).
Warner Brothers Records. BSK 3112.

The Doobie Brothers, *The Best of The Doobies—Volume Two* (1981).
Warner Brothers Records. BSK 3612.

The Doors, *Greatest Hits* (1980).
Elektra Records. Elektra 6E–515.

Foreigner, *Foreigner Records* (1982).
Atlantic Records. Atlantic 7–80999–1.

Grand Funk, *Grand Funk Hits* (1976).

Capitol Records. ST 11579.

The Guess Who, *The Greatest of The Guess Who* (1977).
RCA Records. AYL 1–3746.

Heart, *Greatest Hits/Live* (1980).
Epic Records. KE 2–36888.

Jimi Hendrix, *The Essential Jimi Hendrix* (1978).
Warner Brothers Records. 2 RS 2245.

Joan Jett and The Blackhearts, *I Love Rock 'n' Roll* (1981).
Broadwalk Records. NB 1–33243.

Judas Priest, *Unleashed in the East (Live in Japan)* (1979).
Columbia Records. JC 36179.

The Kinks, *One for the Road* (1980).
Arista Records. A2L–8609.

Led Zeppelin, *Led Zeppelin II* (1969).
Atlantic Records. SD 19127.

Led Zeppelin, *Led Zeppelin IV* (1971).
Atlantic Records. SD 7208.

Huey Lewis and The News, *Sports* (1983).
Crysalis Records. FV 41412.

Metal for Muthas (1980).
EMI Records (Great Britain). EMC 3318.

Metal for Muthas—Volume Two (1980).
EMI Records (Great Britain). EMC 3337.

Ted Nugent, *Double Live Gonzo!* (1978).
Epic Records. KE 2–35069.

Queen, *Greatest Hits* (1981).
Elektra Records. Elektra 5E–564.

The Rolling Stones, *Rewind (1971–1984)* (1984).
Rolling Stone Records. 7–90176.

Mitch Ryder and The Detroit Wheels, *Wheels of Steel* (1982).
PRT Records (Great Britain). DOW 5.

Bob Seger and The Silver Bullet Band, *Nine Tonight* (1981).
Capitol Records. STBK 12182.

Bob Seger and The Silver Bullet Band, *Stranger in Town* (1978).
Capitol Records. SW 11698.

Z Z Top, *The Best of Z Z Top* (1977).
Warner Brothers Records. BSK 3273.

Z Z Top *Eliminator* (1983).
Warner Brothers Records. 1–23774.

G. Rock 'n' Roll Revival
The Blasters, *The Blasters* (1981).
Slash Records. SR 109.

John Lennon, *Rock 'n' Roll* (1975).
Apple Records. SK 3419.

H. Punk, New Wave, and Power Pop
Blondie, *The Best of Blondie* (1981).
Chrysalis Records. CHR 1337.

Elvis Costello, *Armed Forces* (1979).

Columbia Records. JC 35709.

Clash, *London Calling* (1980).
   Epic Records. E 2–36328.

Devo, *Q: Are We Not Men? A: We Are Devo* (1978).
   Warner Brothers Records. BSK 3239.

Joe Jackson, *Look Sharp* (1979).
   A&M Records. SP 4743.

Pebbles—Volume One: Original Artyfacts from the First Punk Era (1979).
   BFD Records (Australia). BFD 5016.

We Do 'Em Our Way (1980).
   Music for Pleasure Records (Great Britain). MFP 50481.

5. Folk Music in Transition
   A. Pop Folk
      Joan Baez, *The First Ten Years* (1978).
         Vanguard Records. VSD 6560/1.
      Joan Baez, *From Every Stage* (1976).
         A & M Records. SP 3704.
      Judy Collins, *Colors of the Day: The Best of Judy Collins* (1972).
         Elektra Records. Elektra 75030.
      Peter, Paul, and Mary, *Ten Years Together: The Best of Peter, Paul, and Mary* (1970).
         Warner Brothers Records. WB 2552.
      Pete Seeger, *Pete Seeger's Greatest Hits* (n.d.).
         Columbia Records. C5 9416.
   B. Protest Music and Folk Rock
      The Bitter End Years (1974).
         Roxbury Records. RLX 300.
      The Byrds, *The Byrds Play Dylan* (1979).
         Columbia Records. PC 36293.
      David Crosby, Stephen Stills, and Graham Nash, *Replay* (1981).
         Atlantic Records. SD 16026.
      Bob Dylan, *Bob Dylan's Greatest Hits* (1967).
         Columbia Records. PC 9463.
      Bob Dylan, *Bob Dylan's Greatest Hits—Volume Two* (1971).
         Columbia Records. PF 31120.
      Greatest Folksingers of the 'Sixties (n.d.).
         Vanguard Records. VSD 17/18.
      Tim Hardin, *The Tim Hardin Memorial Album* (1981).
         Polydor Records. PD 1–6333.
      The Mamas and the Papas, *Farewell to the First Golden Era* (1967).
         ABC Records. DS 50025.
      Moses Moon (Comp.), *Movement Soul: Sounds of the Freedom Movement in the South, 1963–1964* (1980).
         Folkways Records. FD 5486.
      Phil Ochs, *Chords of Fame* (1977).
         A&M Records. SP 4599.
   C. Jazz Pop/Rock
      George Benson, *The George Benson Collection* (1981).

Warner Brothers Records. 2 HW 3577.
The Crusaders, with B. B. King and The Royal Philharmonic Orchestra, *Royal Jam* (1982).
MCA Records. MCA 2–8017.
50 Years of Jazz Guitar (1976).
Columbia Records. CG 33566.
Al Jarreau, *Breakin' Away* (1981).
Warner Brothers Records. BSK 3576.
Chuck Mangione, *Feels So Good* (1977).
A&M Records. SP 3219.
Grover Washington, Jr. *Winelight* (1980).
Elektra Records. Elektra 6E–305.

D. Black and White Gospel Music
James Cleveland, *James Cleveland 'Live' at the Carnegie Hall* (1977).
Savoy Records. DBL 7014.
Sam Cooke, *The Two Sides of Sam Cooke* (1970).
Specialty Records. SPS 2119.
Bob Dylan, *Slow Train Coming* (1979).
Columbia Records. FC 36120.
Aretha Franklin, *Aretha Gospel* (1982).
Checker Records. CH 8500.
Jerry Lee Lewis, *In Loving Memories: The Jerry Lee Lewis Gospel Album* (1970).
Mercury Records. SR 61318.
Little Richard, *I Know the Lord* (1979).
ALA Records. ALA G–903.
The Staples, *Unlock Your Mind* (1978).
Warner Brothers Records. BSK 3192.
Ike and Tina Turner, *The Gospel According to Ike and Tina* (1974).
United Artists Records. UA-LA 203G.

6. Popular Music Expands
A. Traditional Pop Stylists
Cadence Classics—3 Volumes (1975).
Barnaby Records. BR 4000/1/2.
The Chordettes, *The Chordettes' Greatest Hits* (1981).
Everest Records. EV 4115.
Perry Como, *Como's Golden Records* (1958).
RCA Victor Records. LPM 1981.
The 50's Greatest Hits (1972).
Columbia Records. G 30592.
The Fontane Sisters, *Rock Love* (1984).
Charly Records (Great Britain). CR 30229.
The Great Groups are Back—Volume Two (1975).
RCA Records. DPL 2–0119(e).
The Great Ones (1972).
Columbia Records. C2–11003.
Original Early Top 40 Hits (1974).
Paramount Records. PAS 1013.

Linda Ronstadt and The Nelson Riddle Orchestra, *What's New* (1983).
Asylum Records. Asylum 9–60260.

Linda Ronstadt, with Nelson Riddle and His Orchestra, *Lush Life* (1984).
Asylum Records. 60387–1.

Gale Storm, *Gale Storm* (1982).
MCA Records. MCA 1504.

B. Ballad and Teen Idol Rock

Paul Anka, *Paul Anka Gold* (1974).
Sire Records. Sash 3704–2.

Freddy Cannon, *Explosive!* (1980).
Lollipop Records (Germany). 624343 AO.

Connie Francis, *The Very Best of Connie Francis: Connie's 15 Biggest Hits*
(1977).
Polydor Records (Canada). PTV 1013.

Michael Jackson, *Thriller* (1982).
Epic Records. QE 38112.

Cindi Lauper, *She's So Unusual* (1983).
Portrait Records. FR 38930.

Johnny Mathis, *All-Time Greatest Hits* (1972).
Columbia Records. PG 31345.

Rick Nelson, *Rick Nelson—The Decca Years* (1982).
MCA Records. MCA 1517.

Olivia Newton-John, *Olivia Newton-John's Greatest Hits* (1977).
MCA Records. MCA 5226.

Roy Orbison, *The All-Time Greatest Hits of Roy Orbison* (1982).
Monument Records. KWG 38384.

'Til My Dreamin' Comes True: West Coast Teen-Rock, 1958–1964 (1981).
Capitol Records (Holland). 1A 046–78 035.

C. Surf Sounds and Bubblegum Music

The Beach Boys, *Endless Summer* (1974).
Capitol Records. SVBB 11307.

The Beat of the Beach (1982).
Arista Records. A2L 8503.

Bubblegum Music Is the Naked Trust—Volume One (1969).
Buddah Records. BDS 5032.

The Fabulous Bubblegum Years (1976).
Kory Records. KK 3001.

Golden Summer (1976).
United Artists Records. UA-LA 627–H2.

The History of Surf Music—Volume Two: Original Vocal Hits, 1961–1964
(1982).
Rhino Records. RNLP 052.

The History of Surf Music—Volume Three: The Revival, 1980–1982 (1982).
Rhino Records. RNLP 054.

Surfin' Roots (1977).
Festival Records. FR 1010.

D. Pop Rock

Abba, *The Singles: The First Ten Years* (1982).

Atlantic Records. Atlantic 7–80036–1–G.

America, *History—America's Greatest Hits* (1975).
Warner Brothers Records. BSK 3110.

Bread, *The Best of Bread* (1973).
Elektra Records. Elektra 6E–108.

Captain and Tennille, *Captain and Tennille's Greatest Hits* (1977).
A&M Records. SP 4667.

The Carpenters, *The Carpenters' Singles, 1974–1978* (1979).
A&M Records. AMLT 19748.

The Carpenters, *The Singles, 1969–1973* (1973).
A&M Records. SP 3601.

The Fifth Dimension, *Greatest Hits* (1970).
Soul City Records. SCS 33900.

The Four Seasons, *The Four Seasons Story* (1975).
Private Stock Records. PS 7000.

The Mamas and The Papas, *The Best of The Mamas and The Papas* (1982).
MCA Records. MCA 2–6019.

Barry Manilow, *Greatest Hits* (1978).
Arista Records. A 2L 8601.

Anne Murray, *Anne Murray's Greatest Hits* (1980).
Capitol Records. 500 12110.

Olivia Newton-John, *Olivia's Greatest Hits—Volume Two* (1982).
MCA Records. MCA 5347.

Dolly Parton, *9 to 5 and Odd Jobs* (1980).
RCA Records. AHL 1–3852.

Elvis Presley, *Elvis Aron Presley: 25th Anniversary Limited Edition, 1955–1980* (1980).
RCA Records. CLP 8–3699.

Helen Reddy, *Helen Reddy's Greatest Hits* (1975).
Capitol Records. ST 511467.

Barbra Streisand, *Barbra Streisand's Greatest Hits* (1970).
Columbia Records. PC 9968.

Barbra Streisand, *Barbra Streisand's Greatest Hits—Volume Two* (1978).
Columbia Records. FC 35679

Three Dog Night, *The Best of Three Dog Night* (1982).
MCA Records. MCA 2–6018.

A Tribute to Burt Bacharach: Composer, Arranger, Conductor (1972).
Scepter Records. SPS 5100.

Dionne Warwick, *Dionne Warwick Anthology, 1962–1971* (1984).
Rhino Records. RNDA 1100.

E. Symphonic/Classical/Progressive Rock

Chicago, *Chicago Greatest Hits—Volume Two* (1981).
Columbia Records. FC 37682.

Chicago, *Chicago IX: Chicago's Greatest Hits* (1975).
Columbia Records. ST 1–12211.

Duran Duran, *Rio* (1982).
Capitol Records. ST 1–12211.

Electric Light Orchestra, *ELO's Greatest Hits* (1979).

Jet Records. FZ 36310.
Moody Blues, *This Is the Moody Blues* (1974).
Thresold Records. 2 TH 12/13.
Pink Floyd, *The Wall* (1979).
Columbia Records. PC 2-36183.
Steely Dan, *Gold* (1982).
MCA Records. MCA 5324.
Supertramp, *Crime of the Century* (1974).
A&M Records. A&M 3647.
The Who, *Tommy* (1973).
MCA Records. MCA 2-10005.

F. Singer/Songwriter Productions

The Beatles, *The Beatles' Ballads: 20 Original Tracks* (1980).
EMI Parlophone Records (Great Britain). PCS 7214.
The Beatles, *Love Songs* (1977).
Capitol Records. SKBL 11711.
The Beatles, *20 Greatest Hits* (1982).
Capitol Records. SV 12245.
Chuck Berry, *Chuck Berry's Golden Decade* (1972).
Chess/Janus Records. CH 1514.
Chuck Berry, *Chuck Berry's Golden Decade—Volume Two* (1972).
Chess/Janus Records. CH 60023.
Chuck Berry, *Chuck Berry's Golden Decade—Volume Three* (1974).
Chess/Janus Records. CH 60028.
Otis Blackwell, *These Are My Songs!* (1977).
Inner City Records. IC 1032.
Harry Chapin, *Greatest Stories—Live* (1976).
Elektra Records. Elektra E 7-2009.
Sam Cooke, *20 Great Hits* (1981).
Phoenix Records. P 20610.
John Cougar, *American Fool* (1982).
Riva Records. RVL 7601.
Jim Croce, *Bad, Bad Leroy Brown: Jim Croce's Greatest Character Songs* (1978).
Lifesong Records. JZ 35571.
Crosby, Stills, Nash and Young (with Dallas Taylor and Greg Reeves), *Deja Vu* (1970).
Atlantic Records. SD 7200.
Burton Cummings, *My Own Way to Rock* (1977).
Portrait Records. PR 34698.
John Denver, *John Denver's Greatest Hits* (1973).
RCA Records. CPL 1-0374.
John Denver, *John Denver's Greatest Hits—Volume Two* (1977).
RCA Records. CPL 1-2195.
Neil Diamond, *His 12 Greatest Hits* (1974).
MCA Records. MCA 2106.
Neil Diamond, *12 Greatest Hits—Volume Two* (1982).
Columbia Records. TC 38068.

Bob Dylan, *Real Live* (1984).
   Columbia Records. FC 39944.
John Fogerty, *John Fogerty* (1975).
   Asylum Records. Asylum 7E–1046.
George Harrison, *The Best of George Harrison* (1976).
   Capitol Records. ST 11578.
Don Henley, *I Can't Stand Still* (1982).
   Asylum Records. E 1–60048.
Billy Joel, *The Nylon Curtain* (1982).
   Columbia Records. QC 38200.
Billy Joel, *The Stranger* (1977).
   Columbia Records. JC 34987.
Carole King, *Her Greatest Hits: Songs of Long Ago* (1978).
   Ode Records. JE 34967.
Carole King, *Pearls—Songs of Goffin and King* (1980).
   Capitol Records. Soo 12073.
John Lennon, *The John Lennon Collection* (1982).
   Geffen Records. GHSP 2023.
John Lennon and Yoko Ono, *Double Fantasy* (1980).
   Geffen Records. Geffen 2001.
Bob Marley and The Wailers, *Legend* (1984).
   Island Records. 7–90169–1.
Moon Martin, *Escape from Domination* (1979).
   Capitol Records. ST 11933.
Curtis Mayfield, *Curtis Mayfield: His Early Years with The Impressions*
(1973).
   ABC Records. ABCX 780/2.
John Cougar Mellencamp, *Uh-Huh* (1983).
   Riva Records. RVL 7504.
Lee Michaels, *Barrel* (n.d.).
   A&M Records. SP 4249.
Harry Nilsson, *Greatest Hits* (1978).
   RCA Records. AFL 1–2798.
Neil Sedaka, *Neil Sedaka's Greatest Hits* (1977).
   Rocket Records. PIG 2297.
Carly Simon, *The Best of Carly Simon* (1975).
   Elektra Records. Elektra 7E–1048.
Paul Simon, *Greatest Hits, Etc.* (1977).
   Columbia Records. JC 35032.
Paul Simon, *Hearts and Bones* (1983).
   Warner Brothers Records. 23942–1.
Simon and Garfunkel, *Simon and Garfunkel Collected Works* (1981).
   Columbia Records. C5X 37587.
Bruce Springsteen, *Born in the U.S.A.* (1984).
   Columbia Records. QC 38653.
Bruce Springsteen. *Nebraska* (1982).
   Columbia Records. QC 38356.
Bruce Springsteen. *The River* (1980).

Columbia Records. PC 2–36854.

Cat Stevens, *Greatest Hits* (1975).
A&M Records. SP 4519.

James Taylor, *Greatest Hits* (1979).
Warner Brothers Records. BX 2979.

Pete Townshend, *Empty Glass* (1980).
Atco Records. SD 32-100.

Warren Zevon, *Stand in the Fire* (1980).
Asylum Records. Asylum 5E–519.

7. Special Music

    A. Novelty and Comedy Recordings

Alvin, Simon, and Theodore, *Chipmunk Punk* (1982).
Excelsior Records. XLP 6008.

Big Daddy (1983).
Rhino Records. RNLP 852.

Buchanan and Goodman, *The Original Flying Saucers* (n.d.).
IX Chains Records. NCS 9000.

Cheech and Chong, *Cheech and Chong's Greatest Hit* (1981).
Warner Brothers Records. BSK 3614.

Stan Freberg, *The Best of Stan Freberg* (n.d.).
Capitol Records. SM 2020.

Funny Bone Favorites (1978).
Ronco Records. R 2210.

Dickie Goodman, *Dickie Goodman's Greatest Hits* (1983).
Rhino Records. RNLP 811.

Goofy Greats (1979).
K-tel International Records (Canada). NC 511.

Kooky Toones (1976).
K-tel International Records. K-tel 3300.

Looney Tunes (1976).
K-tel International Records. NU 9140.

Randy Newman, *Born Again* (1979).
Warner Brothers Records. HS 3346.

Nutty Numbers (1978).
K-tel International Records (Canada). NC 492.

The Olympics, *The Official Record Album of The Olympics* (1984).
Rhino Records. RNDF 207.

Ray Stevens, *Greatest Hits* (1983).
RCA Records. AHL 1–4727.

25 Years of Recorded Comedy (1977).
Warner Brothers Records. 3 BX 3131. '

    B. Recordings From Festivals, Concert Performances, and Tours

The Beatles, *The Beatles at the Hollywood Bowl* (1977).
Capitol Records. SMAS 11638.

Chuck Berry, *The London Chuck Berry Sessions* (1972).
Chess/Janus Records. CH 60020.

Birdland All-Stars Live at Carnegie Hall (1975).
Roulette Records. RE 127.

James Brown, *Live and Lowdown at the Apollo—Volume One* (1980).
   Solid Smoke Records. SS 806.
Ray Charles, *Ray Charles Live* (1973).
   Atlantic Records. SC 2–503.
Concert for Bangledesh (1971).
   Apple Records. STCH 3385.
Concerts for the People of Kampuchea (1981).
   Atlantic Records. SC 207005.
The Everly Brothers, *The Everly Brothers Reunion Concert—Recorded Live
at the Albert Hall, September 23, 1983* (1983).
   Passport Records (Canada). PD 7003.
Aretha Franklin, *Aretha—Live at the Fillmore West* (1971).
   Atlantic Records. SD 7205.
Janis Joplin, *Joplin in Concert* (1972).
   Columbia Records. C2X 31160.
Jerry Lee Lewis, *The Greatest Live Show on Earth* (1964).
   Smash Records. MGS 27056.
Jerry Lee Lewis, *"Live" at the Star Club in Hamburg* (1980).
   Philips Records (Great Britain). Philips 6336 634.
New Orleans Jazz and Heritage Festival—1976. (1976).
   Island Records. ISLD 9424.
Newport in New York '72: The Soul Sessions—Volume Six (1972).
   Buddah Records. CST 9028.
*No Nukes—From the Muse Concerts for a Non-Nuclear Future in Madison
Square Garden, September 19–23, 1979* (1979).
   Asylum Records. ML 801.
Elvis Presley, *Elvis: The First Live Recordings* (1983).
   Music Works Records. PB 3601.
Elvis Presley, *Elvis, Scotty, and Bill: The First Year* (1983).
   Sun Records (Denmark). Sun 1007.
The Rolling Stones, *"Still Life"—American Concert 1981* (1982).
   Rolling Stone Records. COC 39113.
Simon and Garfunkel, *The Concert in Central Park* (1982).
   Warner Brothers Records. 2 BSK 3654.
Wattstax: The Living Word (1972).
   Stax Records. STS 2–3010.
Wattstax 2: The Living Word (1973).
   Stax Records. STS 2–3018.
C. Motion Picture Soundtracks and Radio Program Transcriptions
   American Graffiti (1973).
      MCA Records. MCA 2–8001.
   American Hot Wax (1978).
      A&M Records. SP 6500.
   American Pop (1981).
      MCA Records. MCA 5021.
   Banjoman (1977).
      Sire Records. SA 7527.
   The Blues Brothers (1980).

Atlantic Records. SD 16017.

Breakin' (1984).

Polydor Records. 821 919–1 Y–1.

Broadway Magic: Volume One—The Best of the Great Broadway Musicals (1981).

Columbia Records. JS 36282.

Broadway Magic: Volume Two—The Great Performers (1981).

Columbia Records. JS 36409.

Broadway Magic: Volume Three—The Showstoppers (1981).

Columbia Records. JS 36599.

Broadway Magic: Volume Four—Super Hits (1981).

Columbia Records. JS 36736.

Broadway Magic: Volume Five—Great Performances (1981).

Columbia Records. JS 36859.

The Buddy Holly Story (1978).

Epic Records. SE 35412.

Bye Bye Birdie (1963).

RCA Records. LSO 1081.

Car Wash (1976).

MCA Records. MCA 2–6000.

Christine (1983).

Motown Records. 6086 ML.

Close Encounters of the Third Kind (1983).

Arista Records. AL 9500.

Eddie Cochran and Gene Vincent, *Rock 'n' Roll Heroes* (1981).

Rockstar Records (Great Britain). RSR LP 1004.

Cooley High (1975).

Motown Records. M7–840 R2.

Cruisin' the Fifties and Sixties: A History of Rock and Roll Radio—13 Volumes (1970, 1972, and 1973).

Increase Records. INCM 2000/12.

Cruising (1980).

Columbia Records. JC 36410.

Neil Diamond, *The Jazz Singer* (1980).

Capitol Records. SWAV 12120.

Diner (1982).

Elektra Records. E1–6010 7E.

Easy Rider (1969).

Dunhill Records. DSX 50063.

Eddie and The Cruisers (1983).

Scotti Brothers Records. BFZ 38929.

The Electric Horseman (1979).

Columbia Records. JS 36327.

Fame (1980).

R.S.O. Records. RX 1–3080.

50 Years on Film: Original Motion Picture Soundtrack Recordings of the Great Scenes and Stars from the Warner Brothers Classics, 1923 to 1973 (1973).

Warner Brothers Records. 3XX 2737.

Flashdance (1983).
    Casablanca Records. 811492–1 M–1.
F.M. (1978).
    MCA Records. MCA 2–12000.
Footloose (1984).
    Columbia Records. JS 39242.
Alan Freed, *Dedication*—3 Volumes (1982).
    Silhouette Music Records. SM 10006/7/8.
The Graduate (1968).
    Columbia Records. OS 3180.
Grease (1978).
    R.S.O. Records. RS 2–4002.
Hair: The American Tribal Love-Rock Musical (1969).
    RCA Records. LSO 1150.
Heavy Metal (1981).
    Full Moon/Asylum Records. DP 90004.
Hollywood Knights (1980).
    Casablanca Records. NBLP 7218.
Honeysuckle Rose (1980).
    Columbia Records. S2–36752.
The Idolmaker (1980).
    A&M Records. SP 4840.
Jesus Christ Superstar—A Rock Opera (1970).
    MCA Records. MCA 2–10000.
Janis Joplin, *Janis* (1975).
    Columbia Records. PG 33345.
The Last Waltz (1978).
    Warner Brothers Records. 3 W5 3146.
Let the Good Times Roll (1973).
    Bell Records. Bell 9002.
Looking for Mr. Goodbar (1977).
    Columbia Records. JS 35029.
Losin' It (1983).
    RCA Records (Canada). RI 8507.
More American Graffiti (1979).
    MCA Records. MCA 2–11006.
National Lampoon's Animal House (1978).
    MCA Records. MCA 3046.
An Officer and a Gentleman (1982).
    Island Records. 7–90017–1.
"Pennies from Heaven" (1981).
    Warner Brothers Records. 2HW 3639.
Prince and The Revolution, *Purple Rain* (1984).
    Warner Brothers Records. 25110–1.
Rock 'n' Roll High School (1979).
    Sire Records. SRK 6070.
Rock 'n' Roll Radio—Starring Alan Freed "The King of Rock 'n' Roll"
(1978).

Radiola Records. MR 1087.

Rocky (1976).

United Artists Records. UA-LA 693G.

The Rose (1979).

Atlantic Records. SD 16010.

Diana Ross, *Lady Sings the Blues* (1972).

Motown Records. M756 D.

Saturday Night Fever (1977).

R.S.O. Records. RS 2–5001.

Sgt. Pepper's Lonely Hearts Club Band (1978).

R.S.O. Records. RS 2–4100.

Paul Simon, *One-Trick Pony* (1980).

Warner Brothers Records. HS 3472.

The Song Remains the Same (1976).

Swan Song Records. SS 2–201.

Stardust (1975).

Arista Records. AL 5000.

The Sting (1973).

MCA Records. MCA 2040.

Streets of Fire (1984).

MCA Records. MCA 5492.

Super Fly (1972)

Curtom Records. CRS 8014–ST.

Superman—The Movie (1978).

Warner Brothers Records. 2 BSK 3257.

"Thank God It's Friday" (1978).

Casablanca Records. NBLP 3–7099.

That's Entertainment (1974).

MCA Records. MCA 2–11002.

That's Entertainment—Part Two (1976).

MGM Records. MG 1–5301.

This Is Elvis (1981).

RCA Records. CPL 2–4031.

Tommy (1975).

Polydor Records. PD 2–9502.

Twenty-Five Years of Recorded Sound, 1945–1970: From the Vaults of M-G-M Records (1979).

DRG Archive Records. DARC 2–2100.

Urban Cowboy (1980).

Full Moon/Asylum Records. DP 90002.

The Wanderers (1979).

Warner Brothers Records. BSK 3359.

The Who, *The Kids Are Alright* (1979).

MCA Records. MCA 2–11005.

The Who, *Quadrophenia* (1979).

Polydor Records. PD 2–6235.

The Wiz (1978).

MCA Records. MCA 2–14000.

Woodstock (1970).
  Cotillion Records. SD 3–500.
Xanadu (1980).
  MMA Records. MCA 6100.
D. Other Special Recordings
Atomic Cafe: Radioactive Rock 'n' Roll, Blues, Country, and Gospel (1982).
  Rounder Records (1982). RR 1034.
The Beatles, *Reel Music* (1982).
  Capitol Records. SV 12199.
Jerry Lee Lewis, Carl Perkins, Johnny Cash, and Elvis Presley, *The Million Dollar Quarter* (1981).
  Sun Records (Great Britain). Sun 1006.
Elvis Presley, *Elvis: A Legendary Performer—Volume One* (1973).
  RCA Records. CPL 1–0341.
Elvis Presley, *Elvis: A Legendary Performer—Volume Two* (1976).
  RCA Records. CPL 1–1349
Elvis Presley, *Elvis: A Legendary Performer—Volume Three* (1978).
  RCA Records. CPL 1–3082.
Elvis Presley, *Elvis: A Legendary Performer—Volume Four* (1983).
  RCA Records. CPL 1–4848.
Phil Spector: The Early Productions, 1958–1961 (1983).
  Rhino Records. RNDF 203.
Phil Spector's Christmas Album (1972).
  Apple Records. SW 3400.
Stevie Wonder, *Stevie Wonder's Journey through the Secret Life of Plants* (1979).
  Tamla Records. T 13–371 C-2.

Selected Bibliography

A. BOOKS AND ANTHOLOGIES

Bane, Michael. *White Boy Singin' the Blues: The Black Roots of White Rock*. New York: Penguin Books, 1982.

Belz, Carl. *The Story of Rock*. 2d ed. New York: Harper and Row, 1972.

Betrock, Alan. *Girl Groups: The Story of a Sound*. New York: Delilah Books, 1982.

Booth, Mark W. *The Experience of Songs*. New Haven, Connecticut: Yale University Press, 1981.

Bowden, Betsy. *Performed Literature: Words and Music by Bob Dylan*. Bloomington: Indiana University Press, 1982.

Broven, John. *Walking to New Orleans: The Story of New Orleans Rhythm and Blues*. Sussex, England: Blues Unlimited, 1974.

Brown, Charles T. *The Rock and Roll Story: From the Sounds of Rebellion to an American Art Form*. Englewood Cliffs, New Jersey: Prentice-Hall, 1983.

Busnar, Gene. *It's Rock 'n' Roll: A Musical History of the Fabulous Fifties*. New York: Wanderer Books, 1979.

Carney, George O., ed. *The Sounds of People and Places: Readings in the Geography of Music*. Washington, D.C.: University Press of America, 1979.

Chapple, Steve, and Reebee Garofalo. *Rock 'n' Roll Is Here to Pay: The History and Politics of the Music Industry*. Chicago: Nelson-Hall, 1977.

Charter, Samuel B. *The Poetry of the Blues*. New York: Oak Publications, 1963.

Christgau, Robert. *Any Old Way You Choose It: Rock and Other Pop Music, 1967–1973*. Baltimore: Penguin Books, 1973.

Cohen, Norm, with music edited by David Cohen. *Long Steel Rail: The Railroad in American Folksong*. Urbana: University of Illinois Press, 1981.

Colman, Stuart. *They Kept on Rockin': The Giants of Rock 'n' Roll*. Poole, Dorset, England: Blandford Press, 1982.

Cone, James H. *The Spirituals and the Blues: An Interpretation*. New York: Seabury Press, 1972.

Cooper, B. Lee. *Images of American Society in Popular Music: A Guide to Reflective Teaching*. Chicago: Nelson-Hall, 1982.

Cott, Johathan, and Christine Doudna, eds. *The Ballad of John and Yoko*. Garden City, New York: Doubleday and Company, 1982.

Craig, Warren, comp. *Sweet and Lowdown: America's Popular Song Writers*. Metuchen, New Jersey: Scarecrow Press, 1978.

Dellar, Fred, comp. *New Musical Express Guide to Rock Cinema*. Middlesex, England: Hamlyn Paperbacks, 1981.

Denisoff, R. Serge. *Great Day Coming: Folk Music and the American Left*. Baltimore: Penguin Books, 1971.

——. *Sing A Song of Social Significance*. Bowling Green, Ohio: Bowling Green University Popular Press, 1972.

Denisoff, R. Serge, and Richard A. Peterson, eds. *The Sounds of Social Change: Studies in Popular Culture*. Chicago: Rand McNally, 1972.

Dennison, Sam. *Scandalize My Name: Black Imagery in American Popular Music*. New York: Garland Publishing, 1982.

DeTurk, David A., and A. Poulin, Jr., eds. *The American Folk Scene: Dimensions of the Folksong Revival*. New York: Dell, 1967.

DeWitt, Howard A. *Chuck Berry: Rock 'n' Roll Music*. Ann Arbor, Michigan: Pierian Press, 1985.

Ehrenstein, David, and Bill Reed. *Rock on Film*. New York: Delilah Books, 1982.

Eisen, Jonathan, ed. *The Age of Rock: Sounds of the American Cultural Revolution*. New York: Vintage Books, 1969.

——. *The Age of Rock—2: Sights and Sounds of the American Cultural Revolution*. New York: Vintage Books, 1970.

——. *Altamont: The Death of Innocence in the Woodstock Nation*. New York: Avon Books, 1970.

——. *Twenty-Minute Fandangos and Forever Changes: A Rock Bazaar*. New York: Vintage Books, 1971.

Elson, Howard. *Early Rockers*. New York: Proteus Books, 1982.

Escott, Colin, and Martin Hawkins. *Sun Records: The Brief History of the Legendary Record Label*. New York: Quick Fox, 1980.

Ewen, David. *All the Years of American Popular Music: A Comprehensive History*. Englewood Cliffs, New Jersey: Prentice-Hall, 1977.

Frith, Simon. *Sound Effects: Youth, Leisure, and the Politics of Rock 'n' Roll*. New York: Pantheon Books, 1981.

Gardner, Carl, ed. *Media, Politics, and Culture: A Socialist View*. Atlantic Highlands, New Jersey: Humanities Press, 1979.

Garon, Paul. *Blues and the Poetic Spirit*. London: Eddison Press, 1975.

Gelt, Andrew L., comp. *Index to Alcohol, Drugs, and Intoxicants in Music*. Albuquerque, New Mexico: A. L. Gelt, 1982.

Gillett, Charlie. *The Sound of the City: The Rise of Rock and Roll*. Rev. ed. New York: Pantheon Books, 1983.

Goldrosen, John. *The Buddy Holly Story*. New York: Quick Fox, 1979.

Gray, Michael. *Song and Dance Man: The Art of Bob Dylan*. New York: E. P. Dutton, 1972.

Grissim, John. *Country Music: White Man's Blues*. New York: Paperback Library, 1970.

Guralnick, Peter. *Feel Like Going Home: Portraits in Blues and Rock 'n' Roll*. New York: Outerbridge and Dienstfrey, 1971.

―――. *Lost Highway: Journeys and Arrivals of American Musicians*. Boston: David R. Godine, 1979.

Hamm, Charles. *Music in the New World*. New York: W. W. Norton, 1983.

―――. *Yesterdays: Popular Song in America*. New York: W. W. Norton, 1979.

Hamm, Charles; Bruno Nettl; and Ronald Byrnside. *Contemporary Music and Music Cultures*. Englewood Cliffs, New Jersey: Prentice-Hall, 1975.

Hanel, Ed, comp. *The Essential Guide to Rock Books*. London: Omnibus Books, 1983.

Haralambos, Michael. *Right On: From Blues to Soul in Black America*. New York: Drake, 1975.

Harker, Dave. *One for the Money: Politics and the Popular Song*. London: Hutchinson, 1980.

Helander, Brock, comp. *The Rock Who's Who*. New York: Schirmer Books, 1982.

Hendler, Herb. *Year by Year in the Rock Era: Events and Conditions Shaping the Rock Generations That Reshaped America*. Westport, Connecticut: Greenwood Press, 1983.

Herbst, Peter, ed. *The Rolling Stone Interviews: Talking with the Legends of Rock and Roll, 1967–1980*. New York: St. Martin's Press/Rolling Stone Press, 1981.

Herdman, John. *Voice without Restraint: A Study of Bob Dylan's Lyrics and Their Background*. New York: Delilah Books, 1982.

Hibbard, Don J., and Carol Kaleialoha. *The Role of Rock*. Englewood Cliffs, New Jersey: Prentice-Hall, 1983.

Hirshey, Gerri. *Nowhere to Run: The Story of Soul Music*. New York: Penguin Books, 1984.

Hoare, Ian; Tony Cummings; Clive Anderson; and Simon Frith. *The Soul Book*. New York: Dell, 1976.

Jahn, Mike. *Rock: From Elvis Presley to the Rolling Stones*. New York: Quadrangle Books, 1973.

Jenkinson, Philip, and Alan Warner. *Celluloid Rock: Twenty Years of Movie Rock*. London: Lorrimer, 1974.

Keil, Charles. *Urban Blues*. Chicago: University of Chicago Press, 1966.

Kingman, Daniel. *American Music: A Panorama*. New York: Schirmer Books, 1979.

Larson, Bob. *Rock: Practical Help for Those Who Listen to the Words and Don't Like What They Hear*. Wheaton, Illinois: Tyndale House, 1980.

Levine, Lawrence W. *Black Culture and Black Consciousness: Afro-American Folk Thought from Slavery to Freedom*. New York: Oxford University Press, 1977.

Litevich, John. *Popular Music as a Learning Tool in the Social Studies*. Clinton, Connecticut: Project Share/J. Litevich, 1983.

Lydon, Michael. *Boogie Lightning*. New York: Dial Press, 1974.

―――. *Rock Folk: Portraits from the Rock 'n' Roll Pantheon*. New York: Dial Press, 1971.

McKee, Margaret, and Fred Chisenhall. *Beale Black and Blue: Life and Music on Black America's Main Street*. Baton Rouge: Louisiana State University Press, 1981.

Macken, Bob; Peter Fornatale; and Bill Ayres. *The Rock Music Source Book*. Garden City, New York: Doubleday, 1980.

Malone, Bill C. *Southern Music/American Music*. Lexington: University Press of Kentucky, 1979.

Marcus, Greil. *Mystery Train: Images of America in Rock 'n' Roll Music*. Rev. ed. New York: E. P. Dutton, 1982.

Marsh, Dave. *Fortunate Son*. New York: Random House, 1985.

Martin, George, ed. *Making Music: The Guide to Writing, Performing, and Recording*. London: Pan Books, 1983.

Meeker, David. *Jazz in the Movies*. Rev. ed. New York: Da Capo Press, 1982.

Middleton, Richard, and David Horn, eds. *Popular Music 1: Folk or Popular? Distinctions, Influences, Continuities*. Cambridge: Cambridge University Press, 1981.

———. *Popular Music 2: Theory and Method*. Cambridge: Cambridge University Press, 1982.

———. *Popular Music 3: Producers and Markets*. Cambridge: Cambridge University Press, 1983.

———. *Popular Music 4: Performers and Audiences*. Cambridge: Cambridge University Press, 1984.

Miller, Jim, ed. *The Rolling Stone Illustrated History of Rock and Roll*. New York: Random House/Rolling Stone Press, 1976.

———. *The Rolling Stone Illustrated History of Rock and Roll*. Rev. ed. New York: Random House/Rolling Stone Press Book, 1980.

Neises, Charles P., ed. *The Beatles Reader: A Selection of Contemporary Views, News, and Reviews of the Beatles in Their Heyday*. Ann Arbor, Michigan: Pierian Press, 1984.

Norman, Philip. *The Road Goes on Forever: Portraits from a Journey through Contemporary Music*. New York: Fireside Books, 1982.

———. *Shout! The Beatles in Their Generation*. New York: Simon and Schuster, 1981.

Oakley, Giles. *The Devil's Music: A History of the Blues*. New York: Harcourt Brace Jovanovich, 1978.

Obst, Lynda R., ed. *The Sixties: The Decade Remembered Now, by the People Who Lived It Then*. New York: Random House/Rolling Stone Press, 1977.

Oliver, Paul. *The Meaning of the Blues*. New York: Collier Books, 1972.

Palmer, Robert. *Baby, That Was Rock and Roll: The Legendary Leiber and Stoller*. New York: Harcourt Brace Jovanovich, 1978.

———. *Deep Blues*. New York: Viking Press, 1981.

Pavletich, Aida. *Sirens of Song: The Popular Female Vocalist in America*. New York: Da Capo Press, 1980. (Originally published under the title of *Rock-a-Bye, Baby*)

Pichaske, David. *Beowulf to Beatles and Beyond: The Varieties of Poetry*. New York: Macmillan, 1981.

———. *A Generation in Motion: Popular Music and Culture in the Sixties*. New York: Schirmer, 1979.

———. *The Poetry of Rock: The Golden Years*. Peoria, Illinois: Ellis Press, 1981.

Pollock, Bruce. *In Their Own Words: Twenty Successful Song Writers Tell How They Write Their Songs*. New York: Collier Books, 1975.

———. *When Rock Was Young: A Nostalgic Review of the Top 40 Era*. New York: Holt, Rinehart and Winston, 1981.

————. *When the Music Mattered: Rock in the 1960s*. New York: Holt, Rinehart and Winston, 1983.

Redd, Lawrence N. *Rock Is Rhythm and Blues: The Impact of Mass Media*. East Lansing: Michigan State University Press, 1974.

Reid, Robert. *Music and Social Problems: A Poster Series*. Portland, Maine: J. Eston Walch, 1971.

Rimler, Walter. *Not Fade Away: A Comparison of Jazz Age with Rock Era Pop Song Composers*. Ann Arbor, Michigan: Pierian Press, 1984.

Rodnitzky, Jerome L. *Minstrels of the Dawn: The Folk-Protest Singer as a Cultural Hero*. Chicago: Nelson-Hall, 1976.

Rogers, Dave. *Rock 'n' Roll*. London: Routledge and Kegan Paul, 1982.

Rogers, Jimmie N. *The Country Music Message*. Englewood Cliffs, New Jersey: Prentice-Hall, 1983.

Rowe, Mike. *Chicago Breakdown*. New York: Drake Publishers, 1975. (Reissued in 1981 by Da Capo Press under the title *Chicago Blues: The City and the Music*.)

Sander, Ellen. *Trips: Rock Life in the Sixties*. New York: Charles Scribner's Sons, 1973.

Sarlin, Bob. *Turn It Up (I Can't Hear the Words): The Best of the New Singer/Song Writers*. New York: Simon and Schuster, 1973.

Savage, William W., Jr. *Singing Cowboys and All That Jazz: A Short History of Popular Music in Oklahoma*. Norman: University of Oklahoma Press, 1982.

Schaffner, Nicholas. *The British Invasion: From the First Wave to the New Wave*. New York: McGraw Hill, 1982.

Schroeder, Fred E. H., ed. *Twentieth-Century Popular Culture in Museums and Libraries*. Bowling Green, Ohio: Bowling Green University Popular Press, 1981.

Schultheiss, Tom, comp. *The Beatles—A Day in the Life: A Day-by-Day Diary, 1960–1970*. New York: Quick Fox, 1981.

Scott, John Anthony. *The Ballad of America: The History of the United States in Song and Story*. Carbondale: Southern Illinois University Press, 1983.

Shaw, Arnold. *Honkers and Shouters: The Golden Years of Rhythm and Blues*. New York: Collier Books, 1978.

————. *The Rockin' 50's: The Decade That Transformed the Pop Music Scene*. New York: Hawthorn Books, 1974.

————. *The World of Soul*. New York: Paperback Library, 1971.

Stewart, Tony. *Cool Cats: 25 Years of Rock 'n' Roll Style*. New York: Delilah Books, 1982.

Swenson, John. *Bill Haley: The Daddy of Rock and Roll*. New York: Stein and Day, 1983.

————. *The Year in Rock, 1981–82*. New York: Delilah Books, 1981.

Tharpe, Jac L., ed. *Elvis: Images and Fancies*. Jackson: University Press of Mississippi, 1979.

Titon, Jeff Todd. *Early Downhome Blues: A Musical and Cultural Analysis*. Urbana: University of Illinois Press, 1977.

Tobler, John, and Stuart Grundy. *The Record Producers*. New York: St. Martin's Press, 1983.

Torgoff, Martin, ed. *The Complete Elvis*. New York: Delilah Books, 1982.

Tosches, Nick. *Country: The Biggest Music in America*. New York: Stein and Day, 1977.

———. *Hellfire: The Jerry Lee Lewis Story*. New York: Dell, 1982.

———. *Unsung Heroes of Rock 'n' Roll: The Birth of Rock 'n' Roll in the Dark and Wild Years Before Elvis*. New York: Charles Scribner's Sons, 1984.

Vassal, Jacques. *Electric Children: Roots and Branches of Modern Folkrock*. New York: Taplinger, 1976.

Vulliamy, Graham, and Ed Lee. *Pop, Rock, and Ethnic Music in School*. Cambridge: Cambridge University Press, 1982.

Weiner, Rex, and Deanne Stillman. *Woodstock Census: The Nationwide Survey of the Sixties Generation*. New York: Viking Press, 1979.

Weissman, Dick. *Music Making in America*. New York: Frederick Ungar, 1982.

Whetmore, Edward Jay. *Mediamerica: Form, Content, and Consequence of Mass Communication*. 3rd ed. Belmont, California: Wadsworth, 1985.

Whitcomb, Ian. *After the Ball: Pop Music from Rag to Rock*. Baltimore: Penguin Books, 1972.

———. *Rock Odyssey: A Musician's Guide to the Sixties*. Garden City, New York: Dolphin Books, 1983.

Wiegand, Wayne A., ed. *Popular Culture and the Library: Current Issues Symposium II*. Lexington: College of Library Science at the University of Kentucky, 1978.

Williams, Brett. *John Henry: A Bio-Bibliography*. Westport, Connecticut: Greenwood Press, 1983.

Williams, Paul. *Dylan—What Happened?* Glenn Ellen, California: Entwhistle Books, 1980.

Williams, Richard. *Out of His Head: The Sound of Phil Spector*. New York: Outerbridge and Lazard, 1972.

York, William. *Who's Who in Rock Music*. Rev. ed. New York: Charles Scribner's Sons, 1982.

Zalkind, Ronald, comp. *Contemporary Music Almanac 1980/81*. New York: Schirmer Books, 1980.

B. SONG LYRIC COLLECTION

Aldridge, Alan, ed. *The Beatles Illustrated Lyrics*. New York: Delacort Press, 1969.

———. *The Beatles Illustrated Lyrics—2*. New York: Delacort Press, 1971.

Aldridge, Alan, and Mike Dempsey, eds. *Bernie Taupin—The One Who Writes the Words for Elton John: Complete Lyrics from 1968 to Goodbye, Yellow Brick Road*. New York: Alfred A. Knopf, 1976.

American Rock and Roll—Volume One. Ojai, California: Creative Concepts, n.d.

American Rock and Roll—Volume Two. Ojai, California: Creative Concepts, n.d.

American Rock and Roll—Volume Three. Ojai, California: Creative Concepts, n.d.

American Rock and Roll—Volume Four. Ojai, California: Creative Concepts, n.d.

Arnett, Hazel, ed. *I Hear America Singing! Great Folk Songs from the Revolution to Rock*. New York: Praeger, 1975.

Atkinson, Bob, ed. *Songs of the Open Road: The Poetry of Folk Rock*. New York: New American Library, 1974.

Bacharach, Burt, and Hal David. *The Bacharach and David Song Book.* New York: Simon and Schuster, 1970.

The Best of Album Oriented Rock—Volume One. Hialeah, Florida: Columbia Pictures Publications, 1979.

The Best of Album Oriented Rock—Volume Two. Hialeah, Florida: Columbia Pictures Publications, 1980.

The Best of New Wave Rock. New York: Warner Brothers Publications, 1978.

The Best of Popular Music: First Omnibus of Popular Songs. Miami Beach, Florida: Hansen Publications, 1968.

The Best Pop Songs of the 70's. Hialeah, Florida: Columbia Pictures Publications, 1980.

The Best Soul Songs of the 70's. Hialeah, Florida: Columbia Pictures Publications, 1980.

The Big Disco Rock Book. Hialeah, Florida: Columbia Pictures Publications, 1976.

The Big Rock Standards Books. Hialeah, Florida: Columbia Pictures Publications, 1976.

The Big 77 Songbook. New York: Warner Brothers Publications, 1976.

Birnie, W.A.H., ed. *Reader's Digest Family Songbook.* Pleasantville, New York: Reader's Digest Association, 1969.

Blansky, Bob, comp. *The Motown Era.* Detroit: Jobete Music Company, 1971.

Bob Dylan Song Book. New York: M. Witmark and Sons, n.d.

The Book of Golden Disco. Hialeah, Florida: Columbia Pictures Publications, 1979.

The Book of Rock—Volume One. New York: Warner Brothers Publications, 1976.

The Book of Rock—Volume Two. New York: Warner Brothers Publications, 1976.

Broderick, Richard, comp. *The New York Times 100 Great Country Songs.* New York: Quadrangle Books, 1973.

The Bubblegum Book. Miami: Screen Gems–Columbia Publications, 1972.

Campbell, Colin, and Allan Murphy, comps. *Things We Said Today: The Complete Lyrics and a Concordance to The Beatles' Songs, 1962–1970.* Ann Arbor, Michigan: Pierian Press, 1980.

Carawan, Guy, and Candie Carawan, comps. *Freedom Is a Constant Struggle.* New York: Oak Publications, 1964.

———. *Voices from the Mountains: Life Struggle in the Appalachian South—The Words, the Faces, the Songs, and the Memories of the People Who Live It.* New York: Alfred A. Knopf, 1975.

———. *We Shall Overcome! Songs of the Southern Freedom Movement.* New York: Oak Publications, 1963.

Chartbusters: Hits of Today. New York: Chappel and Company, 1979.

Chipman, Bruce L., comp. *Hardening Rock: An Organic Anthology of the Adolescence of Rock 'n' Roll.* Boston: Little, Brown, 1972.

Chuck Berry—The Golden Decade, 1955–1965. New York: ARC Music, n.d.

Conly, John M., ed. *The Joan Baez Songbook.* New York: Ryerson Music, 1964.

Cohen, Norm. *Long Steel Rail: The Railroad in American Folksong.* Urbana: University of Illinois Press, 1981.

Dalton, David, ed. *The Rolling Stones: An Unauthorized Biography in Words, Photographs, and Music.* New York: Amsco Music, 1972.

Damsker, Matt, ed. *Rock Voices: The Best Lyrics of an Era.* New York: St. Martin's Press, 1980.

Dane, Barbara, and Irvin Sibler, comps. *The Vietnam Songbook.* New York: Guardian Press, 1965.

Darling, Charles W., comp. *The New American Songster: Traditional Ballads and Songs of North America.* Lanham, England: University Press of America, 1983.

David, Hal. *What the World Needs Now and Other Love Lyrics.* New York: Trident Press, 1970.

The Diana Ross Songbook. Hollywood, California: Jobete Music, 1979.

Dicks, Ted, ed. *A Decade of The Who: An Authorized History in Music, Paintings, Words, and Photographs.* London: Fabulous Music, 1977.

Disco Fever. New York: Chappell, 1979.

Disco Pops. Hialeah, Florida: Columbia Pictures Publications, 1979.

The Discotheque Sound. New York: Screen Gems–Columbia Pictures, 1975.

Don Kirshner's Rock Concert. Miami: Screen Gems–Columbia Publications, 1975.

Dowded, Landon Gerald, comp. *Journey to Freedom: A Casebook with Music.* Chicago: Swallow Press, 1969.

Dust in the Wind and 50 Rock Classics. New York: Warner Brothers Publications, 1978.

80 for the 80's. Hialeah, Florida: Columbia Pictures Publications, 1980.

Emrick, Duncan, comp. *American Folk Poetry: An Anthology.* Boston: Little, Brown, 1974.

Engel, Lyle Kenton, comp. *500 Songs That Made the All Time Hit Parade.* New York: Bantam Books, 1964.

The Female Superstar Songbook. Hialeah, Florida: Columbia Pictures Publications, 1980.

The Festival Songbook. New York: AMSCO, 1973.

50 Golden Giants. New York: Warner Brothers Publications, 1976.

50 Swinging Sounds. New York: Charles Hansen Educational Music and Books, 1973.

The Folk Decade: A Retrospective. New York: Warner Brothers Publications, 1976.

Folk Music Greatest Hits. Ojai, California: Creative Concepts, n.d.

Folk Rock: Top Recorded Hits. New York: M. Witmark and Sons, n.d.

40 Blockbusters. Hialeah, Florida: Columbia Pictures Publications, 1979.

40 Top Chart Songs. Hialeah, Florida: Columbia Pictures Publications, 1979.

44 New Superhits of the Superstars. Hialeah, Florida: Columbia Pictures Publications, 1979.

43 New Superhits of the Superstars Hialeah, Florida: Columbia Pictures Publications, 1978.

Francis, Steve, comp. *Anthology—Stevie Wonder.* Miami: Screen Gems–Columbia Publications, 1975.

Glazer, Tom, ed. *A New Treasury of Folk Songs.* 2d ed. New York: Bantam Books, 1964.

———. *Songs of Peace, Freedom, and Protest.* Greenwich, Connecticut: Fawcett Publications, 1970.

The Golden Book of Rock. Hialeah, Florida: Columbia Pictures Publications, 1976.

Goldstein, Richard, ed. *The Poetry of Rock.* New York: Bantam Books, 1969.

Graves, Barbara Farris, and Donald J. McBain, eds. *Lyric Voices: Approaches to the Poetry of Contemporary Song.* New York: John Wiley and Sons, 1972.

Great Music Festivals from Monterey to Woodstock. New York: Charles Hansen Music and Books, n.d.

Haag, John L., comp. *Steppenwolf Gold: Their Greatest Hits.* Los Angeles: West Coast Publications, n.d.

————. *Super Stars: Collectors Series No. 9.* Los Angeles: West Coast Publications, n.d.

Handy, W. C. (ed. Jerry Silvermann). *Blues: An Anthology.* New York: Macmillan, 1972.

History of Rhythm and Blues: The Big Beat, 1958–1960. New York: Progressive Music, 1969.

History of Rhythm and Blues: The Golden Years, 1953–55. New York: Progressive Music, 1969.

History of Rhythm and Blues: Rock and Roll, 1956–57. New York: Progressive Music, 1969.

The History of Rock Music. New York: Charles Hansen Music and Books, n.d.

Horstman, Dorothy. *Sing Your Heart Out, Country Boy.* New York: E. P. Dutton, 1975.

The House of Soul/The House of the Blues. New York: Conrad Music, n.d.

Houston, Cisco (ed. Moses Asch and Irwin Silber). *900 Miles: The Ballads, Blues, and Folksongs of Cisco Houston.* New York: Oak Publications, 1965.

In Concert ABC—Volume One. Miami: Screen Gems–Columbia Publications, 1973.

In Concert ABC—Volume Two. Miami: Screen Gems–Columbia Publications, 1974.

In Concert ABC—Volume Three. Miami: Screen Gems–Columbia Publications, 1974.

Ives, Burl. *Songs in America.* New York: Duell, Sloan, and Pearce, 1962.

Jackson, Bruce. *Wake Up Dead Man: Afro-American Worksongs from Texas Prisons.* Cambridge, Massachusetts: Harvard University Press, 1972.

Jim Croce—I Got a Name. New York: Blendingwell Music, 1974.

Ledbetter, Hudie (comp. Moses Asch and Alan Lomax). *The Leadbelly Songbook.* New York: Oak Publications, 1963.

The Legal Fake Book. Rev. ed. New York: Warner Brothers Publishing, 1979.

Live at the Fillmore. New York: Warner Brothers Publications, n.d.

Lomax, Alan, comp. *Hard Hitting Songs for Hard-Hit People.* New York: Oak Publications, 1967.

Lomax, John A., and Alan Lomax, comps. *Folk Song U.S.A.* New York: New American Library, 1975.

Mellow Rock. Hialeah, Florida: Columbia Pictures Publications, 1977.

The Memphis Sound. Hollywood, California: Almo Publications, 1978.

Morse, David, comp. *Grand Father Rock: The New Poetry and the Old.* New York: Dell, 1972.

Morse, Jim, and Nancy Mathews, comps. *Survival Songbook.* San Francisco: Sierra Club, 1971.

The New Big Folk-Rock Book. 3d ed. Hialeah, Florida: Columbia Pictures Publications, 1978.

The New Big Top 100. Hialeah, Florida: Columbia Pictures Publications, 1979.

The New Smash Hits of '79. Hollywood, California: Almo Publications, 1979.

The New Super 79. Hialeah, Florida: Columbia Pictures Publications, 1979.

Nicholas, A. X., ed. *The Poetry of Soul.* New York: Bantam Books, 1971.

————. *Woke up This Mornin': Poetry of the Blues.* New York: Bantam Books, 1973.

Norback, Peter and Craig, eds. *Great Songs of Madison Avenue*. New York: Quadrangle Books, 1976.

#1 Songs of the Seventies. New York: Warner Brothers Publications, 1978.

Ochs, Phil. *Songs of Phil Ochs*. New York; Appleseed Music, 1964.

———. *The War Is Over*. New York: Collier Books, 1971.

Offen, Carol, ed. *Country Music: The Poetry*. New York: Ballantine Books, 1977.

Ohrlin, Glenn. *The Hell-Bound Train: A Cowboy Songbook*. Urbana: University of Illinois Press, 1973.

Okun, Milton, ed. *Great Songs of Lennon and McCartney*. New York: Quadrangle Press, 1973.

———. *Great Songs . . . of the Sixties*. Chicago: Quadrangle Press, 1970.

———. *The New York Times Country Music's Greatest Songs*. New York: Times Books, 1978.

———. *The New York Times Great Songs of the Seventies*. New York: Times Books, 1977.

———. *Something to Sing About: The Personal Choices of America's Folk Singers*. New York: Macmillan, 1968.

100 of the Greatest Rock and Roll Hits. New York: Big 3, n.d.

111 Hits of the Super Stars. 4th ed. Hialeah, Florida: Columbia Pictures Publications, 1979.

120 Greatest Hits of the 50's, 60's, and 70's. New York: Big 3, 1979.

120 Super Songs of the Super Stars. New York: Warner Brothers Publications, 1978.

122 Superhits of the Super Stars. Hialeah, Florida: Columbia Pictures Publications, 1978.

Palmer, Robert, comp. *Baby, That Was Rock and Roll: The Legendary Leiber and Stoller*. New York: Harcourt Brace Jovanovich, 1978.

Paul Simon—Greatest Hits, Etc. New York: Charing Cross Music, 1977.

Paxton, Tom. *Ramblin' Boy and Other Songs*. New York: Oak Publications, 1964.

Peck, Richard, ed. *Sounds and Silences: Poetry for Now*. New York: Dell, 1970.

Pichaske, David R., ed. *Beowulf to Beatles and Beyond: The Varieties of Poetry*. New York: Macmillan, 1981.

———. *Beowulf to Beatles: Approaches to Poetry*. New York: Free Press, 1972.

Platinum '78: Songbook of the Superstars. New York: Warner Brothers Publications, 1979.

Platinum '79. New York: Warner Brothers Publications, 1979.

Popular Rhythm and Blues. Hollywood, California: Jobete Music, 1976.

Progressive Rock Classics. New York: Warner Brothers Publications, n.d.

Punk/Rock 'N' Roll/New Wave. Hollywood, California: Almo Publications, 1978.

Raim, Ethel, and Irwin Silber, eds. *American Favorite Ballads: Tunes and Songs as Sung by Pete Seeger*. New York: Oak Publications, 1961.

Raph, Theodore, comp. *The Songs We Sang: A Treasury of American Popular Music*. New York: A. S. Barnes, 1964.

Rhythm and Blues Folio. New York: Progressive Music, 1963.

Rock Anthology. Miami: Screen Gems–Columbia Publications, 1975.

Rock Anthology: Top of the Charts. Hialeah, Florida: Columbia Pictures Publications, 1979.

Rock Lives! Los Angeles: ATV Music Publications, 1980.

Ryan, Betsy, ed. *Sounds of Silence*. New York: Scholastic Book Services, 1972.

Sackheim, Eric, comp. *The Blues Line: A Collection of Blues Lyrics.* New York: Grossman, 1969.

Savary, Louis M., ed. *Popular Song and Youth Today: Fifty Songs—Their Meaning and You.* New York: Association Press, 1971.

Scott, John Anthony, comp. *The Ballad of America: The History of the United States in Song and Story.* New York: Bantam Books, 1966.

Seeger, Pete, ed. *American Favorite Ballads.* New York: Oak Publications, 1961.

———. *The Nearly Complete Collection of Woody Guthrie Folksongs.* New York: Ludlow Music, 1963.

77 Giant Hits of Today. New York: Big 3 Music, 1978.

Siegmeister, Elie, ed. *The Joan Baez Songbook.* New York: Ryerson Music, 1966.

Silber, Fred and Irwin, comps. *Folksinger's Wordbook.* New York: Oak Publications, 1973.

Silber, Irwin, ed. *Folksong Festival.* New York: Scholastic Magazine, 1967.

Silber, Irwin, and Earl G. Robinson. *Songs of the Great American West.* New York: Macmillan, 1967.

Silverman, Jerry, comp. *Folk Blues.* Rev. ed. New York: Oak Publications, 1968.

———. *The Liberated Women's Songbook.* New York: Collier Books, 1971.

Simon, Peter, comp. *Carly Simon Complete.* New York: Alfred A. Knopf, 1975.

Simon, William L., ed. *Reader's Digest Festival of Popular Songs.* Pleasantville, New York: Reader's Digest Association, 1977.

———. *Reader's Digest Treasury of Best Loved Songs: 114 All-Time Family Favorites.* Pleasantville, New York: Reader's Digest Association, 1972.

Sing Along! Pleasantville, New York: Reader's Digest Association, 1977.

Solid Gold Rock and Roll. Hialeah, Florida: Screen Gems–Columbia Productions, 1975.

Solid Gold Rock and Roll. New York: Big 3 Music, 1975.

The Songs of Bob Dylan: From 1966 through 1975. New York: Alfred A. Knopf/ Cherry Lane, 1978.

The Songs of Leonard Cohen. New York: Amsco Music, 1969.

The Songs of Paul Simon. New York: Alfred A. Knopf/Big Bells, 1972.

Songs Recorded by Elvis Presley—Volume One. New York: Elvis Presley Music, 1968.

Songs Recorded by Elvis Presley—Volume Two. New York: Elvis Presley Music, 1968.

Spinner, Stephanie, ed. *Rock Is Beautiful: An Anthology of American Lyrics, 1953– 1968.* New York: Dell, 1970.

Stairway to Heaven plus 24 Heavy Hits. New York: Warner Brothers Publications, 1977.

Staying Alive plus 24 Super Songs. New York: Warner Brothers Publications, 1978.

Stevie Winwood and Friends. New York: Collier Books, 1970.

Still and I'll Never Love This Way Again plus 24 Solid Gold Songs. Hialeah, Florida: Columbia Pictures Publications, 1979.

Super Chart Songs of 1979. Hialeah, Florida: Columbia Pictures Publications, 1980.

Super Hits of the 70's. Hollywood, California: Almo Publications, 1979.

Super Stars. Los Angeles: West Coast Publications, n.d.

Superstar Songbook. Trenton, New Jersey: Big Bells, 1975.

Tinsley, Jim Bob, comp. *He Was Singing' This Song: A Collection of Forty-Eight Traditional Songs of the American Cowboy—With Words, Music, Pictures and Stories.* Orlando: University of Central Florida Press, 1981.

Titon, Jeff. *Down Home Blues Lyrics: An Anthology from the Post–World War II Era*. Boston: Twayne Publishers, 1981.

Today's Fantastic Hits. New York: Robbins Music, 1970.

Top Hits of 1970 and Great Standards. New York: Robbins Music, 1971.

Walker, Jerry L. ed. *Favorite Pop/Rock Lyrics*. New York: Scholastic Book Service, 1969.

———. *Pop/Rock Lyrics 3*. New York: Scholastic Book Service, 1971.

———. *Pop/Rock Lyrics 2*. New York: Scholastic Book Service, 1970.

———. *Pop/Rock Songs of the Earth*. New York: Scholastic Book Service, 1972.

White, John I., *Git Along, Little Dogies: Songs and Songmakers of the American West*. Urbana: University of Illinois Press, 1976.

Whitman, Wanda Willson, ed. *Songs That Changed the World*. New York: Crown, 1970.

The Who Complete: A Complete Collection of the Best of The Who. New York: Charles Hansen Music and Books, n.d.

Wise, Herbert H., ed. *Professional Rock and Roll*. New York: Collier Books, 1967.

Wolfe, Richard, comp. *Legit Professional Fake Book: More Than 1010 Songs*. New York: Big 3 Music, n.d.

Woodstock. New York: Warner Brothers Publications, 1970.

C. CHART LISTS, DISCOGRAPHIES, AND ENCYCLOPEDIAS

Chart Lists and Discographies

Albert, George and Frank Hoffmann, comps. *The Cash Box Country Charts, 1958–1982*. Metuchen, New Jersey: Scarecrow Press, 1984.

Berry, Peter E. *"... And the Hits Just Keep on Comin' "*. Syracuse, New York: Syracuse University Press, 1977.

Blair, John, ed. *The Illustrated Discography of Surf Music, 1961–1965*. Rev. ed. Ann Arbor, Michigan: Pierian Press, 1984.

Castleman, Harry, and Walter J. Podrazik, comps. *All Together Now: The First Complete Beatles Discography, 1961–1975*. New York: Ballantine Books, 1975.

———. *The Beatles Again?* Ann Arbor, Michigan: Pierian Press, 1977.

———. *The End of the Beatles?* Ann Arbor, Michigan: Pierian Press, 1985.

Clee, Ken, comp. *The Directory of American 45 R.P.M. Records—3 Volumes*. Philadelphia: Stax-O-Wax, 1981. (Supplements for 1982 are also available).

Cotten, Lee, and Howard A. DeWitt. *Jailhouse Rock: The Bootleg Records of Elvis Presley, 1970–1983*. Ann Arbor, Michigan: Pierian Press, 1983.

DeFoe, George, and Martha DeFoe, with Henry Beck, Nancy Breslow, and Jim Linderman, eds. *International Discography of the New Wave: Volume 1982–83*. New York: Omnibus Books, 1982.

———. *Volume II: International Discography of the New Wave, 1982–83*. New York: One Ten Records, 1982.

Denisoff, R. Serge, comp. *Songs of Protest, War, and Peace: A Bibliography and Discography*. Santa Barbara, California: American Bibliography Center–CLIO Press, 1973.

Edwards, Joe, comp. *Top 10's and Trivia of Rock and Roll and Rhythm and Blues*,

1950–1980. St. Louis: Blueberry Hill, 1981. (Annual Supplements are also available.)

Ferlingere, Robert D., comp. *A Discography of Rhythm and Blues and Rock 'n' Roll Vocal Groups, 1945 to 1965.* Hayward: California Trade School, 1976.

The 45 RMP Handbook of Oldies: A Complete Guide to All the Available Hit Singles of the Past. Los Angeles: Record Rack, 1976.

Gambaccini, Paul, comp. *Rock Critics' Choice: The Top 200 Albums.* New York: Quick Fox, 1978.

Gilbert, Bob, and Gary Theroux. *The Top Ten: 1956 to the Present.* New York: Simon and Schuster, 1982.

Goldmann, Frank, and Klaus Hiltscher, comps. *The Gimmix Book of Records: An Almanac of Unusual Records, Sleeves, and Pictures Discs.* London: Virgin Books, 1981.

Goldstein, Stewart, and Alan Jacobson, comps. *Oldies but Goodies: The Rock 'n' Roll Years.* New York: Mason/Charter, 1977.

Gonzalez, Fernando, comp. *Disco-File: The Discographical Catalog of American Rock and Roll and Rhythm and Blues Vocal Harmony Groups, 1902 to 1976.* 2d ed. Flushing, New York: F. L. Gonzalez, 1977.

Gray, Michael H., comp. *Bibliography of Discographies—Volume 3: Popular Music.* New York: R. R. Bowker, 1983.

Guralnick, Peter. *Listener's Guide to the Blues.* New York: Facts on File, 1982.

Havlice, Patrice Pate, comp. *Popular Song Index.* Metuchen, New Jersey: Scarecrow Press, 1978.

———. *Popular Song Index—First Supplement.* Metuchen, New Jersey: Scarecrow Press, 1978.

Helander, Brock, comp. *The Rock Who's Who: A Biographical Dictionary and Critical Discography.* New York: Schirmer Books, 1982.

———. *The Miles Chart Display of Popular Music, Volume II: Top 100, 1971–1975.* New York: Arno Press, 1977.

Hibbert, Tom, ed. *The Perfect Collection.* New York: Proteus Books, 1982.

———, ed. *Rare Records: Wax Trash and Vinyl Treasures.* New York: Proteus Books, 1982.

Hoffmann, Frank, comp. *The Cash Box Singles Charts, 1950–1981.* Metuchen, New Jersey: Scarecrow Press, 1983.

Houndsome, Terry, comp. *New Rock Record.* New York: Facts on File, 1983.

Jasper, Tony, comp. *The Top Twenty Book: The Official British Record Charts, 1955–1982.* Poole, England: Blandford Press, 1983.

Leadbitter, Mike and Neil Slaven, comps. *Blues Records, 1943–66: A Discography.* New York: Oak Publications, 1968.

Leichter, Albert, comp. *Discography of Rhythm and Blues and Rock and Roll, Circa 1946–1964: A Reference Manual.* Staunton, Virginia: A. Leichter, 1975.

Lifton, Sarah, *The Listener's Guide to Folk Music.* New York: Facts on File, 1983.

Lyons, Len, comp. *The 101 Best Jazz Albums: A History of Jazz on Records.* New York: William Morrow, 1980.

Marsh, Dave and John Swenson, eds. *The New Rolling Stone Record Guide* (Revised Edition). New York: Random House/Rolling Stone Press Book, 1983.

Mawhinney, Paul C., comp. *Musicmaster: The 45 RPM Record Directory, 1947 to 1982—2 Volumes.* Allison Park, Pennsylvania: Record-Rama, 1983.

Miles, Daniel J., Betty T. Miles, and Martin J. Miles, comps. *The Miles Chart Display, Volume I: Top 100, 1955–1970*. Boulder, Colorado: Convex Industries, 1973.

Miron, Charles, comp. *Rock Gold: All the Hit Charts from 1955 to 1976*. New York: Drake, 1977.

Murrells, Joseph, comp. *The Book of Golden Discs: The Records That Sold a Million*. Rev. ed. London: Barrie and Jenkins, 1978.

Music/Records/200: Billboard's July 4, 1976 Spotlight on America. New York: Billboard Publications, 1976.

Nugent, Stephen, and Charlie Gillett, comps. *Rock Almanac: Top Twenty American and British Singles and Albums of the '50's, '60's, and '70's*. Garden City, New York: Anchor Press/Doubleday, 1976.

Oermann, Robert K., and Douglas B. Green. *The Listener's Guide to Country Music*. New York: Facts on File, 1983.

Osborne, Jerry, comp. *Rock and Roll Record Albums Price Guide*. 5th ed. Phoenix: O'Sullivan, Woodside, 1983.

Osborne, Jerry, and Bruce Hamilton, comps. *Blues/Rhythm and Blues/Soul: Original Record Collector's Price Guide*. Phoenix: O'Sullivan, Woodside, 1980.

————. *55 Years of Recorded Country/Western Music*. Phoenix: O'Sullivan, Woodside, 1976.

————. *A Guide to Record Collecting*. Phoenix: O'Sullivan, Woodside, 1979.

————. *Movie/TV Soundtracks and Original Cast Albums Price Guide*. Phoenix: O'Sullivan, Woodside, 1981.

————. *Popular and Rock Price Guide for 45's*. 3d ed. Phoenix: O'Sullivan, Woodside, 1981.

————. *Presleyana*. Phoenix: O'Sullivan, Woodside, 1981.

Pavlow, Al, comp. *Big Al Pavlow's the R & B Book: A Disc-History of Rhythm and Blues*. Providence, Rhode Island: Music House, 1983.

Pitts, Michael R., and Louis H. Harrison, comps. *Hollywood on Record: The Film Star's Discography*. Metuchen, New Jersey: Scarecrow Press, 1978.

Propes, Steve. *Golden Goodies: A Guide to 50's and 60's Popular Rock & Roll Record Collecting*. Radnor, Pennsylvania: Chilton, 1975.

————. *Golden Oldies: A Guide to 60's Record Collecting*. Radnor, Pennsylvania: Chilton, 1974.

————. *Those Oldies but Goodies: A Guide to 50's Record Collecting*. New York: Collier Books, 1973.

Quirin, Jim, and Barry Cohen, comps. *Chartmasters' Rock 100: An Authoritative Ranking of the 100 Most Popular Songs for Each Year, 1956 through 1981*. Covington, Louisiana: Chartmasters, 1982. (Annual Supplements are also available.)

Raymond, Jack. *Show Music on Record: From the 1890's to the 1980's*. New York: Ungar Books, 1982.

Reinhart, Charles. *You Can't Do That: Beatles' Bootlegs and Novelty Records, 1963–1980*. Ann Arbor, Michigan: Pierian Press, 1981.

Reuss, Richard A., ed. *Songs of American Labor, Industrialization, and the Urban Work Experience: A Discography*. Ann Arbor: Labor Studies Center in the Institute of Labor and Industrial Relations at the University of Michigan, 1983.

Rice, Jo; Tim Rice; Paul Gambaccini; and Mike Read, comps. *The Guinness Book of British Hit Singles*. 4th ed. London: Guinness Superlatives, 1983.

————. *The Guinness Book of 500 Number One Hits*. London: Guinness Superlatives, 1983.

————. *The Guinness Book of Hits of the 70s*. London: Guinness Superlatives, 1983.

————. *The Guinness Book of Hits of the 60s*. London: Guinness Superlatives, 1984.

Robbins, Ira A., comp. *The Trouser Press Guide to New Wave Records*. New York: Charles Scribner's Sons, 1983.

Ruppli, Michel, comp. *Atlantic Records: A Discography—4 Volumes*. Westport, Connecticut: Greenwood Press, 1979.

————. *The Chess Labels: A Discography—2 Volumes*. Westport, Connecticut: Greenwood Press, 1983.

————. *The Savoy Label: A Discography*. Westport, Connecticut: Greenwood Press, 1980.

Russel, Jeff P., comp. *The Beatles on Record*. New York: Charles Scribner's Sons, 1982.

Scott, Frank, et al., comps. *The Blues Catalog*. El Cerrito, California: Down Home Music, 1982.

————. *Country Music Catalog—Including Western Swing, Steel Guitar, and Cowboy Songs*. El Cerrito, California: Down Home Music, 1983.

————. *Vintage Rock and Roll Catalog*. El Cerrito, California: Down Home Music, 1983.

Shapiro, Nat, ed. *Popular Music: An Annotated Index of American Popular Songs, Vol. I: 1950–1959*. New York: Adrian Press, 1964.

————. *Popular Music: An Annotated Index of American Popular Songs, Vol. III: 1960–1964*. New York: Adrian Press, 1967.

————. *Popular Music: An Annotated Index of American Popular Songs, Vol. VI: 1965–1969*. New York: Adrian Press, 1973.

Solomon, Clive, comp. *Record Hits: The British Top 50 Charts, 1954–1976*. London: Omnibus Press, 1977.

Tharin, Frank C., Jr., comp. *Chart Champions: 40 Years of Rankings and Ratings*. San Francisco: Chart Champions, 1980.

Tudor, Dean, comp. *Popular Music: An Annotated Guide to Recordings*. Littleton, Colorado: Libraries Unlimited, 1983.

Tudor, Dean, and Nancy Tudor, comps. *Black Music*. Littleton, Colorado: Libraries Unlimited, 1979.

————. *Contemporary Popular Music*. Littleton, Colorado: Libraries Unlimited, 1979.

Whitburn, Joel, comp. *The Billboard Book of Top 40 Hits, 1955 to the Present*. New York: Billboard Publications, 1983.

————. *Bubbling under the Hot 100, 1959–1981*. Menomonee Falls, Wisconsin: Record Research, 1982.

————. *Music Yearbook 1983*. Menomonee Falls, Wisconsin: Record Research, 1984.

————. *Music Yearbook 1984*. Menomonee Falls, Wisconsin: Record Research, 1985.

————. *Pop Annual, 1955–1982*. Menomonee Falls, Wisconsin: Records Research, 1983.

————. *Top Country and Western Records, 1949–1971*. Menomonee Falls, Wisconsin: Record Research, 1972. (Annual Supplements through 1982 are also available.)

————. *Top Easy Listening Records, 1961–1974*. Menomonee Falls, Wisconsin: Record Research, 1975. (Annual Supplements through 1982 are also available.)

——. *Top LP Records, 1945–1972.* Menomonee Falls, Wisconsin: Record Research, 1973. (Annual Supplements through 1982 are also available.)

——. *Top Pop, 1955–1982.* Menomonee Falls, Wisconsin: Record Research, 1983.

——. *Top Pop Albums, 1955–1985.* Menomonee Falls, Wisconsin: Record Research, 1985.

——. *Top Pop Records, 1940–1955.* Menomonee Falls, Wisconsin: Record Research, 1973.

——. *Top Rhythm and Blues Records, 1949–1971.* Menomonee Falls, Wisconsin: Record Research, 1972. (Annual Supplements through 1982 are also available.)

Encyclopedias

Anderson, Robert, and Gail North, comps. *Gospel Music Encyclopedia.* New York: Sterling, 1979.

Baggelaar, Kristin, and Donald Milton, comps. *Folk Music: More Than a Song.* New York: Thomas Y. Crowell, 1976.

Baker, Glenn A., and Stuart Coupe. *The New Music.* New York: Harmony Books, 1980.

Bane, Michael, ed. *Who's Who in Rock.* New York: Facts on File, 1981.

Bianco, Dave. *Who's New Wave in Music: An Illustrated Encyclopedia, 1976–1982.* Ann Arbor, Michigan: Pierian Press, 1985.

Bonds, Ray, ed. *The Harmony Illustrated Encyclopedia of Rock.* 3d ed. New York: Harmony Books, 1982.

——. *The Illustrated Encyclopedia of Black Music.* New York: Harmony Books, 1982.

Carlton, Joseph R., comp. *Carlton's Complete Reference Book of Music.* Studio City, California: Carlton Publications, 1980.

Carr, Patrick, ed. *The Illustrated History of Country Music.* Garden City, New York: Doubleday, 1980.

Case, Brian, and Stan Britt, eds. *The Illustrated Encyclopedia of Jazz.* New York: Harmony Books, 1978.

Charlesworth, Chris. *A-Z of Rock Guitarists.* New York: Proteus Press, 1982.

Cross, Colin, with Paul Kendall and Mick Farren, comps. *Encyclopedia of British Beat Groups and Solo Artists of the Sixties.* London: Omnibus Press, 1980.

Dellar, Fred; Roy Thompson; and Douglas B. Green, comps. *The Illustrated Encyclopedia of Country Music.* New York: Harmony Books, 1977.

Feather, Leonard. *The Encyclopedia of Jazz in the Sixties.* New York: Horizon Books, 1967.

——. *The New Edition of the Encyclopedia of Jazz.* New York: Horizon Books, 1960.

Feather, Leonard and Ira Gitler. *The Encyclopedia of Jazz in the Seventies.* New York: Horizon Books, 1977.

Fricke, David; John Morthland; John Swenson; and Mark Mehler, comps. "Who's Who—Artists." In *Contemporary Music Almanac 1980/81.* Comp. Ronald Zalkind. New York: Schirmer Books, 1980, pp. 157–349.

Friede, Goldie; Robin Titone; and Sue Weiner, comps. *The Beatles A to Z: The Complete Illustrated Beatle Encyclopedia.* New York: Methuen Books, 1980.

Hardy, Phil, and Dave Laing, comps. *Encyclopedia of Rock 1955–1975*. London: Aquarius Books, 1977.

Harrigan, Brian, comp. *Heavy Metal A-Z: The Definitive Encyclopedia of Heavy Metal*. London: Bopcat Books, 1981.

Harrigan, Brian, and Malcolm Dome, comps. *Encyclopedia Metallica: The Bible of Heavy Metal*. London: Bopcat Books, 1980.

Harris, Sheldon, comp. *Blues Who's Who: A Biographical Dictionary of Blues Singers*. New Rochelle, New York: Arlington House, 1979.

Helander, Brock, comp. *The Rock Who's Who*. New York: Schirmer Books, 1982.

Hume, Martha. *You're So Cold I'm Turning Blue: Martha Hume's Guide to the Greatest in Country Music*. New York: Penguin Books, 1982.

Jablonski, Edward, comp. *The Encyclopedia of American Music*. Garden City, New York: Doubleday, 1981.

Kinkle, Roger D. *The Complete Encyclopedia of Popular Music and Jazz, 1900–1950*. New Rochelle, New York: Arlington House, 1974.

Marchbank, ?earce, and Barry Miles, comps. *The Illustrated Rock Almanac*. New York Paddington Press, 1977.

May, Chris, and Tim Phillips, comps. *British Beat*. London: Socion Books, 1974.

Naha, Ed, comp. *Lillian Roxon's Rock Encyclopedia*. Rev. ed. New York: Grosset and Dunlap, 1978.

Nite, Norm N. comp. *Rock On: The Illustrated Encyclopedia of Rock 'n' Roll—Volume One: The Solid Gold Years*. Rev. ed. New York: Harper and Row, 1982.

———. *Rock On—Volume Two: The Illustrated Encyclopedia of Rock 'n' Roll—The Modern Years, 1964 to the Present*. New York: Thomas Y. Crowell, 1978.

Noble, Peter L. *Future Pop: Music for the Eighties*. New York: Delilah Books, 1983.

Palmer, Trisha, ed. *The Illustrated Encyclopedia of Country Music*. New York: Harmony Books, 1977.

Pareles, Jon, and Patricia Romanowski, eds. *The Rolling Stone Encyclopedia of Rock and Roll*. New York: Rolling Stone Press/Summit Books, 1983.

Rachlin, Harvey, comp. *The Encyclopedia of the Music Business*. New York: Harper and Row, 1981.

Roxon, Lillian, comp. *Lillian Roxon's Rock Encyclopedia*. New York: Grosset and Dunlap, 1969.

Russell, Tony, ed. *Encyclopedia of Rock*. London: Crescent Books, 1983.

Shapiro, Harry. *A-Z of Rock Drummers*. New York: Proteus Books, 1982.

Shestack, Melvin, comp. *The Country Music Encyclopedia*. New York: Thomas Y. Crowell, 1974.

Simon, George T., and Friends, comps. *The Best of the Music Makers*. Garden City, New York: Doubleday, 1979.

Stambler, Irwin, and Grelun Landon, eds. *The Encyclopedia of Folk, Country, and Western Music*. 2d ed. New York: St. Martin's Press, 1983.

York, William, comp. *Who's Who in Rock Music*. Rev. ed. New York: Charles Scribner's Sons, 1982.

D. ARTICLES, BOOK REVIEWS, AND RECORD REVIEWS

Aquilla, Richard. "Images of the West in Rock Music." *Western Historical Quarterly* 11 (October 1980): 415–432.

Auslander, H. Ben. " 'If Ya Wanna End War and Stuff, You Gotta Sing Loud': A Survey of Vietnam-Related Protest Music." *Journal of American Culture* 4 (Summer 1981): 108–113.

Baker, Glenn A. "Recording the Right." *Goldmine* 66 (November 1981): 176–178.

————. "Rock's Angry Voice." *Goldmine* 75 (July 1982): 10–11.

Campbell, Gregg M. "Bob Dylan and the Pastoral Apocalypse." *Journal of Popular Culture* 8 (Spring 1975): 696–707.

Carey, James T. "Changing Courtship Patterns in the Popular Song." *American Journal of Sociology* 74 (May 1969): 720–731.

————. "The Ideology of Autonomy in Popular Lyrics: A Content Analysis." *Psychiatry* 22 (May 1969): 150–164.

Carney, George O. "Music and Dance." In *This Remarkable Continent: An Atlas of United States and Canadian Society and Cultures.* Ed. John F. Rooney, Jr., Wilbur Zelinsky, and Dean R. Louder. College Station, Texas: For the Society of the North American Cultural Survey by Texas A&M University Press, 1982, pp. 234–253.

————. "The Roots of American Music." In *The Sounds of People and Places: Readings in the Geography of Music.* Ed. George O. Carney. Washington, D.C.: University Press of America, 1979, pp. 286–323.

Chenoweth, Lawrence. "The Rhetoric of Hope and Despair: A Study of The Jimi Hendrix Experience and The Jefferson Airplane." *American Quarterly* 23 (Spring 1981): 25–45.

Cobb, James M. "From Muskogee to Luckenbach: Country Music and the Southernization of America." *Journal of Popular Culture* 16 (Winter 1982): 81–91.

Cole, Richard. "Top Songs of the Sixties: A Content Analysis of Popular Lyrics." *American Behavioral Scientist* 14 (January-February 1971): 389–400.

Cooper, B. Lee. "Audio Images of the City." *Social Studies* 72 (May-June 1981): 129–136.

————. "Chuck Berry and the American Motor Car." *Music World* no. 86 (June 1981): 18–23.

————. "Folk History, Alternative History, and Future History." *Teaching History: A Journal of Methods* 2 (Spring 1977): 58–62.

————. "Foreword." In *Popular Culture and Libraries.* Ed. Frank W. Hoffmann. Hamden, Connecticut: Library Professional Publications, Shoe String Press, 1984, pp. vii-xv.

————. "The Image of the Black Man: Contemporary Lyrics as Oral History." *The Journal of the Interdenominational Theological Center* 5 (Spring 1978): 105–122.

————. "The Image of the Outsider in Contemporary Lyrics." *Journal of Popular Culture* 12 (Summer 1978): 168–178.

————. "Information Services, Popular Culture, and the Librarian: Promoting a Contemporary Learning Perspective." *Drexel Library Quarterly* 16 (July 1980): 24–42.

————. " 'It's A Wonder I Can Think at All': Vinyl Images of American Public Education, 1950–1980." *Popular Music and Society* 9 (Fall 1984): 47–65.

————. "Music and the Metropolis: Lyrical Images of Life in American Cities, 1950–1980." *Teaching History: A Journal of Methods* 6 (Fall 1981); 72–84.

————. "Popular Culture: Teaching Problems and Challenges." In *Popular Culture and the Library.* Ed. Wayne A. Wiegand. Lexington: College of Library Science at the University of Kentucky, 1978, pp. 10–26.

———. "Popular Music in the Social Studies Classroom: Audio Resources for Teachers." How-To-Do-It—Series 2, no. 13. Washington, D.C.: National Council for the Social Studies, 1981.

———. "A Popular Music Perspective: Challenging Sexism in the Social Studies Class." *Social Studies* 71 (March-April 1980): 71–76.

———. "Rock Music and Religious Education: A Proposed Synthesis." *Religious Education* 70 (May-June 1975): 289–299.

———. "Shifting Images of Transportation Technology and American Society in Railroad Songs, 1920–1980." *International Journal of Instructional Media* 10 (1982–1983): 131–146.

———. "Social Change, Popular Music, and the Teacher." In *Ideas for Teaching Gifted Students: Social Studies (Secondary).* Ed. Jackie Mallis. Austin, Texas: Multi Media Arts, 1979, pp. 9–19.

Denisoff, R. Serge. "Folk-Rock: Folk Music, Protest, or Commercialism?" *Journal of Popular Culture* 3 (Fall 1969): 214–230.

———. "Protest Songs, Those on the Top Forty and Those of the Streets." *American Quarterly* 22 (Winter 1970): 807–823.

———. "Songs of Persuasion: A Sociological Analysis of Urban Propaganda Songs." *Journal of American Folklore* 79 (October-December 1966): 581–589.

Denisoff, R. Serge, and David Fandray. " 'Hey, Hey Woody Guthrie I Wrote You a Song': The Political Side of Bob Dylan." *Popular Music and Society* 5 (1977): pp. 31–42.

Denisoff, R. Serge, and Mark H. Levine. "The Popular Protest Song: The Case of 'Eve of Destruction.' " *Public Opinion Quarterly* 35 (Spring 1971): 117–122.

Denisoff, R. Serge, and Richard A. Peterson. "Theories of Culture, Music, and Society." In *The Sounds of Social Change: Studies in Popular Culture.* Ed. R. Serge Denisoff and Richard A. Peterson. Chicago: Rand McNally, 1972, pp. 1–12.

Dimaggio, Paul; Richard A. Peterson; and Jack Esco, Jr. "Country Music: Ballad of the Silent Majority." In *The Sounds of Social Change: Studies in Popular Culture.* Ed. R. Serge Denisoff and Richard A. Peterson. Chicago: Rand McNally, 1972, pp. 38–55.

Dixon, Richard D.; Fred R. Ingram; Richard M. Levinson; and Catherine L. Putnam. "The Cultural Diffusion of Punk Rock in the United States." *Popular Music and Society* 6 (1979): 210–218.

Ferrandino, Joe. "Rock Culture and the Development of Social Consciousness." In *Side-Saddle on the Golden Calf: Social Structure and Popular Culture in America.* Ed. George H. Lewis. Pacific Palisades, California: Goodyear, 1972, pp. 263–290.

Flippo, Chet. "The History of *Rolling Stone*—A Three-Part Study." *Popular Music and Society* 3 (1974): 159–188, 258–280, 281–298.

Ford, Larry. "Geographical Factors in the Origin, Evolution, and Diffusion of Rock and Roll Music." *Journal of Geography* 70 (November 1971): 455–464.

Fox, William S., and Michael H. Wince. "Feminist Attitudes and Preferences for a Feminist 'Message' Song: A Research Note." *Popular Music and Society* 4 (1975): 156–169.

Francaviglia, Richard V. "Diffusion of Popular Culture: Comments on the Spatial Aspects of Rock Music." In *An Invitation to Geography*. Ed. David A. Lanegran and Risa Palm. New York: McGraw-Hill, 1973, pp. 117–126.

Friedberg, Harris. "Bob Dylan: Psychohistorian of a Generation." *The Chronicle of Higher Education* 8 (January 28, 1974): 15–16.

Frith, Simon. " 'The Magic That Can Set You Free': The Ideology of Folk and the Myth of the Rock Community." In *Popular Music I: Folk or Popular? Distinctions, Influences, Continuities*. Ed. Richard Middleton and David Horn. Cambridge: Cambridge University Press, 1981, pp. 159–168.

———. "Popular Music, 1950–1980." In *Making Music: The Guide to Writing, Performing, and Recording*. Ed. George Martin. London: Pan Books, 1983, pp. 18–48.

Fruediger, Patricia. "Love Lauded and Love Lamented: Men and Women in Popular Music." *Popular Music and Society* 6 (1978): 1–10.

Fryer, Paul. " 'Can You Blame the Colored Man?' The Topical Song in Black American Popular Music," *Popular Music and Society* 8 (1981): 19–31.

Garofalo, Reebee, and Steve Chapple. "From ASCAP to Alan Freed: The Pre-History of Rock 'n' Roll," *Popular Music and Society* 6 (1978): 72–80.

Geltman, Max. "The Hot Hundred: A Surprise." *National Review* 18 (September 6, 1966): 894–896.

Gleason, Ralph J. "Like a Rolling Stone." *American Scholar* 36 (Autumn 1967): 555–563.

———. "The Times They Are A-Changin'." *Ramparts* 3 (April 1965): 36–48.

Goldberg, Steven. "Bob Dylan and the Poetry of Salvation." *Saturday Review* 53 (May 30, 1970): 43–46ff.

Graebner, William. "Teaching The History of Rock 'n' Roll." *Teaching History: A Journal of Methods* 9 (Spring 1984): 2–20.

Greenway, John. "Folk Songs as Socio-Historical Documents." *Western Folklore* 19 (January 1960): 1–9.

Gritzner, Charles F. "Country Music: A Reflection of Popular Culture." *Journal of Popular Culture* 11 (Fall 1978): 857–864.

Hamm, Charles. "Changing Patterns in Society and Music: The U.S. since World War II." In *Contemporary Music and Music Cultures*. Ed. Charles Hamm, Bruno Nettl, and Ronald Byrnside. Englewood Cliffs, New Jersey: Prentice-Hall, 1975, pp. 35–70.

Haralambos, Michael. "Soul Music and Blues: Their Meaning and Relevance in Northern United States Black Ghettos." In *Afro-American Anthropology*. Ed. Norman E. Whitten, Jr., and John F. Szwed. New York: Free Press, 1970, pp. 367–384.

Harmon, James E. "Meaning in Rock Music: Notes toward a Theory of Communication." *Popular Music and Society* 2 (Fall 1972): pp. 18–32.

———. "The New Music and Counter-Culture Values." *Youth and Society* 4 (September 1972): 61–82.

Heckman, Don. "Black Music and White America." In *Black America*. Ed. John F. Szwed. New York: Basic Books, 1970, pp. 158–170.

Hellmann, John M., Jr. " 'I'm a Monkey': The Influence of the Black American Blues Argot on The Rolling Stones." *Journal of American Folklore* 86 (October-December 1973): 367–373.

Henderson, Floyd M. "The Image of New York City in American Popular Music of 1890–1970." *New York Folklore Quarterly* 30 (December 1974): 267–278.

Hesbacher, Peter, and Les Waffen. "War Recordings: Incidence and Change, 1940–1980." *Popular Music and Society* 8 (1982): 77–101.

Hey, Kenneth R. "I Feel A Change Comin' On: The Counter-Cultural Image of the South in Southern Rock 'n' Roll." *Popular Music and Society* 5 (1977): 93–99.

Hirsch, Paul M. "Sociological Approaches to the Pop Music Phenomenon." *American Behavioral Scientist* 14 (January-February 1971): 371–388.

Hirsch, Paul; John Robinson; Elizabeth Keogh Taylor; and Stephen B. Withey. "The Changing Popular Song: An Historical Overview." *Popular Music and Society* 1 (Winter 1972): 83–93.

Horton, Donald. "The Dialogue of Courtship in Popular Songs." *American Journal of Sociology* 62 (May 1957): 569–578.

Hugunin, Marc. "ASCAP, BMI, and the Democratization of American Popular Music." *Popular Music and Society* 7 (1979): 8–17.

Hyden, Colleen, and N. Jane McCandless. "Men and Women as Portrayed in the Lyrics of Contemporary Music." *Popular Music and Society* 9 (1983): 19–26.

Janeti, Joseph. "Folk Music's Affair with Popular Culture: A Redefinition of the 'Revival.' " In *New Dimensions in Popular Culture*. Ed. Russell B. Nye. Bowling Green, Ohio: Bowling Green University Popular Press, 1972, pp. 224–225.

Johnson, Eric P. "The Use of Folk Songs in Education: Some Examples of the Use of Folk Songs in the Teaching of History, Geography, Economics, and English Literature." *The Vocational Aspect of Education* 21 (Summer 1969): 89–94.

Johnstone, John, and Elihu Katz. "Youth and Popular Music: A Study of the Sociology of Taste." *American Journal of Sociology* 62 (May 1957): 563–568.

Jordania, Redjeb. "Essay in Semiotics: Boris Vian and the Popular Song." *Popular Music and Society* 6 (1978): 45–63.

Kamin, Jonathan. "Parallels in the Social Reactions to Jazz and Rock." *Journal of Jazz Studies* 2 (December 1974): 95–125.

———. "Taking the Roll Out of Rock 'n' Roll: Reverse Acculturation." *Popular Music and Society* 2 (Fall 1972): 1–17.

———. "The White R & B Audience and the Music Industry, 1952–1956." *Popular Music and Society* 4, (1975): 170–187.

King, Florence. "Rednecks, White Socks, and Blue-Ribbon Fear: The Nashville Sound of Discontent." *Harper's Magazine* 249 (July 1974): 30–34.

King, Woodie, Jr. "Searching for Brothers Kindred: Rhythm and Blues of the 1950's." *The Black Scholar* 6 (November 1974): 19–30.

Korall, Burt. "The Music of Protest." *Saturday Review* 51 (November 16, 1968): 36–39ff.

Lees, Gene. "1918–1968: From *Over There* to *Kill for Peace*." *High Fidelity* 18 (November 1968): 56–60.

———. "War Songs: Bathos and Acquiescence." *High Fidelity* 28 (December 1978): 41–44.

———. "War Songs II: Music Goes AWOL." *High Fidelity* 29 (January 1979): 20–22.

Levine, Mark H., and Thomas J. Harig. "The Role of Rock: A Review and Critique of Alternative Perspectives on the Impact of Rock Music." *Popular Music and Society* 4 (1975): 195–207.

Lewis, George H. "Country Music Lyrics." *Journal of Communication* 26 (Autumn 1976): 37–40.

———. "Cultural Socialization and the Development of Taste Cultures and Culture Classes in American Popular Music: Existing Evidence and Proposed Research Directions." *Popular Music and Society* 4 (1975): 226–241.

———. "Popular Music, Musical Preference, and Drug Use among Youth." *Popular Music and Society* 7 (1980): 176–181.

———. "Social Class and Cultural Communication: An Analysis of Song Lyrics." *Popular Music and Society* 5 (1977): 23–30.

———. "Social Protest and Self-Awareness in Black Popular Music." *Popular Music and Society* 2 (Summer 1973): 327–333.

London, Herbert. "The Charles Reich Typology and Early Rock Music." *Popular Music and Society* 1 (Winter 1972): 65–72.

Lund, Jens. "Country Music Goes to War: Songs for the Red-Blooded American." *Popular Music and Society* 2 (Summer 1972): 210–230.

———. "Fundamentalism, Racism, and Political Reaction in Country Music." In *The Sounds of Social Change: Studies in Popular Culture*. Ed. R. Serge Denisoff and Richard A. Peterson. Chicago: Rand McNally, 1972, pp. 79–91.

Lund, Jens, and R. Serge Denisoff. "The Folk Music Revival and the Counter Culture." *Journal of American Folklore* 84 (October/December 1971): 394–405.

Lyons, Anne W. "Creative Teaching in Interdisciplinary Humanities: The Human Values in Pop Music." *Minnesota English Journal* 10 (Winter 1974): 23–31.

Mahrmann, G. P., and F. Eugene Scott. "Popular Music and World War II: The Rhetoric of Continuation." *Quarterly Journal of Speech* 62 (February 1976): 145–156.

Maultsby, Portia K. "Soul Music: Its Sociological and Political Significance in American Popular Culture." *Journal of Popular Culture* 17 (Fall 1983): 51–60.

McCarthy, John D.; Richard A. Peterson; and William L. Yancey. "Singing Along with the Silent Majority." In *Popular Culture: Mirror of American Life*. Ed. David Manning White and John Pendleton. Del Mar, California: Publisher's, 1977, pp. 169–173.

McConnell, Frank D. "Rock and the Politics of Frivolity." *The Massachusetts Review* 12 (Winter 1971): 119–134.

McCourt, Tom. "Bright Lights, Big City: A Brief History of Rhythm and Blues, 1945–1957." *Popular Music and Society* 9 (1983): 1–18.

McGuigan, Cathleen, with Mark D. Vehling, Jennifer Smith, Sherry Keene-Osborn, Barbara Burgower, and Nadine Joseph. "Breaking Out: America Goes Dancing." *Newsweek* 104 (July 2, 1984): 46–52.

Miller, Lloyd, and James K. Skipper, Jr. "Sound of Protest: Jazz and the Militant Avant-Garde." In *Approaches to Deviance: Theories, Concepts, and Research Findings*. Ed. Mark Lefton, James K. Skipper, Jr., and Charles H. McCaghy. New York: Appleton-Century-Crofts, 1968, pp. 129–140.

Mooney, Hughson F. "Commercial 'Country' Music in the 1970s: Some Special and Historical Perspectives." *Popular Music and Society* 7 (1980): 208–213.

————. "Just before Rock: Pop Music 1950–1953 Reconsidered." *Popular Music and Society* 3 (1974): 65–108.

————. "Popular Music since the 1920's: The Significance of Shifting Taste." *Popular Music and Society* 1 (Spring 1972): 129–143.

————. "Rock as an Historical Phenomenon." *Popular Music and Society* 1 (Spring 1972): 129–143.

————. "Songs, Singers, and Society." *American Quarterly* 6 (Fall 1954): 221–232.

————. "Twilight of the Age of Aquarius? Popular Music in the 1970s." *Popular Music and Society* 7 (1980): 182–198.

Morgan, John P., and Thomas C. Tulloss. "The Jake Walk Blues: A Toxicologic Tragedy Mirrored in American Popular Music." *Annals of Internal Medicine* 85 (December 1976): 804–808.

Morse, David E. "Avant-Rock in the Classroom." *English Journal* 58 (February 1969): 196–200ff.

Mosher, Harold F., Jr. "The Lyrics of American Pop Music: A New Poetry." *Popular Music and Society* 1 (Spring 1972): 167–176.

Murray, Ronald S. "From Memphis to Motown: Some Geographical Implications of the Origin and Diffusion of Rock 'n' Roll Music." In *The Sounds of People and Places: Readings in the Geography of Music.* Ed. George O. Carney. Washington, D.C.: University Press of America, 1979, pp. 233–246.

Peterson, Richard A. "Disco!" *The Chronicle Review* 17 (October 2, 1978): R.26–27.

————. "The Production of Cultural Change: The Case of Contemporary Country Music." *Social Research* 45 (Summer 1978): 292–314.

————. "Taking Popular Music Too Seriously," *Journal of Popular Culture* 4 (Winter 1971): 590–594.

————. "The Unnatural History of Rock Festivals: An Instance of Media Facilitation." *Popular Music and Society* 2 (Winter 1973): 97–123.

Peterson, Richard A., and David G. Berger. "Cycles in Symbol Production: The Case of Popular Music." *American Sociological Review* 40 (April 1975): 158–173.

————. "Three Eras in the Manufacture of Popular Music Lyrics." In *The Sounds of Social Change: Studies in Popular Culture.* Ed. R. Serge Denisoff and Richard A. Peterson. Chicago: Rand McNally, 1972, pp. 282–303.

Poirer, Richard. "Learning from The Beatles," *Partisan Review* 34 (Fall 1967): 526–546.

Pollock, Bruce. "Paul Simon: Survivor from the Sixties." *Saturday Review* 3 (June 12, 1976): 43–44ff.

Reinartz, Kay F. "The Paper Doll: Images of American Women in Popular Songs." In *Women: A Feminist Perspective.* Ed. Jo Freeman. Palo Alto, California: Mayfield, 1975, pp. 293–308.

Rice, Ronald E. "The Content of Popular Recordings." *Popular Music and Society* 7 (1980): 140–158.

Ridgeway, Cecilia L., and John M. Roberts. "Urban Popular Music and Interaction: A Semantic Relationship." *Ethnomusicology* 20 (May 1976): 233–251.

Rieger, Jon H. "The Coming Crisis in the Youth Music Market." *Popular Music and Society* 4 (1975): 19–35.

Riesman, David. "Listening to Popular Music." *American Quarterly* 2 (Winter 1950): 359–371.

Robinson, John P., and Paul Hirsch. "It's the Sound That Does It." *Psychology Today* 3 (October 1969): 42–45.

Robinson, John P.; Robert Pilskaln; and Paul Hirsch. "Protest Rock and Drugs." *Journal of Communication* 26 (Autumn 1976): 125–136.

Rodnitzky, Jerome L. "The Decline of Contemporary Protest Music." *Popular Music and Society* 1 (Fall 1971): 44–50.

———. "The Evolution of the American Protest Song." *Journal of Popular Culture* 3 (Summer 1969): 35–45.

———. "The New Revivalism: American Protest Songs, 1945–1968." *South Atlantic Quarterly* 70 (Winter 1971): 13–21.

———. "Popular Music in American Studies." *History Teacher* 7 (August 1974): 503–510.

———. "Songs of Sisterhood: The Music of Women's Liberation." *Popular Music and Society* 4 (1975): 77–85.

Rose, Cynthia. "Raves from the Grave: The Eternal Appeal of Rock's Death Songs." *History of Rock* no. 29 (1982): 574–575.

Rosenstone, Richard A. " 'The Times They Are A-Changin': The Music of Protest." *The Annals of the American Academy of Political and Social Science* 381 (March 1969): 131–144.

Seeger, Charles. "Music and Class Structure in the United States." *American Quarterly* 9 (Fall 1957): 281–295.

Seidman, Laurence I. " 'Get on the Raft with Taft' and Other Musical Treats." *Social Education* 40 (October 1976): 436–437.

———. "Teaching about the American Revolution through Its Folk Songs." *Social Education* 38 (November 1973): 654–664.

Shaw, Greg. "Punk Politics: The Kids Are Mostly Right. . . . " *Bomp!* no. 17 (November 1977): 16–17.

Shelton, Robert. "Cat Clothes and the Curtis Cut: The Look of Rockabilly." *History of Rock* no. 6 (1982): 116–117.

Shepherd, John. "Music and Social Control: An Essay on the Sociology of Musical Knowledge." *Catalyst: Social Science Controversy* no. 13 (Spring 1979): 1–54.

Sievert, William A. "For Every Bob Dylan, a Joni Mitchell." *The Chronicle of Higher Education* 11 (January 12, 1976): 17.

———. "Progressive Rock: Poetry, Politics, and Powerful Music." *The Chronicle Review* 17 (February 20, 1979): 22–23.

Skipper, James K. "How Popular Is Popular Music? Youth and Diversification of Musical Preferences." *Popular Music and Society* 2 (Winter 1973): 145–154.

Stevenson, Gordon. "Popular Culture and the Public Library." In *Advances in Librarianship—Vol. VII*. Ed. Melvin J. Voight and Michael H. Harris. New York: Academic Press, 1977, pp. 177–229.

———. "Race Records: Victims of Benign Neglect in Libraries." *Wilson Library Bulletin* 50 (November 1975): 224–232.

———. "The Wayward Scholar: Resources and Research in Popular Culture." *Library Trends* 25 (April 1977): 779–818.

Taylor, A.J.W. "Beatlemania—The Adulation and Exhuberance of Some Adolescents." In *Sociology and Everyday Life*. Ed. Marcello Truzzi. Englewood Cliffs, New Jersey: Prentice-Hall, 1968, pp. 161–170.

Thorpe, Peter. "I'm Movin' On: The Escape Theme in Country and Western Music." *Western Humanities Review* 24 (Autumn 1970): 307–318.

Thrush, John C., and George S. Paulus. "The Concept of Death in Popular Music: A Social Psychological Perspective." *Popular Music and Society* 6 (1979): 219–228.

Tillman, Robert H. "Punk Rock and the Construction of 'Pseudo-Political' Movements." *Popular Music and Society* 7 (1980): 165–175.

Titon, Jeff Todd. "Thematic Pattern in Downhome Blues Lyrics: The Evidence of Commercial Phonograph Records since World War II." *Journal of American Folklore* 90 (July-September 1977): 316–330.

Waffen, Les, and Peter Hesbacher. "War Songs: Hit Recordings During the Vietnam Period." *ARSC Journal* 13 (1981): 4–18.

Wanzenried, John, and Robert Henly Woody. "Country and Western Song Lyrics: Intentional and Extensional Orientations." *Popular Music and Society* 32 (March 1975): 31–42.

Watts, Michael. "The Call and Response of Popular Music: The Impact of American Pop Music in Europe." In *Superculture: American Popular Culture and Europe*. Ed. C.W.E. Bigsby. Bowling Green, Ohio: Bowling Green University Popular Press, 1975, pp. 123–139.

Wells, John. "Bent Out of Shape from Society's Pliers: A Sociological Study of the Grotesque in the Songs of Bob Dylan." *Popular Music and Society* 6 (1978): 27–38.

Wright, David. "Rock Music, Media, and the Counter Culture." In *New Dimensions in Popular Culture*. Ed. Russel B. Nye. Bowling Green, Ohio: Bowling Green University Popular Press, 1962, pp. 211–223.

Wright, John L. "Croonin' about Cruisin'." In *The Popular Culture Reader*. Ed. Jack Nachbar, Deborah Weiser, and John L. Wright. Bowling Green, Ohio: Bowling Green University Popular Press, 1978, pp. 109–117.

E. CONFERENCE PAPERS, DISSERTATIONS, THESES, AND OTHER UNPUBLISHED SOURCES

Bailey, Robert T. "A Study of the Effect of Popular Music on Achievement in and Attitude toward Contemporary United States History." Research project for the degree of specialist in education: West Georgia College, 1979.

Banes, Ruth A. "The Image of Women in Southern Country and Western Music." Mimeographed paper presented at the eleventh annual convention of the Popular Culture Association in Cincinnati, Ohio, March 1981.

Berger, David G. "The Unchanging Popular Tune Lyric, 1910–1955." Doctoral dissertation: Columbia University, 1966.

Bridges, John. "Changing Courtship Patterns in the Popular Song: A Replication of Horton and Carey." Masters thesis: Bowling Green State University, 1980.

Bucci, Jerry Michael. "Love, Marriage, and Family Life Themes in the Popular Song: A Comparison of the Years 1940 and 1965." Doctoral dissertation: Columbia University, 1968.

Burns, Gary Curtis. "Trends in Lyrics in the Annual Top Twenty Songs in the United States, 1963–1972." Mimeographed paper presented at the twelfth annual convention of the Popular Culture Association in Louisville, Kentucky, April 1982.

———. "Utopia and Dystopia in Popular Song Lyrics: Rhetorical Visions in the United States, 1963–1972." Doctoral dissertation: Northwestern University, 1981.

Butchart, Ronald E., and B. Lee Cooper. " 'Teacher, Leave Them Kids Alone!': Perceptions of Schooling and Education in American Popular Music." Mimeographed paper presented at the annual convention of the American Education Studies Association in Boston, Massachusetts, November 1981.

Cantor, Louis. "Bob Dylan and the Protest Movement of the 1960's: The Electronic Medium Is the Apocalyptic Message." Mimeographed paper presented at the eighth annual convention of the Popular Culture Association in Cincinnati, Ohio, April 1978.

Charles, Norman. "Social Values in American Popular Songs, 1890–1950." Doctoral dissertation: University of Pennsylvania, 1958.

Cheeseboro, James W.; Jay Nachman; and Andrew Yannelli. "Popular Music as a Mode of Communication." Mimeographed paper presented at the tenth annual convention of the Popular Culture Association in Detroit, Michigan, April 1980.

Chilcoat, George W. "History of America: A Popular Music Approach." Mimeographed paper presented at the Rocky Mountain regional conference of the National Council for the Social Studies in Phoenix, Arizona, April 1984.

Cooper, B. Lee. "Popular Music and American History: Exploring Unusual Audio Teaching Resources." Mimeographed paper presented at the annual Missouri Valley History Conference in Omaha, Nebraska, March 1981.

———. "Sounds Like a Train A-Comin': Audio Imitations of Locomotives in Contemporary Songs, 1955–1980." Mimeographed paper and audio tape presentation delivered at the twelfth annual convention of the Popular Culture Association in Louisville, Kentucky, April 1982.

DeWitt, Howard A. "Using Popular History in the American Survey: Rock and Roll as an Expression of American Culture in the 1950s." Mimeographed paper presented at the seventh annual convention of the Popular Culture Association in Baltimore, Maryland, April 1977.

Fuchsman, Kenneth A. "Between the Garden and the Devil's Bargain: The 1960's Counter Culture in Rock Music." Mimeographed paper presented at the sixth annual convention of the American Culture Association in Toronto, March 1984.

———. "Deliver Me from the Days of Old: Lyrical Themes in 1950's Rock and Roll." Mimeographed paper presented at the thirteenth annual convention of the Popular Culture Association in Wichita, Kansas, April 1983.

Harmon, James Elmer. "The New Music and the American Youth Subculture." Doctoral dissertation: United States International University, 1971.

Heath, Julia A. "Courtship Patterns Expressed in Popular Songs." Mimeographed paper presented at the eighth annual convention of the Popular Culture Association in Cincinnati, Ohio, April 1978.

Johnson, Mary Jane Carle. "Rock Music as a Reflector of Social Attitudes among Youth of the 1960s." Doctoral dissertation: St. Louis University, 1978.

Kamin, Jonathan. "Rhythm and Blues in White America: Rock and Roll as Acculturation and Perceptual Learning." Doctoral dissertation: Princeton University, 1976.

Keesing, Hugo A. "Culture in the Grooves: American History at 78, 45, and 33 1/3 r.p.m." Mimeographed paper presented at the eighth annual convention of the Popular Culture Association in Cincinnati, Ohio, April 1978.

———. "Pop Goes to War: The Music of World War II and Vietnam." Mimeographed paper presented at the ninth annual convention of the Popular Culture Association in Pittsburgh, Pennsylvania, April 1979.

———. "The Pop Message: A Trend Analysis of the Psychological Content of Two Decades of Music." Mimeographed paper presented at the annual meeting of the Eastern Psychological Society in Philadelphia, Pennsylvania, April 1974.

———. "Popular Music in American Society." Mimeographed paper and audio tape presented at the seventh annual convention of the Midwest Popular Culture Association at Bowling Green, Ohio, October 1979.

———. "Popular Recordings and the American Presidency: From John F. Kennedy to Ronald Reagan." Mimeographed paper presented at the thirteenth annual convention of the Popular Culture Association in Wichita, Kansas, April 1983.

———. "Youth in Transition: A Content Analysis of Two Decades of Popular Music." Doctoral dissertation: Adelphi University, 1972.

Kizer, Elizabeth J. "Protest Song Lyrics as Rhetoric." Mimeographed paper presented at the twelfth annual convention of the Popular Culture Association in Louisville, Kentucky, April 1982.

Lance, Larry M. "Singing Along with the Sexual Revolution: Sexual Messages in Popular Music during the 1960's and 1970's." Mimeographed paper presented at the ninth annual convention of the Popular Culture Association in Pittsburgh, Pennsylvania, April 1979.

McLaughlin, Mary. "The Social World of American Popular Songs." Master's thesis: Cornell University, 1968.

Meese, Elizabeth A. " 'Country Music Is for Lovers': A Comparative Analysis of Sex Roles." Mimeographed paper presented at the sixth annual convention of the Popular Culture Association in Chicago, Illinois, April 1976.

O'Leary, J.F. "Lyrics: Images of Self." Mimeographed paper presented at the thirteenth annual convention of the Popular Culture Association in Wichita, Kansas, April 1983.

Peterson, James. "Using Popular Music to Teach Topics in American History since 1950 for High School Students." Master's thesis: University of Southern California, 1977.

Peterson, Richard A. "No Mule Sings It: Folk Purity, Avant-Gardism, and Nostalgia in American Country Music." Mimeographed paper presented at the fourteenth annual convention of the Popular Culture Association in Toronto, March 1984.

Rogers, Jimmie N.; Raymond S. Rodgers; and Peggy J. Beasley-Rodgers. "The Country Music Message: An Analysis of the Most Popular Country Songs from 1965 to 1980." Mimeographed paper presented at the eleventh annual convention of the Popular Culture Association in Cincinnati, Ohio, March 1981.

Root, Robert L., Jr. "A Listener's Guide to the Rhetoric of Popular Music." Mimeographed paper presented at the twelfth annual convention of the Popular Culture Association in Louisville, Kentucky, April 1982.

Ryan, John. "Organization, Environment, and Culture Change: The ASCAP-BMI Controversy." Doctoral dissertation: Vanderbilt University, 1982.

Slater, Thomas J. "Rock Music, Youth, and Society: The Uses of Rock Music in the Movies, 1955–1981." Mimeographed paper presented at the twelfth annual convention of the Popular Culture Association in Louisville, Kentucky, April 1982.

Swindell, Warren C. "Selected Black Influences on Popular Music." Mimeographed paper presented at the eleventh annual convention of the Popular Culture Association in Cincinnati, Ohio, March 1981.

Tungate, James Lester. "Romantic Images in Popular Songs, 1950–1959." Doctoral dissertation: Northwestern University, 1972.

Weinstein, Deena. "Rock: Youth and Its Music." Mimeographed paper presented at the fourteenth annual convention of the Popular Culture Association in Toronto, April 1984.

Weller, Donald J. "Rock Music: Its Role and Political Significance as a Channel of Communication." Doctoral dissertation: University of Hawaii, 1971.

Song Title Index

Recording Artist Index

About the Author

B. LEE COOPER is Professor of History and Vice President for Academic Affairs. His earlier works include *Images of American Society in Popular Music* (winner of the 1983 ASCAP-Deems Taylor Award) and *The Popular Music Handbook*. Articles by Dr. Cooper have appeared in *Goldmine*, *Popular Music and Society*, *Social Education*, *JEMF Quarterly*, *American Music*, *Record Profile Magazine*, and *Drexel Library Quarterly*.

DATE DUE

APR 0 2 2001	

GAYLORD   PRINTED IN U.S.A.